FAIRY TAIL S

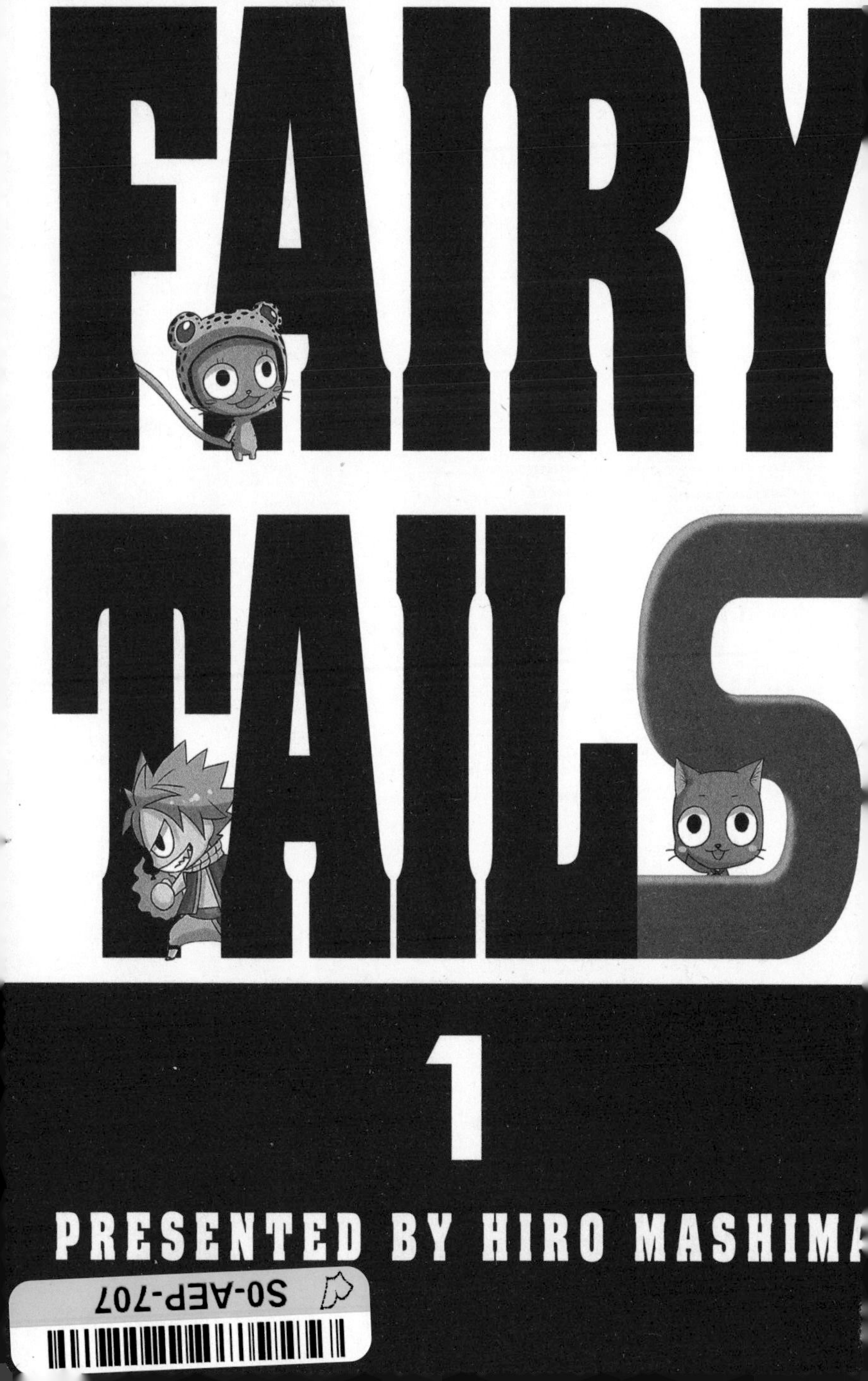

1

PRESENTED BY HIRO MASHIMA

CONTENTS

HAPPY THE BLUE CAT — 003
FIRST PUBLISHED IN THE GREAT TOHOKU EARTHQUAKE CHARITY DOUJINSHI "PRAY FOR JAPAN."

THE FAIRIES' BOOBY PRIZES — 011
FIRST PUBLISHED IN *MAGAZINE SPECIAL*, 2013, ISSUE 8

WELCOME HOME, FROSCH — 036
FIRST PUBLISHED IN *BESSATSU SHONEN MAGAZINE*, 2014, ISSUE 4

413 DAYS — 058
FIRST PUBLISHED IN *MAGAZINE SPECIAL*, 2014, ISSUE 4

THAT WOMAN, ERZA — 080
FIRST PUBLISHED IN *YOUNG MAGAZINE*, 2014, ISSUE 18

NATSU VS. MAVIS — 101
FIRST PUBLISHED IN *MAGAZINE SPECIAL*, 2015, ISSUE 2

FAIRY TAIL OF THE DEAD MEEEEEEEEN — 110
FIRST PUBLISHED IN *WEEKLY SHONEN MAGAZINE*, 2015, ISSUE 17

A MERRY, FAIRY CHRISTMAS — 153
FIRST PUBLISHED IN *MAGAZINE SPECIAL*, 2015, ISSUE 12

SPECIAL MISSION: BEWARE OF GUYS WHO SHOW A KEEN INTEREST! — 175
FIRST PUBLISHED IN *WEEKLY SHONEN MAGAZINE*, 2007, ISSUE 50

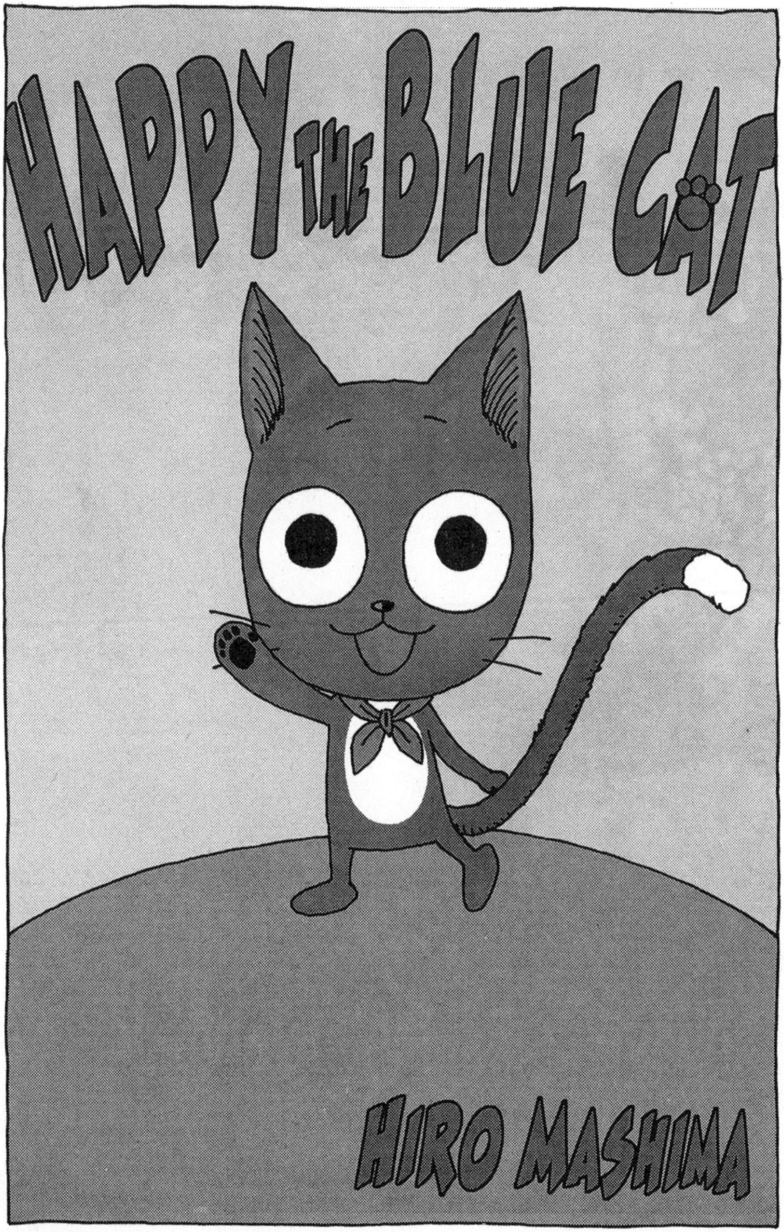
HAPPY THE BLUE CAT
HIRO MASHIMA

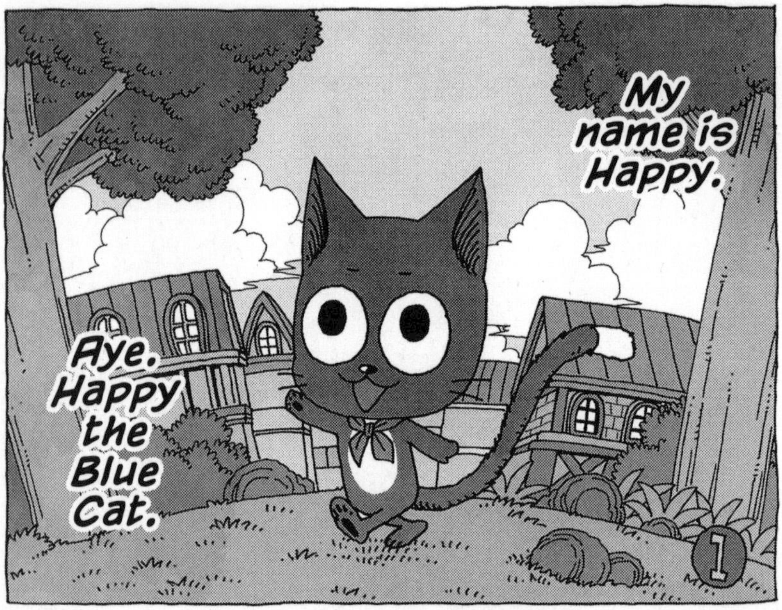
My name is Happy.
Aye. Happy the Blue Cat.
1

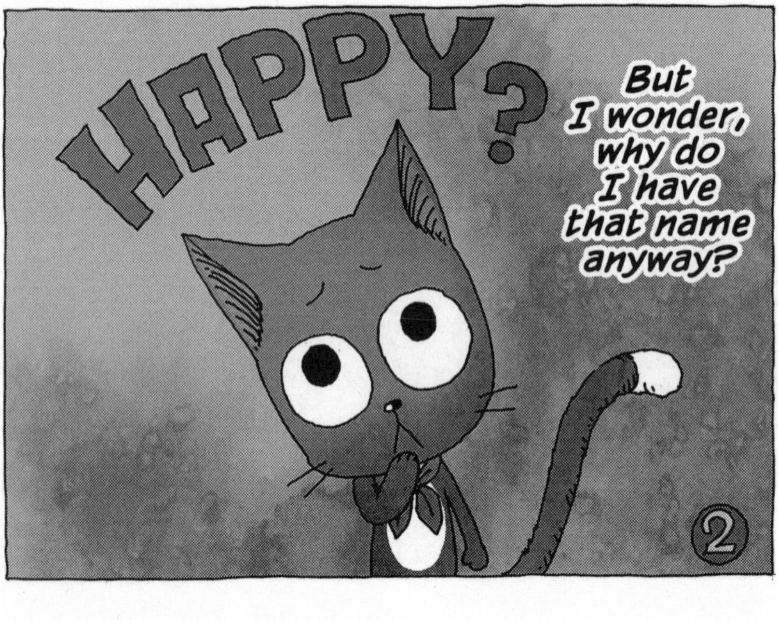
But I wonder, why do I have that name anyway?
HAPPY?
2

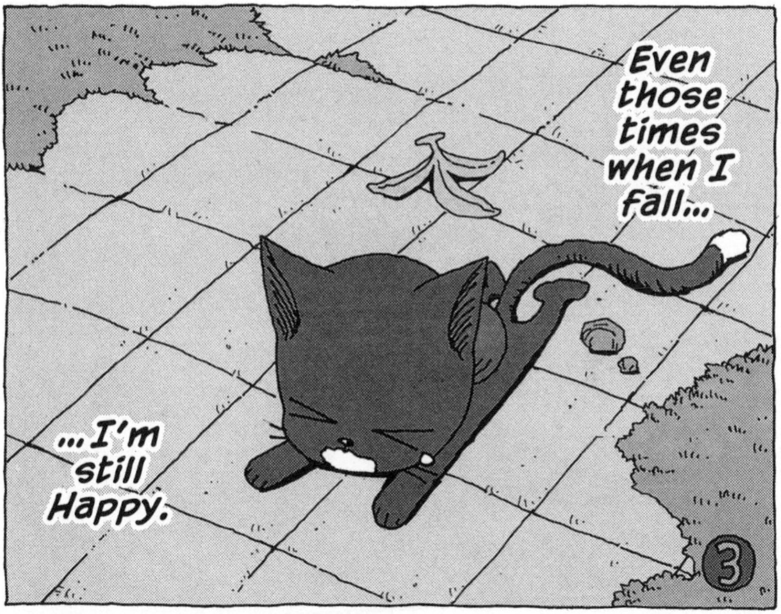
Even those times when I fall...
...I'm still Happy.
3

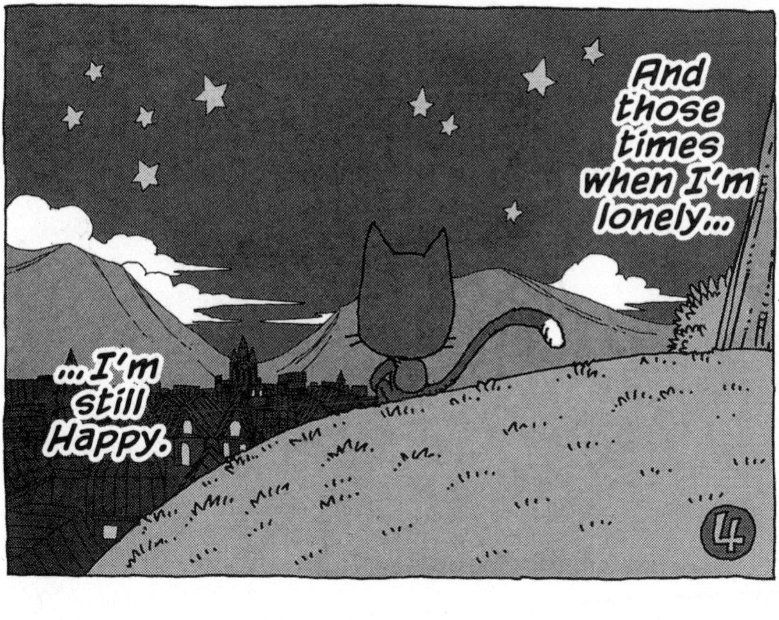
And those times when I'm lonely...
...I'm still Happy.
4

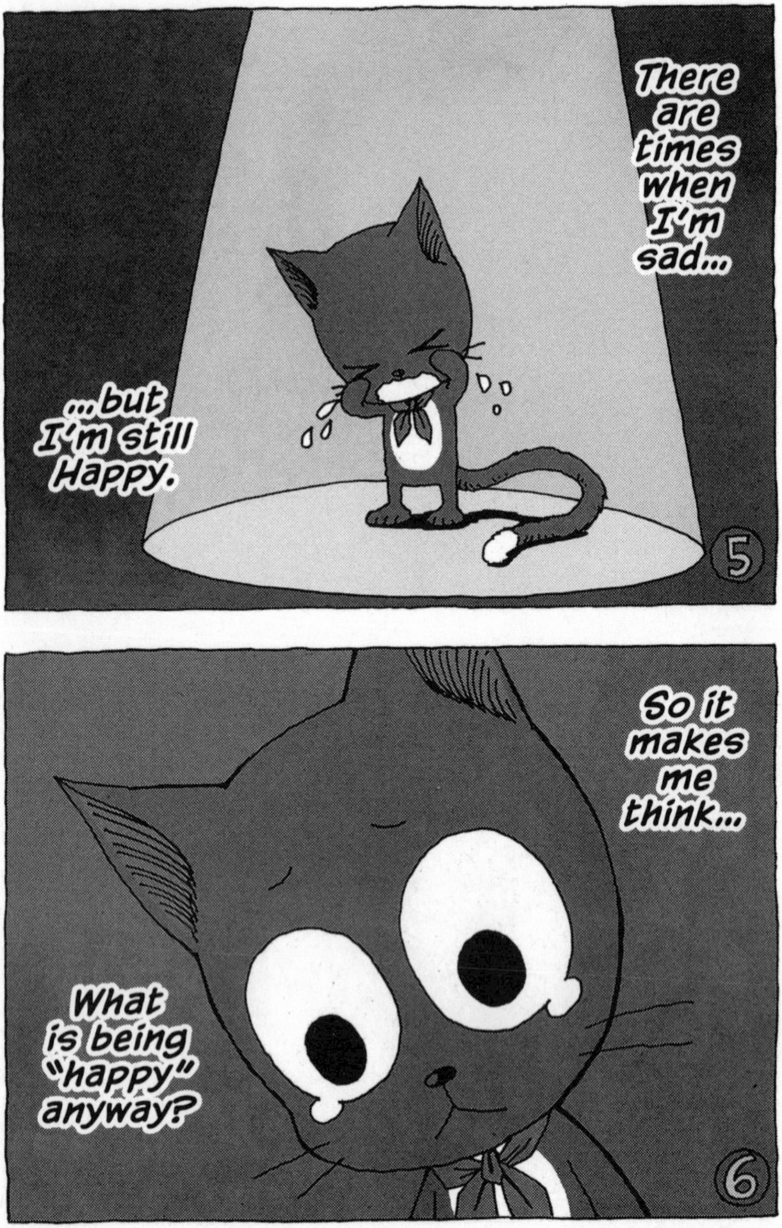
There are times when I'm sad...
...but I'm still Happy.
5
So it makes me think...
What is being "happy" anyway?
6

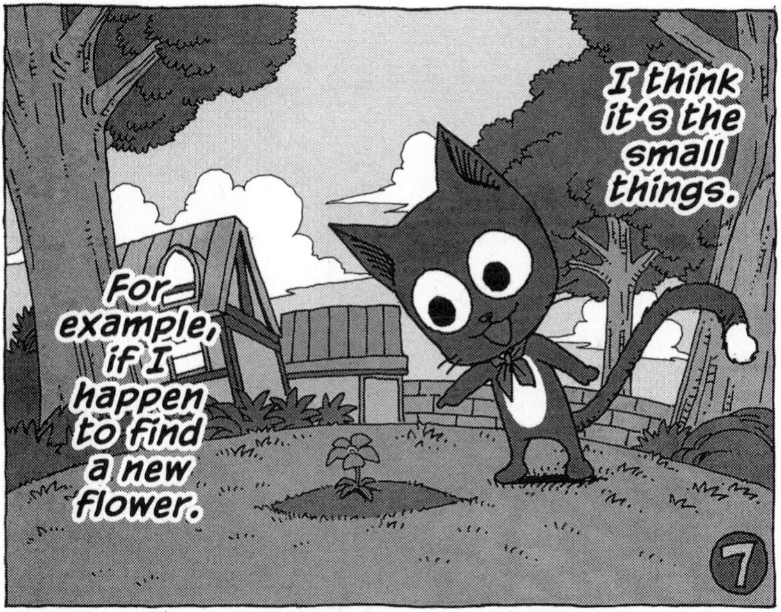
I think it's the small things.
For example, if I happen to find a new flower.
7

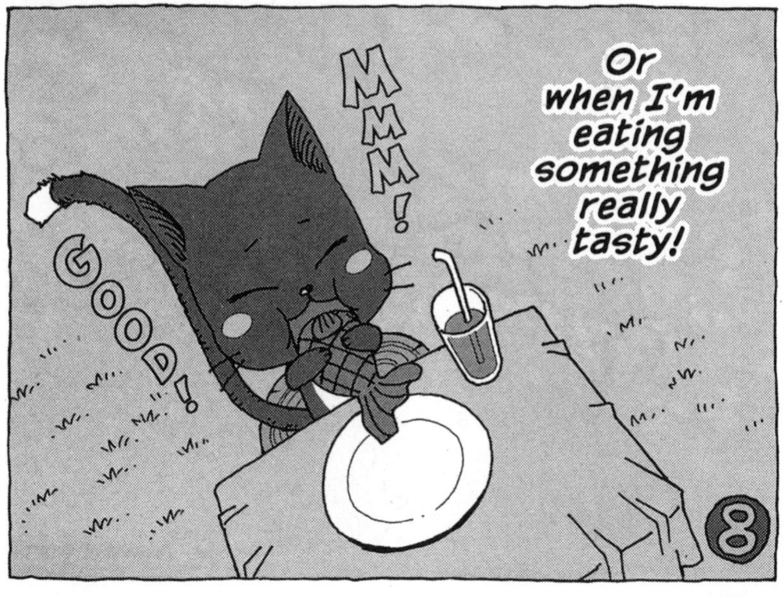
Or when I'm eating something really tasty!
MMMM!
GOOD!
8

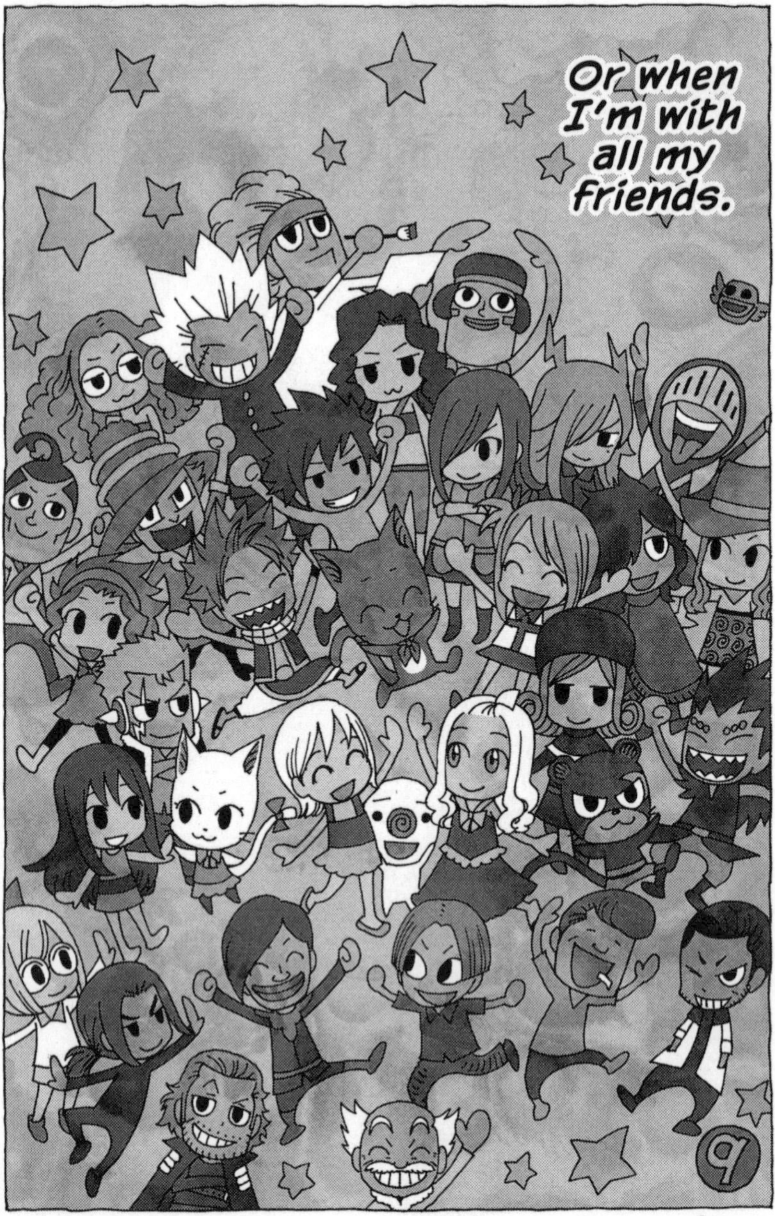
Or when I'm with all my friends.

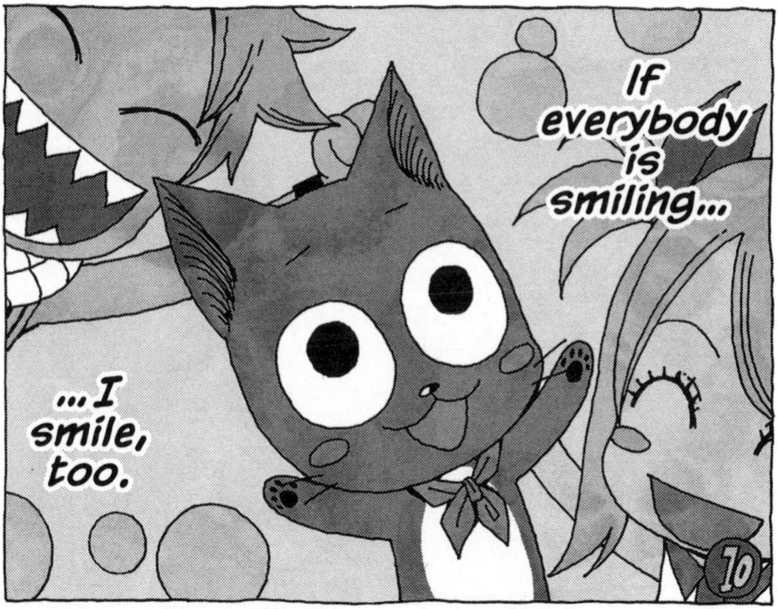
If everybody is smiling...
...I smile, too.
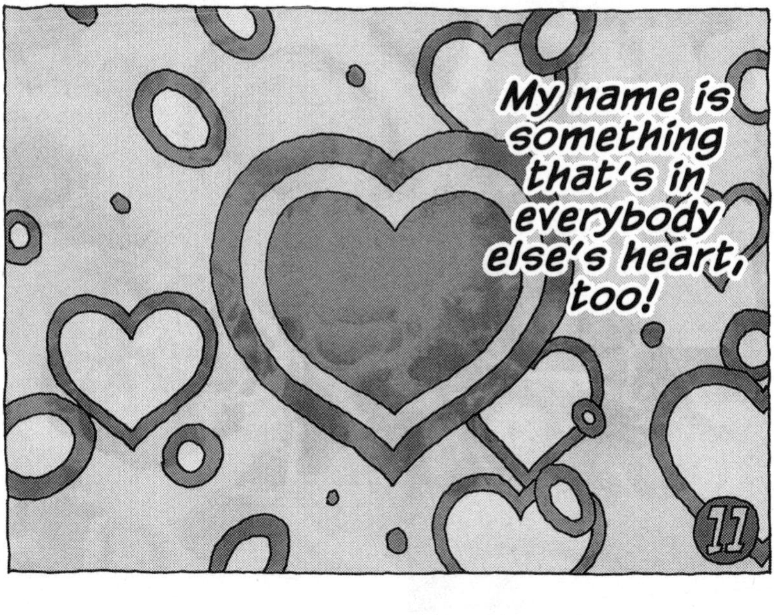
My name is something that's in everybody else's heart, too!

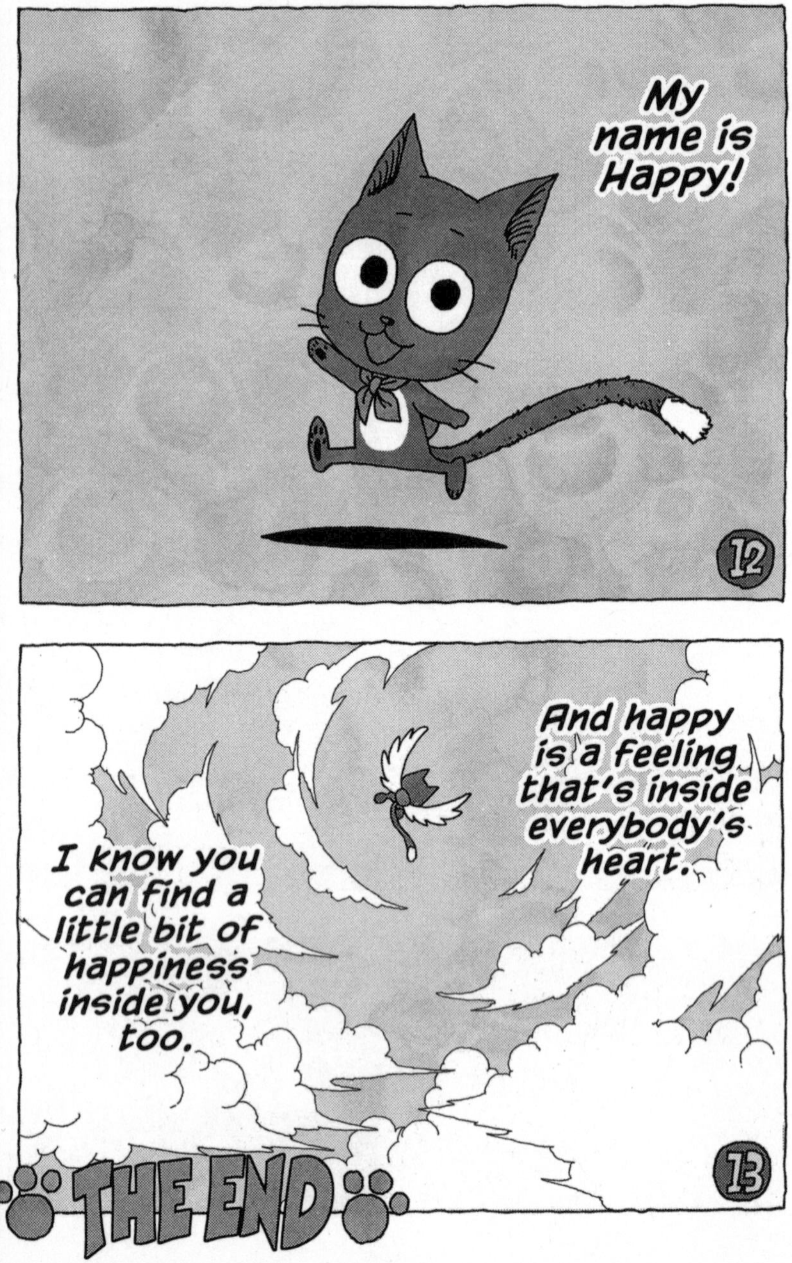
My name is Happy!
12
And happy is a feeling that's inside everybody's heart.
I know you can find a little bit of happiness inside you, too.
13
THE END

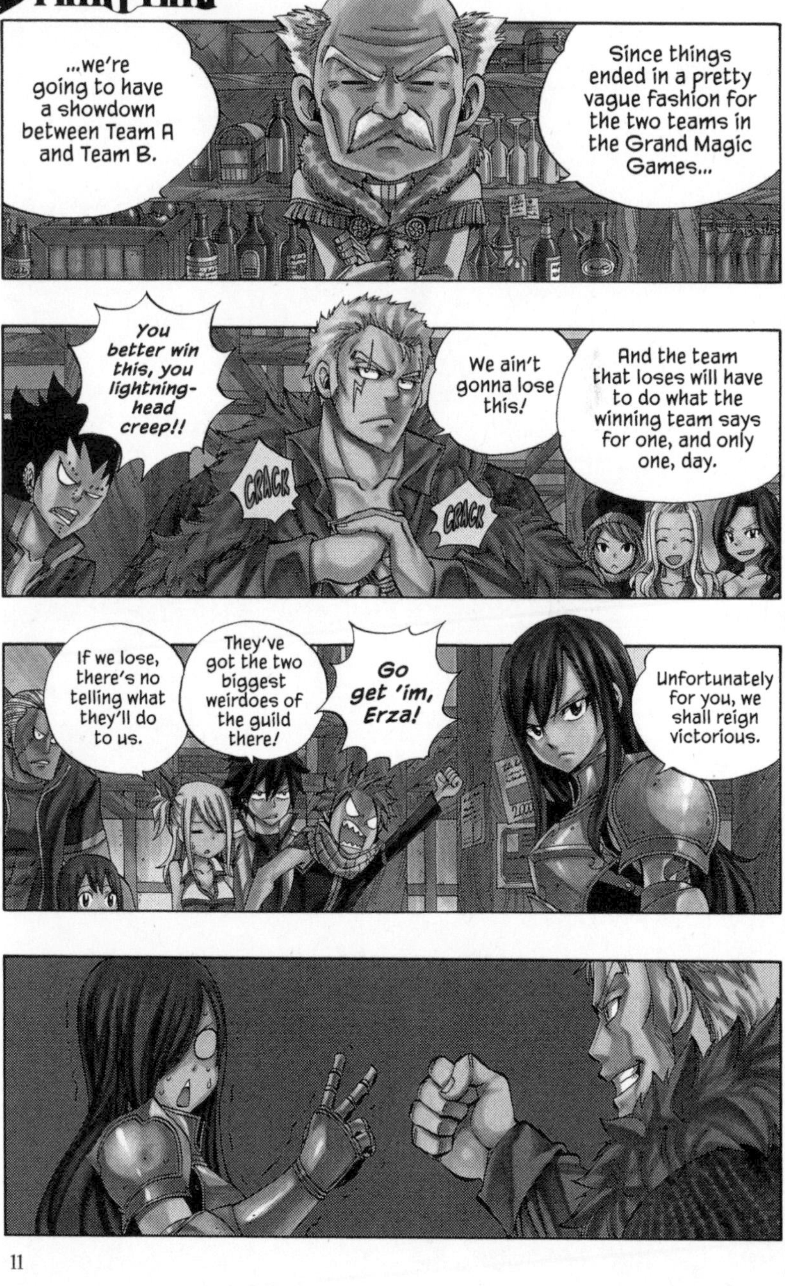
Since things ended in a pretty vague fashion for the two teams in the Grand Magic Games...
...we're going to have a showdown between Team A and Team B.
And the team that loses will have to do what the winning team says for one, and only one, day.
We ain't gonna lose this!
You better win this, you lightning-head creep!!
CRACK
CRACK
Unfortunately for you, we shall reign victorious.
Go get 'im, Erza!
They've got the two biggest weirdoes of the guild there!
If we lose, there's no telling what they'll do to us.

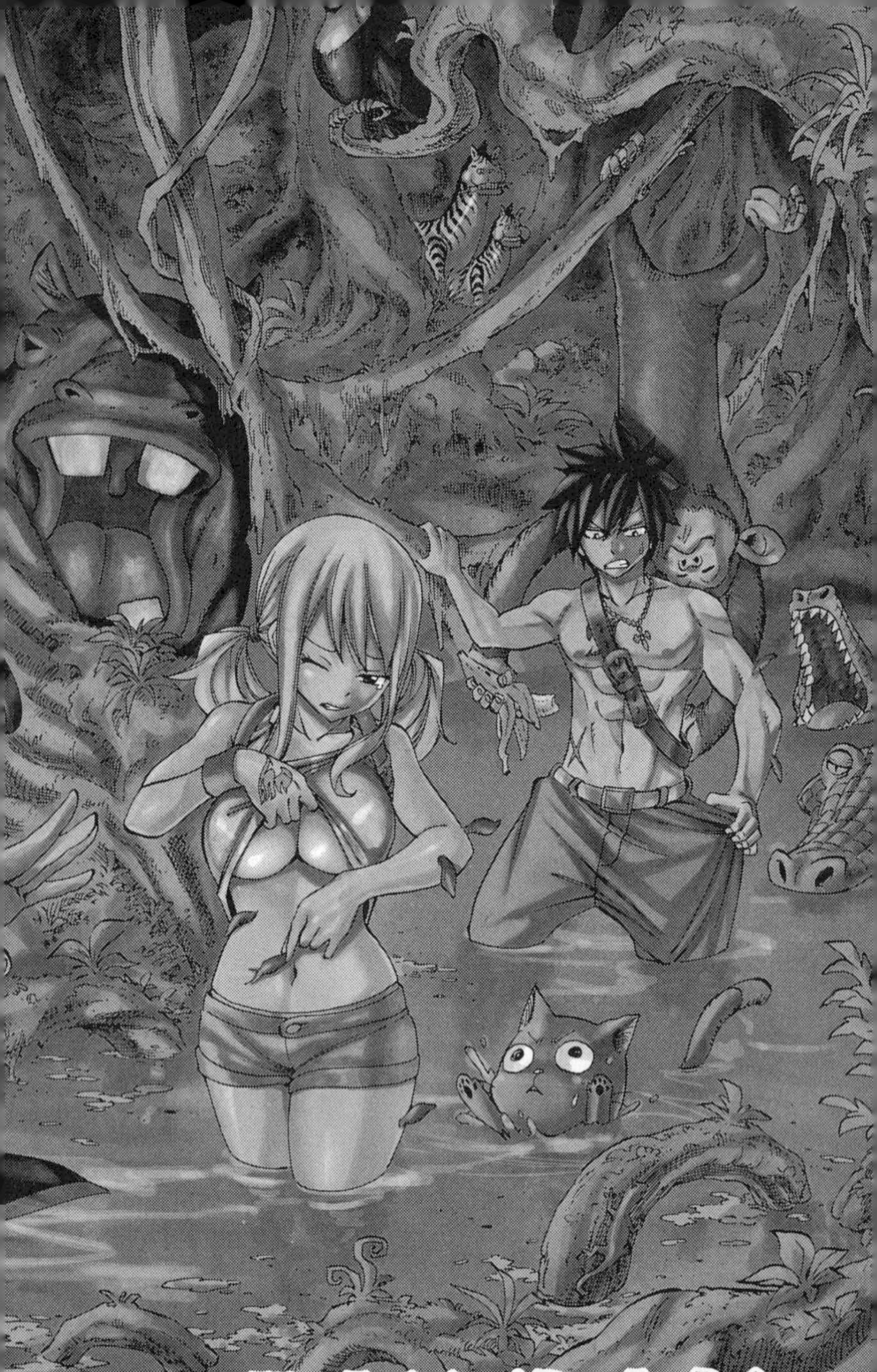

The Fairies' Booby Prizes

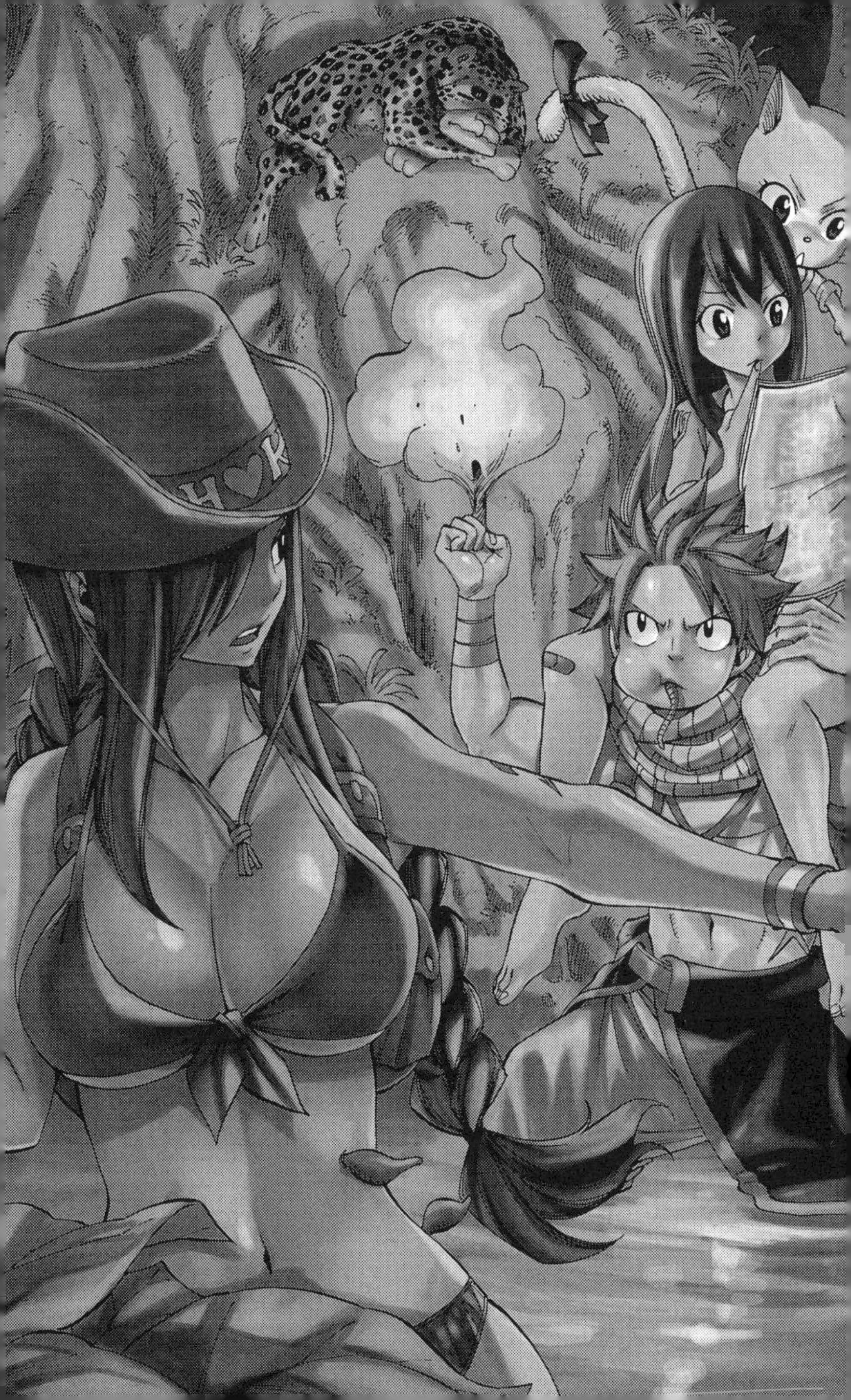

FT✦S

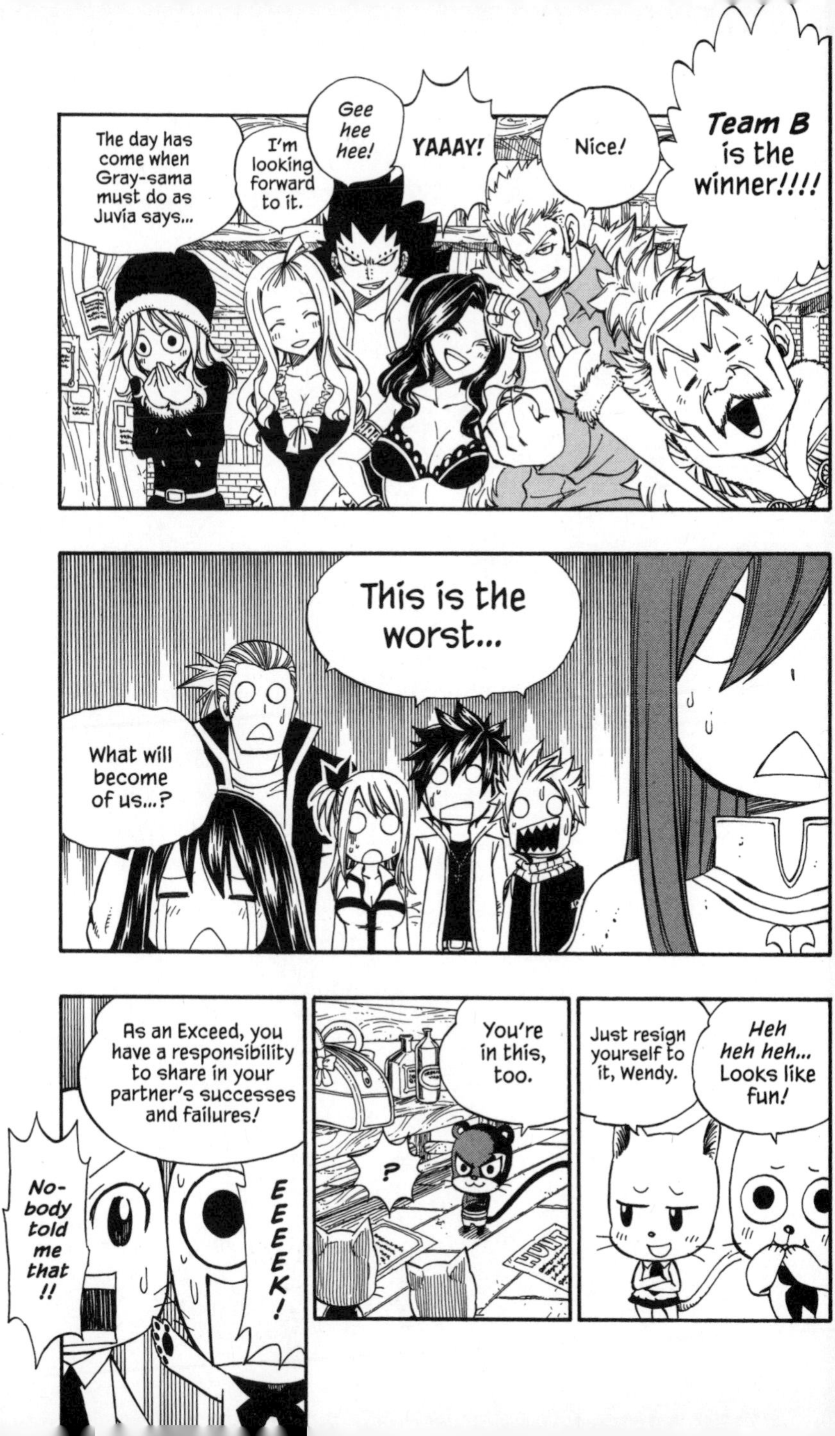
Team B is the winner!!!!
Nice!
YAAAY!
Gee hee hee!
I'm looking forward to it.
The day has come when Gray-sama must do as Juvia says...
This is the worst...
What will become of us...?
Heh heh heh... Looks like fun!
Just resign yourself to it, Wendy.
You're in this, too.
?
As an Exceed, you have a responsibility to share in your partner's successes and failures!
EEEEEK!
Nobody told me that!!

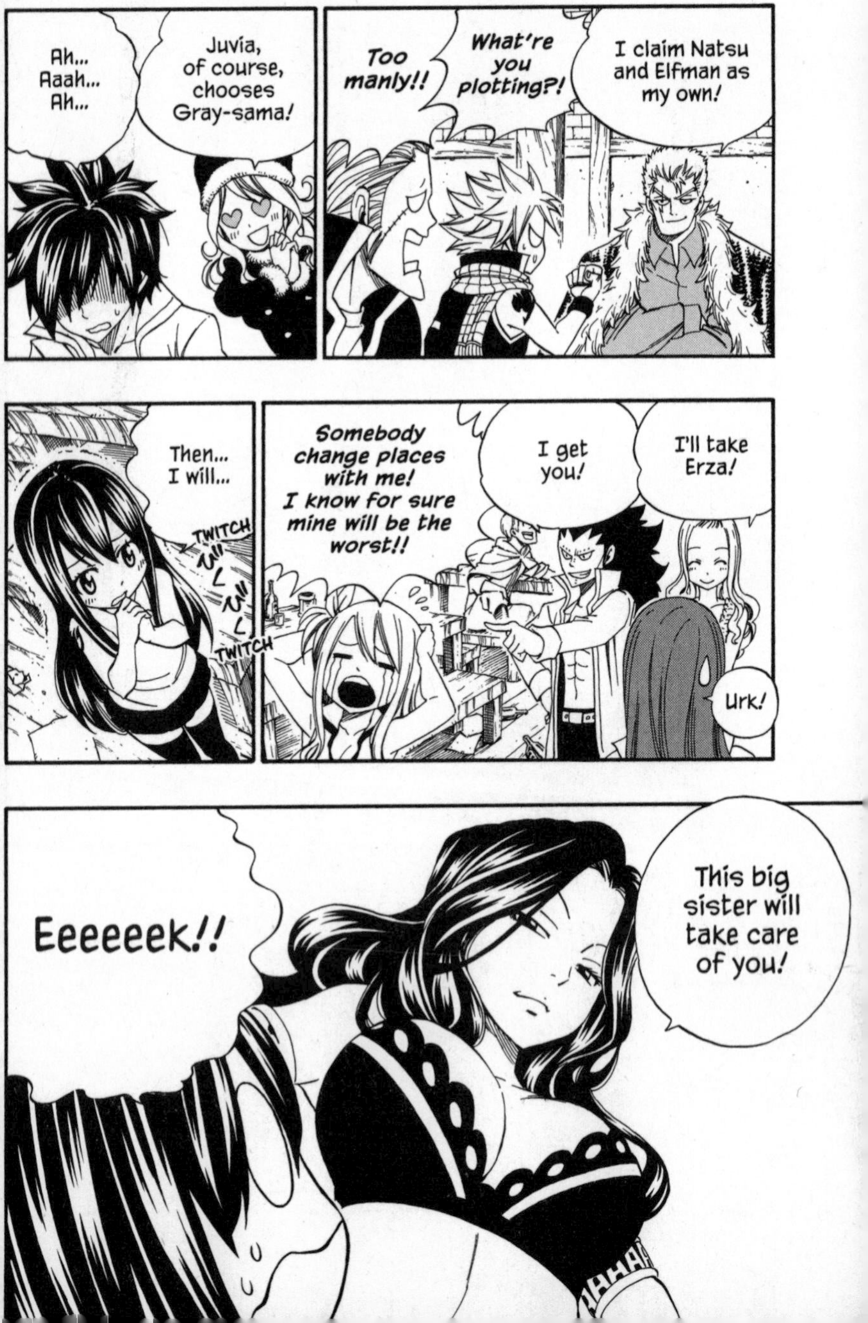
I claim Natsu and Elfman as my own!
What're you plotting?!
Too manly!!
Juvia, of course, chooses Gray-sama!
Ah... Aaah... Ah...
I'll take Erza!
I get you!
Somebody change places with me! I know for sure mine will be the worst!!
Urk!
Then... I will...
TWITCH
TWITCH
This big sister will take care of you!
Eeeeeek!!

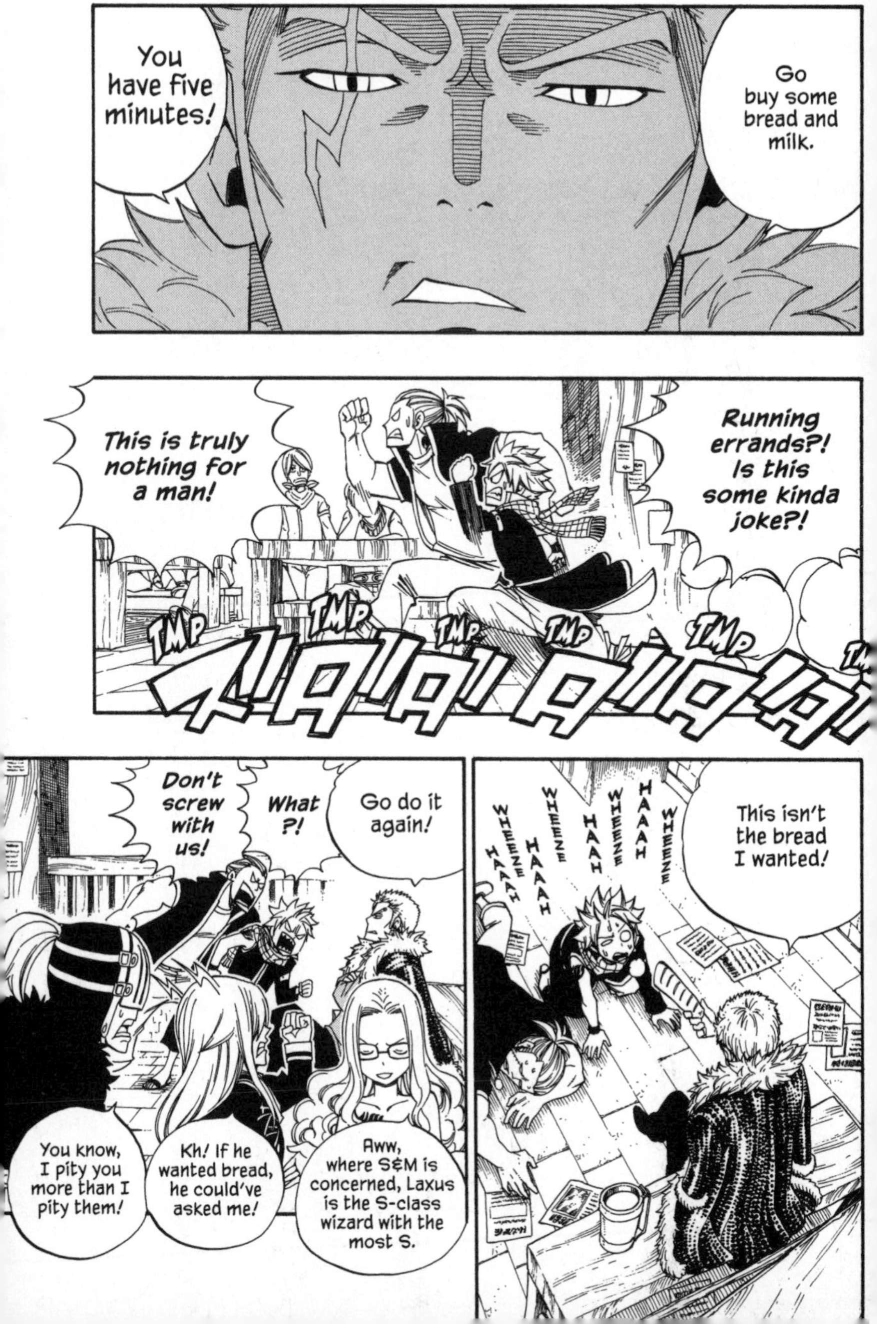
Go buy some bread and milk.
You have five minutes!
Running errands?! Is this some kinda joke?!
This is truly nothing for a man!
TMP TMP TMP TMP TMP
This isn't the bread I wanted!
WHEEZE
HAAAH
WHEEZE
HAAH
WHEEZE
HAAAH
WHEEZE HAAAH
Go do it again!
What?!
Don't screw with us!
Aww, where S&M is concerned, Laxus is the S-class wizard with the most S.
Kh! If he wanted bread, he could've asked me!
You know, I pity you more than I pity them!

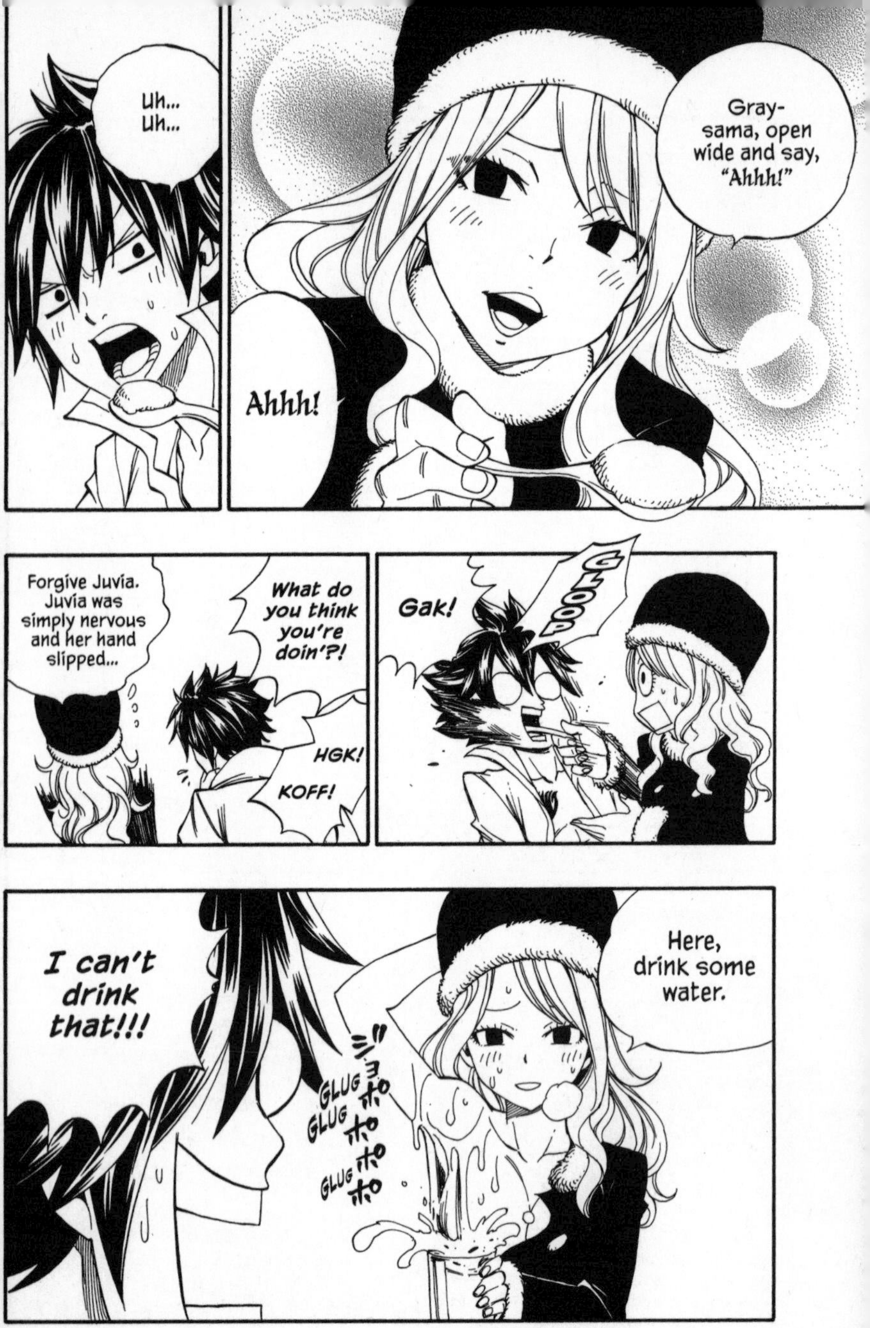
Gray-sama, open wide and say, "Ahhh!"
Ahhh!
Uh... Uh...
GLOOP
Gak!
What do you think you're doin'?!
HGK!
KOFF!
Forgive Juvia. Juvia was simply nervous and her hand slipped...
Here, drink some water.
ジョポポポポ
GLUG GLUG GLUG
I can't drink that!!!

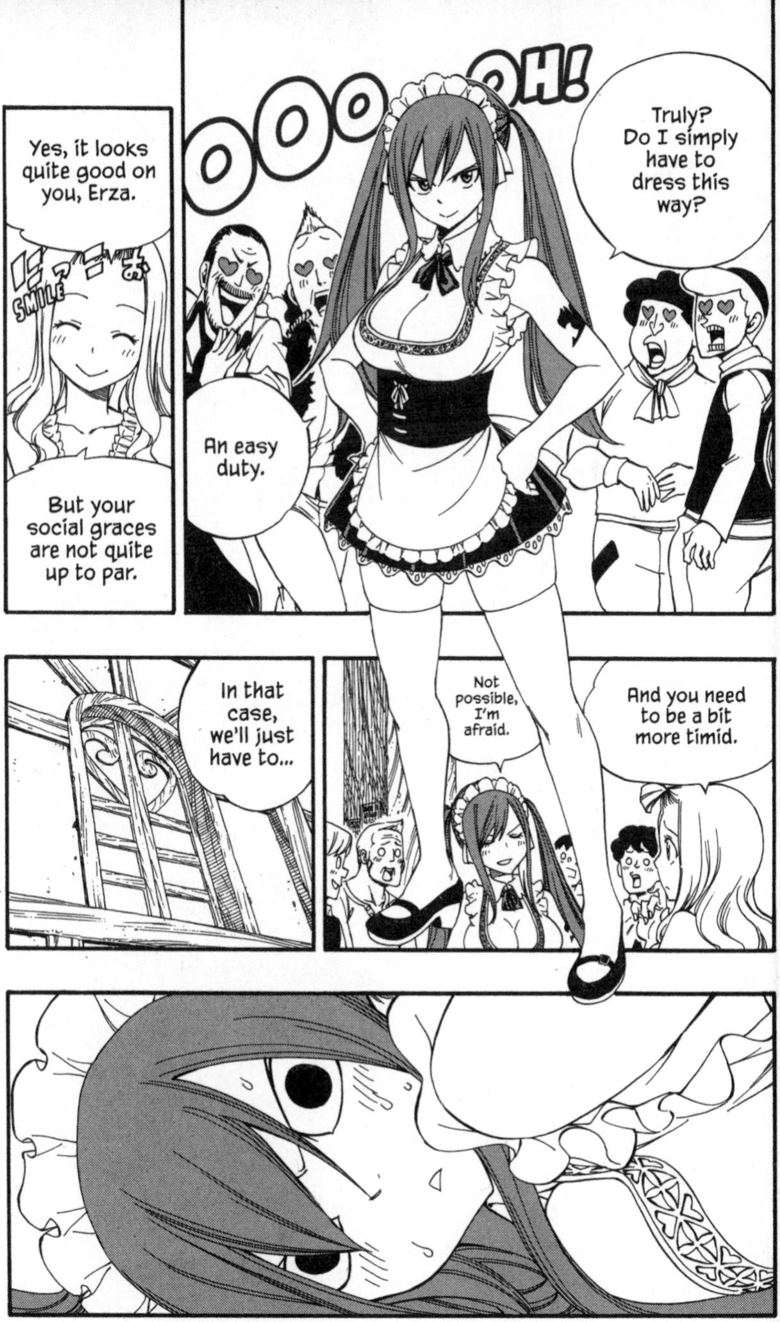

OOO OH!
Truly? Do I simply have to dress this way?
An easy duty.
SMILE
Yes, it looks quite good on you, Erza.
But your social graces are not quite up to par.
And you need to be a bit more timid.
Not possible, I'm afraid.
In that case, we'll just have to...

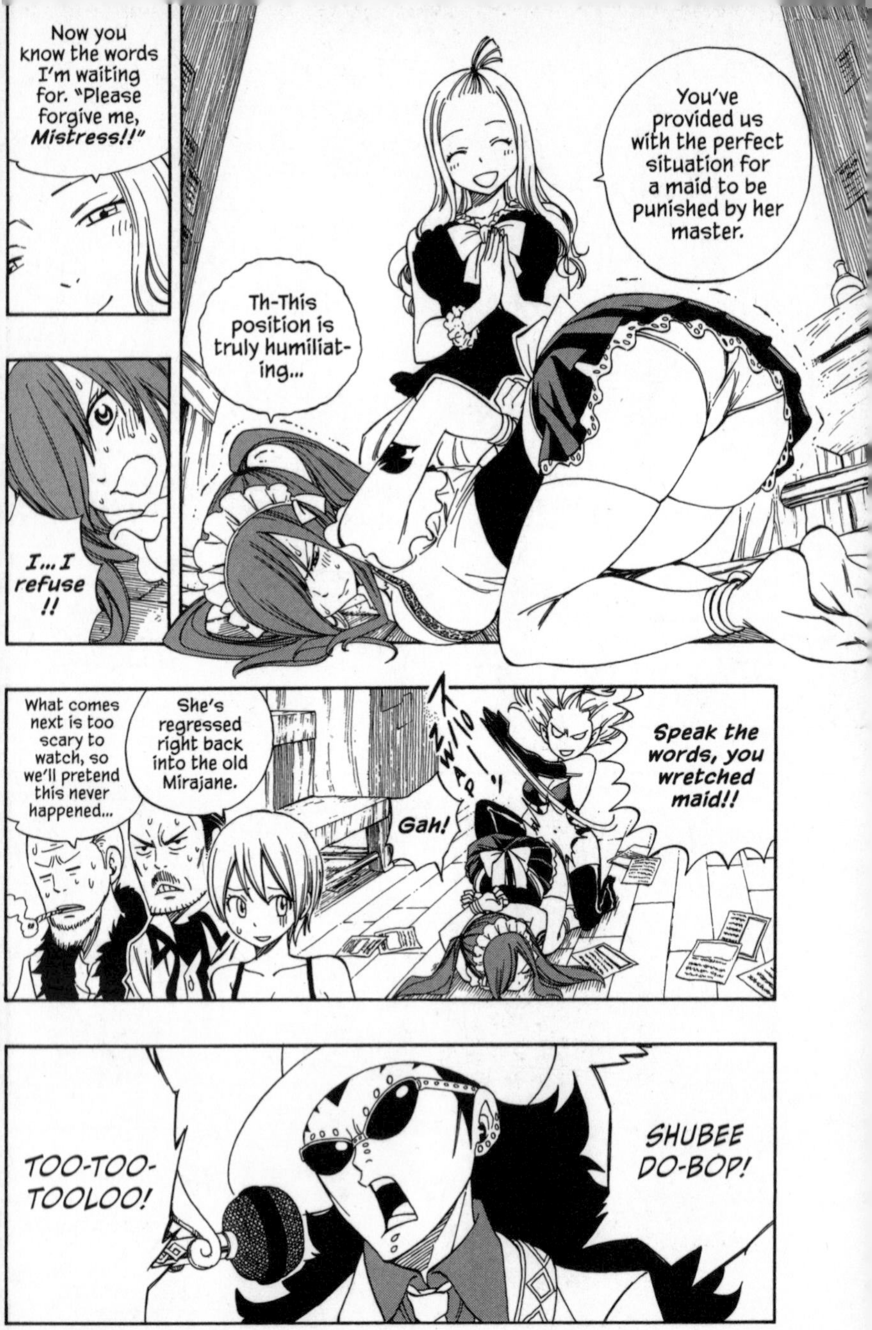
You've provided us with the perfect situation for a maid to be punished by her master.
Th-This position is truly humiliating...
Now you know the words I'm waiting for. "Please forgive me, Mistress!!"
I...I refuse!!
Speak the words, you wretched maid!!
Gah!
She's regressed right back into the old Mirajane.
What comes next is too scary to watch, so we'll pretend this never happened...
SHUBEE DO-BOP!
TOO-TOO-TOOLOO!

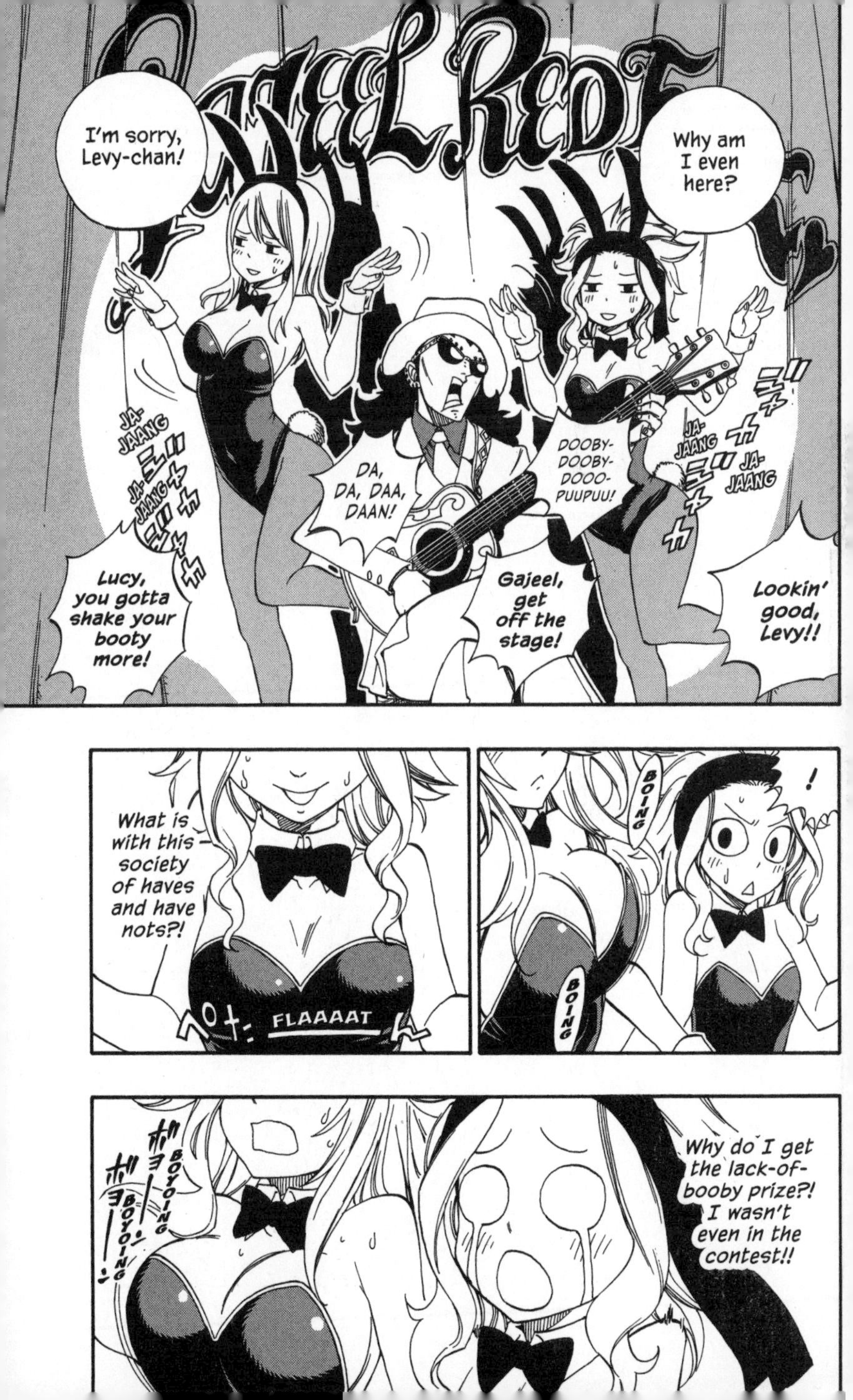
Why am I even here?
JA-JAANG
JA-JAANG
DOOBY-DOOBY-DOOO-PUUPUU!
Lookin' good, Levy!!
Gajeel, get off the stage!
DA, DA, DAA, DAAN!
I'm sorry, Levy-chan!
JA-JAANG
JA-JAANG
Lucy, you gotta shake your booty more!
!
BOING
BOING
What is with this society of haves and have nots?!
FLAAAAT
Why do I get the lack-of-booby prize?! I wasn't even in the contest!!
BOYOING
BOYOING

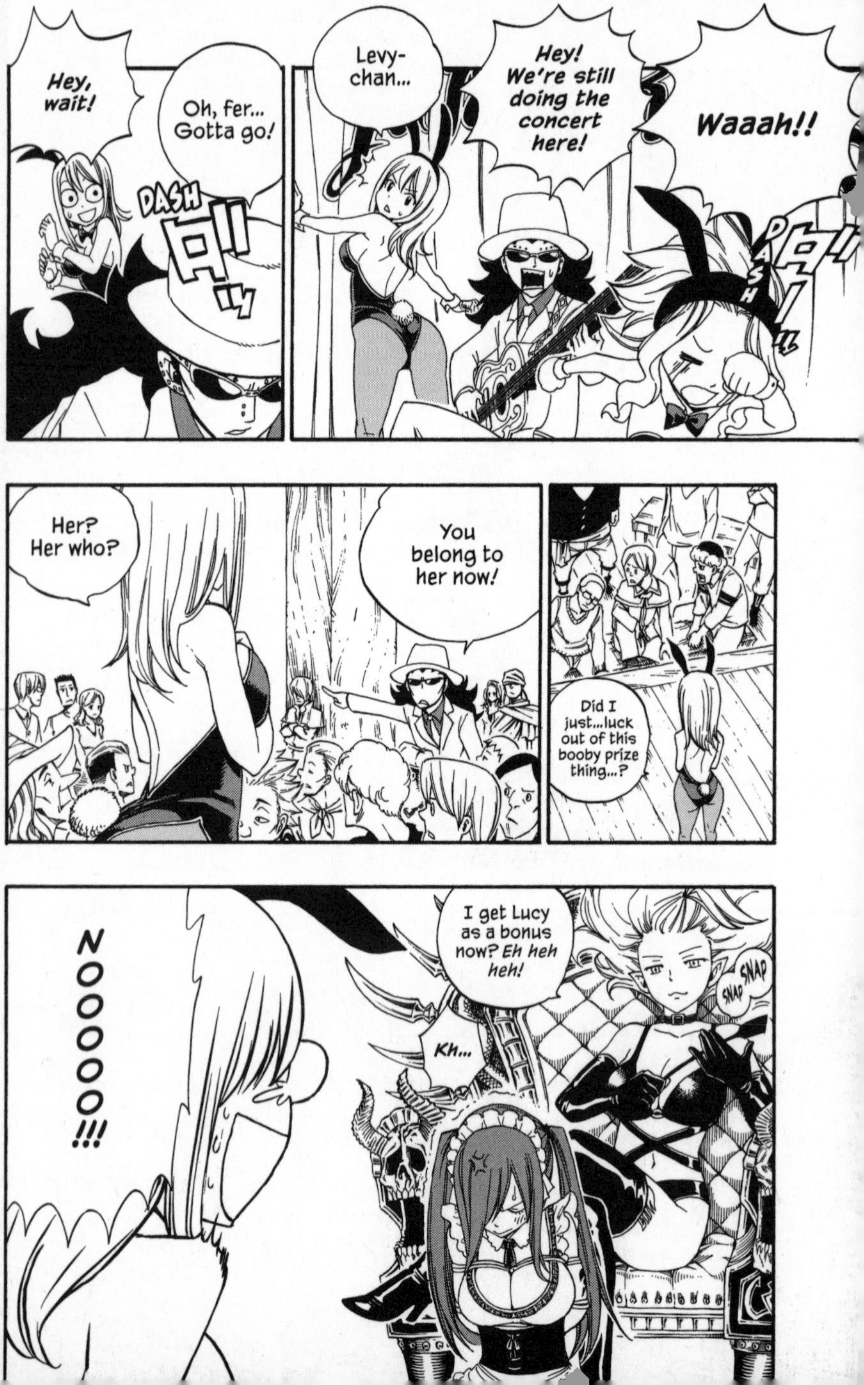
Waaah!!
Hey! We're still doing the concert here!
Levy-chan...
DASH
Oh, fer... Gotta go!
Hey, wait!
DASH
Did I just...luck out of this booby prize thing...?
You belong to her now!
Her? Her who?
I get Lucy as a bonus now? Eh heh heh!
SNAP
SNAP
Kh...
NOOOOOOO!!!

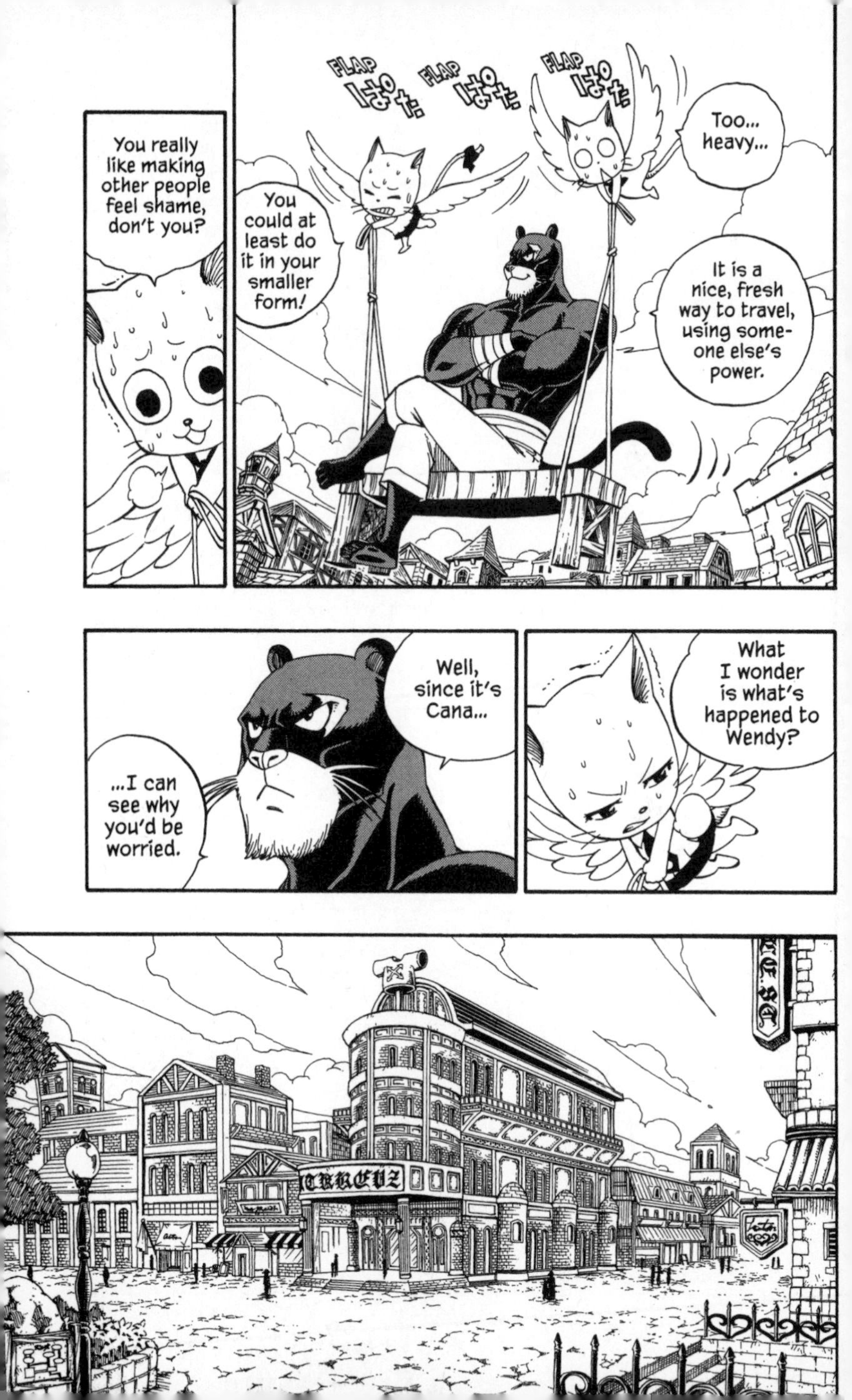
FLAP
FLAP
FLAP
Too... heavy...
You could at least do it in your smaller form!
It is a nice, fresh way to travel, using some-one else's power.
You really like making other people feel shame, don't you?
What I wonder is what's happened to Wendy?
Well, since it's Cana...
...I can see why you'd be worried.

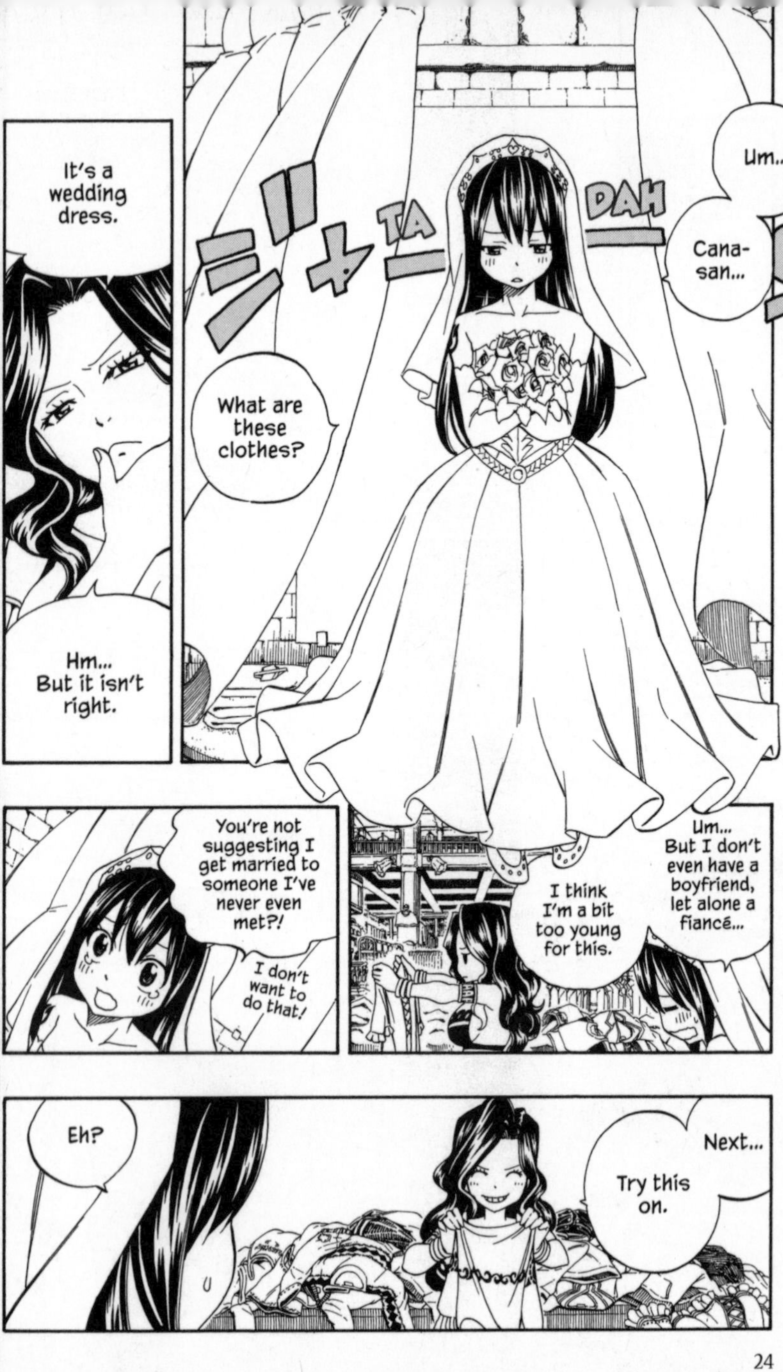
Um...
Cana-san...
TA DAH
What are these clothes?
It's a wedding dress.
Hm... But it isn't right.
Um... But I don't even have a boyfriend, let alone a fiancé...
I think I'm a bit too young for this.
You're not suggesting I get married to someone I've never even met?!
I don't want to do that!
Next...
Try this on.
Eh?

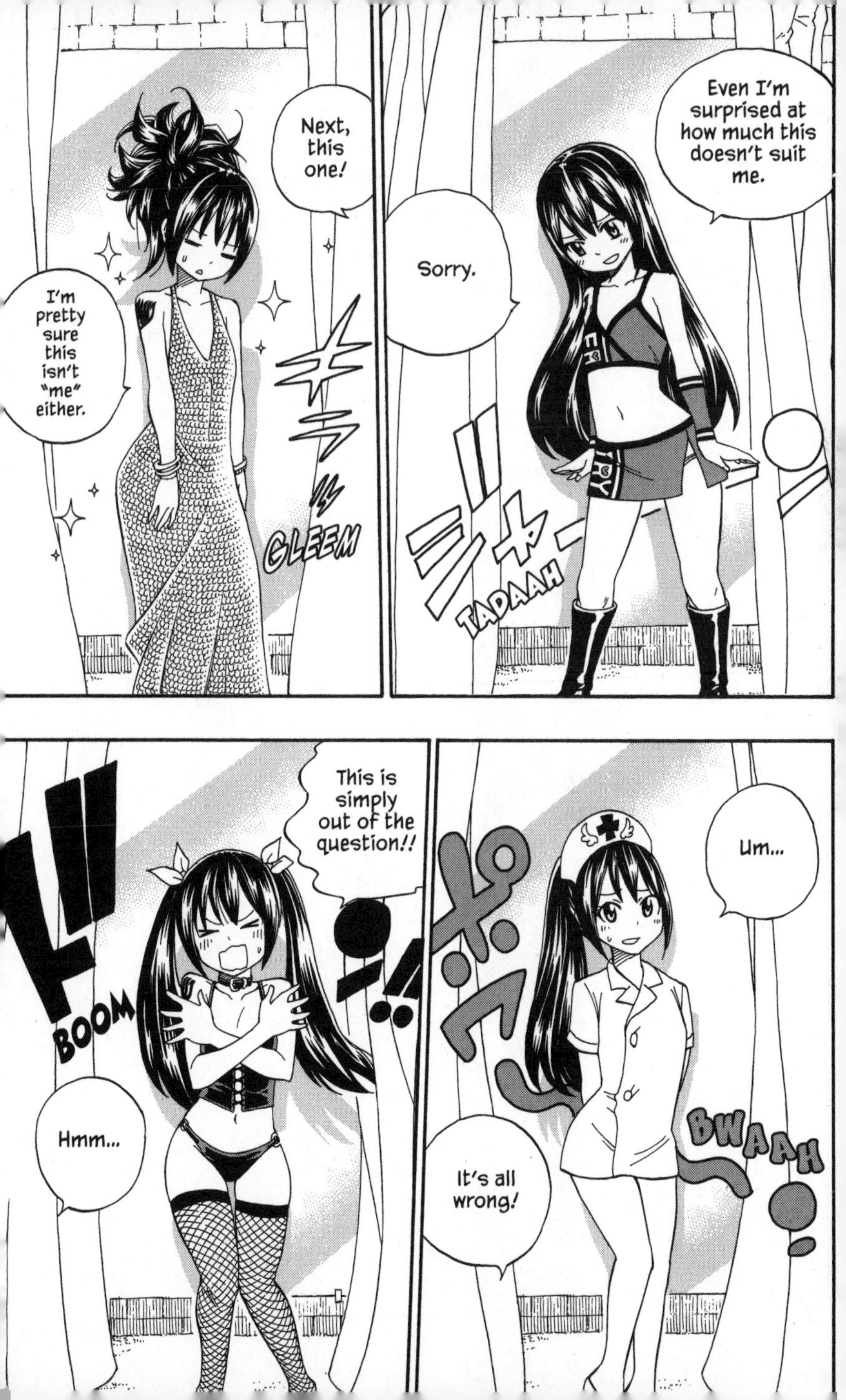
Even I'm surprised at how much this doesn't suit me.
Sorry.
TADAAH
Next, this one!
I'm pretty sure this isn't "me" either.
GLEEM
Um...
BWAAH
It's all wrong!
This is simply out of the question!!
BOOM
Hmm...

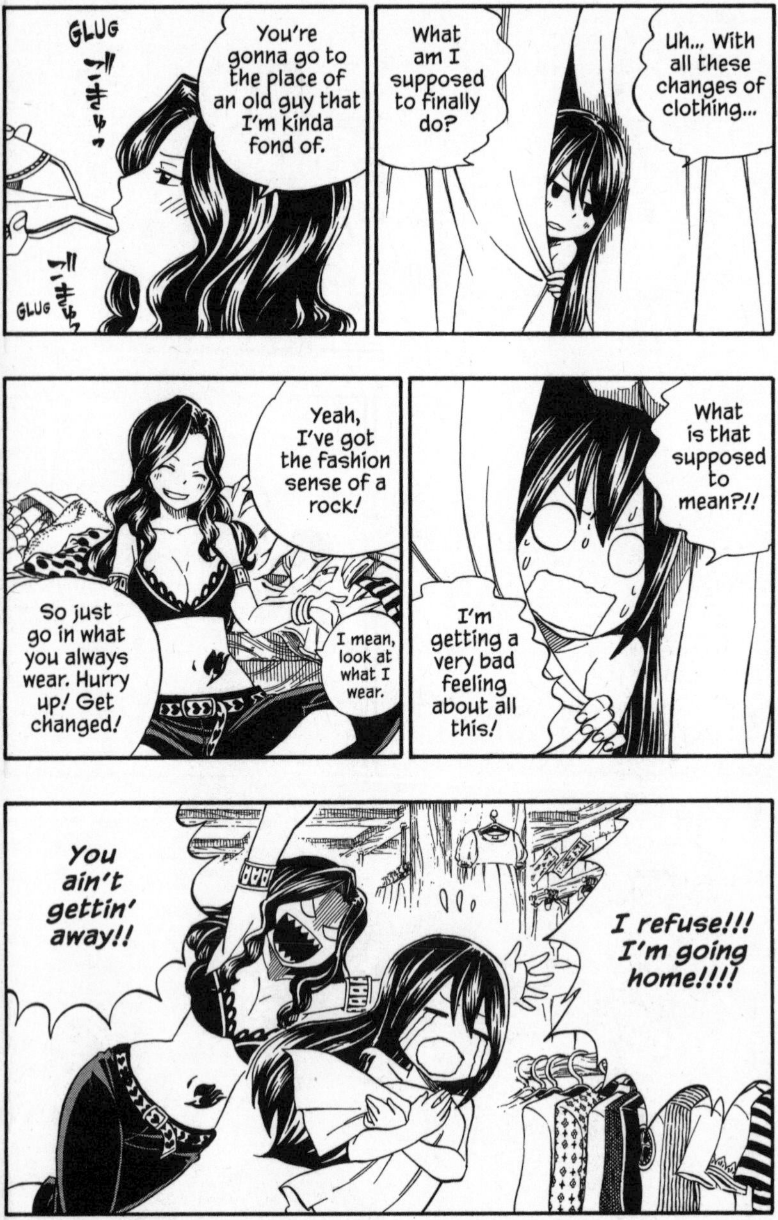
Uh... With all these changes of clothing...
What am I supposed to finally do?
You're gonna go to the place of an old guy that I'm kinda fond of.
GLUG
ごきゅっ
GLUG
ごきゅっ
What is that supposed to mean?!!
I'm getting a very bad feeling about all this!
Yeah, I've got the fashion sense of a rock!
I mean, look at what I wear.
So just go in what you always wear. Hurry up! Get changed!
I refuse!!! I'm going home!!!!
You ain't gettin' away!!

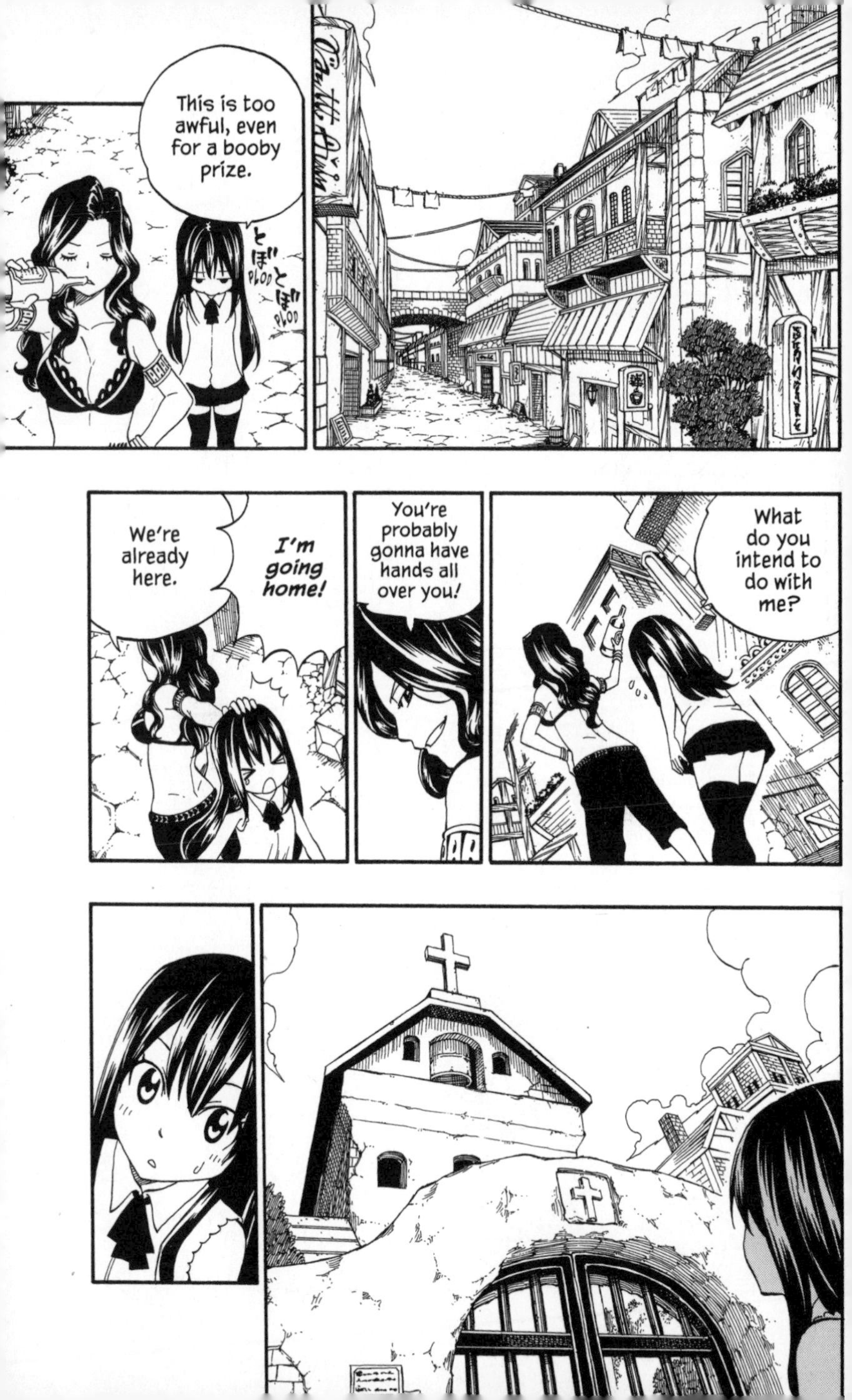
This is too awful, even for a booby prize.
とぼ PLOD とぼ PLOD
What do you intend to do with me?
You're probably gonna have hands all over you!
I'm going home!
We're already here.

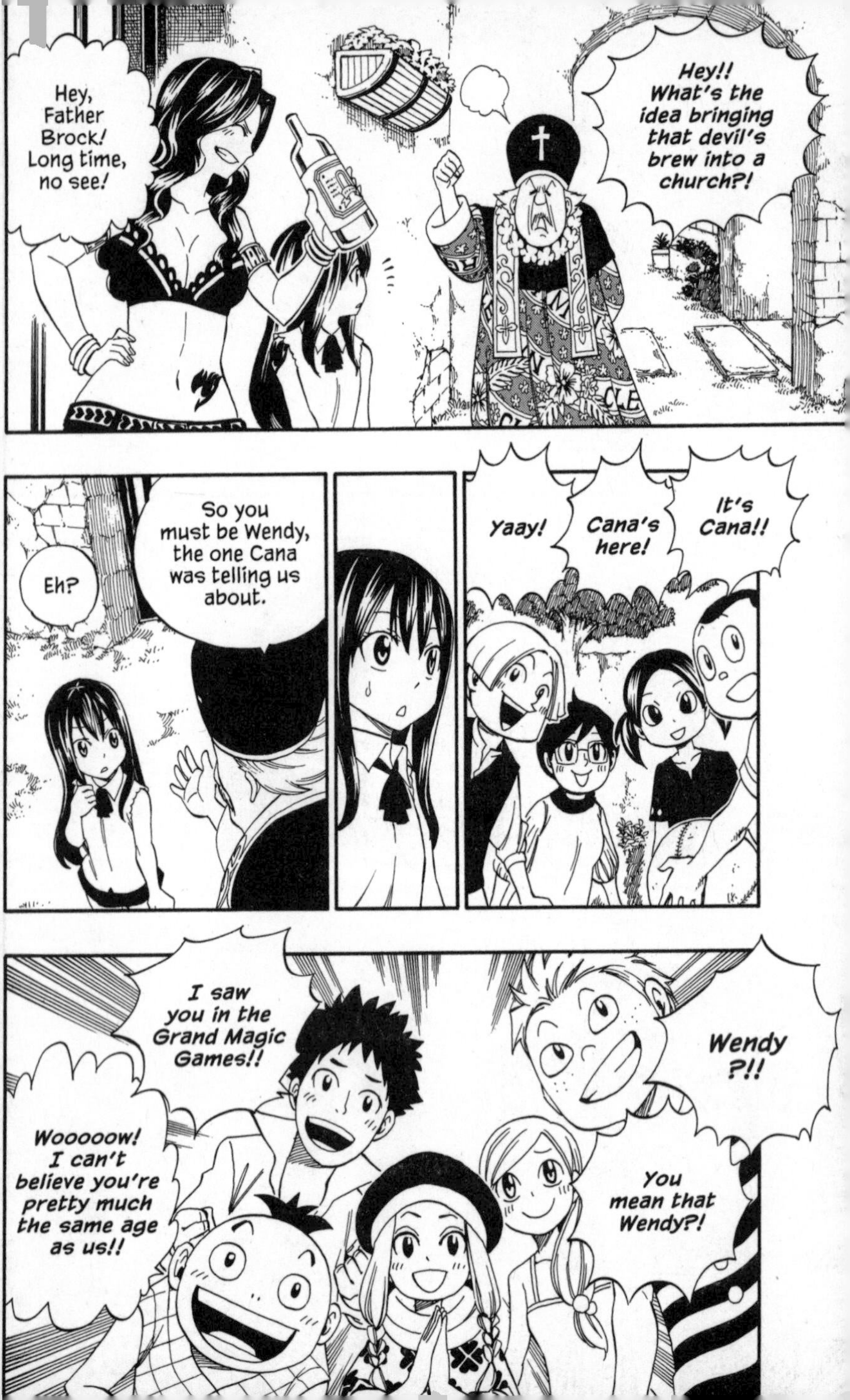
Hey!! What's the idea bringing that devil's brew into a church?!
Hey, Father Brock! Long time, no see!
It's Cana!!
Cana's here!
Yaay!
So you must be Wendy, the one Cana was telling us about.
Eh?
Wendy ?!!
I saw you in the Grand Magic Games!!
You mean that Wendy?!
Woooow! I can't believe you're pretty much the same age as us!!

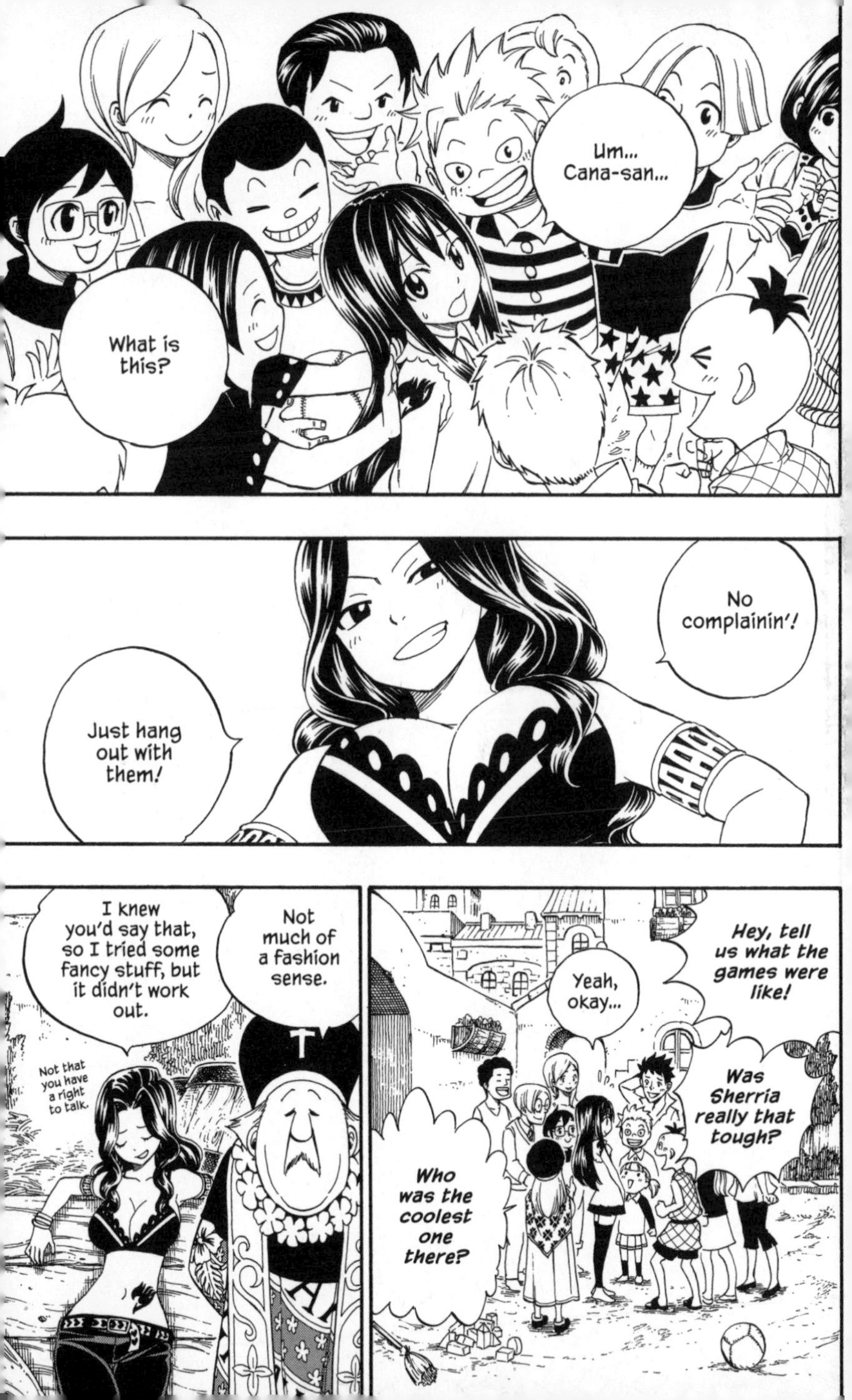
Um... Cana-san...
What is this?
No complainin'!
Just hang out with them!
Hey, tell us what the games were like!
Yeah, okay...
Was Sherria really that tough?
Who was the coolest one there?
Not much of a fashion sense.
I knew you'd say that, so I tried some fancy stuff, but it didn't work out.
Not that you have a right to talk.

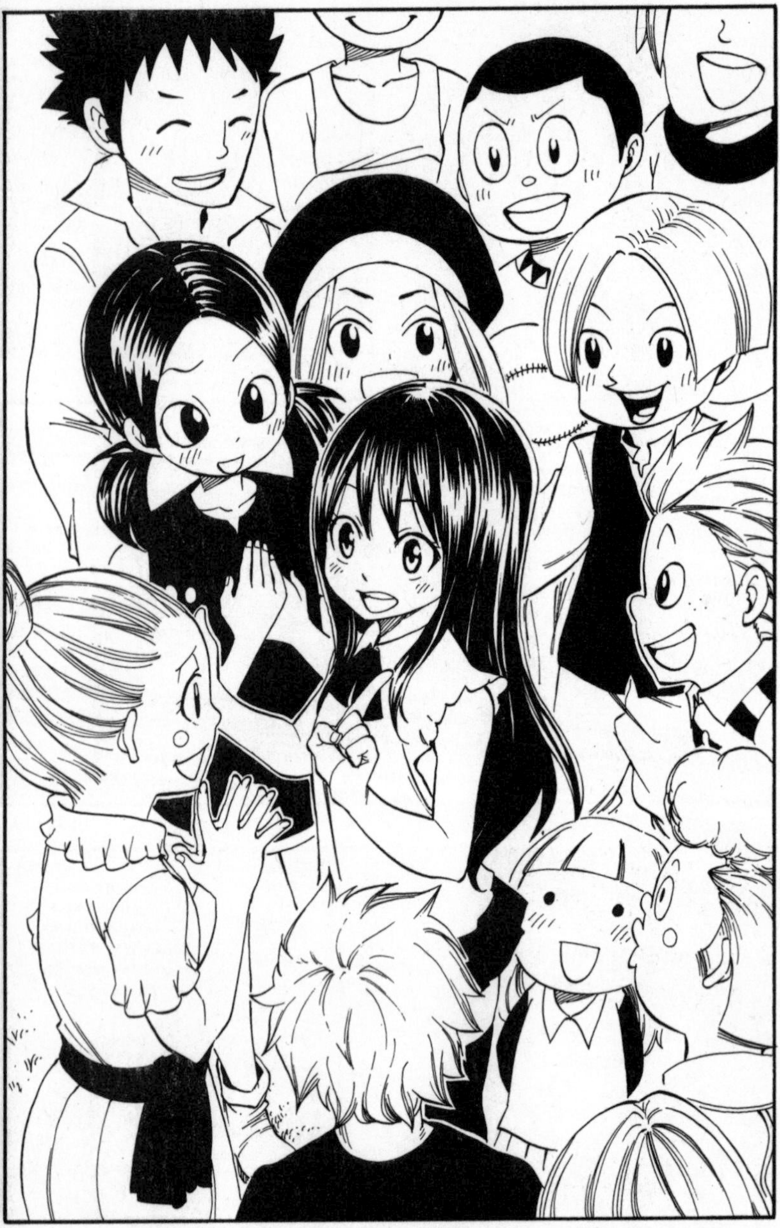

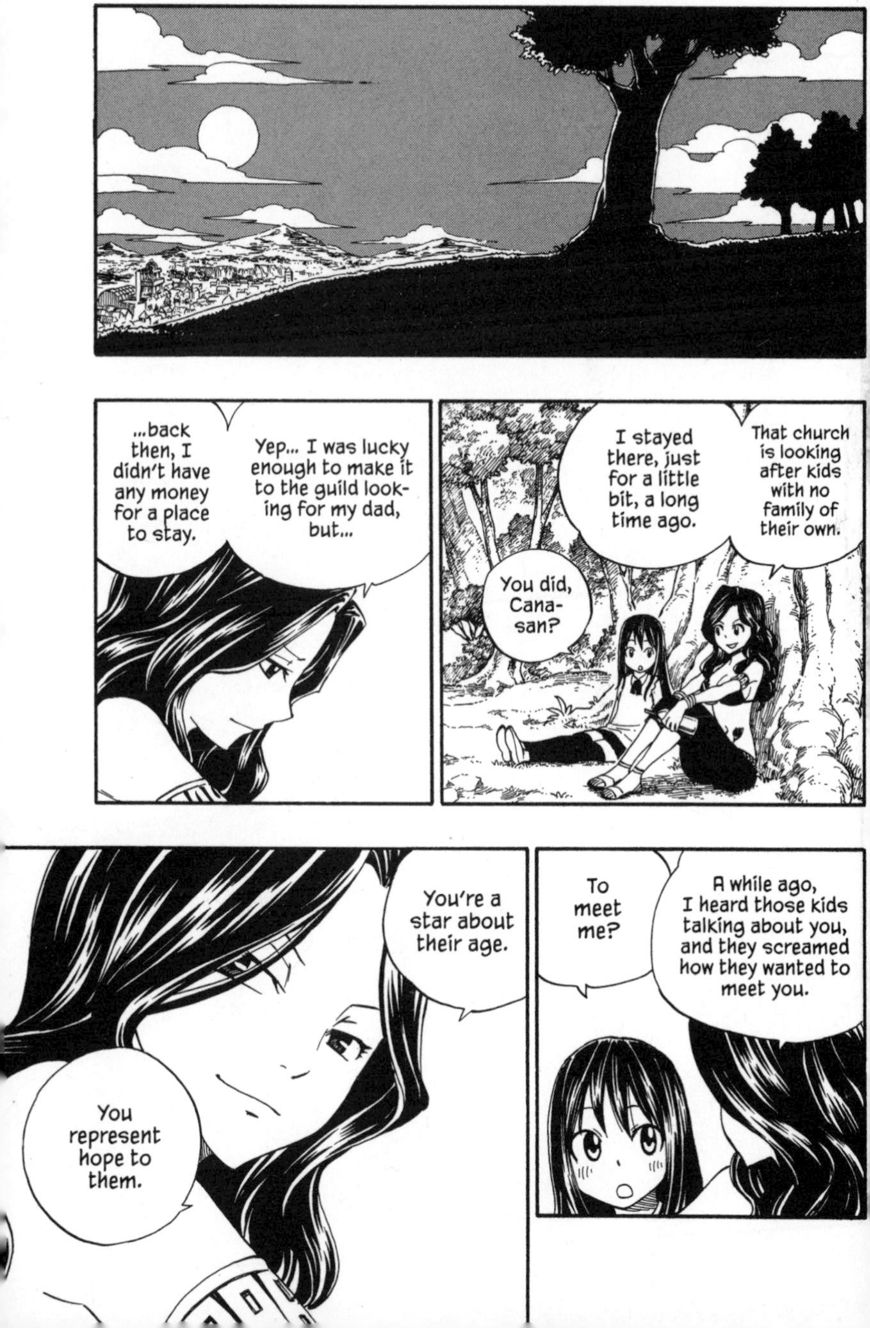
That church is looking after kids with no family of their own.
I stayed there, just for a little bit, a long time ago.
You did, Cana-san?
Yep... I was lucky enough to make it to the guild looking for my dad, but...
...back then, I didn't have any money for a place to stay.
A while ago, I heard those kids talking about you, and they screamed how they wanted to meet you.
To meet me?
You're a star about their age.
You represent hope to them.

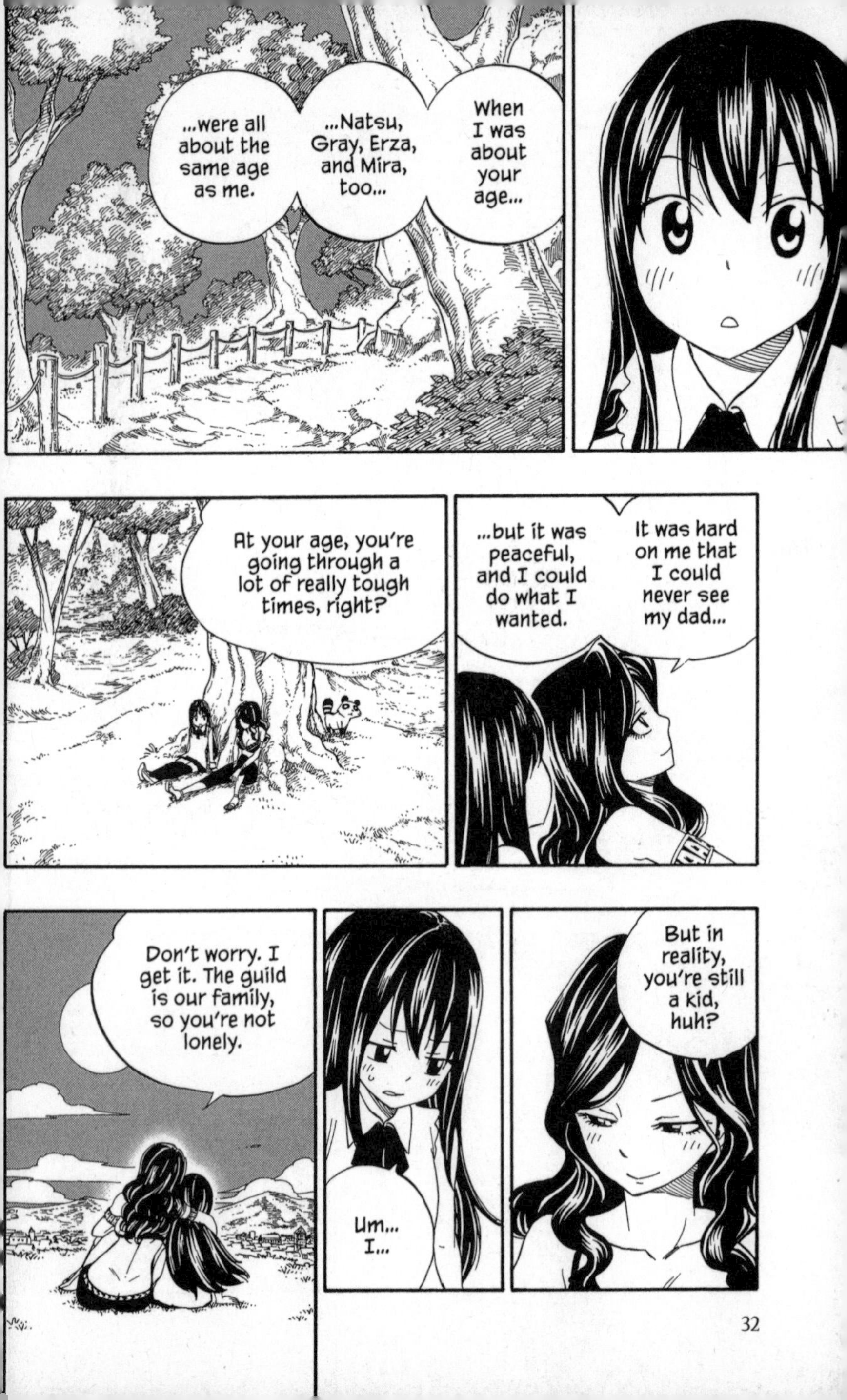
When I was about your age...
...Natsu, Gray, Erza, and Mira, too...
...were all about the same age as me.
It was hard on me that I could never see my dad...
...but it was peaceful, and I could do what I wanted.
At your age, you're going through a lot of really tough times, right?
But in reality, you're still a kid, huh?
Um... I...
Don't worry. I get it. The guild is our family, so you're not lonely.

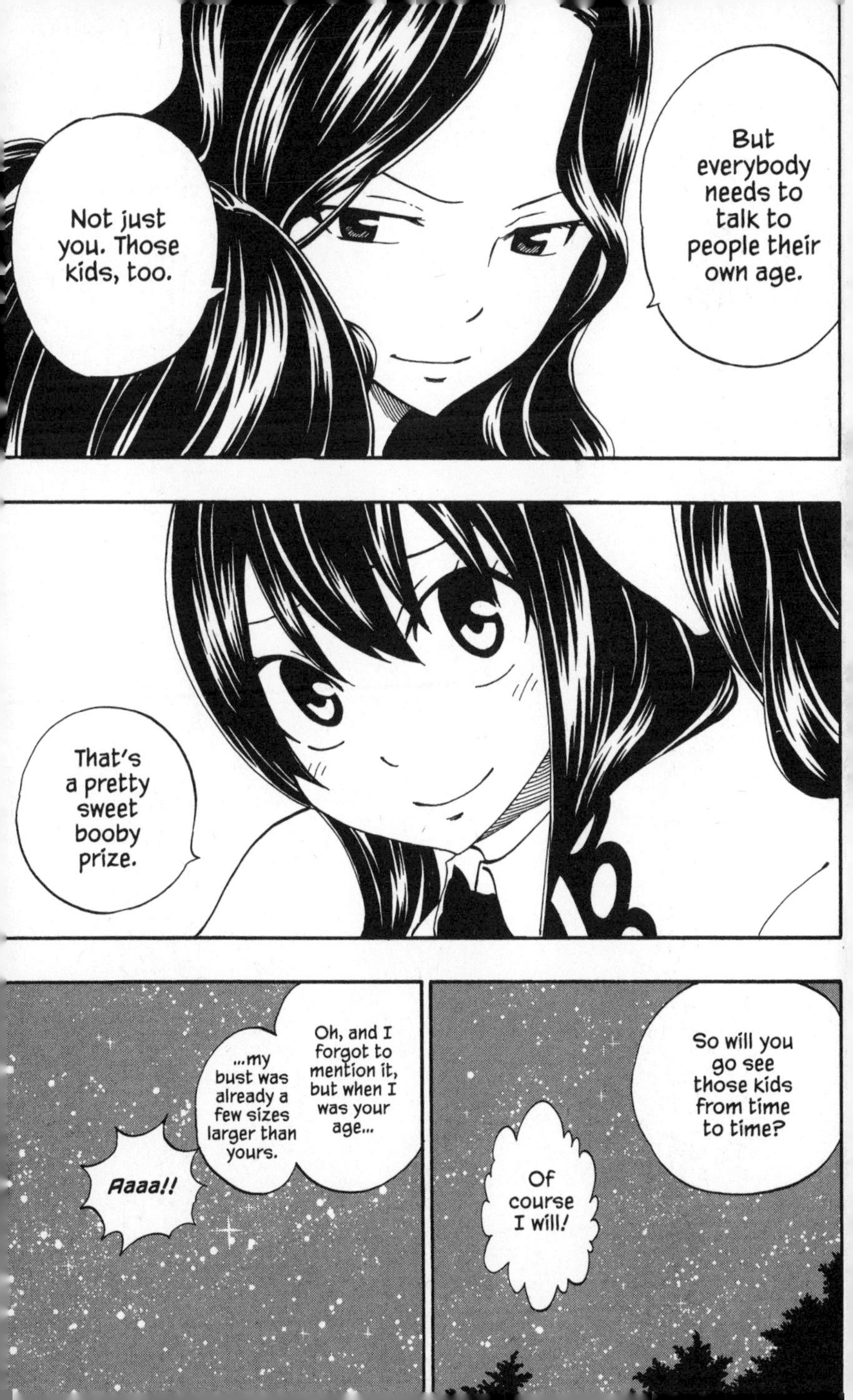
But everybody needs to talk to people their own age.
Not just you. Those kids, too.
That's a pretty sweet booby prize.
So will you go see those kids from time to time?
Of course I will!
Oh, and I forgot to mention it, but when I was your age...
...my bust was already a few sizes larger than yours.
Aaaa!!

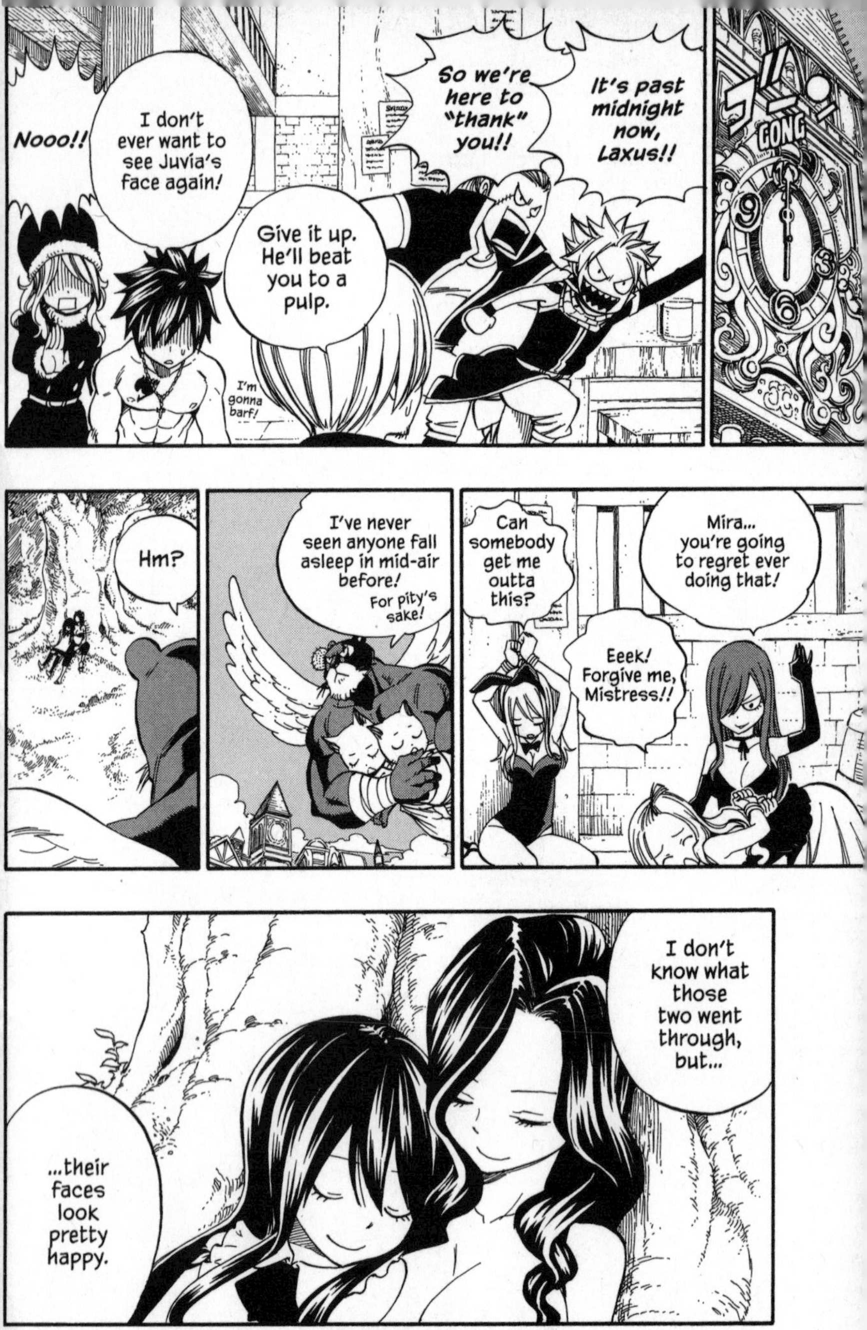
GONG
It's past midnight now, Laxus!!
So we're here to "thank" you!!
Give it up. He'll beat you to a pulp.
I don't ever want to see Juvia's face again!
Nooo!!
I'm gonna barf!
Mira... you're going to regret ever doing that!
Eeek! Forgive me, Mistress!!
Can somebody get me outta this?
I've never seen anyone fall asleep in mid-air before!
For pity's sake!
Hm?
I don't know what those two went through, but...
...their faces look pretty happy.

★The End★

FOUR-PANEL COMICS!

SUBJECT: VALENTINE'S DAY

THE ORIGINAL CHOICE WAS ABOUT CURRY

Maybe I wrapped this a little *too* nicely.
I don't... want him to get any wrong ideas.
Um...
I wouldn't choose either one!
But if you absolutely *had* to make the choice?
But "Chocolate-flavored poop" or "Poop-flavored chocolate"?! I don't wanna eat either!
And whose poop are we talkin' about?!
That doesn't really matter.
Lucy, what's *your* answer?!
GRR
I choose to not give you anything.

FROM *MAGAZINE SPECIAL*, 2009, ISSUE 2.

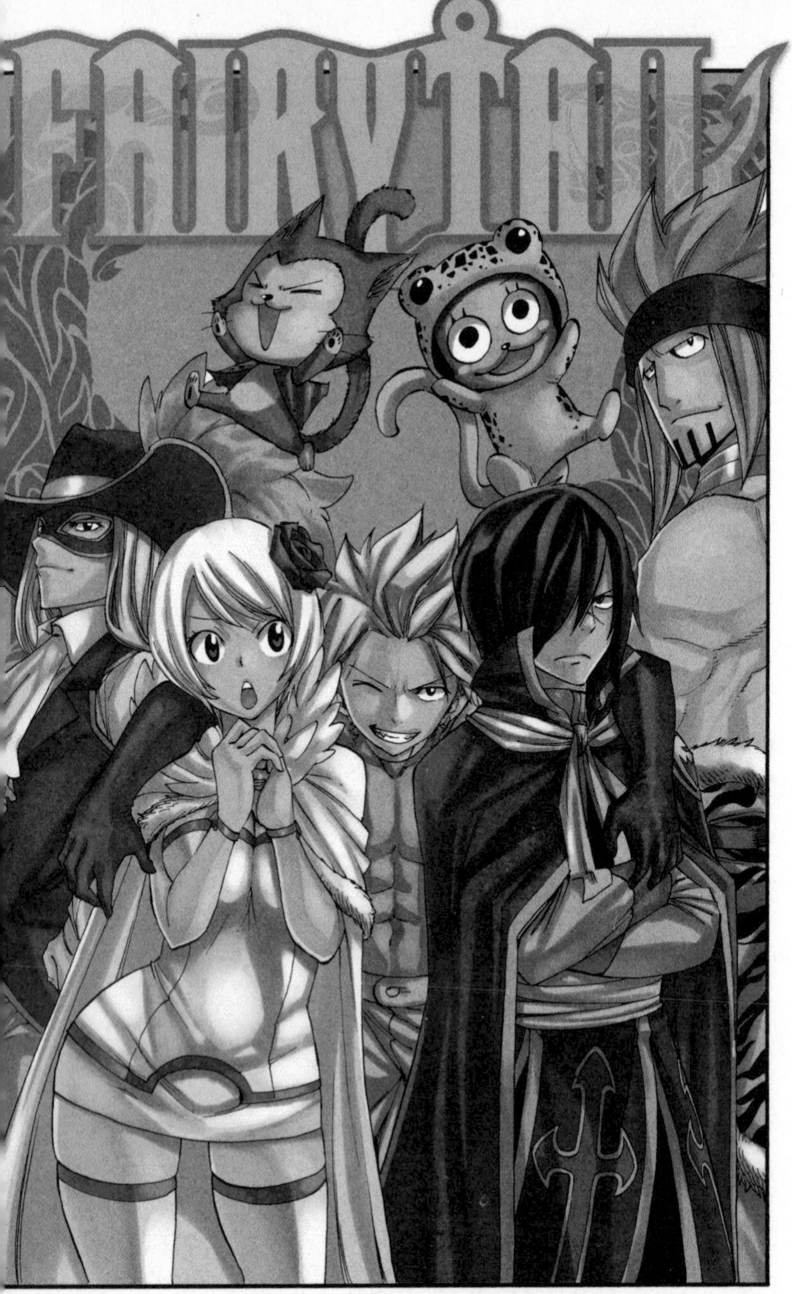
FAIRY TAIL

Welcome Home, Frosch

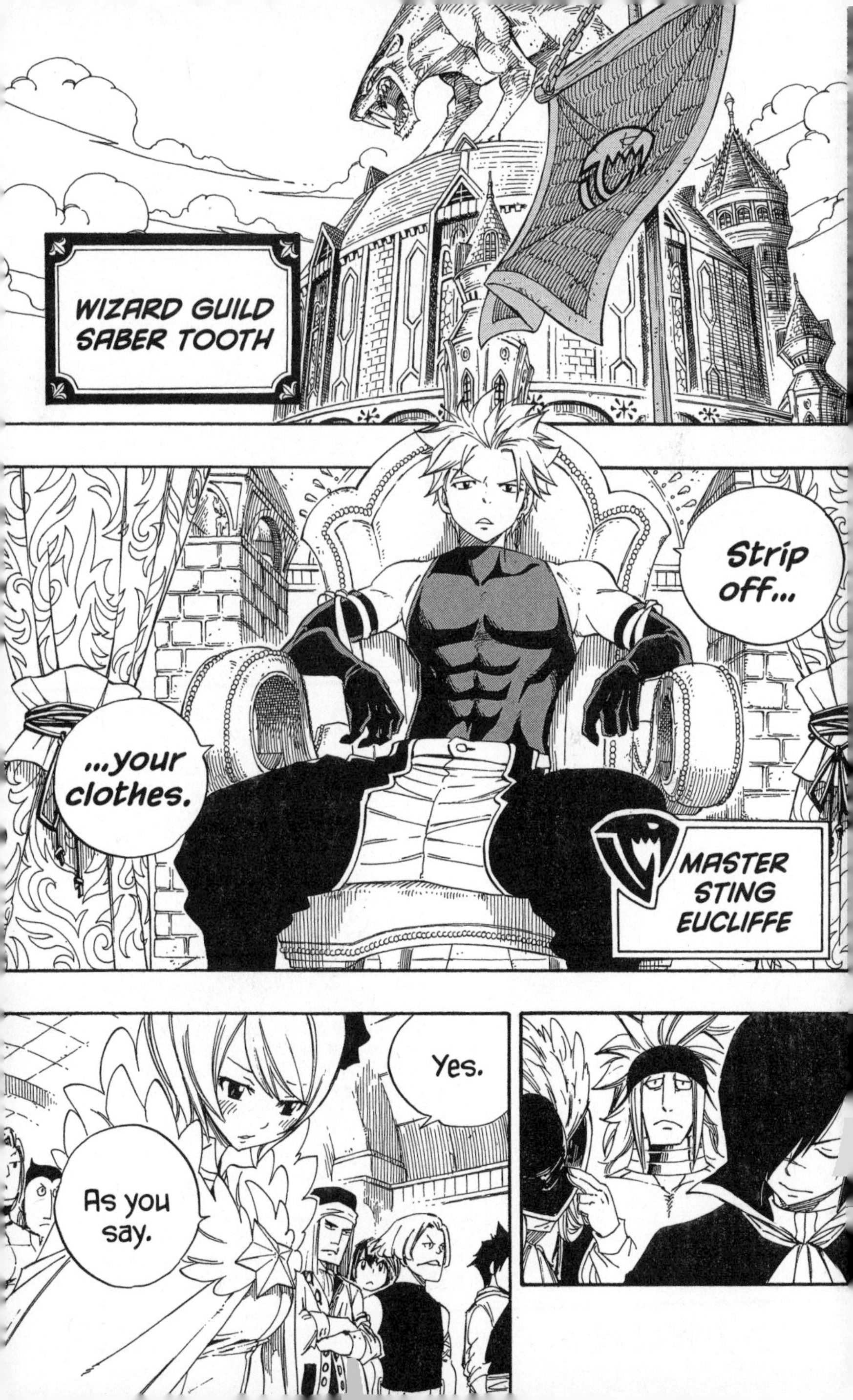
WIZARD GUILD SABER TOOTH
Strip off...
...your clothes.
MASTER STING EUCLIFFE
Yes.
As you say.

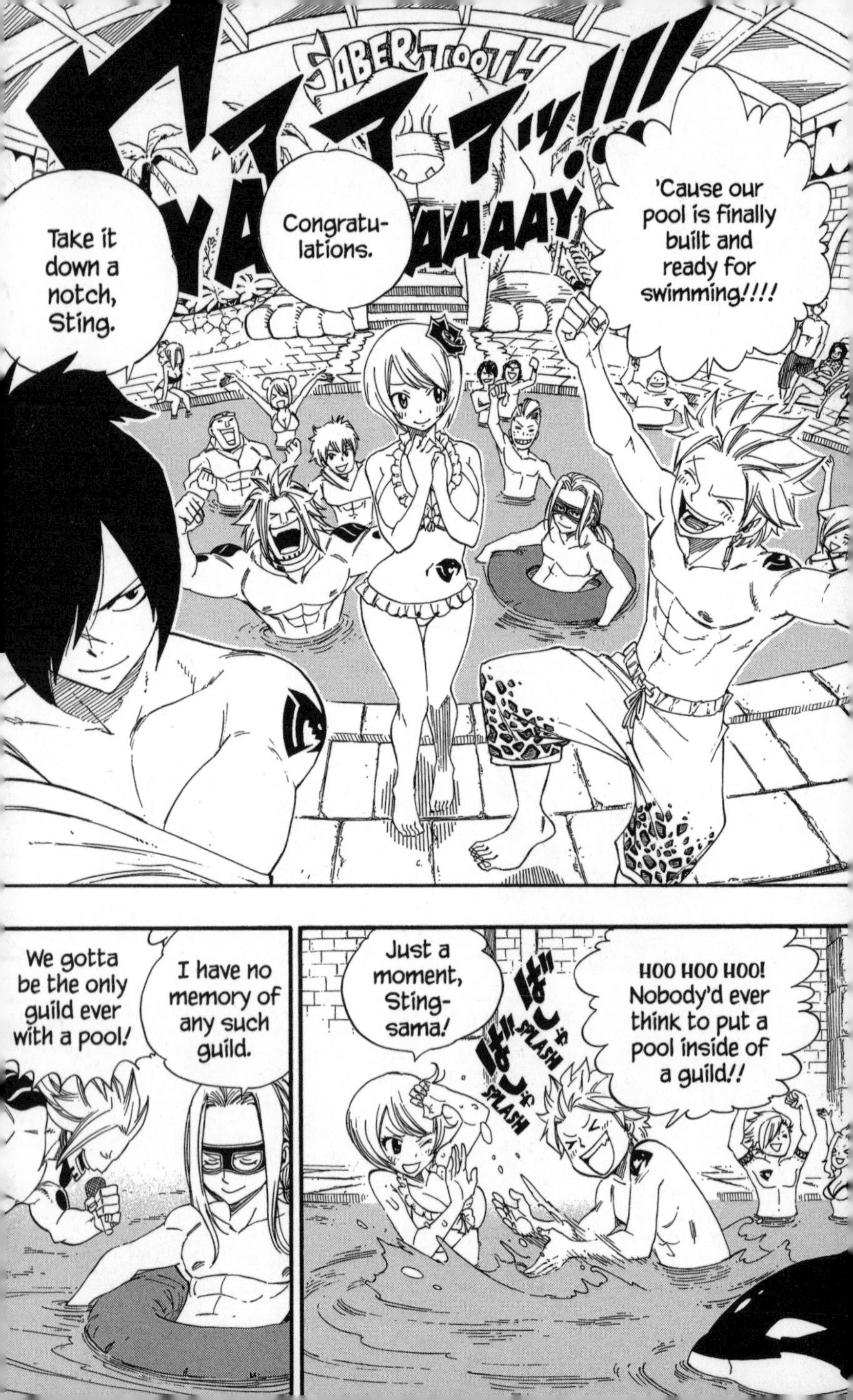
SABERTOOTH
YAAAAAY
'Cause our pool is finally built and ready for swimming!!!!
Congratu-lations.
Take it down a notch, Sting.
HOO HOO HOO! Nobody'd ever think to put a pool inside of a guild!!
Just a moment, Sting-sama!
SPLASH
SPLASH
We gotta be the only guild ever with a pool!
I have no memory of any such guild.

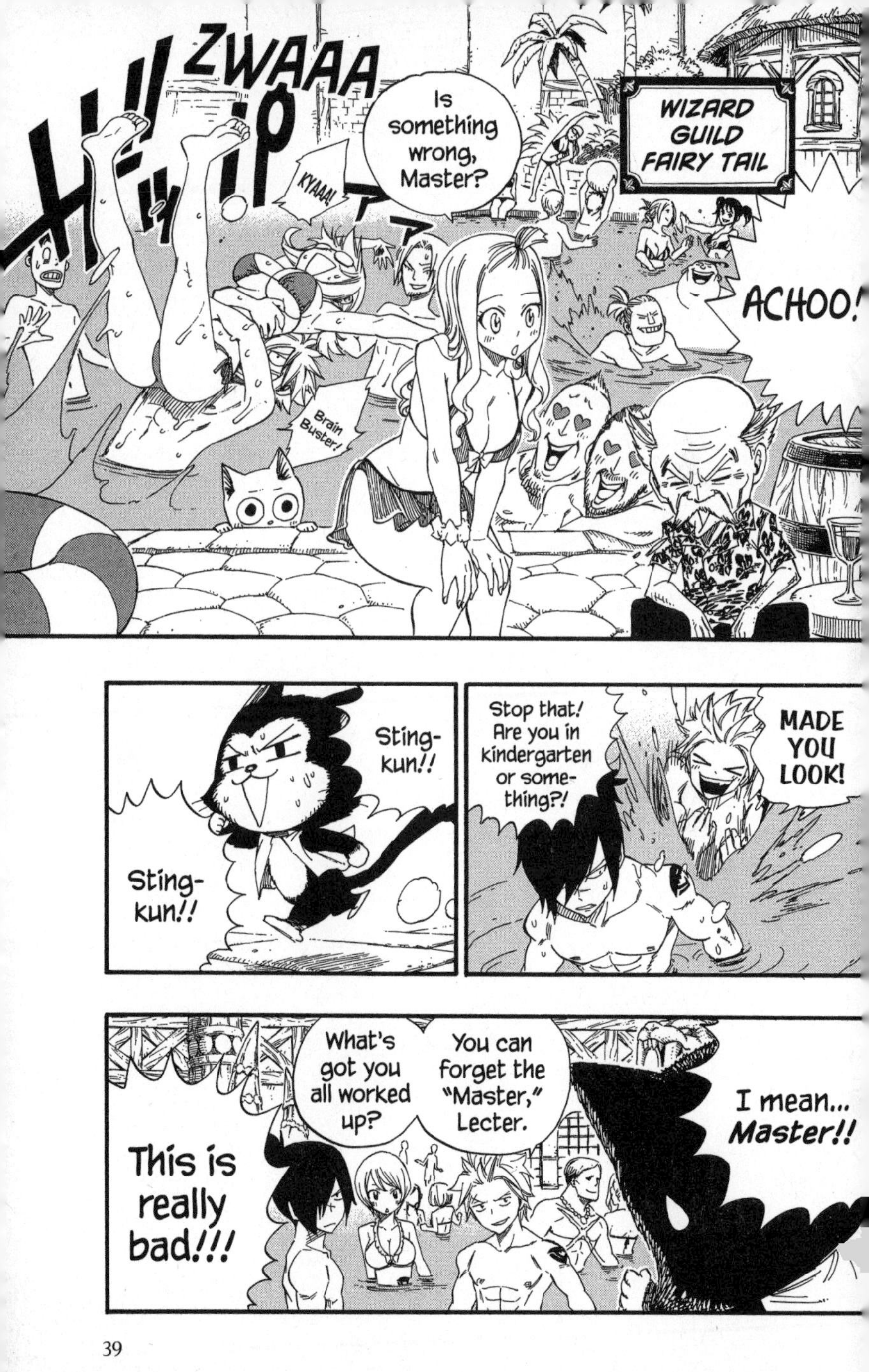
WIZARD GUILD FAIRY TAIL
ACHOO!
Is something wrong, Master?
KYAAA!
ZWAAAP
Brain Buster!
MADE YOU LOOK!
Stop that! Are you in kindergarten or some-thing?!
Sting-kun!!
Sting-kun!!
I mean... *Master!!*
You can forget the "Master," Lecter.
What's got you all worked up?
This is really bad!!!

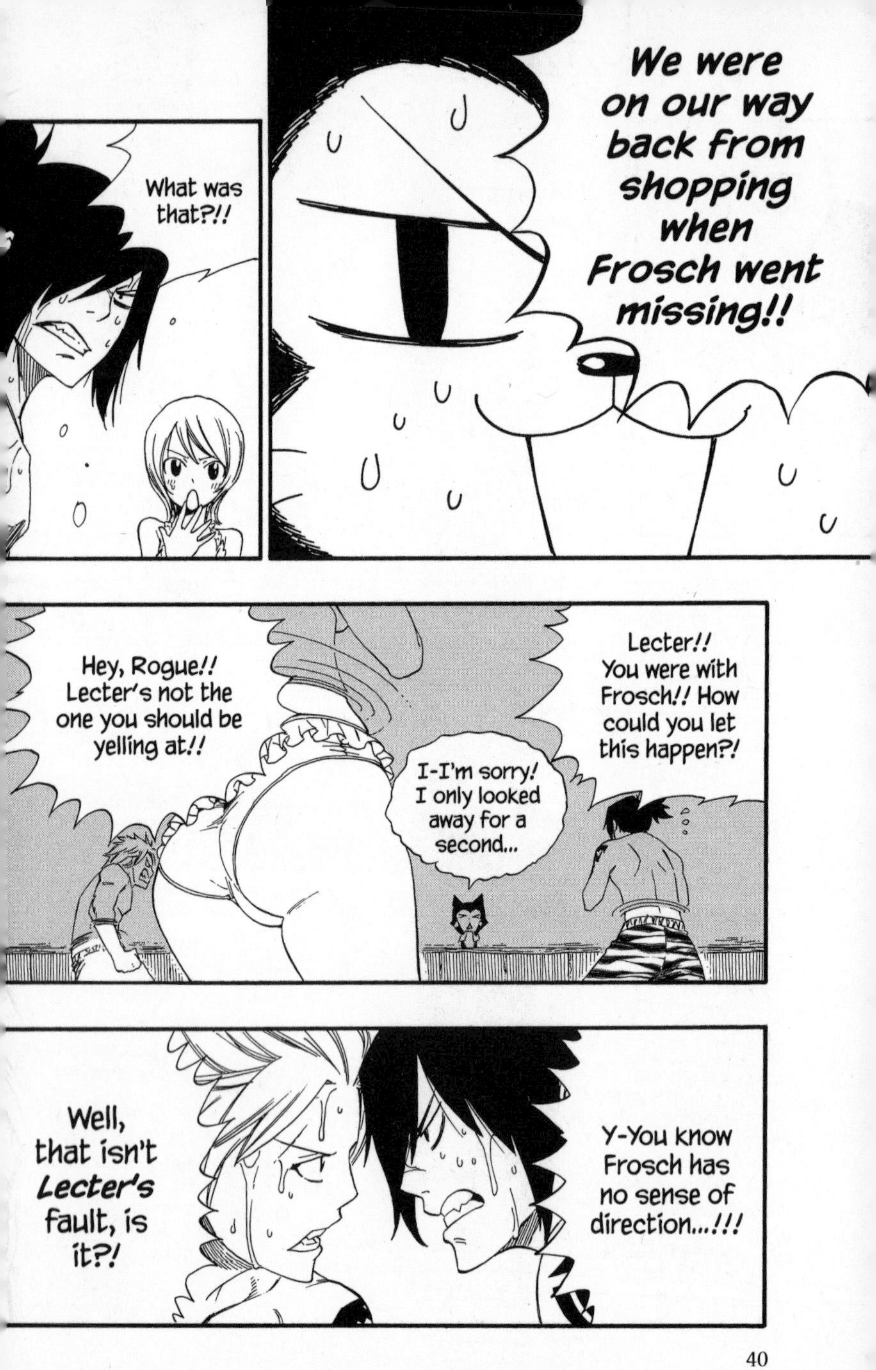
We were on our way back from shopping when Frosch went missing!!
What was that?!!
Lecter!! You were with Frosch!! How could you let this happen?!
I-I'm sorry! I only looked away for a second...
Hey, Rogue!! Lecter's not the one you should be yelling at!!
Y-You know Frosch has no sense of direction...!!!
Well, that isn't Lecter's fault, is it?!

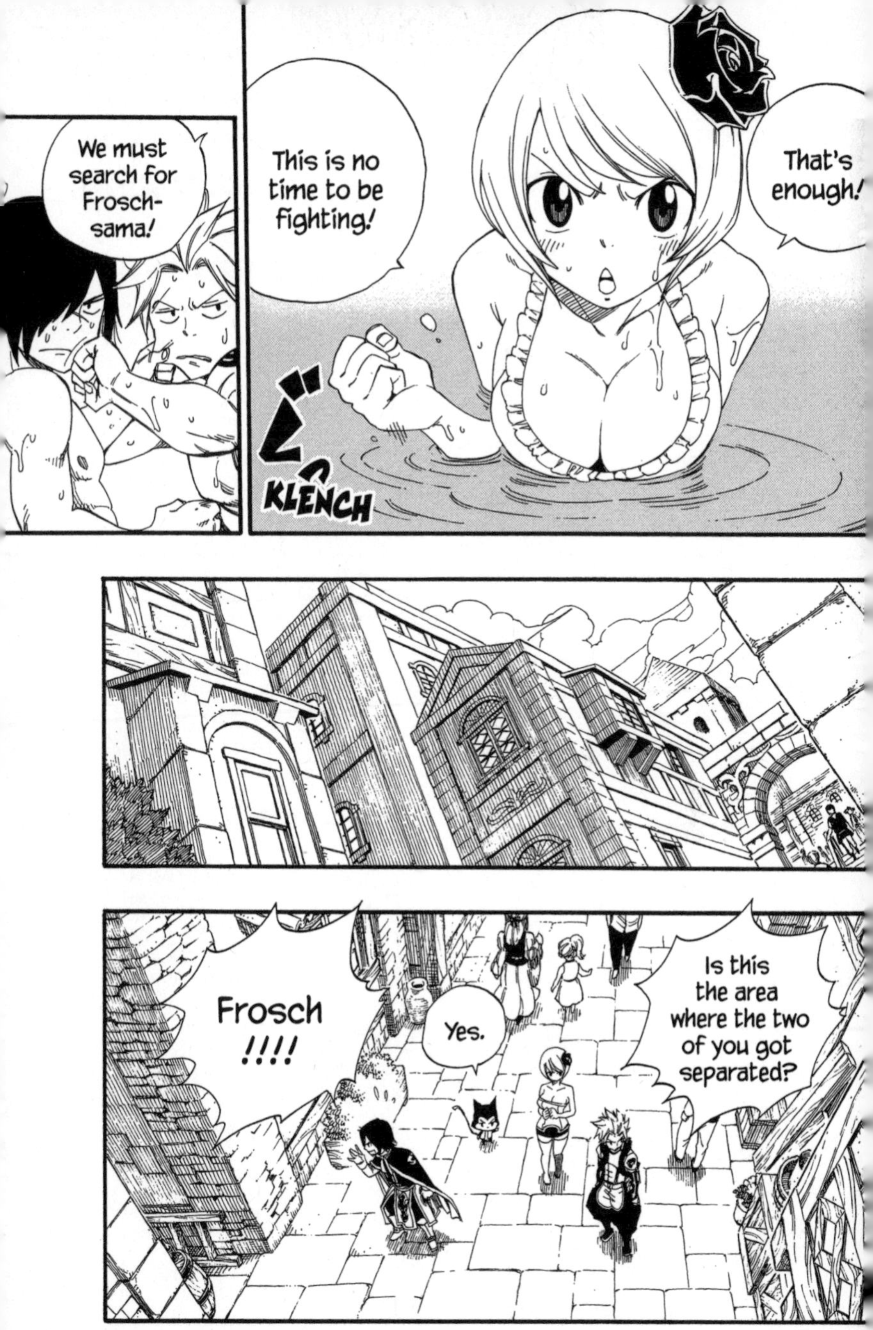
That's enough!
This is no time to be fighting!
KLENCH
We must search for Frosch-sama!
Is this the area where the two of you got separated?
Yes.
Frosch !!!!

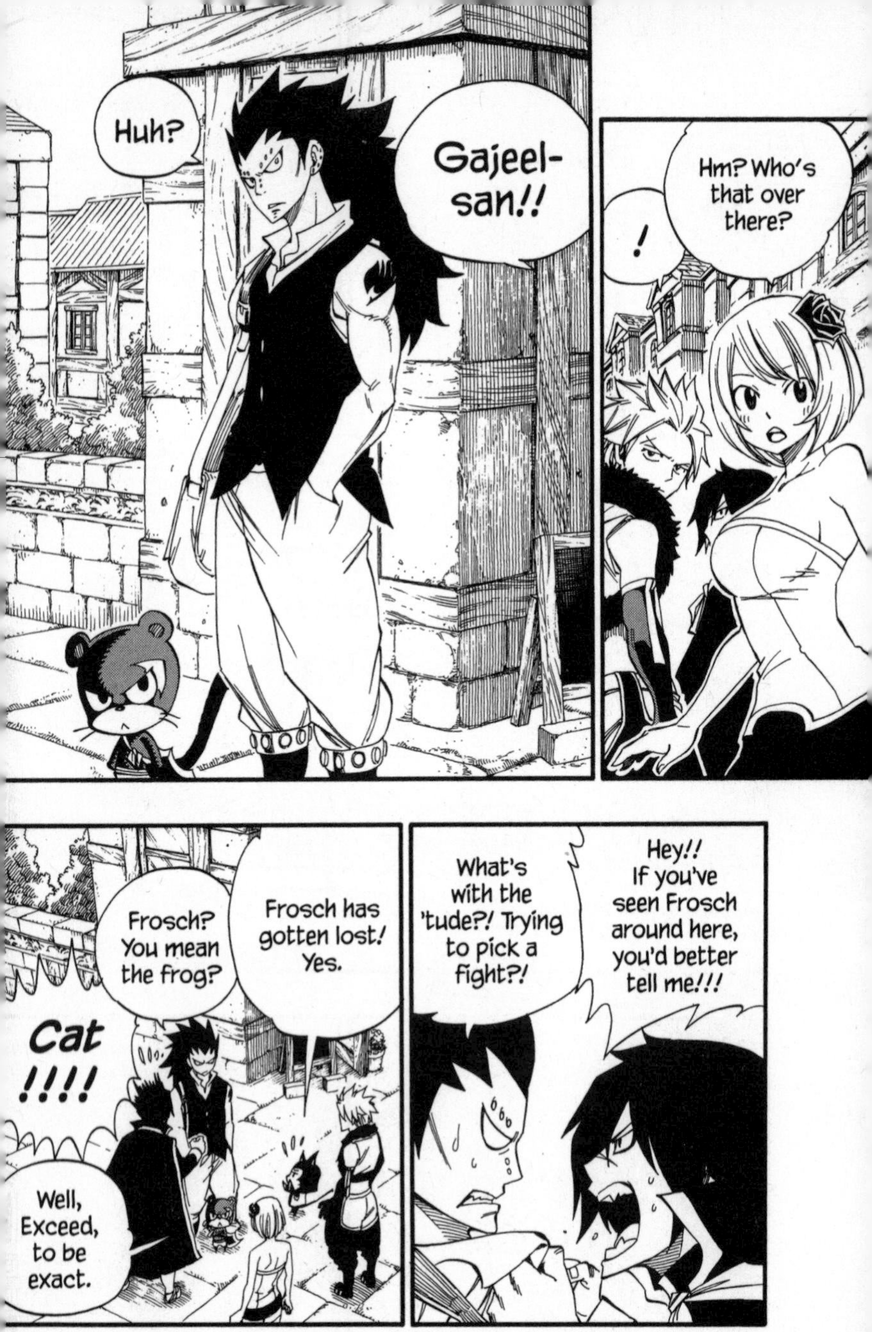
Hm? Who's that over there?
!
Gajeel-san!!
Huh?
Hey!! If you've seen Frosch around here, you'd better tell me!!!
What's with the 'tude?! Trying to pick a fight?!
Frosch has gotten lost! Yes.
Frosch? You mean the frog?
Cat !!!!
Well, Exceed, to be exact.

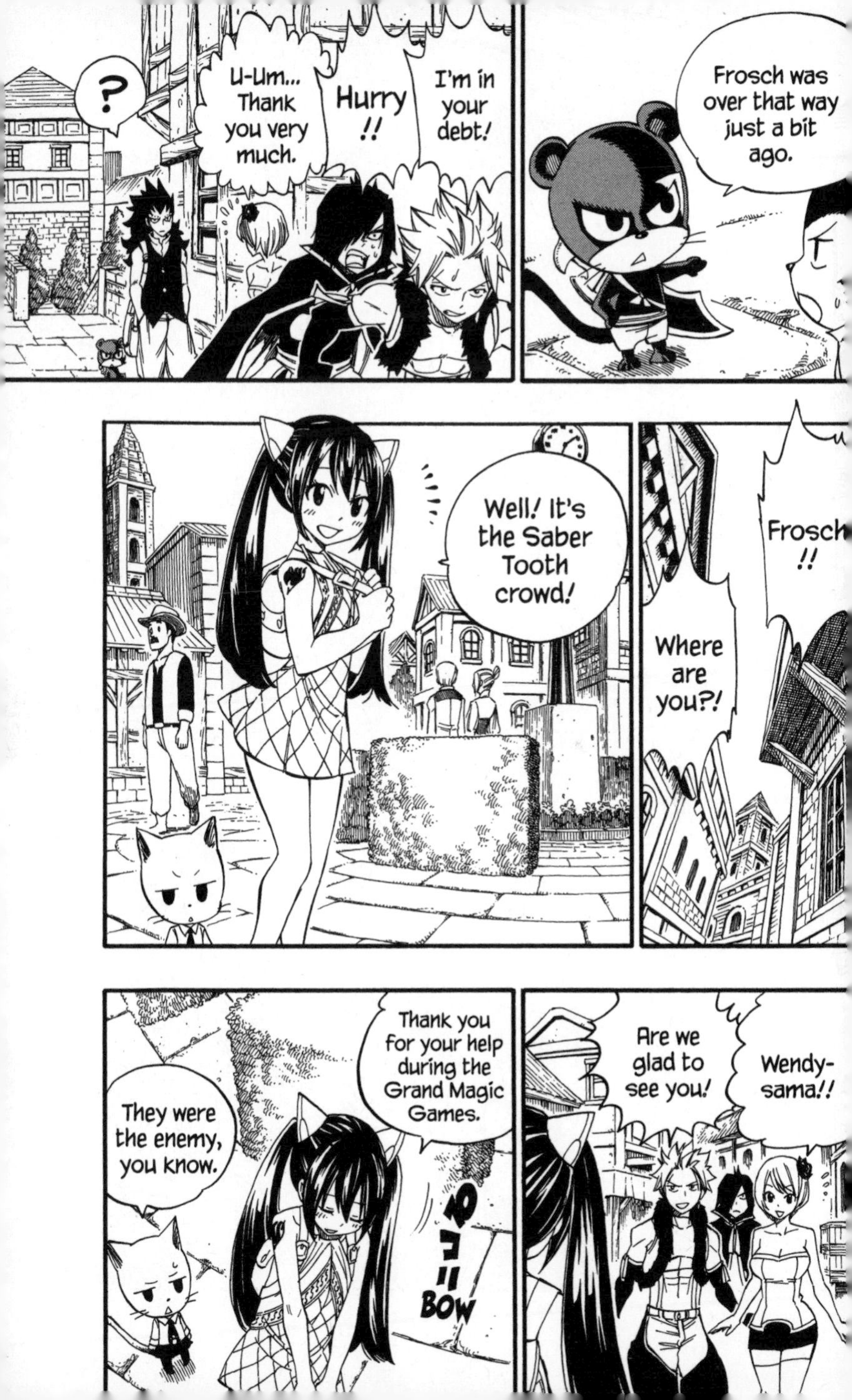
Frosch was over that way just a bit ago.
I'm in your debt!
Hurry!!
U-Um... Thank you very much.
?
Frosch!!
Where are you?!
Well! It's the Saber Tooth crowd!
Wendy-sama!!
Are we glad to see you!
Thank you for your help during the Grand Magic Games.
BOW
They were the enemy, you know.

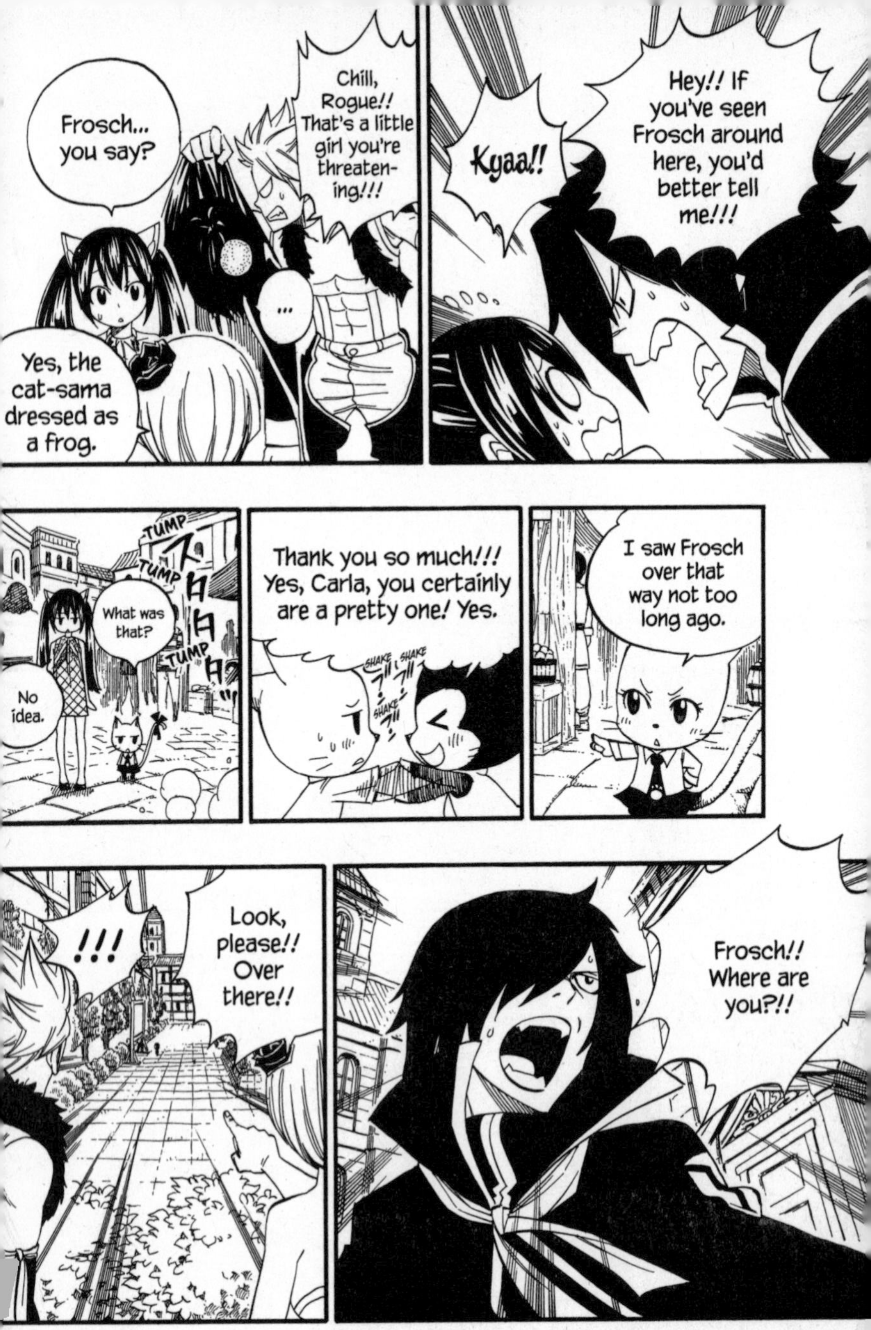
Hey!! If you've seen Frosch around here, you'd better tell me!!!
Kyaa!!
Chill, Rogue!! That's a little girl you're threaten-ing!!!
Frosch... you say?
...
Yes, the cat-sama dressed as a frog.
I saw Frosch over that way not too long ago.
Thank you so much!!! Yes, Carla, you certainly are a pretty one! Yes.
SHAKE
SHAKE
SHAKE
TUMP
TUMP
TUMP
What was that?
No idea.
Frosch!! Where are you?!!
!!!
Look, please!! Over there!!

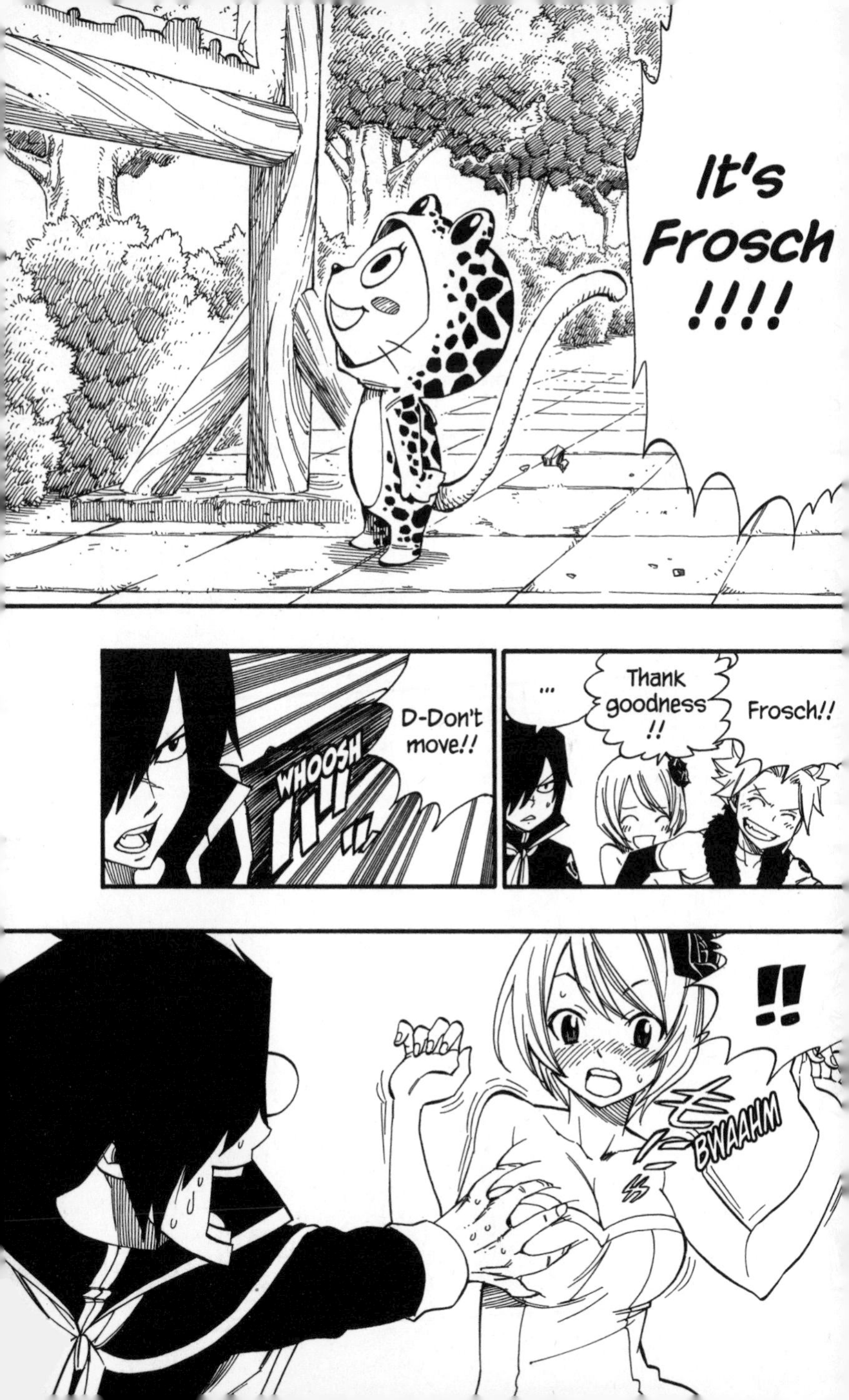
It's Frosch!!!!
Frosch!!
Thank goodness!!
...
D-Don't move!!
WHOOSH
!!
BWAAHM

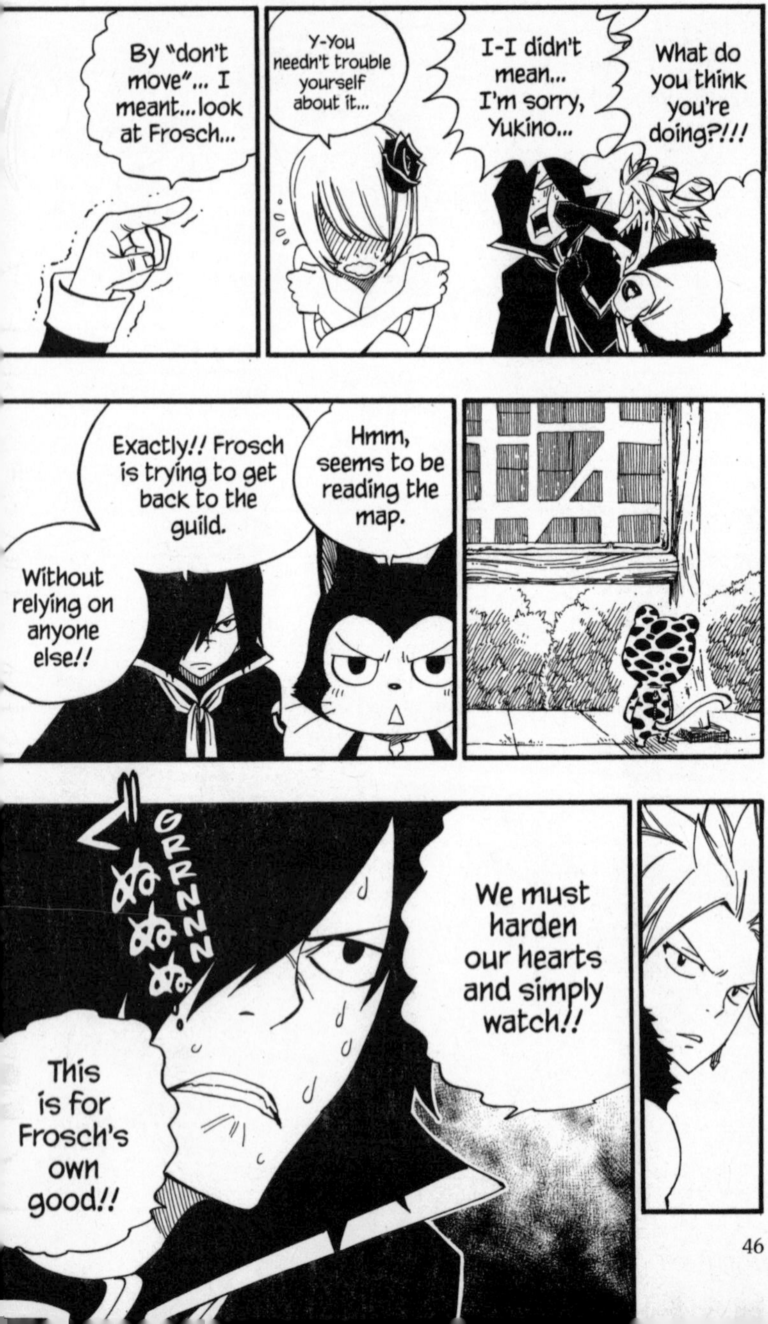
What do you think you're doing?!!!
I-I didn't mean... I'm sorry, Yukino...
Y-You needn't trouble yourself about it...
By "don't move"... I meant...look at Frosch...
Hmm, seems to be reading the map.
Exactly!! Frosch is trying to get back to the guild.
Without relying on anyone else!!
We must harden our hearts and simply watch!!
GRRNNN
ぬぬぬ
This is for Frosch's own good!!

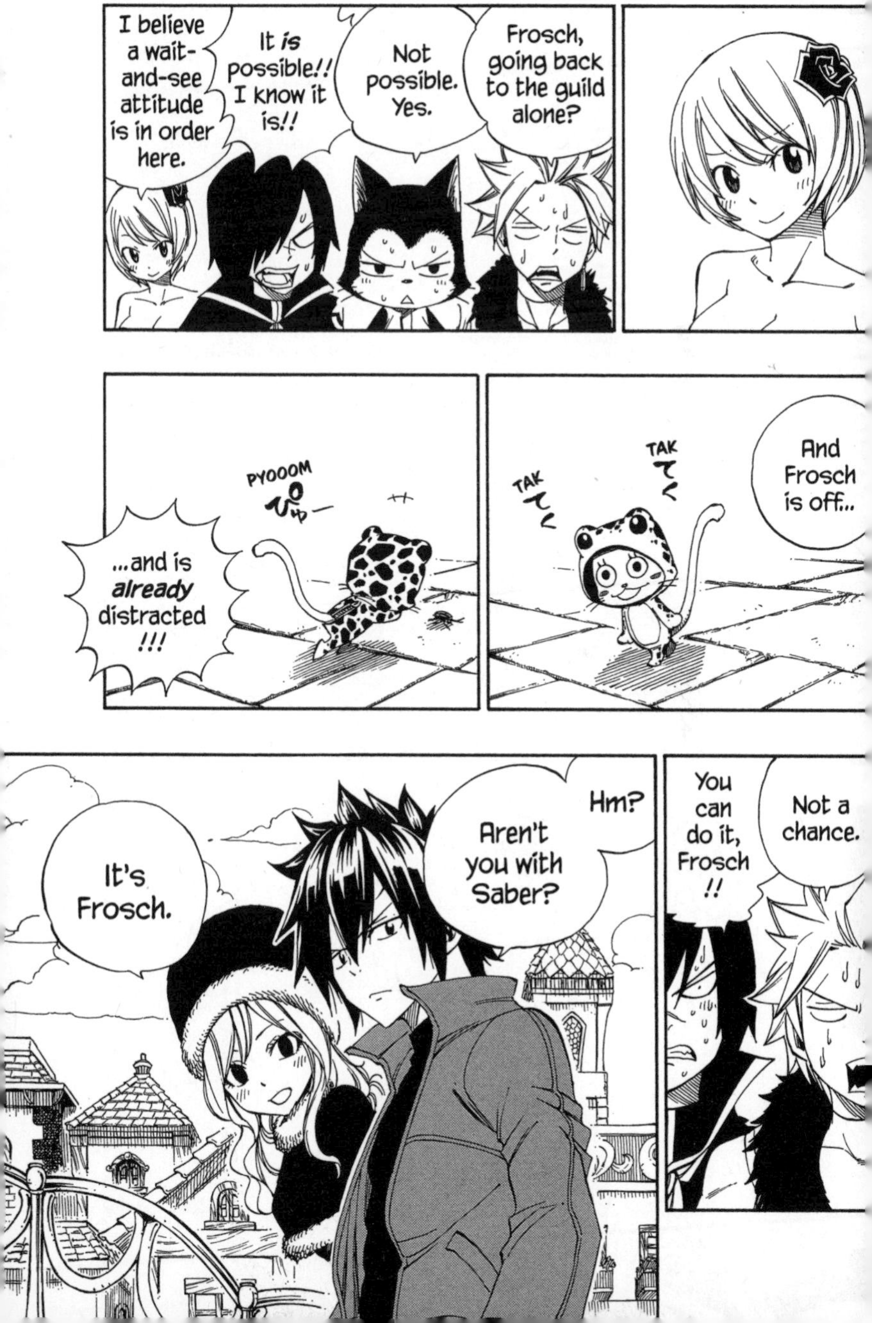
Frosch, going back to the guild alone?
Not possible. Yes.
It *is* possible!! I know it is!!
I believe a wait-and-see attitude is in order here.
And Frosch is off...
TAK
TAK
PYOOOM
...and is *already* distracted!!!
Not a chance.
You can do it, Frosch!!
Hm?
Aren't you with Saber?
It's Frosch.

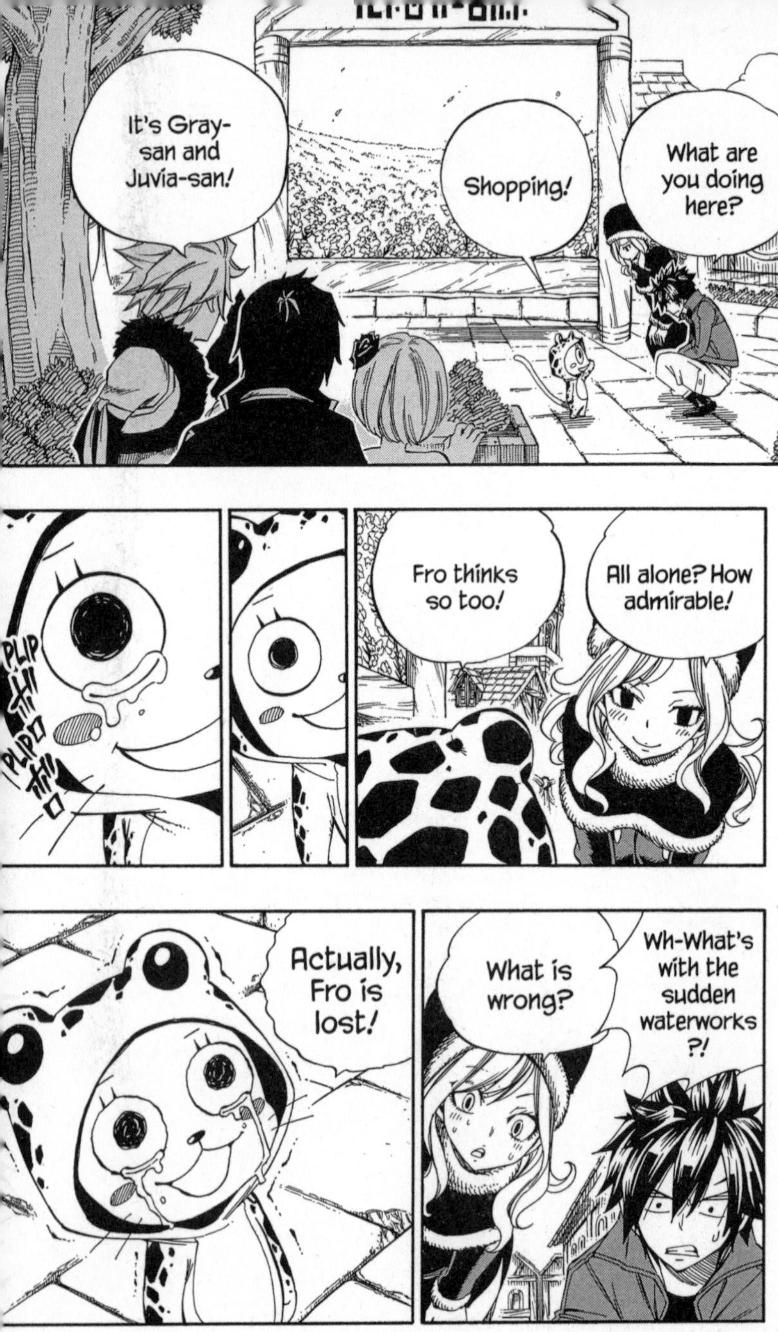
What are you doing here?
Shopping!
It's Gray-san and Juvia-san!
All alone? How admirable!
Fro thinks so too!
PLIP
PLIP
Wh-What's with the sudden waterworks?!
What is wrong?
Actually, Fro is lost!

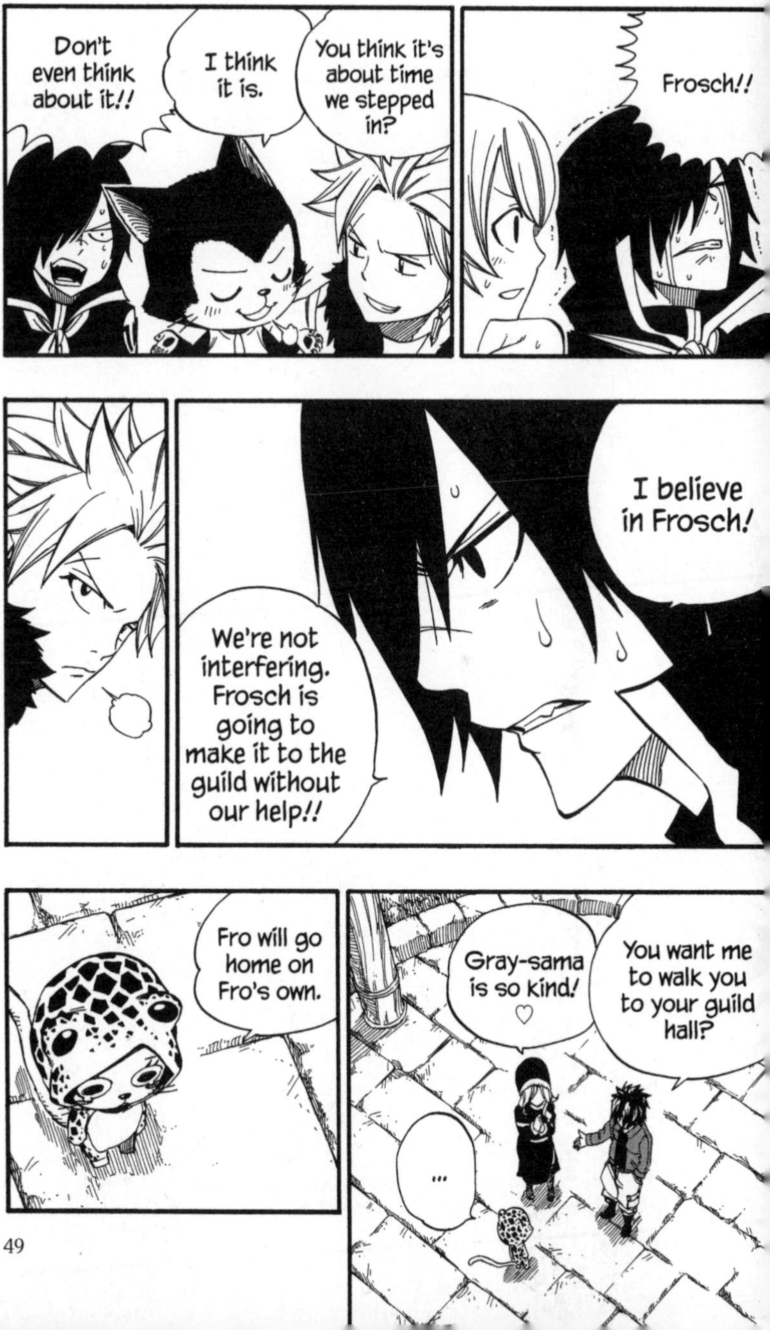
Frosch!!
You think it's about time we stepped in?
I think it is.
Don't even think about it!!
I believe in Frosch!
We're not interfering. Frosch is going to make it to the guild without our help!!
You want me to walk you to your guild hall?
Gray-sama is so kind! ♡
...
Fro will go home on Fro's own.

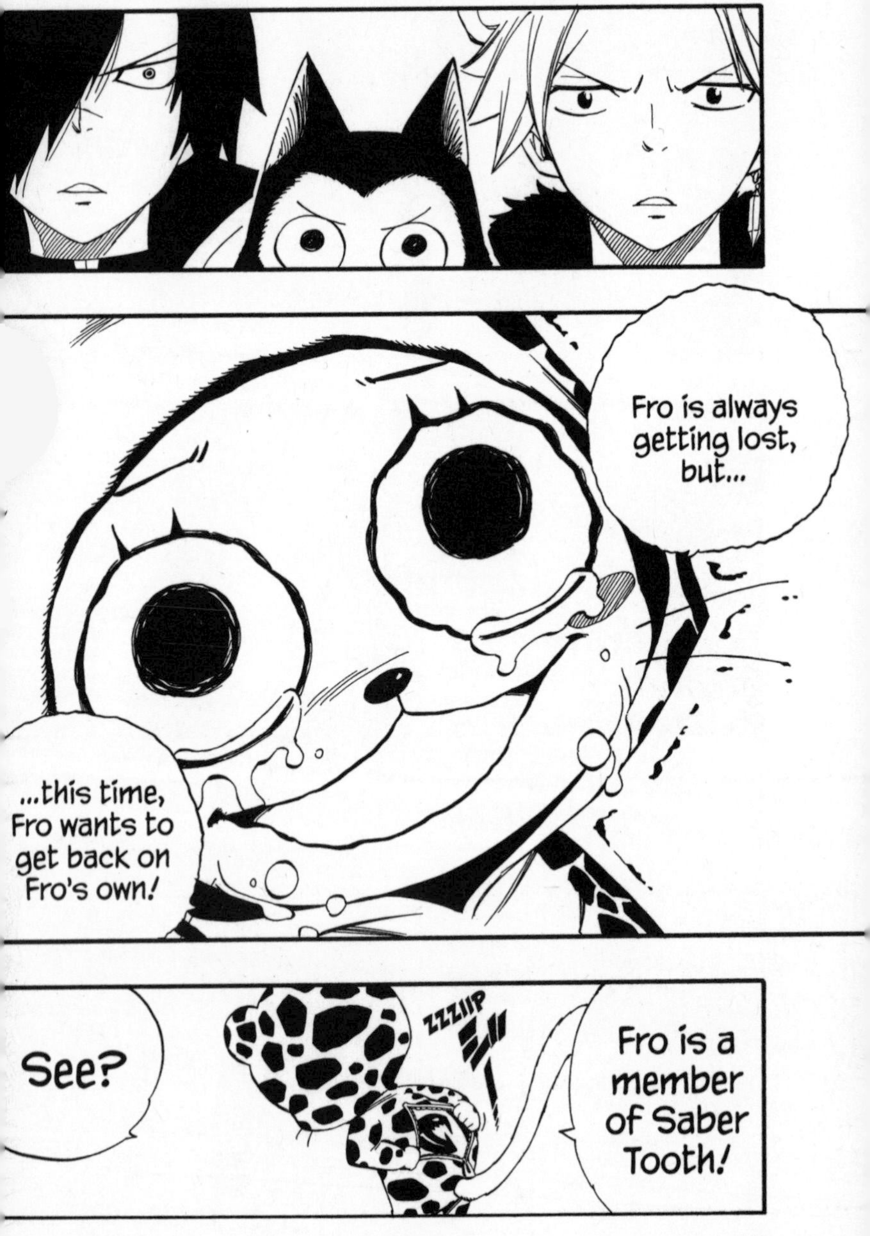
Fro is always getting lost, but...
...this time, Fro wants to get back on Fro's own!
Fro is a member of Saber Tooth!
ZZZIIP
See?

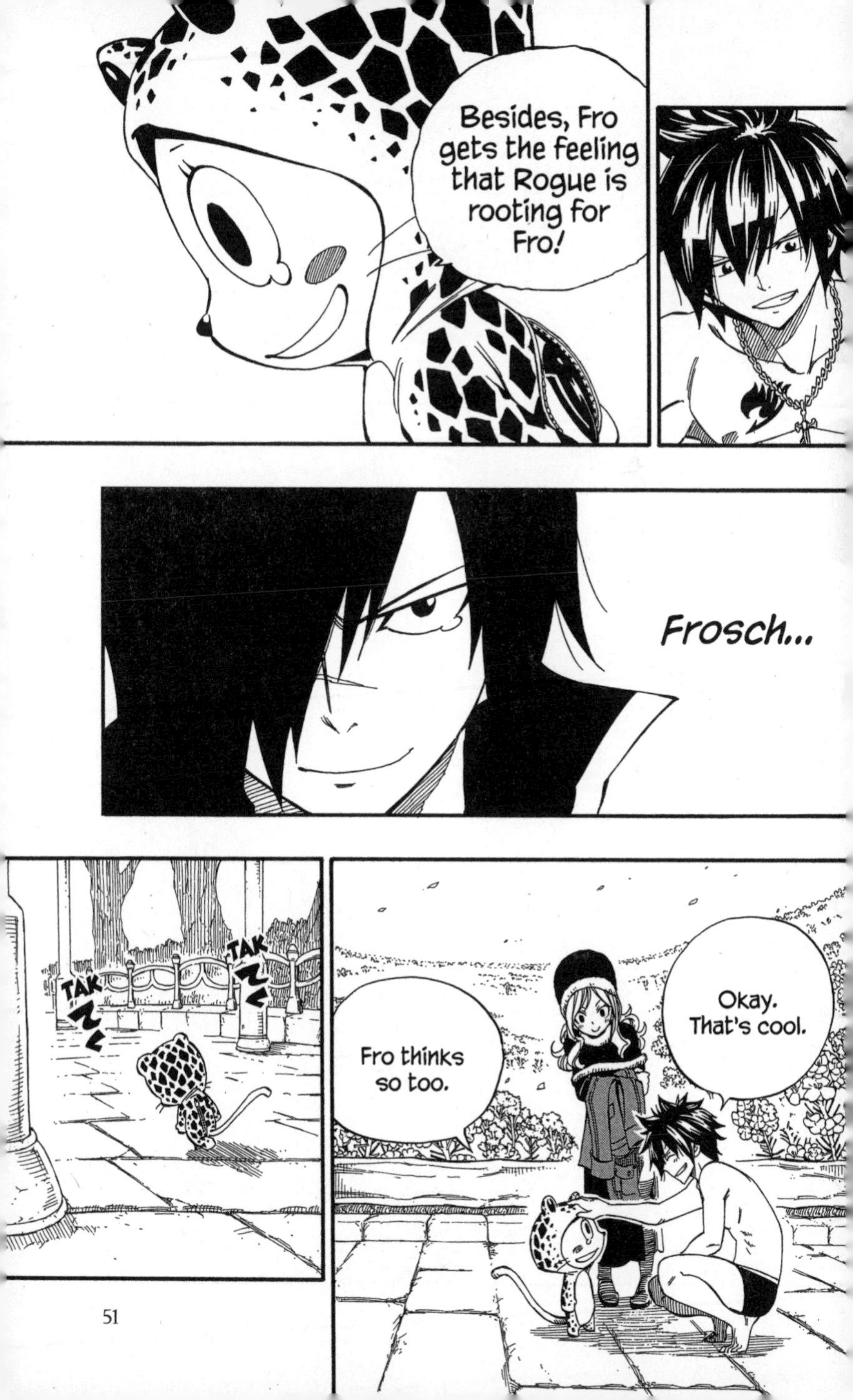
Besides, Fro gets the feeling that Rogue is rooting for Fro!
Frosch...
Okay. That's cool.
Fro thinks so too.
TAK
TAK

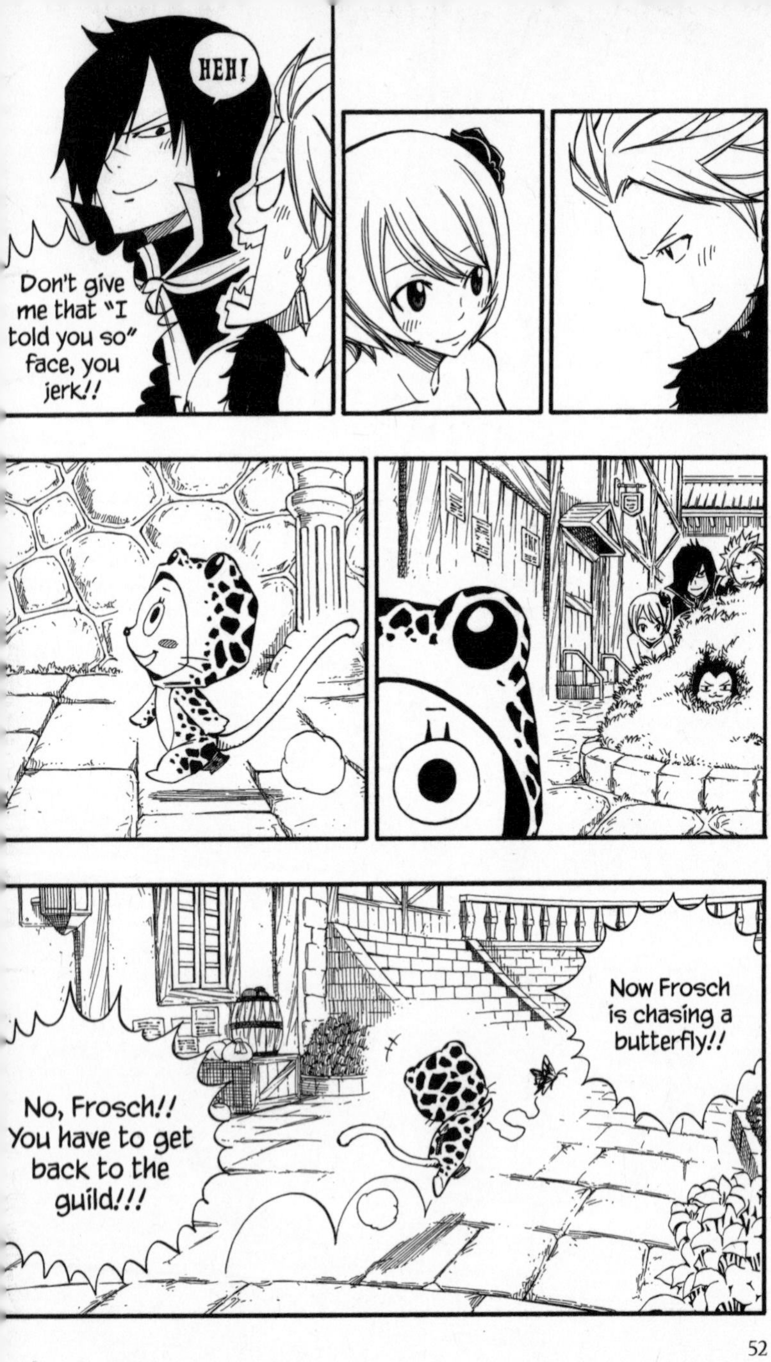
HEH!
Don't give me that "I told you so" face, you jerk!!
Now Frosch is chasing a butterfly!!
No, Frosch!! You have to get back to the guild!!!

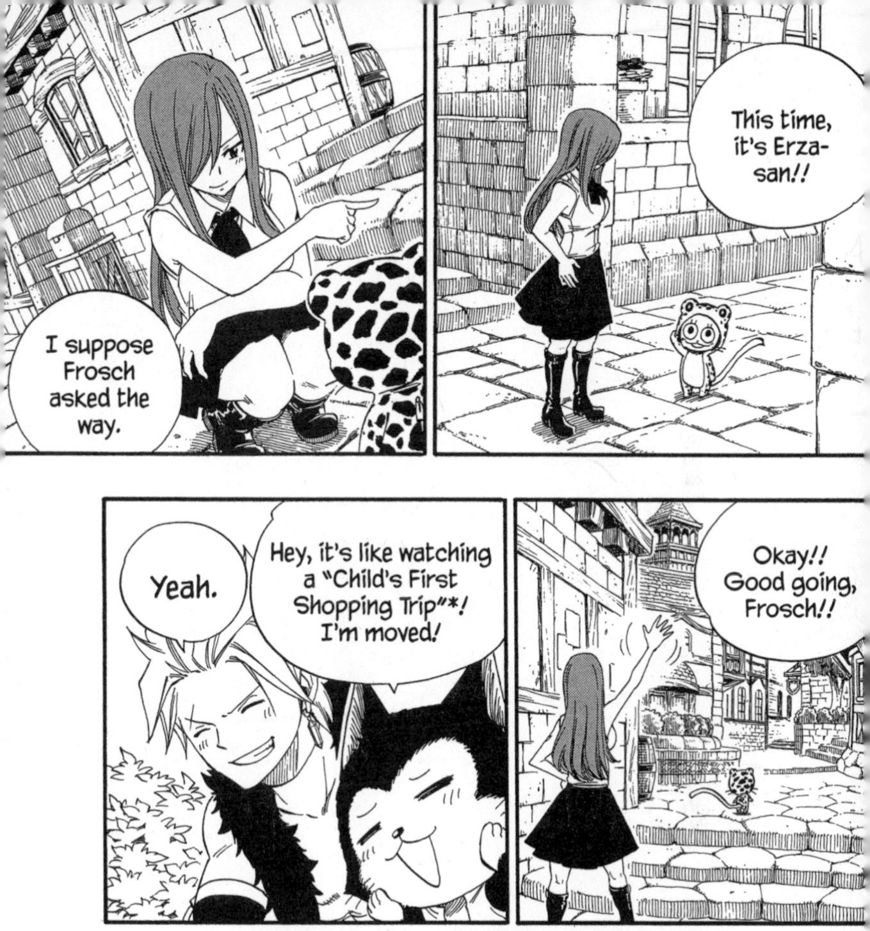
This time, it's Erza-san!!
I suppose Frosch asked the way.
Okay!! Good going, Frosch!!
Hey, it's like watching a "Child's First Shopping Trip"*! I'm moved!
Yeah.

*A popular Japanese TV program.

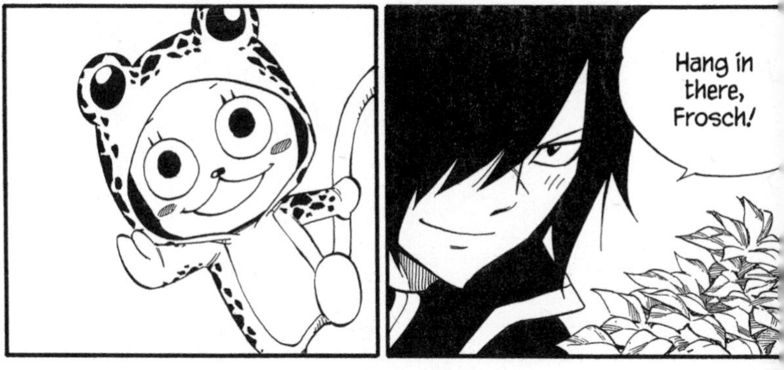
Hang in there, Frosch!

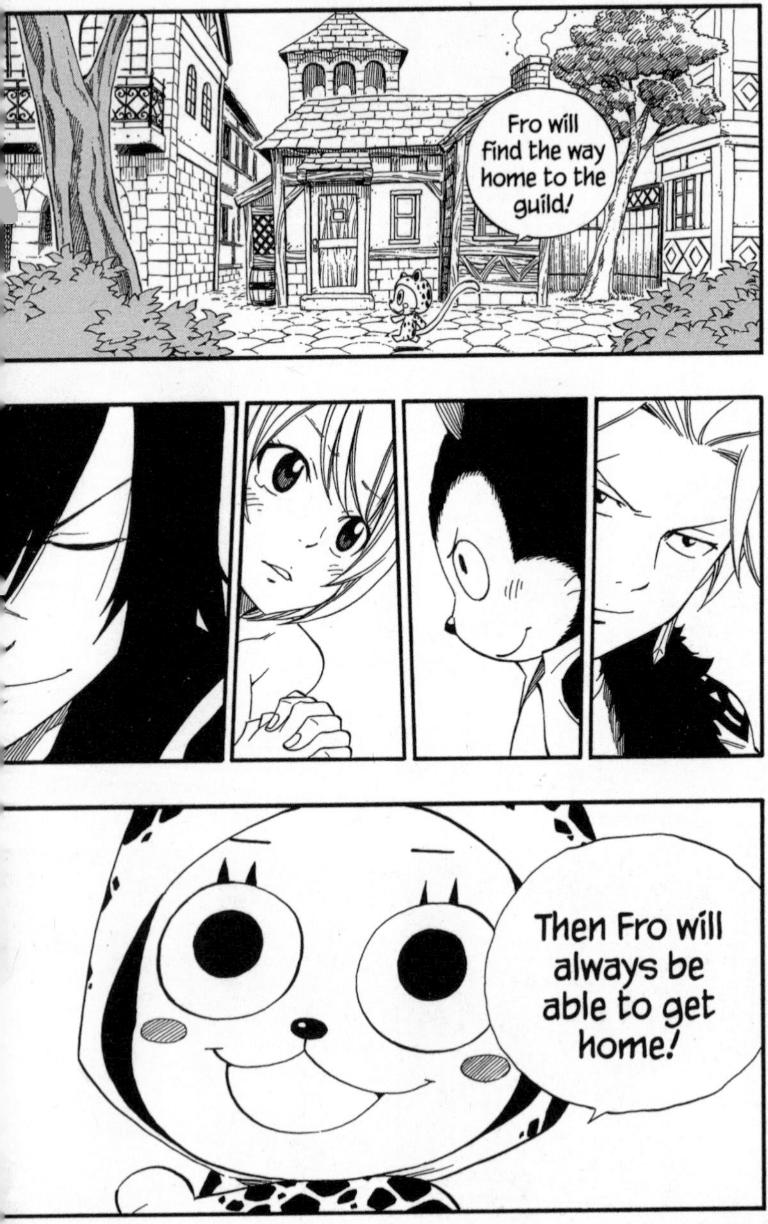
Fro will find the way home to the guild!
Then Fro will always be able to get home!

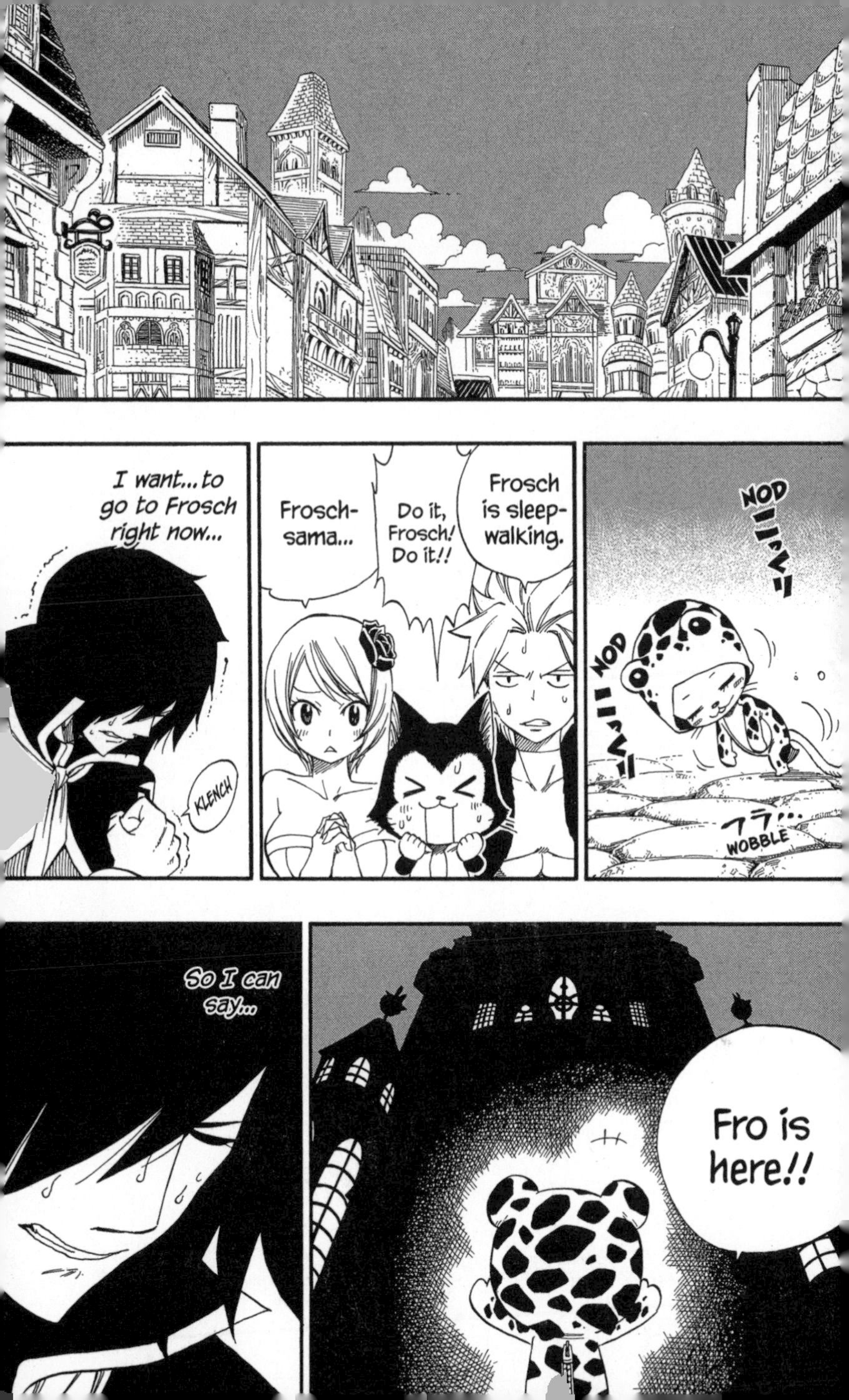
NOD
NOD
フラ…
WOBBLE
Frosch is sleep-walking.
Do it, Frosch! Do it!!
Frosch-sama...
I want...to go to Frosch right now...
KLENCH
Fro is here!!
So I can say...

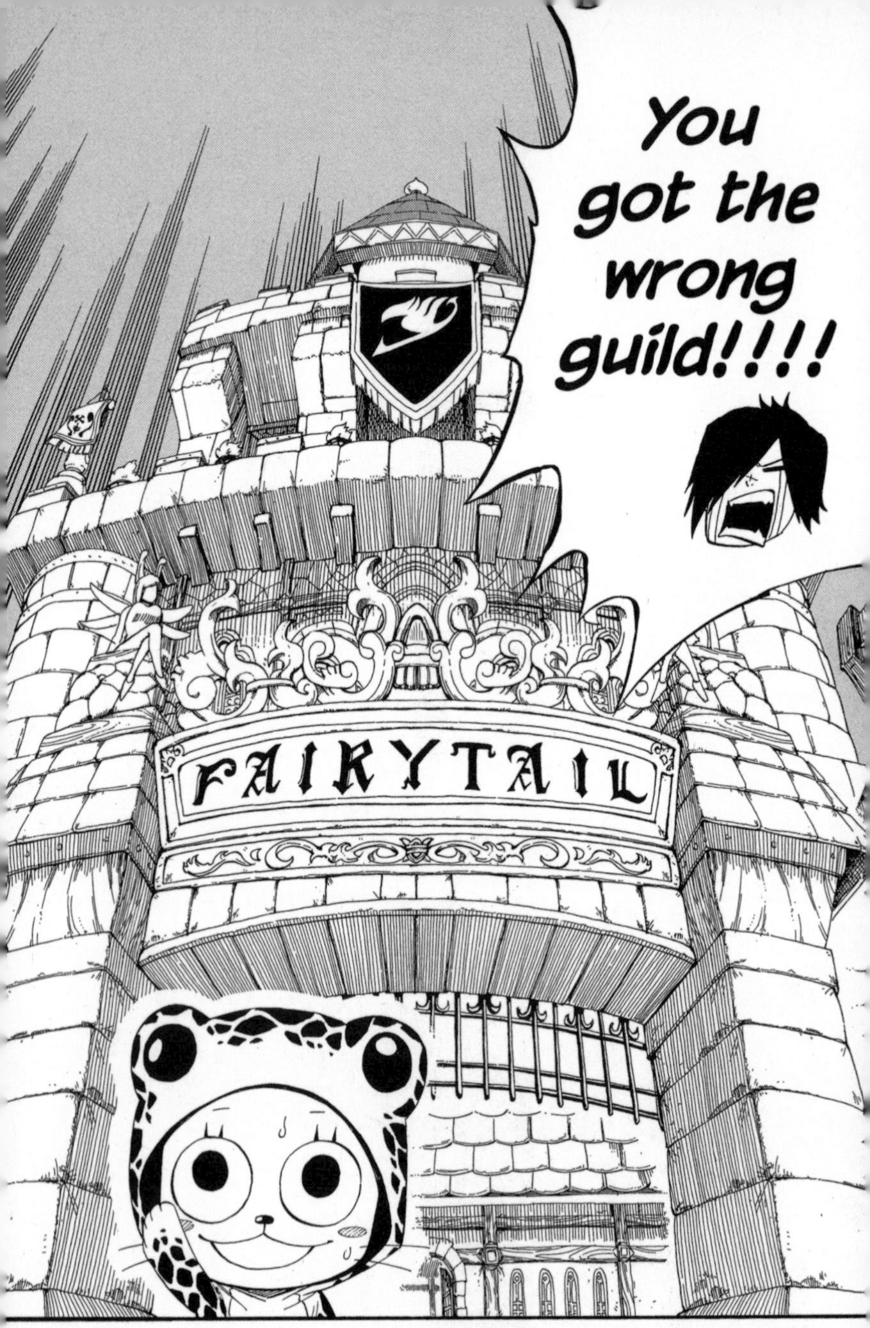
You got the wrong guild!!!!
FAIRY TAIL

★THE END★

FT☆S

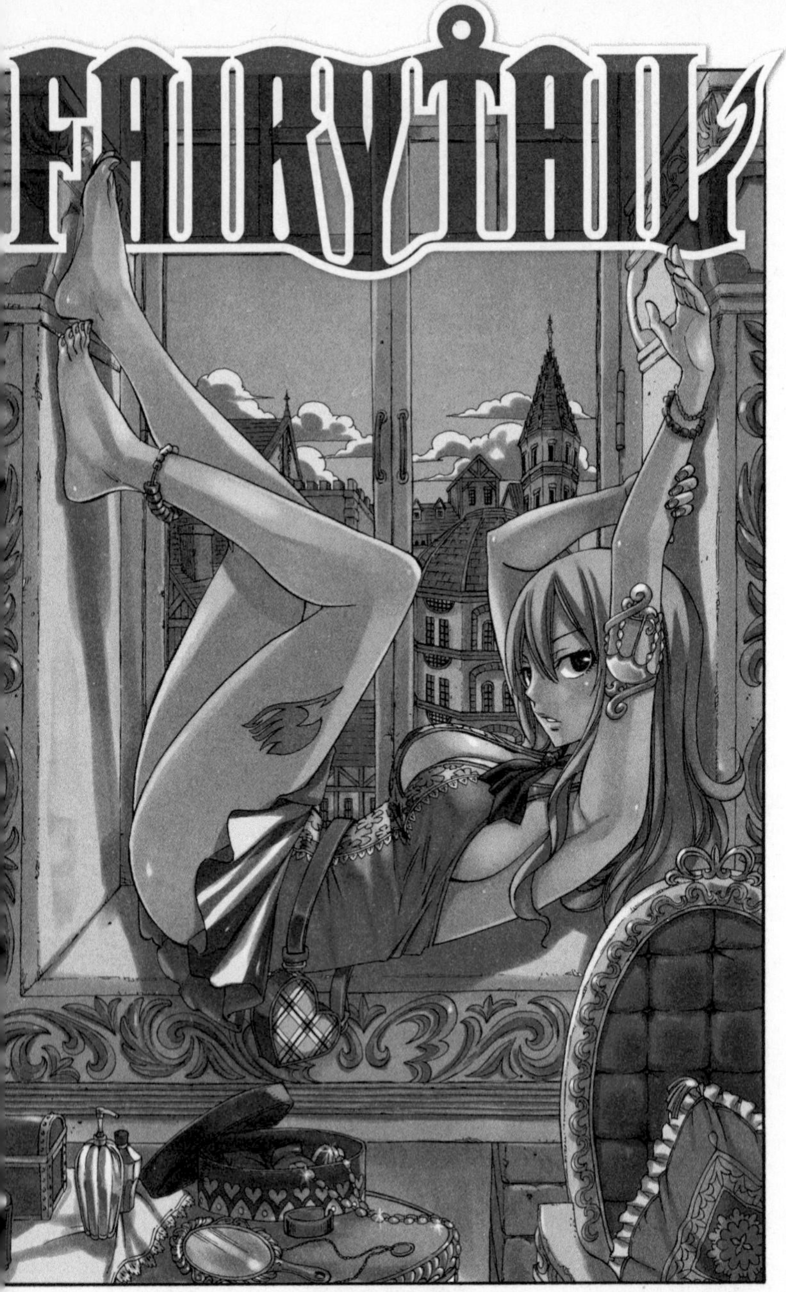
FAIRY TAIL

413 DAYS

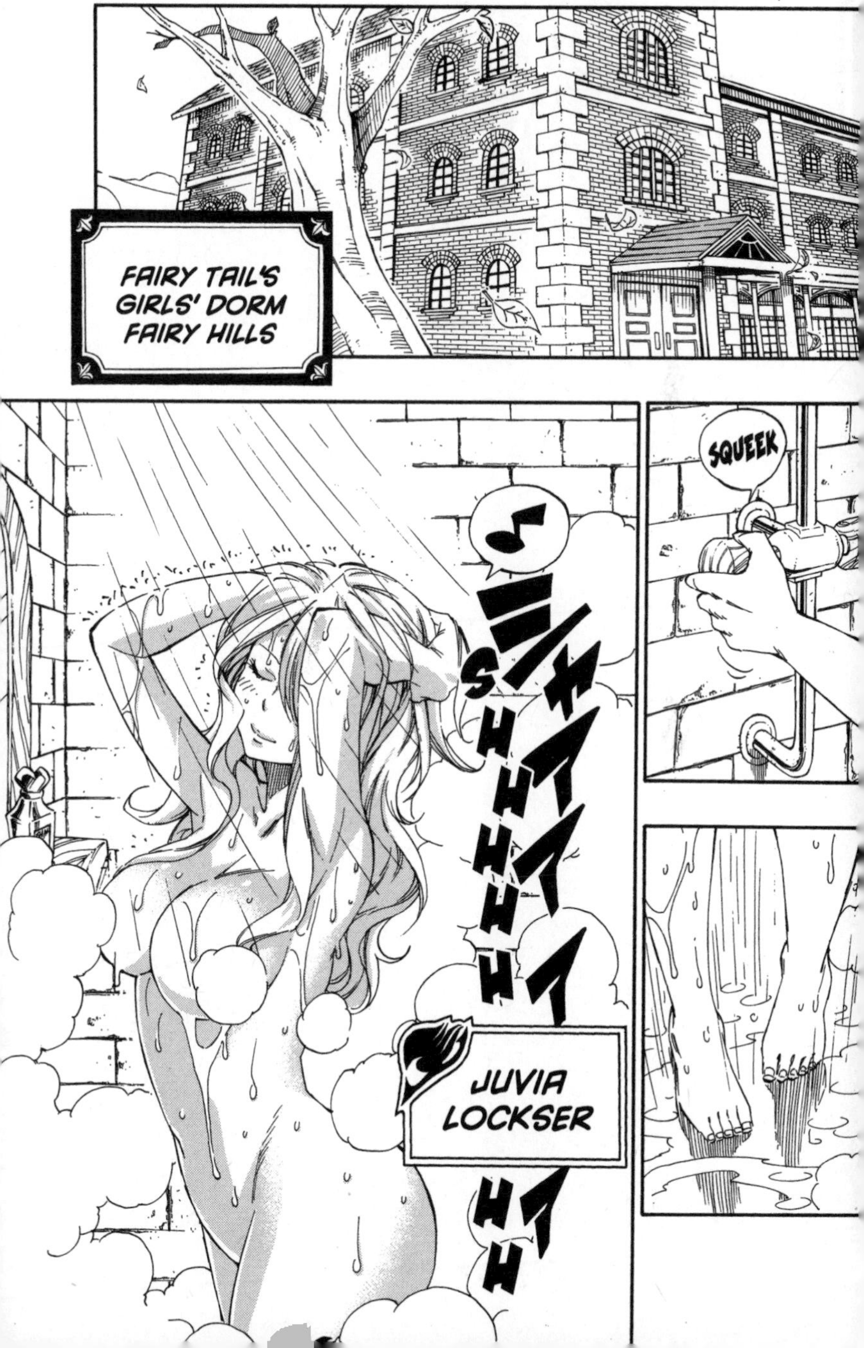
FAIRY TAIL'S
GIRLS' DORM
FAIRY HILLS
SQUEEK
♪
SHHHHHHHHH
JUVIA
LOCKSER

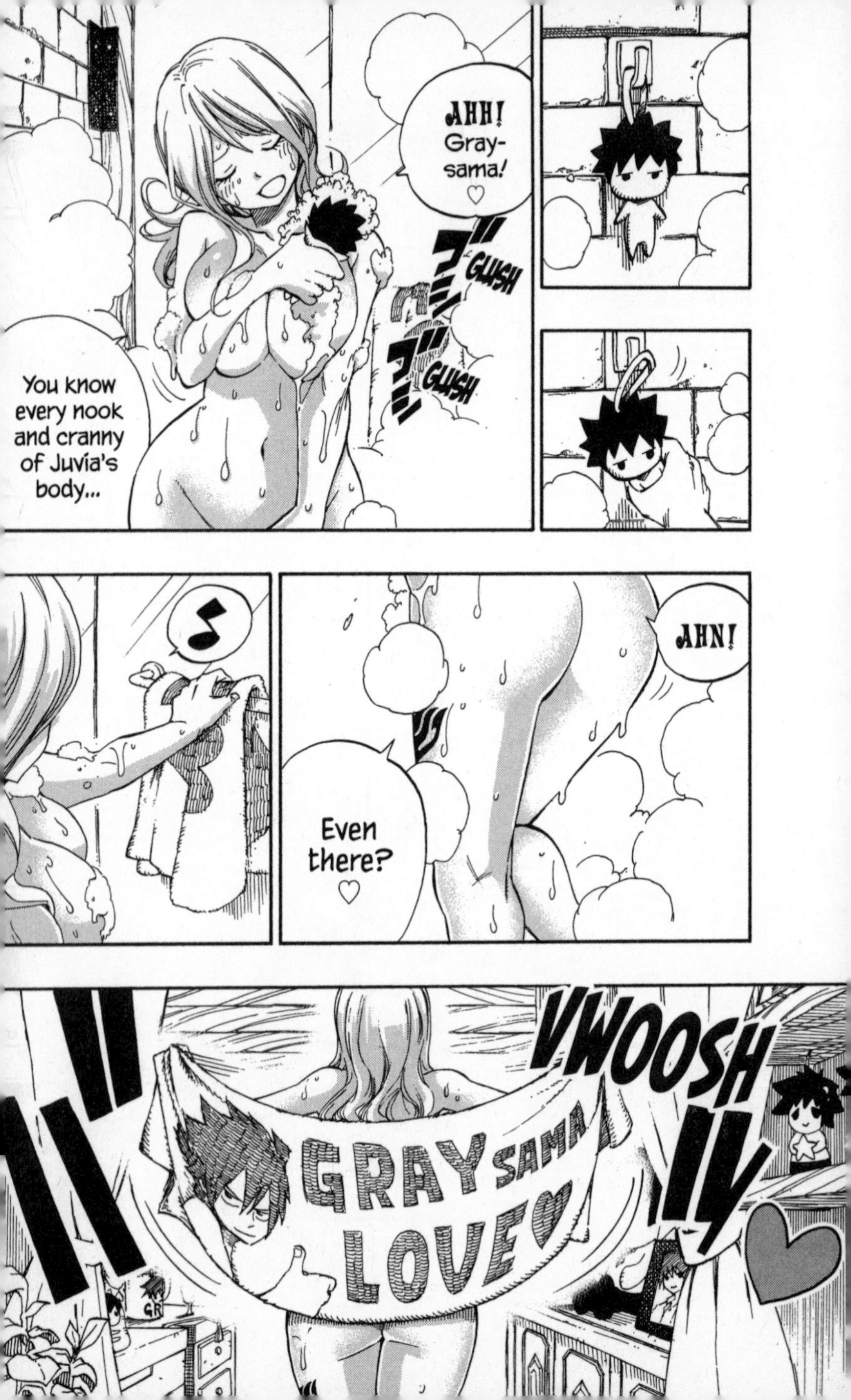
AHH! Gray-sama! ♡
GLUSH
GLUSH
You know every nook and cranny of Juvia's body...
AHN!
Even there? ♡
VWOOSH
GRAY SAMA LOVE ♡
GR

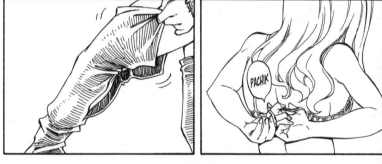

...Gray-sama!

SMAK

Time for Juvia to go...

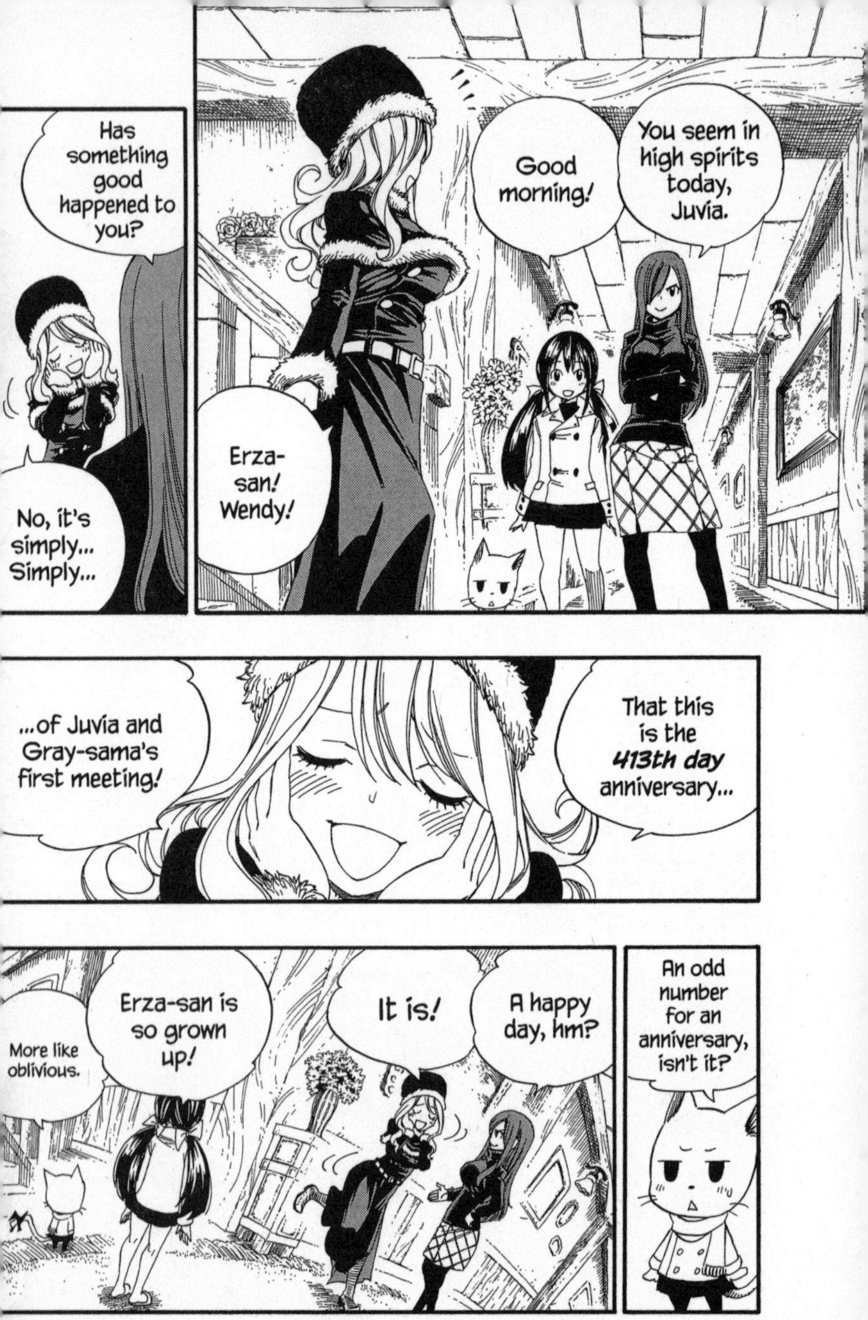
You seem in high spirits today, Juvia.
Good morning!
Erza-san! Wendy!
Has something good happened to you?
No, it's simply... Simply...
That this is the ***413th day*** anniversary...
...of Juvia and Gray-sama's first meeting!
An odd number for an anniversary, isn't it?
A happy day, hm?
It is!
Erza-san is so grown up!
More like oblivious.

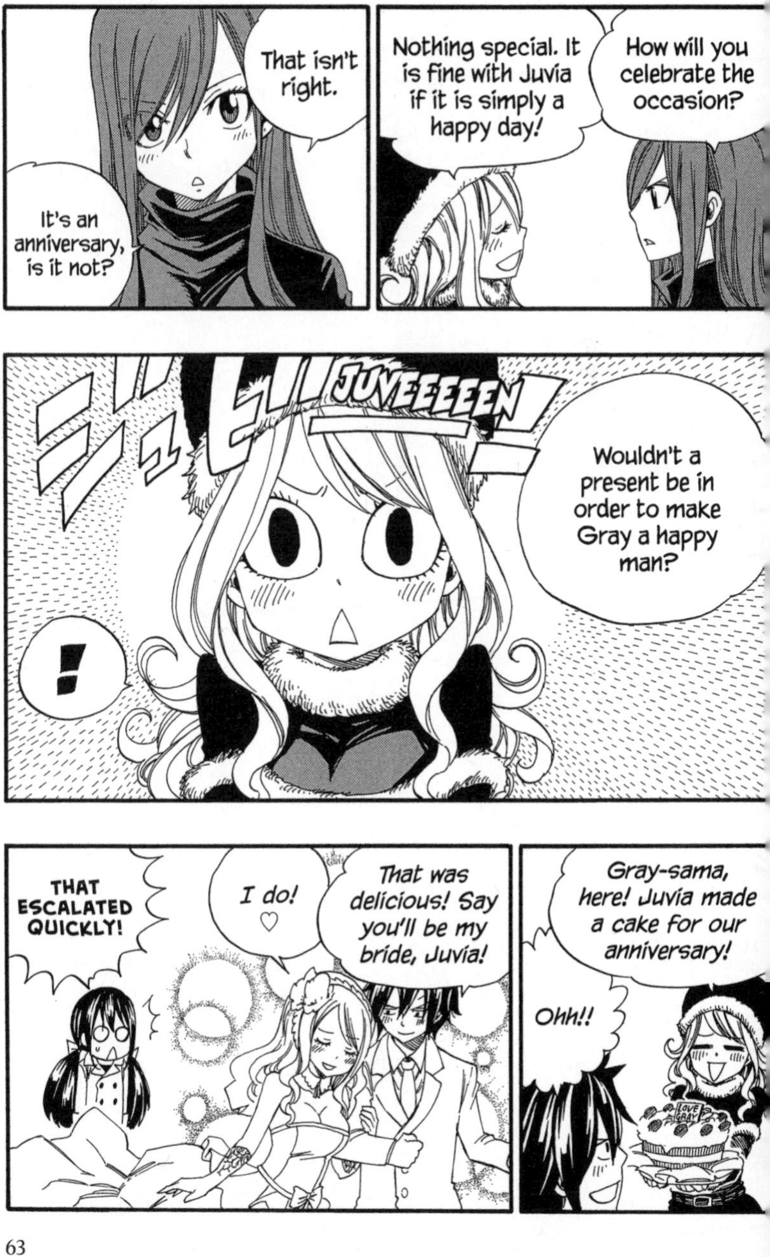
How will you celebrate the occasion?
Nothing special. It is fine with Juvia if it is simply a happy day!
That isn't right.
It's an anniversary, is it not?
JUVEEEEEN
Wouldn't a present be in order to make Gray a happy man?
!
Gray-sama, here! Juvia made a cake for our anniversary!
Ohh!!
LOVE GRAY
That was delicious! Say you'll be my bride, Juvia!
I do! ♡
THAT ESCALATED QUICKLY!

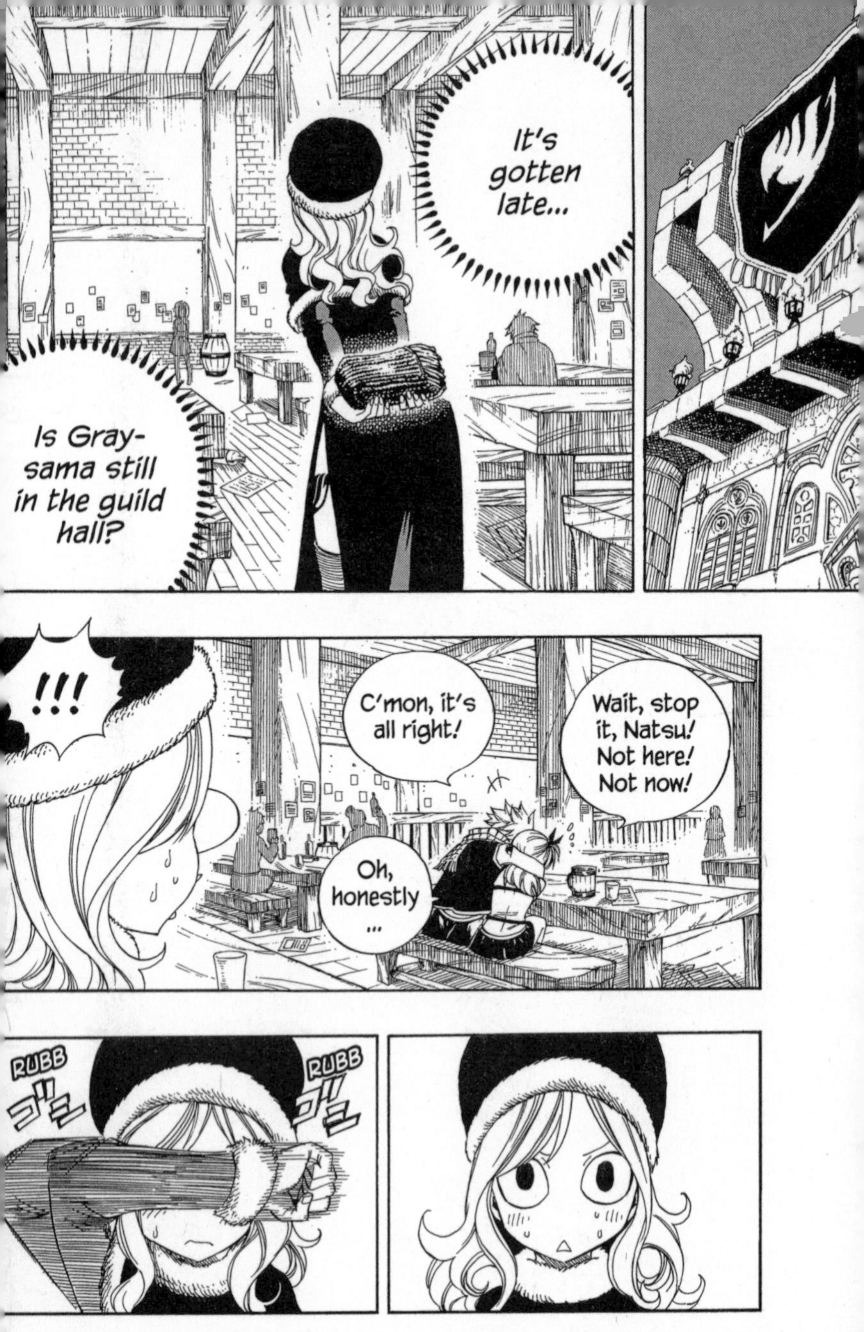
It's gotten late...
Is Gray-sama still in the guild hall?
Wait, stop it, Natsu! Not here! Not now!
C'mon, it's all right!
!!!
Oh, honestly ...
RUBB
RUBB

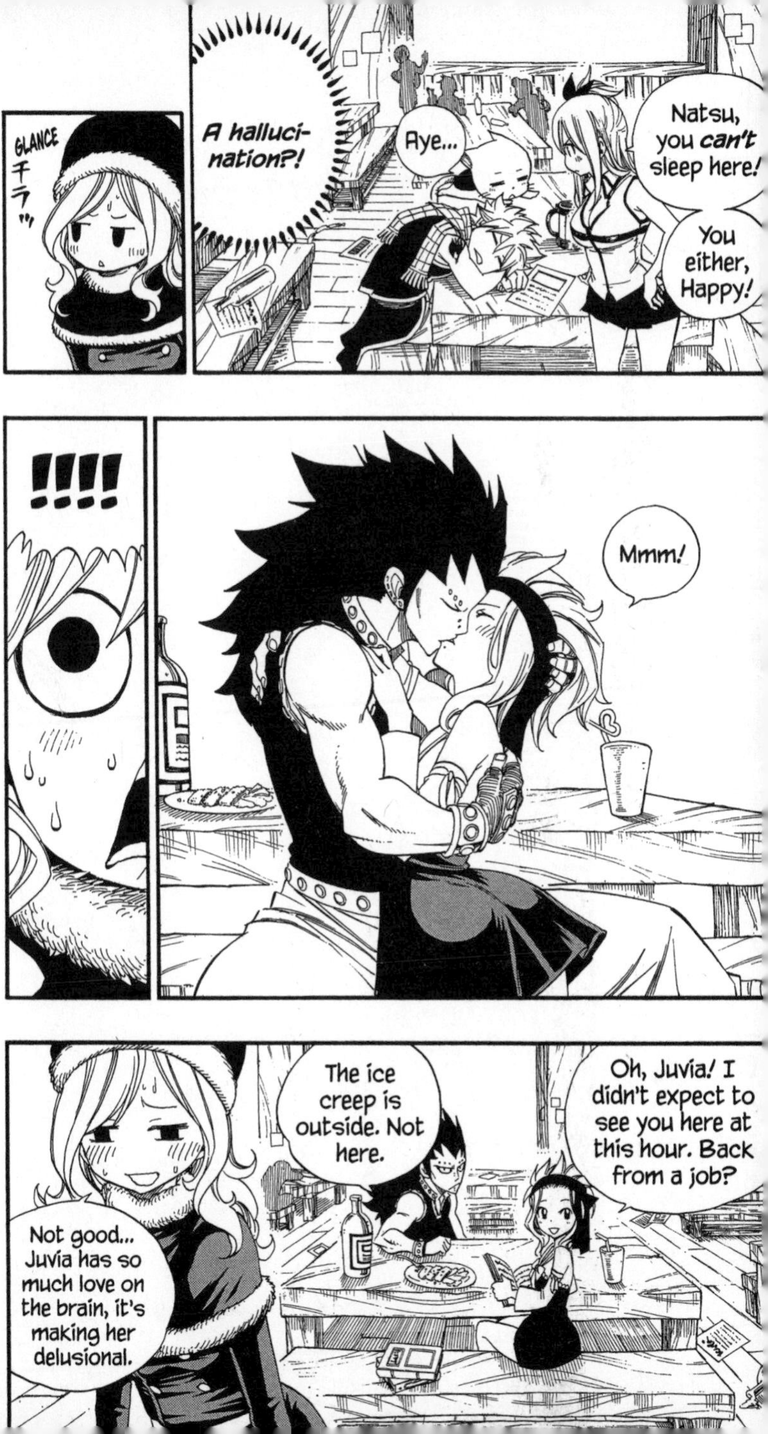
Natsu, you *can't* sleep here!
You either, Happy!
Aye...
A halluci-nation?!
GLANCE
チラッ
Mmm!
!!!!
Oh, Juvia! I didn't expect to see you here at this hour. Back from a job?
The ice creep is outside. Not here.
Not good... Juvia has so much love on the brain, it's making her delusional.

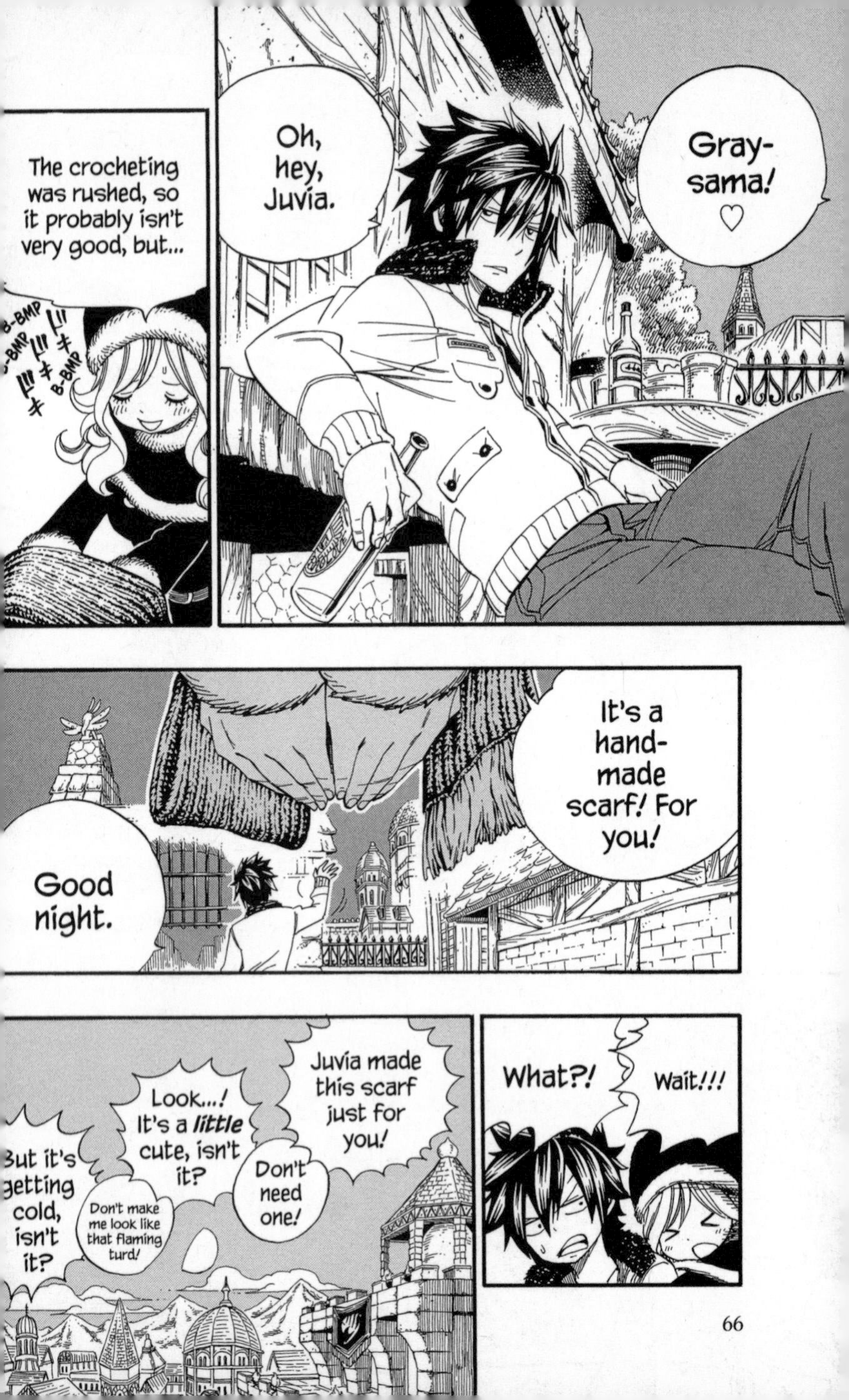
Gray-sama! ♡
Oh, hey, Juvia.
The crocheting was rushed, so it probably isn't very good, but...
B-BMP B-BMP B-BMP
It's a hand-made scarf! For you!
Good night.
Wait!!!
What?!
Juvia made this scarf just for you!
Look...! It's a *little* cute, isn't it?
Don't need one!
But it's getting cold, isn't it?
Don't make me look like that flaming turd!

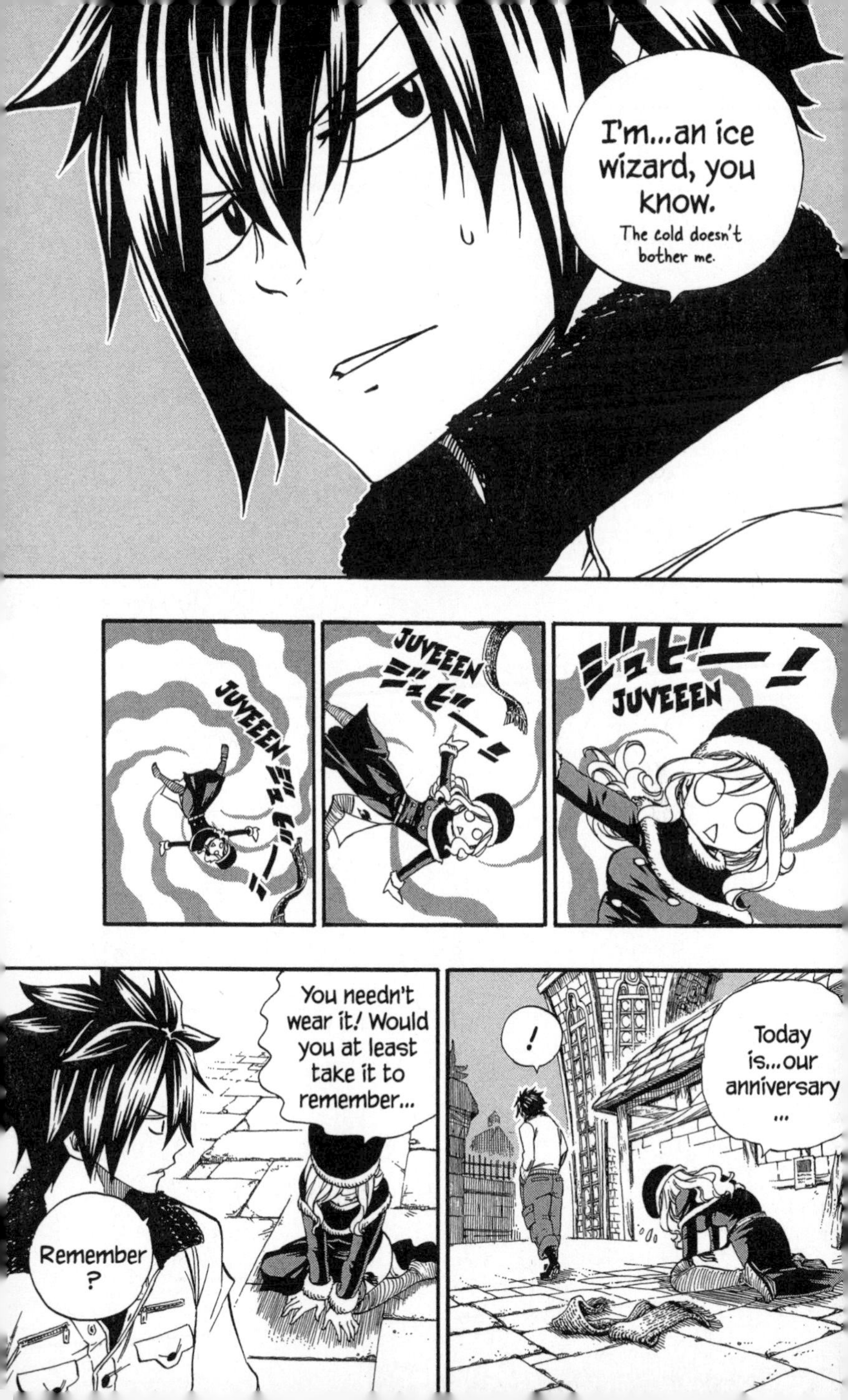
I'm...an ice wizard, you know.
The cold doesn't bother me.
JUVEEEN
JUVEEEN
JUVEEEN
!
Today is...our anniversary...
You needn't wear it! Would you at least take it to remember...
Remember?

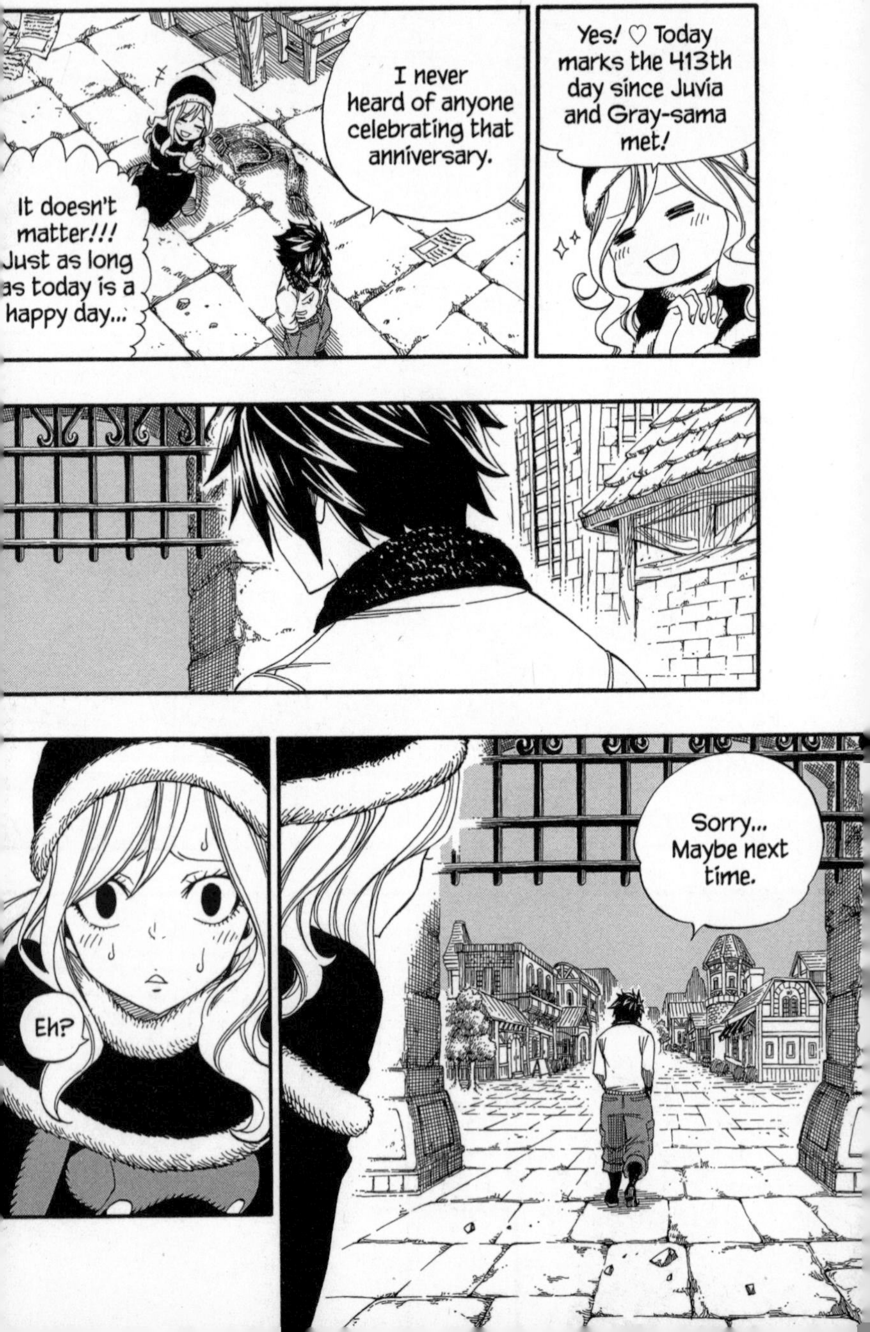
Yes! ♡ Today marks the 413th day since Juvia and Gray-sama met!
I never heard of anyone celebrating that anniversary.
It doesn't matter!!! Just as long as today is a happy day...
Sorry... Maybe next time.
Eh?

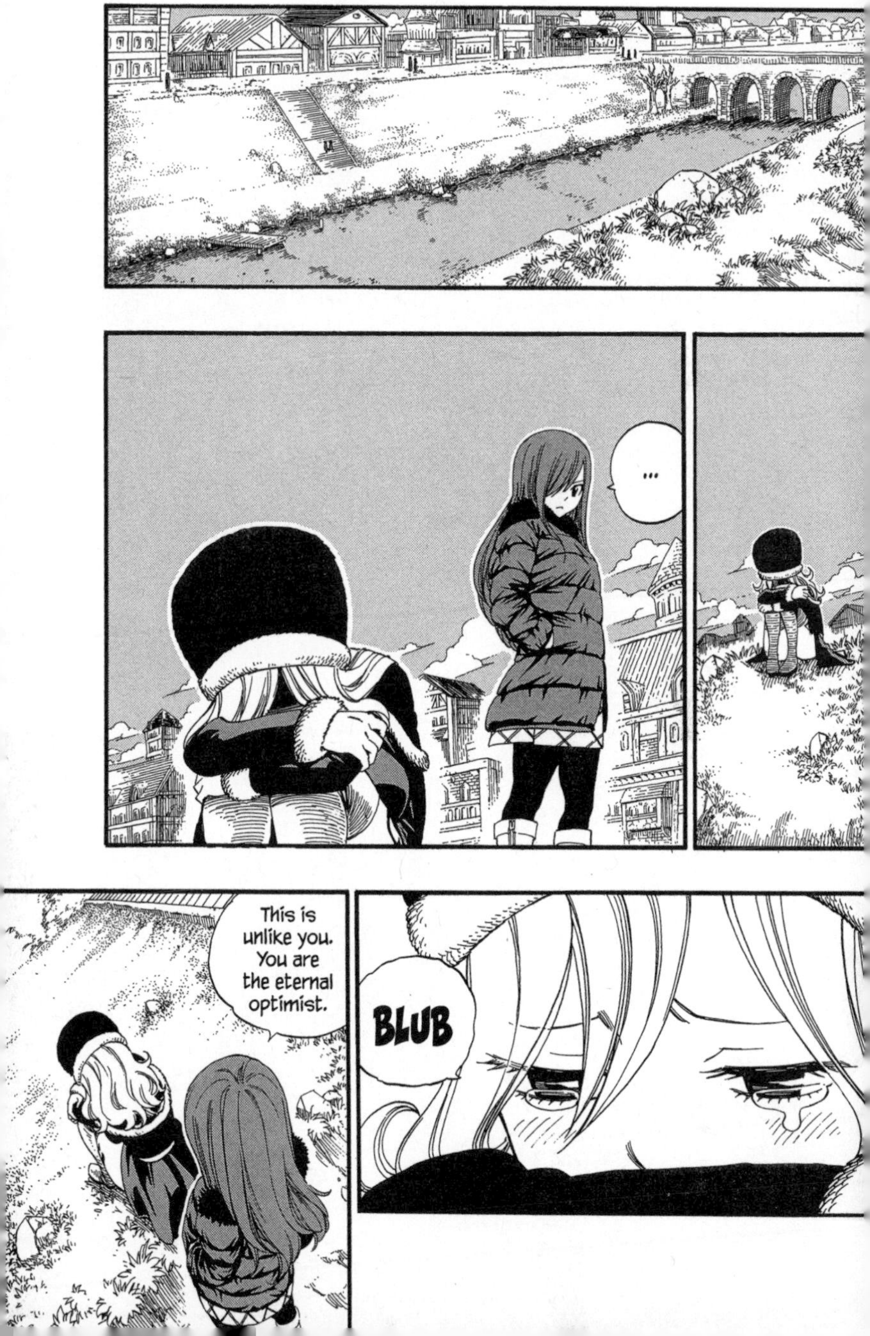
...
BLUB
This is unlike you. You are the eternal optimist.

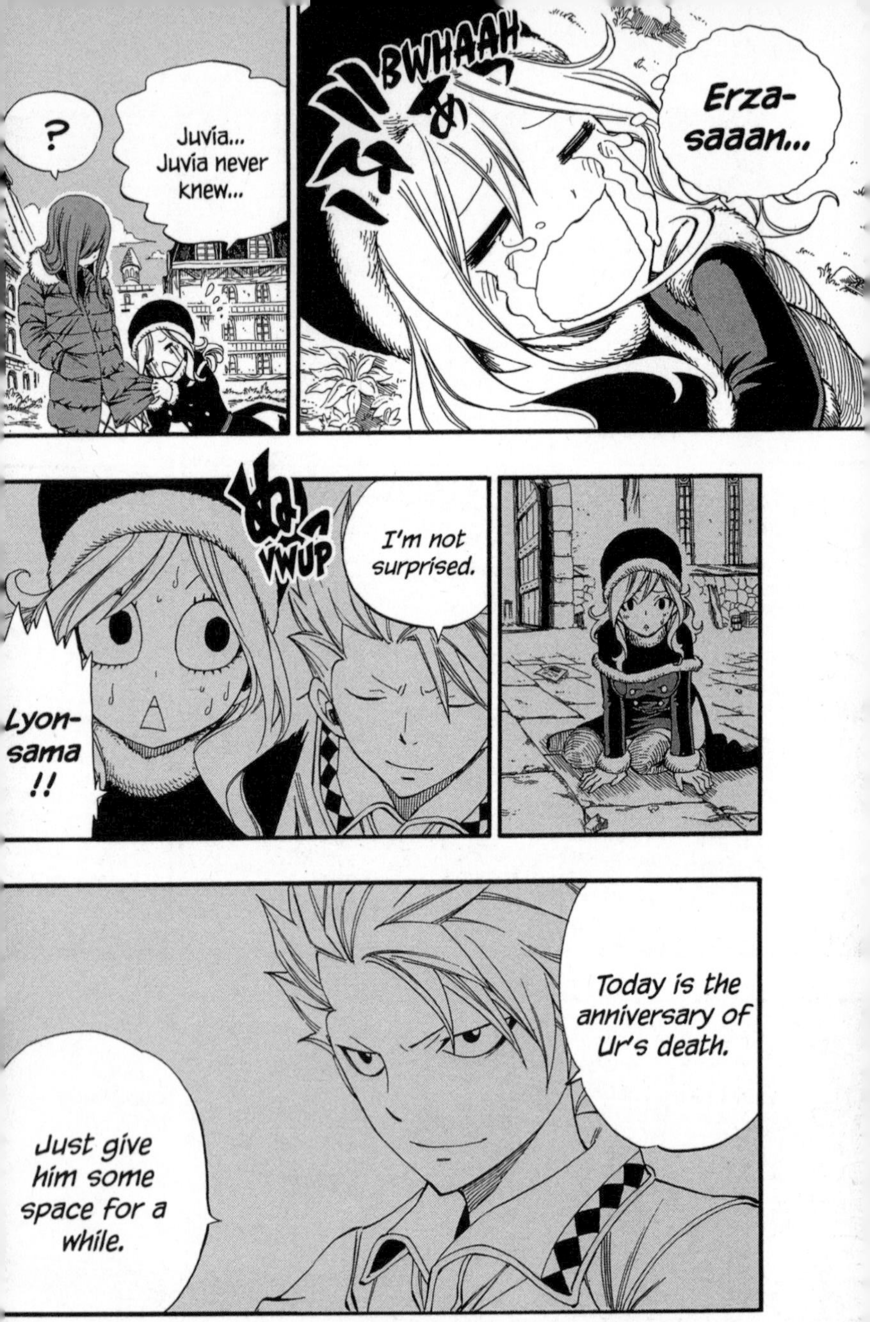
BWHAAH
Erza-saaan...
Juvia... Juvia never knew...
?
I'm not surprised.
VWUP
Lyon-sama!!
Today is the anniversary of Ur's death.
Just give him some space for a while.

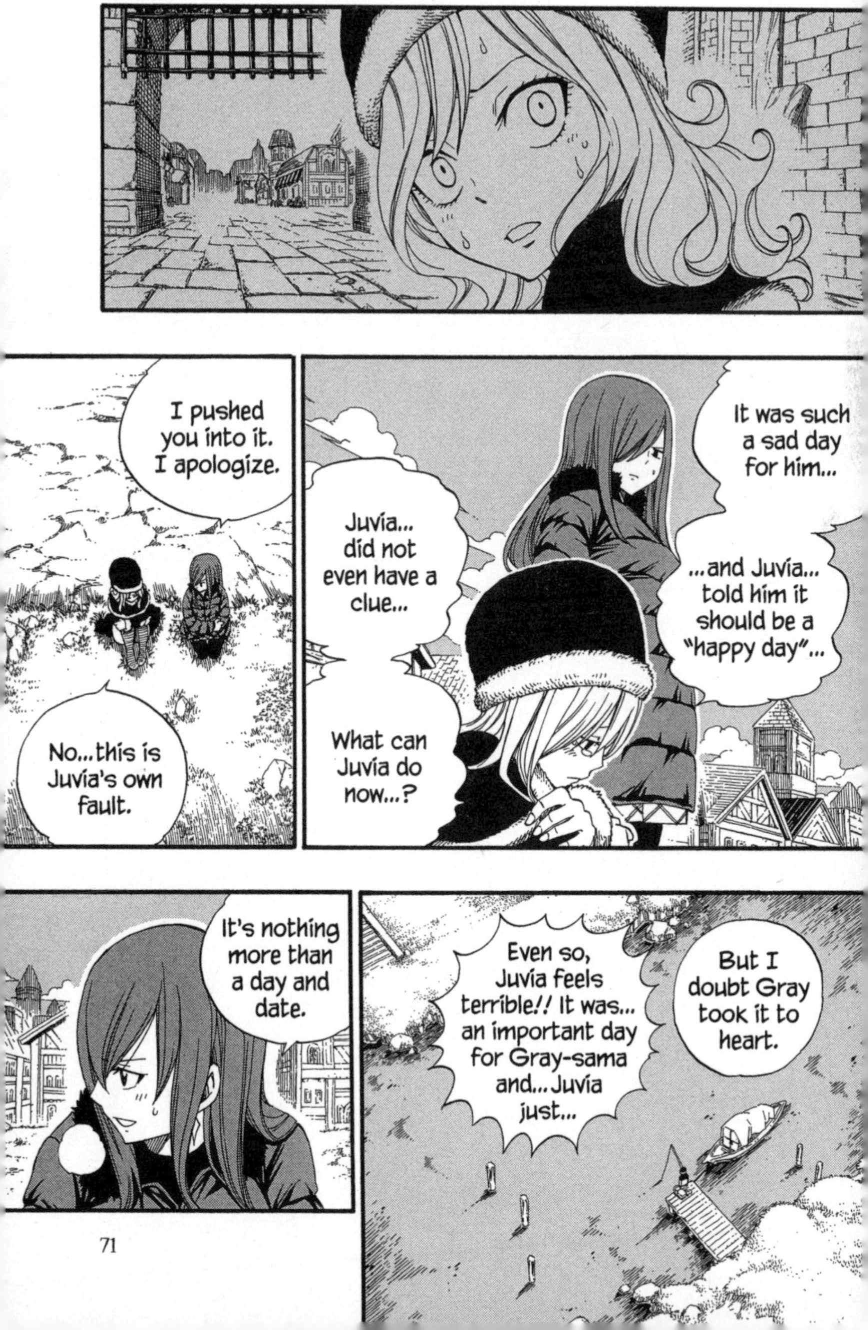
It was such a sad day for him...
...and Juvia... told him it should be a "happy day"...
Juvia... did not even have a clue...
What can Juvia do now...?
I pushed you into it. I apologize.
No...this is Juvia's own fault.
But I doubt Gray took it to heart.
Even so, Juvia feels terrible!! It was... an important day for Gray-sama and... Juvia just...
It's nothing more than a day and date.

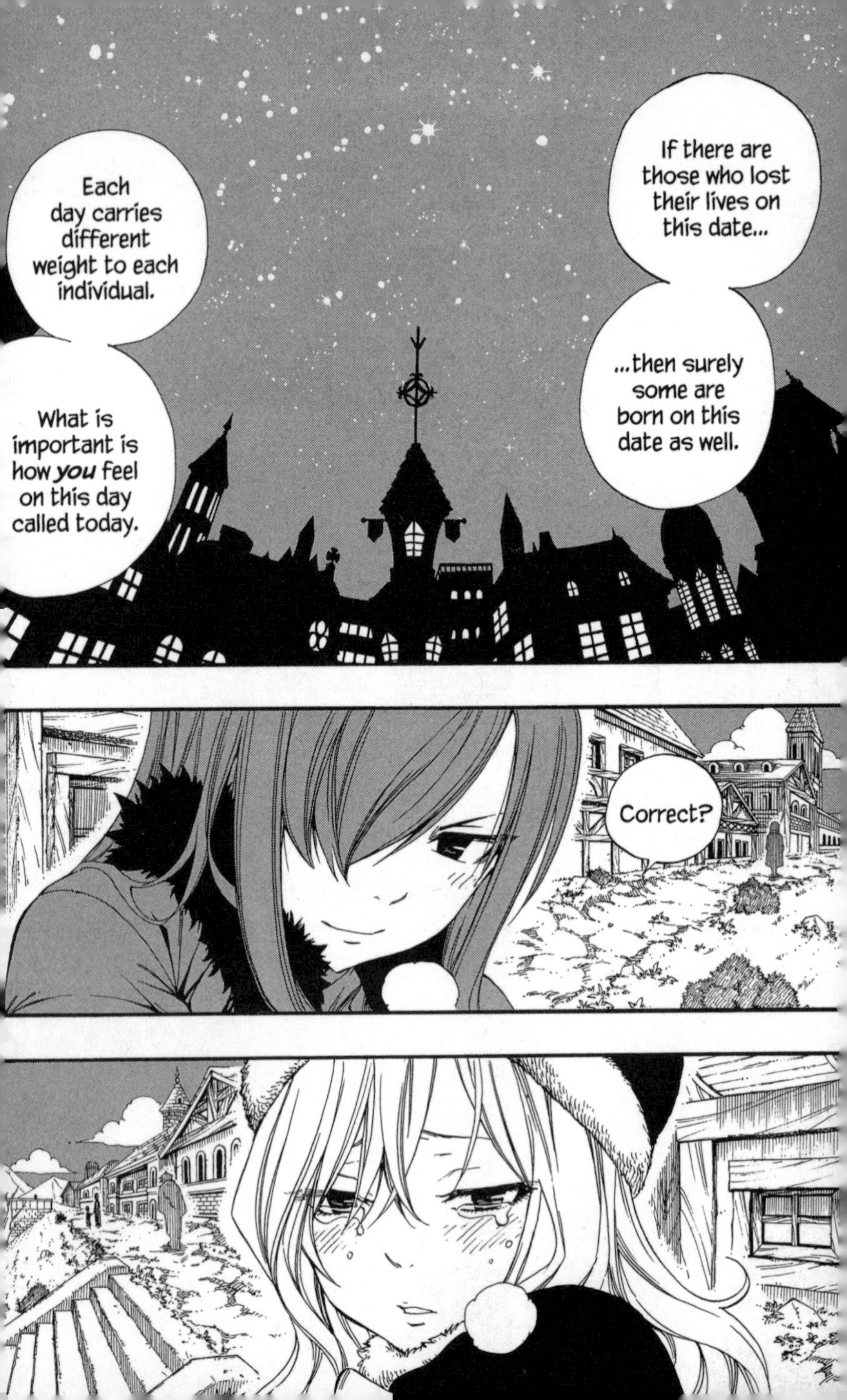
If there are those who lost their lives on this date...
...then surely some are born on this date as well.
Each day carries different weight to each individual.
What is important is how *you* feel on this day called today.
Correct?

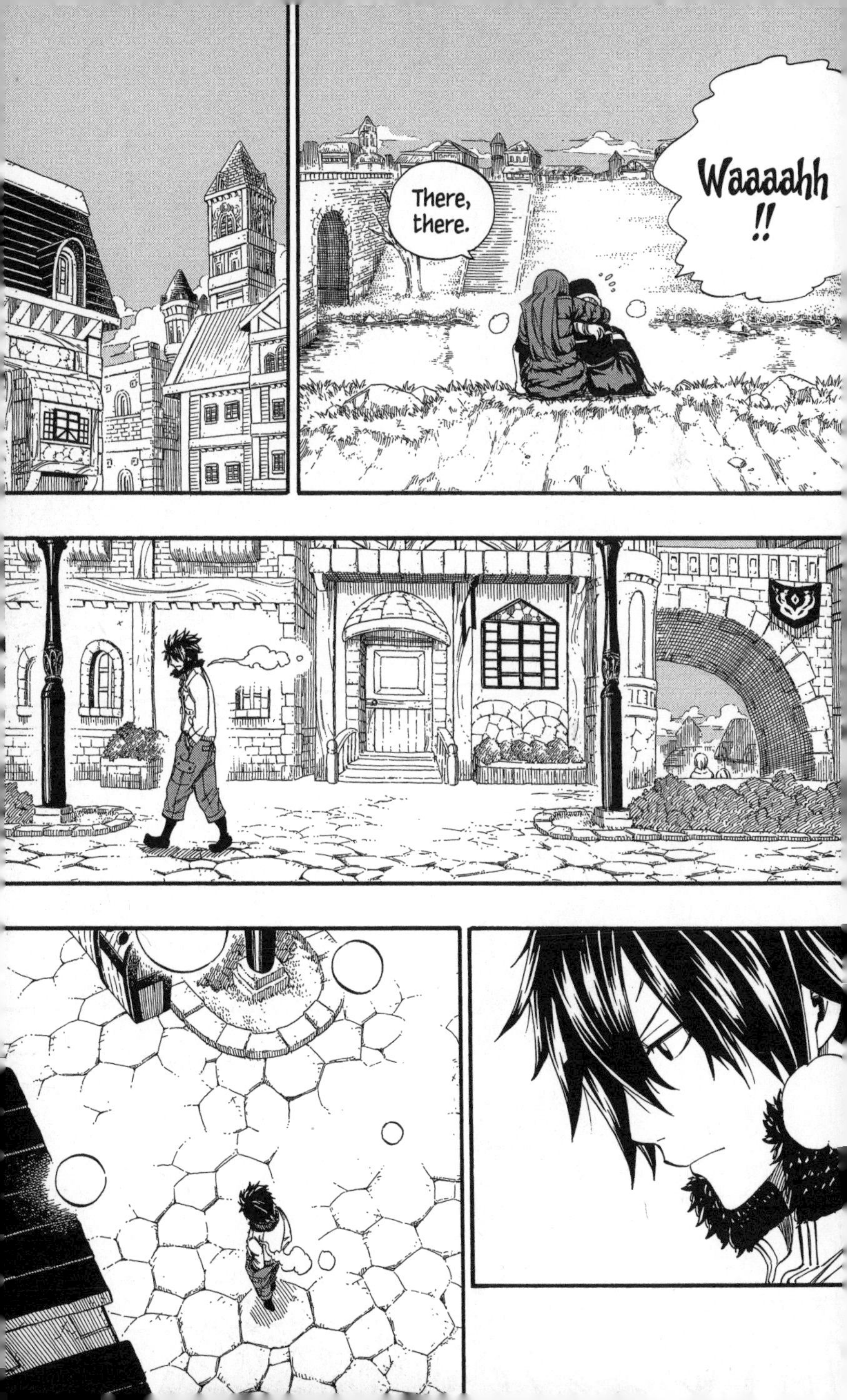
Waaaahh !!
There, there.

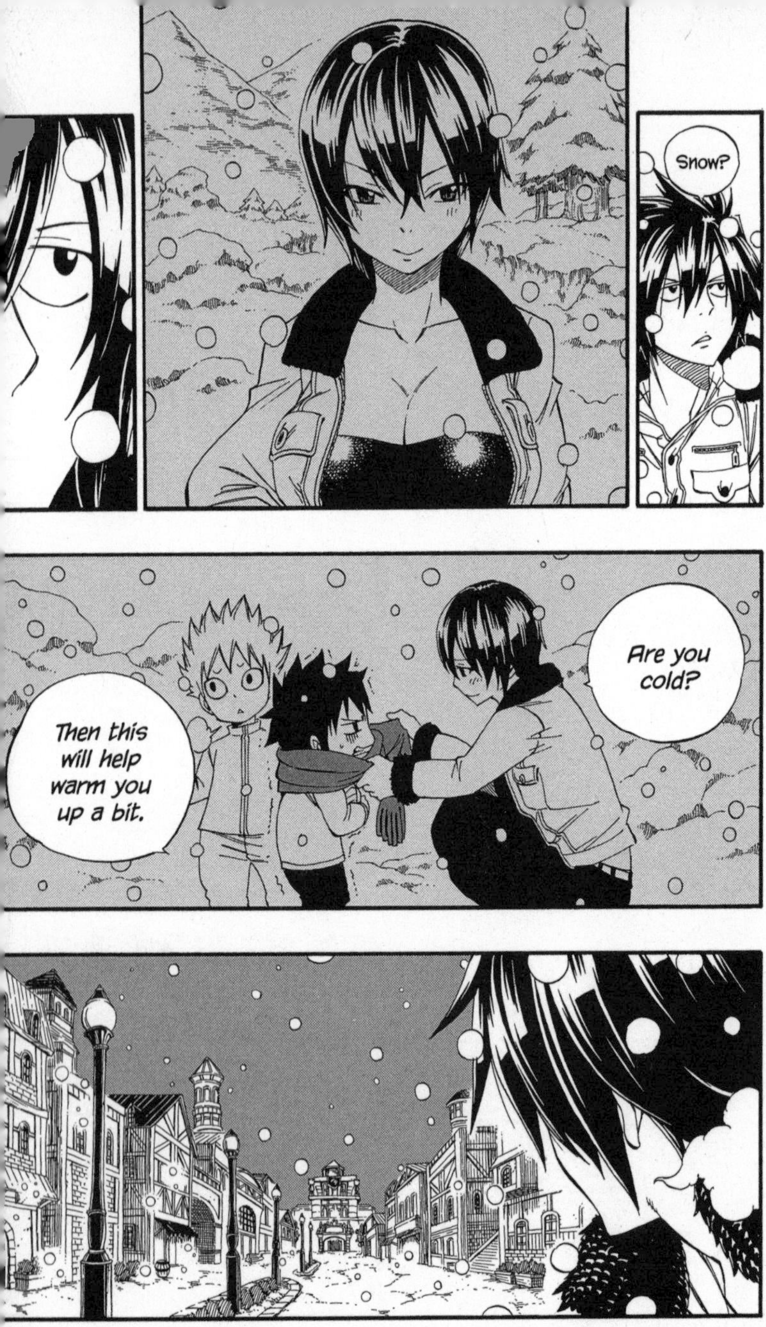
Snow?
Are you cold?
Then this will help warm you up a bit.

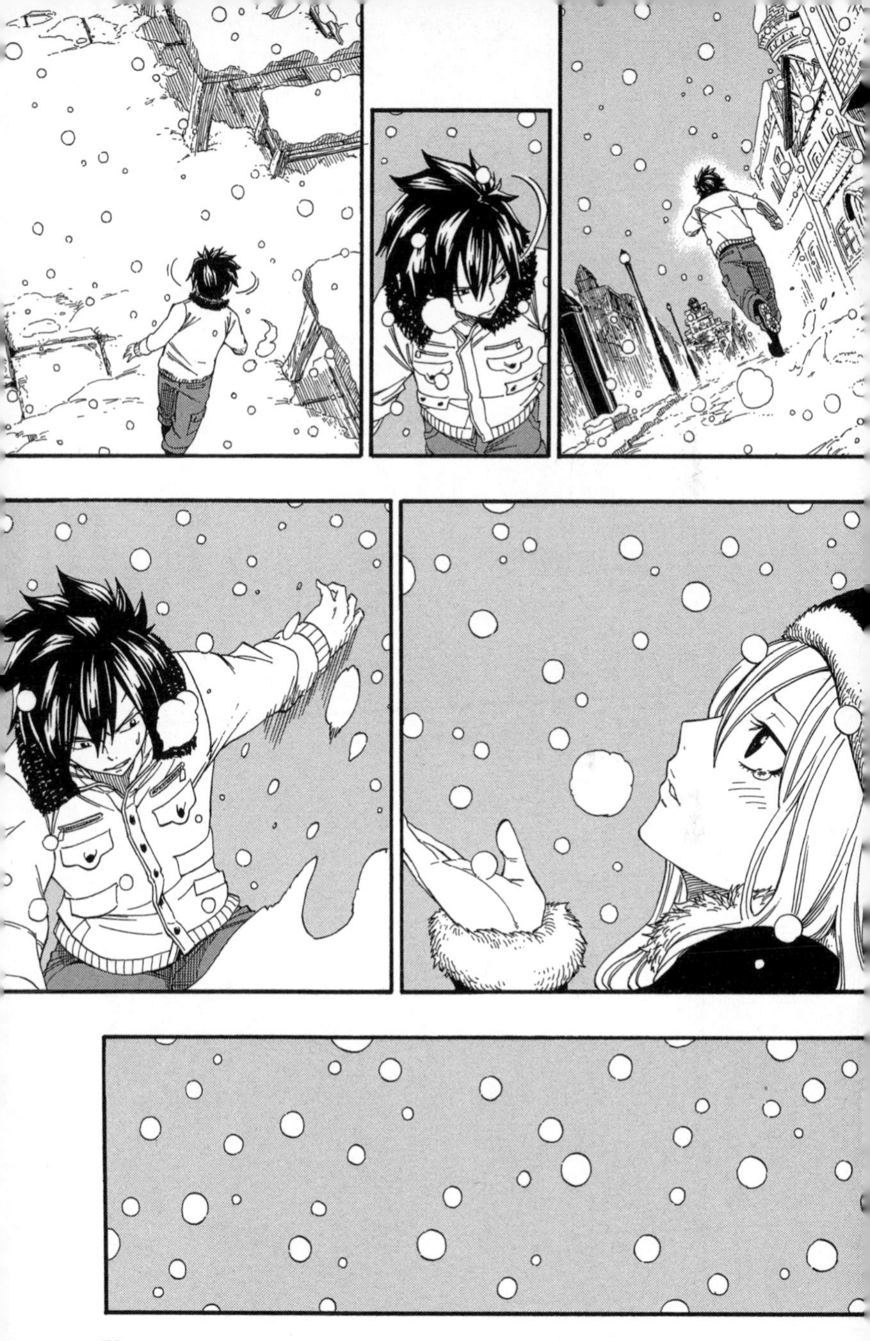

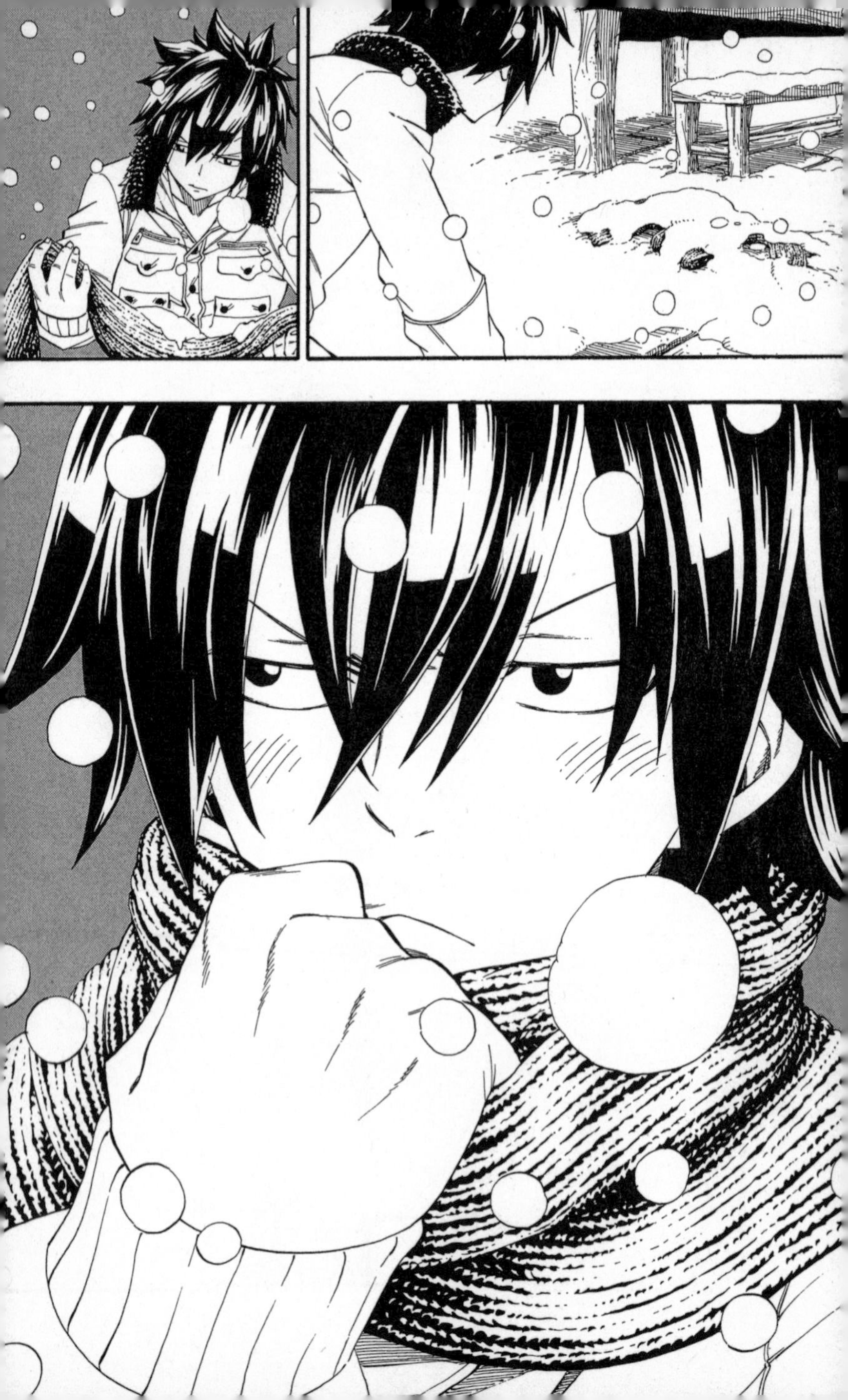

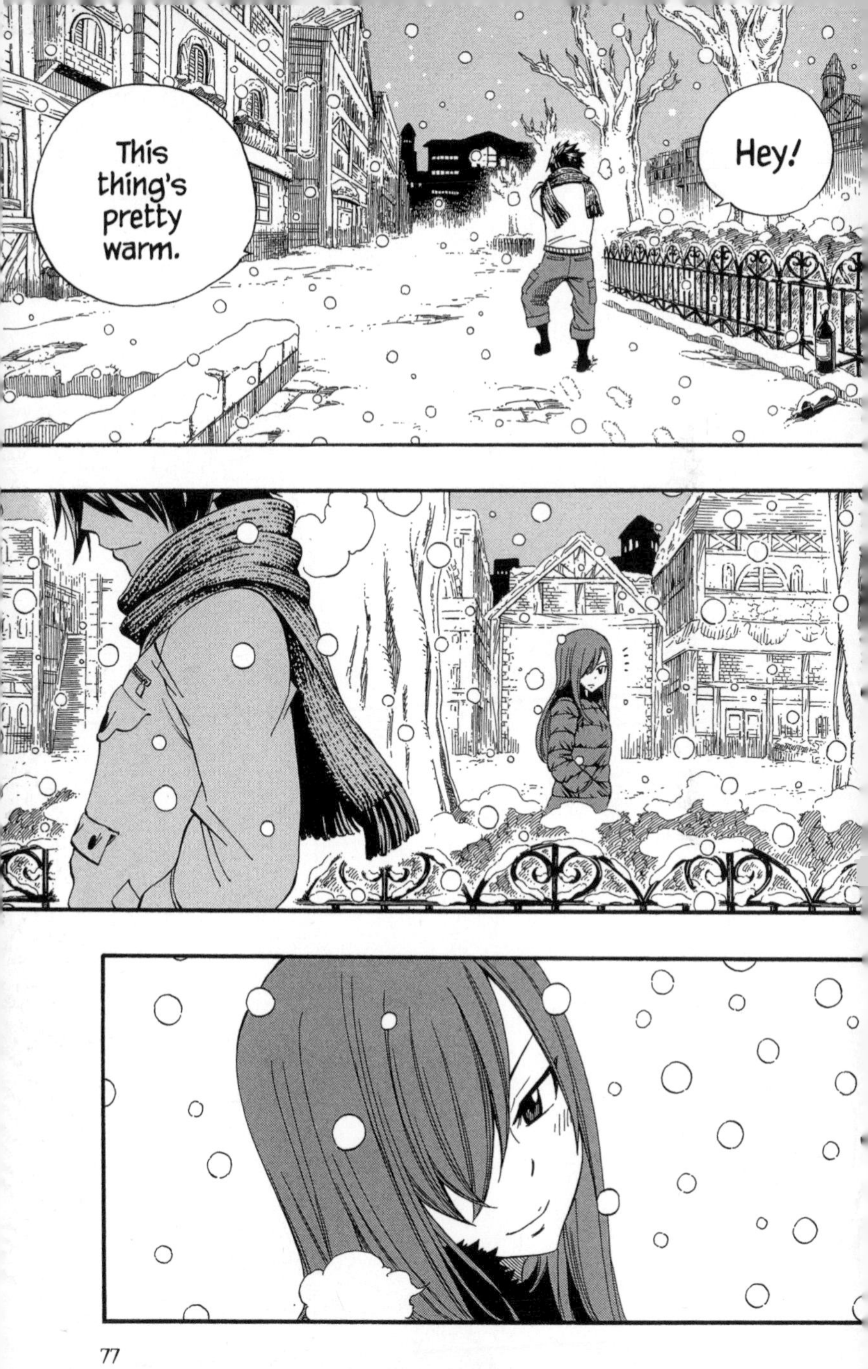
Hey!
This thing's pretty warm.

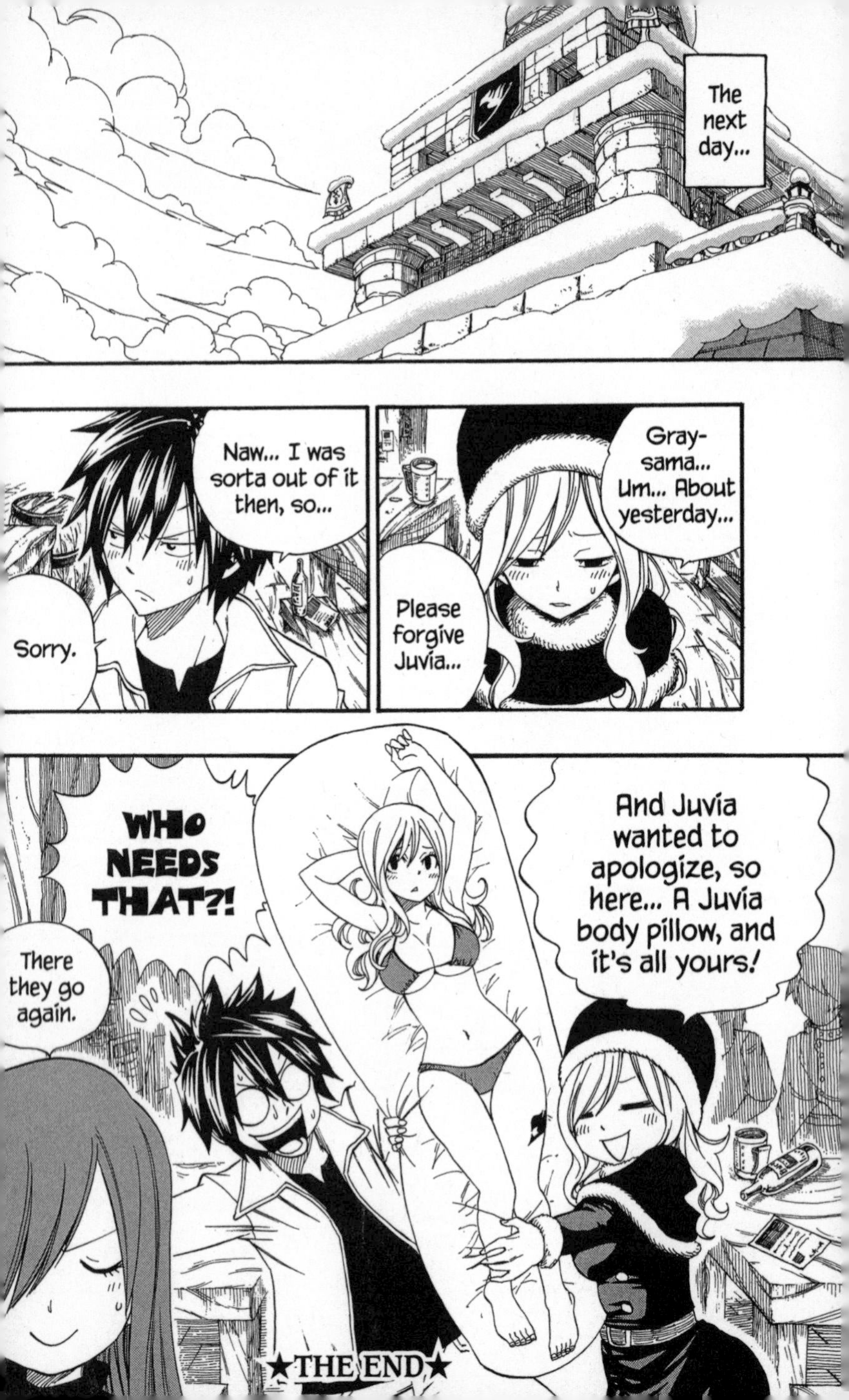
The next day...
Gray-sama... Um... About yesterday...
Please forgive Juvia...
Naw... I was sorta out of it then, so...
Sorry.
And Juvia wanted to apologize, so here... A Juvia body pillow, and it's all yours!
WHO NEEDS THAT?!
There they go again.
★THE END★

FT☆S

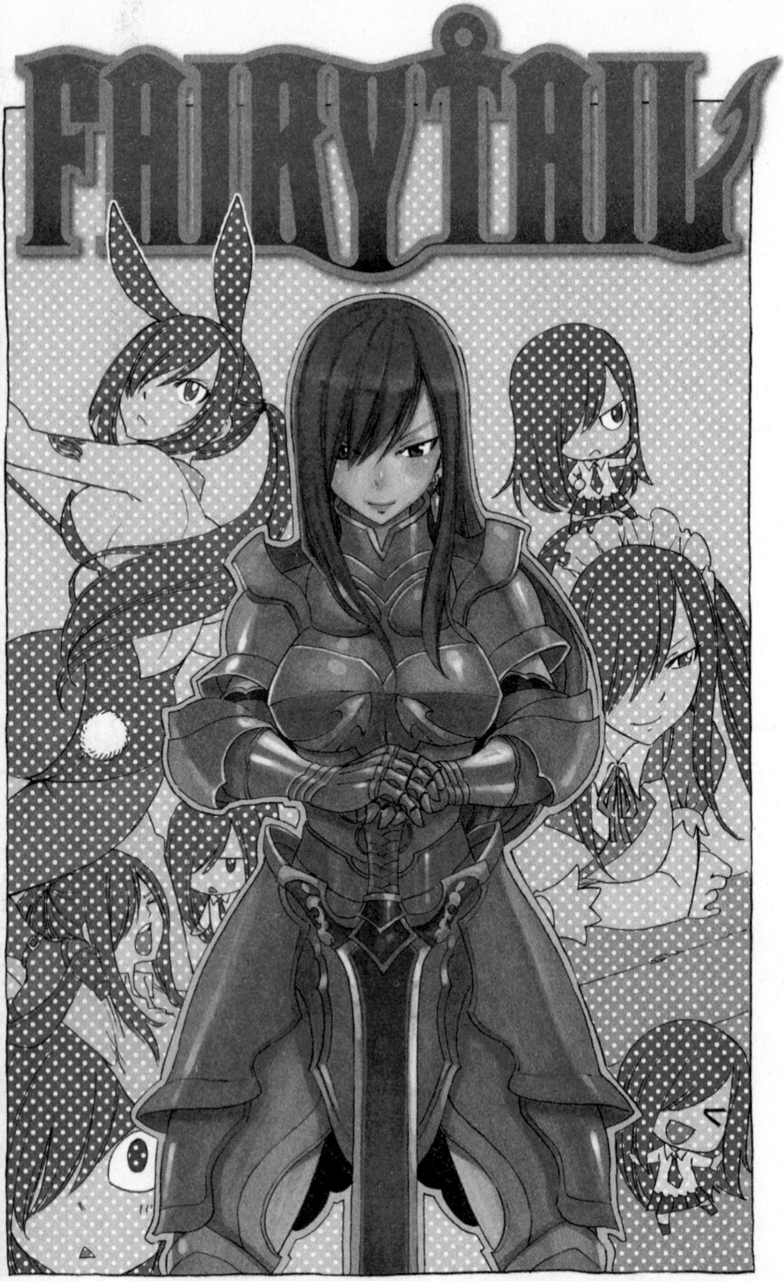
FAIRY TAIL

That Woman, Erza

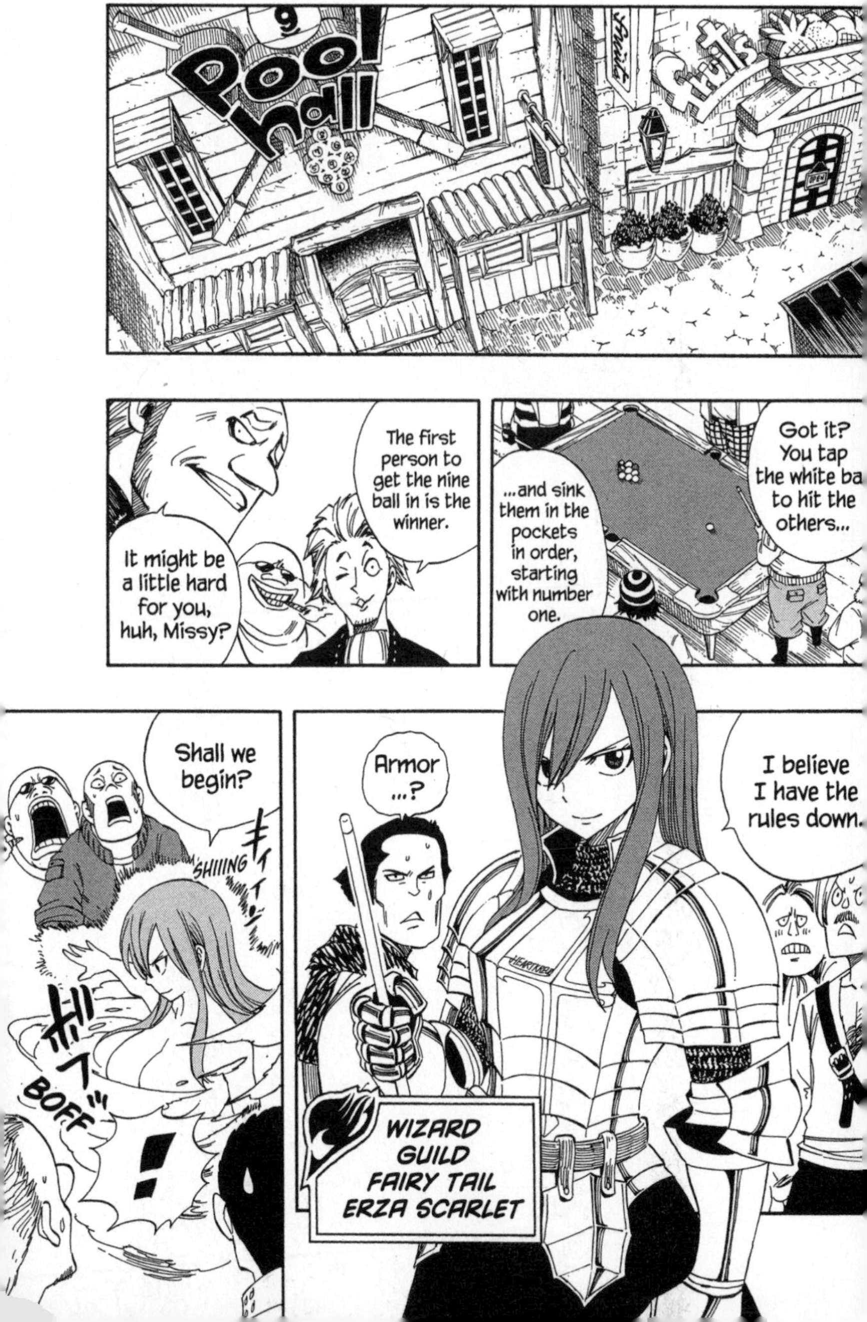
Pool hall
fruits
Got it? You tap the white ba to hit the others...
...and sink them in the pockets in order, starting with number one.
The first person to get the nine ball in is the winner.
It might be a little hard for you, huh, Missy?
I believe I have the rules down.
Armor ...?
WIZARD GUILD FAIRY TAIL ERZA SCARLET
Shall we begin?
SHIIING
BOFF

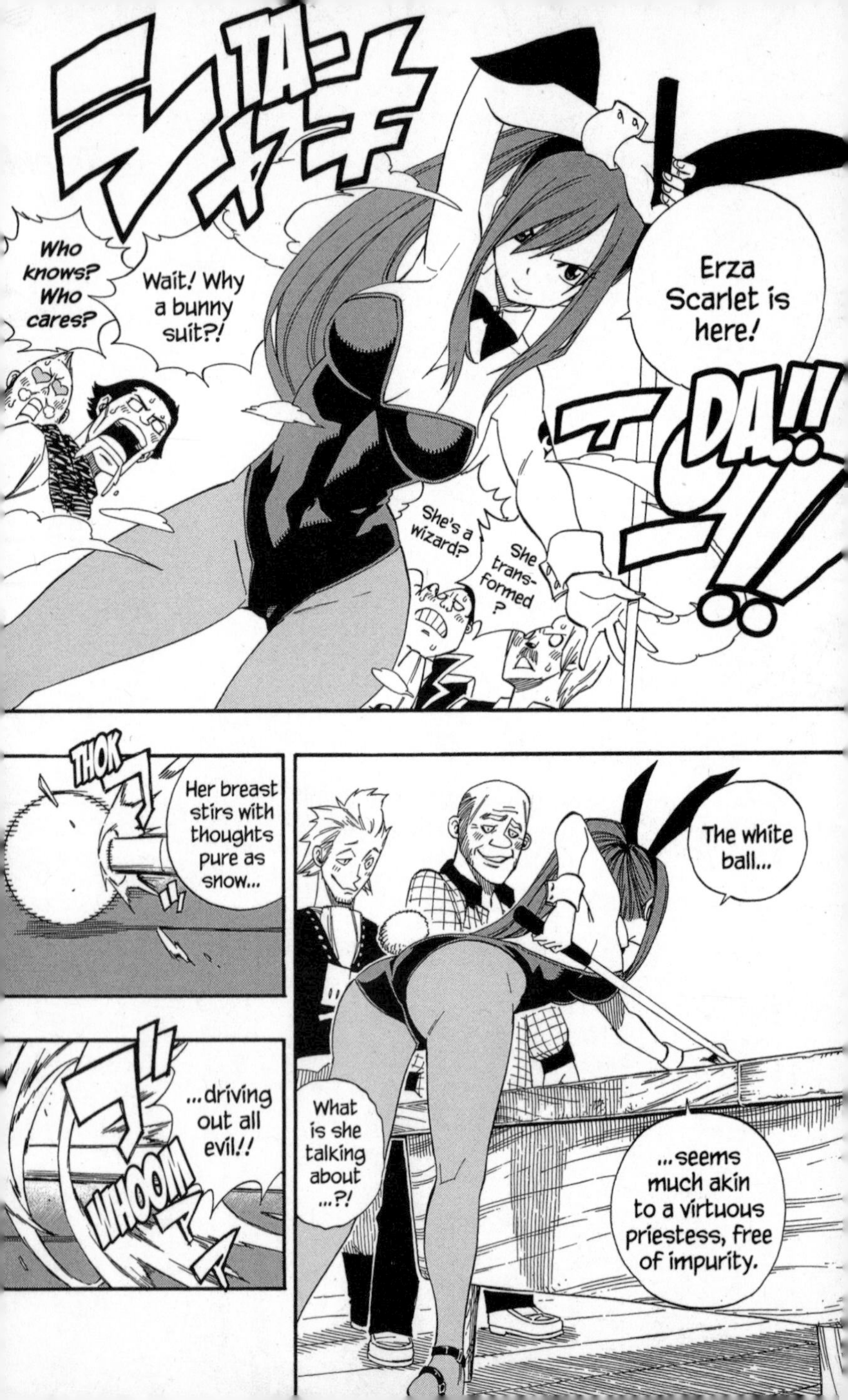
TA-
Erza Scarlet is here!
DA!!
Wait! Why a bunny suit?!
Who knows? Who cares?
She transformed?
She's a wizard?
The white ball...
...seems much akin to a virtuous priestess, free of impurity.
What is she talking about ...?!
THOK
Her breast stirs with thoughts pure as snow...
...driving out all evil!!
WHOOM

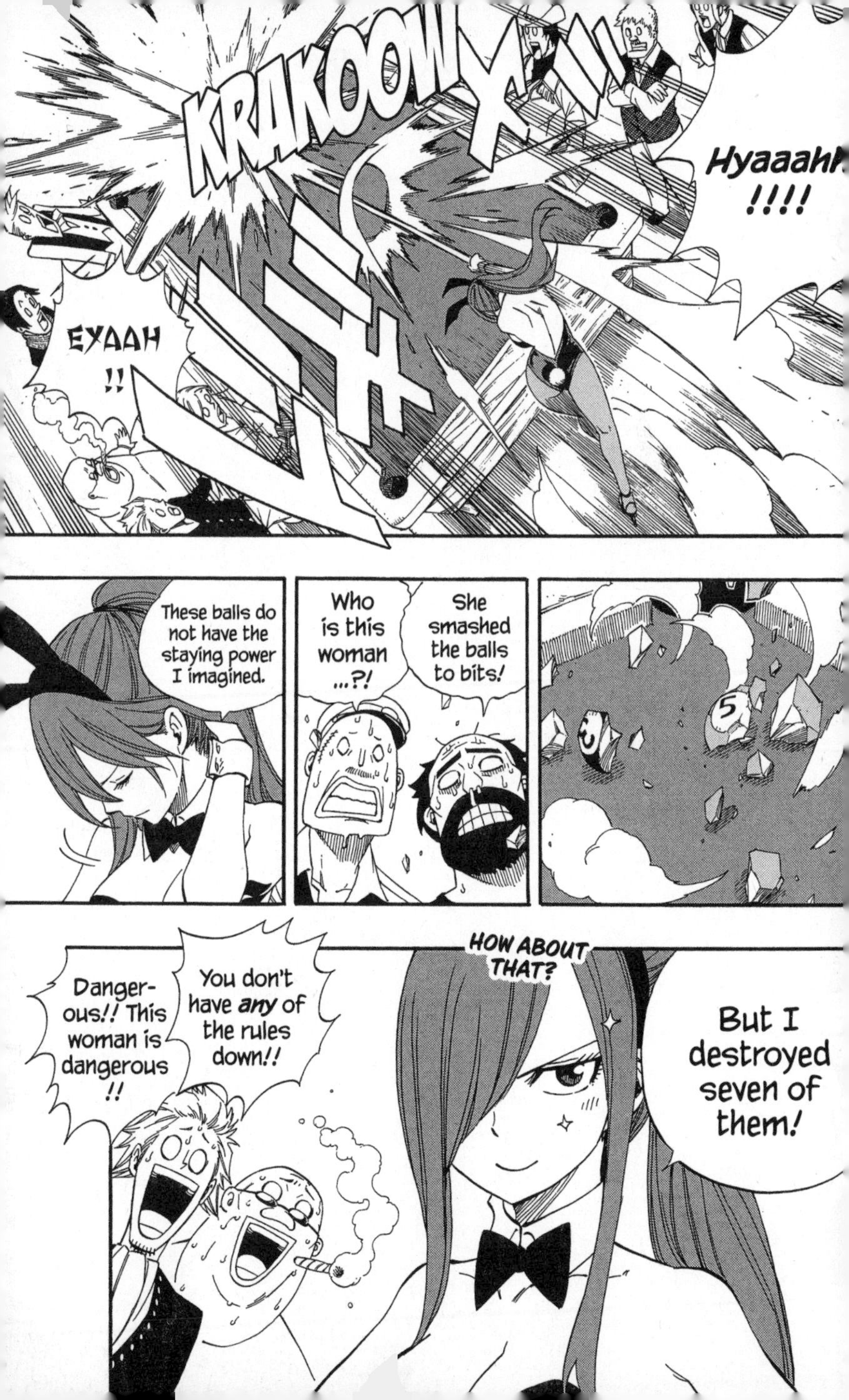

Hyaaah!
!!!!
KRAKOOM!!!
EYAAH
!!
She smashed the balls to bits!
Who is this woman ...?!
These balls do not have the staying power I imagined.
HOW ABOUT THAT?
But I destroyed seven of them!
You don't have *any* of the rules down!!
Danger-ous!! This woman is dangerous!!

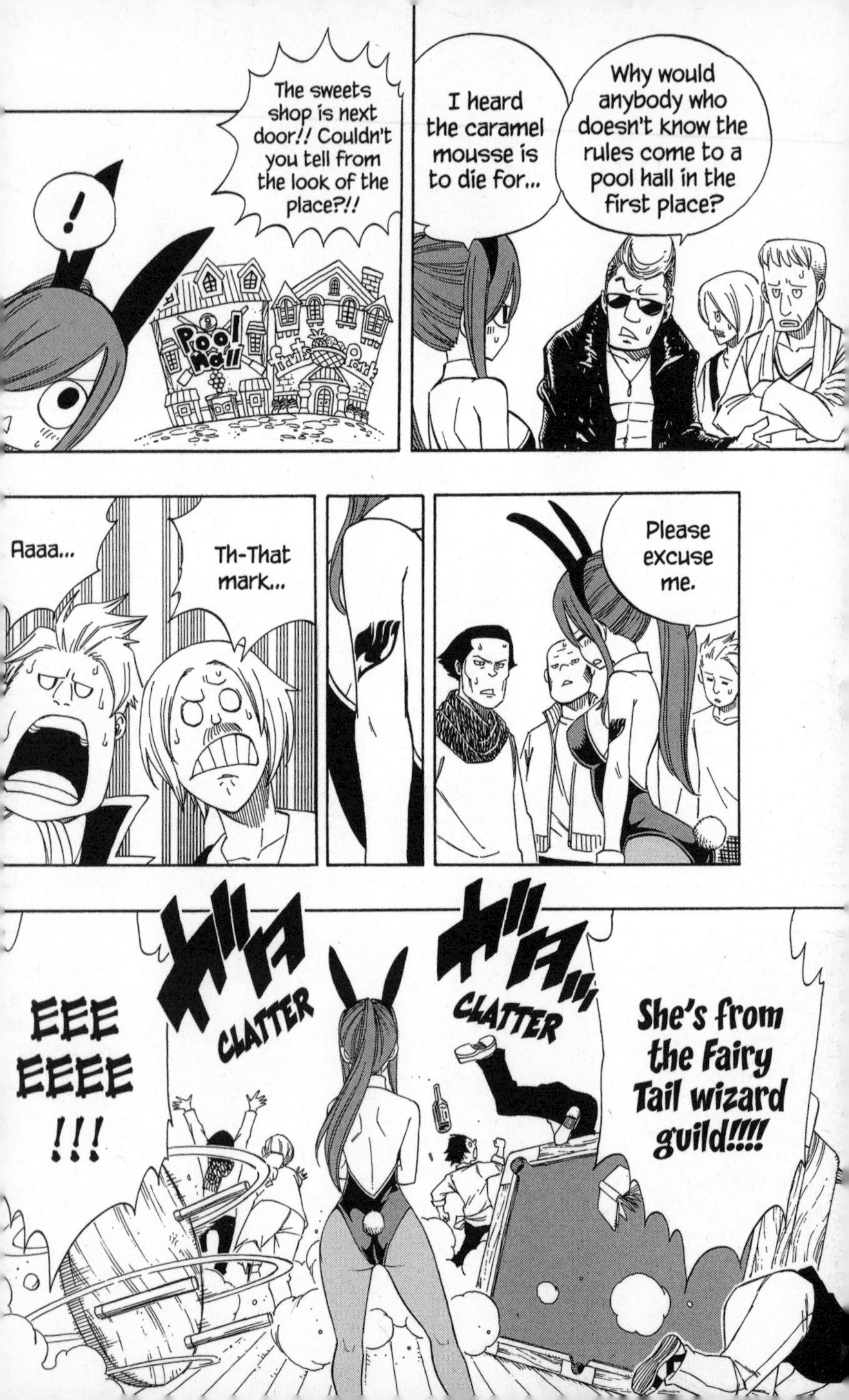
Why would anybody who doesn't know the rules come to a pool hall in the first place?
I heard the caramel mousse is to die for...
The sweets shop is next door!! Couldn't you tell from the look of the place?!!
!
Please excuse me.
Th-That mark...
Aaaa...
She's from the Fairy Tail wizard guild!!!!
CLATTER
CLATTER
EEE EEEE !!!

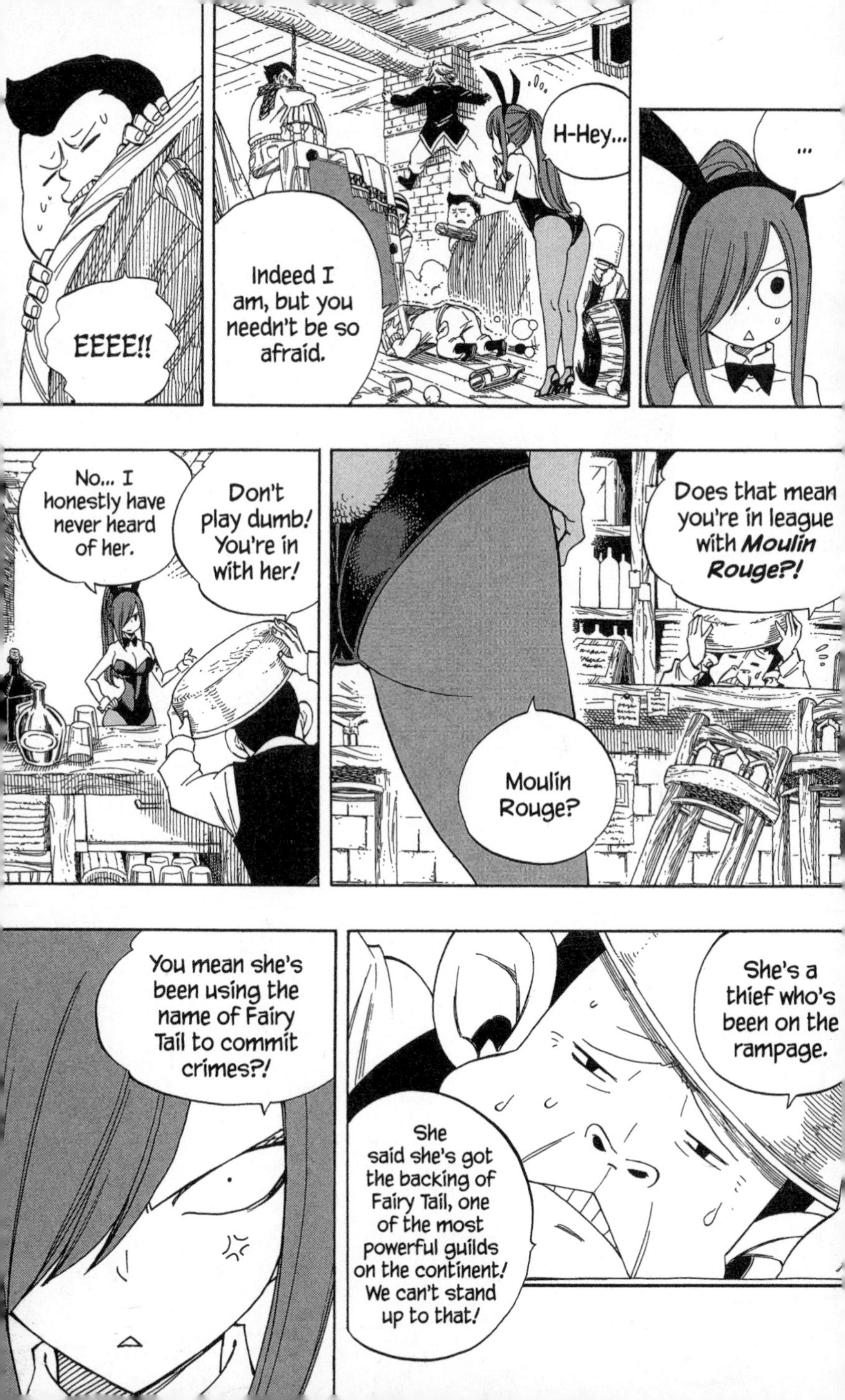
...
H-Hey...
Indeed I am, but you needn't be so afraid.
EEEE!!
Does that mean you're in league with *Moulin Rouge?!*
Moulin Rouge?
Don't play dumb! You're in with her!
No... I honestly have never heard of her.
She's a thief who's been on the rampage.
She said she's got the backing of Fairy Tail, one of the most powerful guilds on the continent! We can't stand up to that!
You mean she's been using the name of Fairy Tail to commit crimes?!

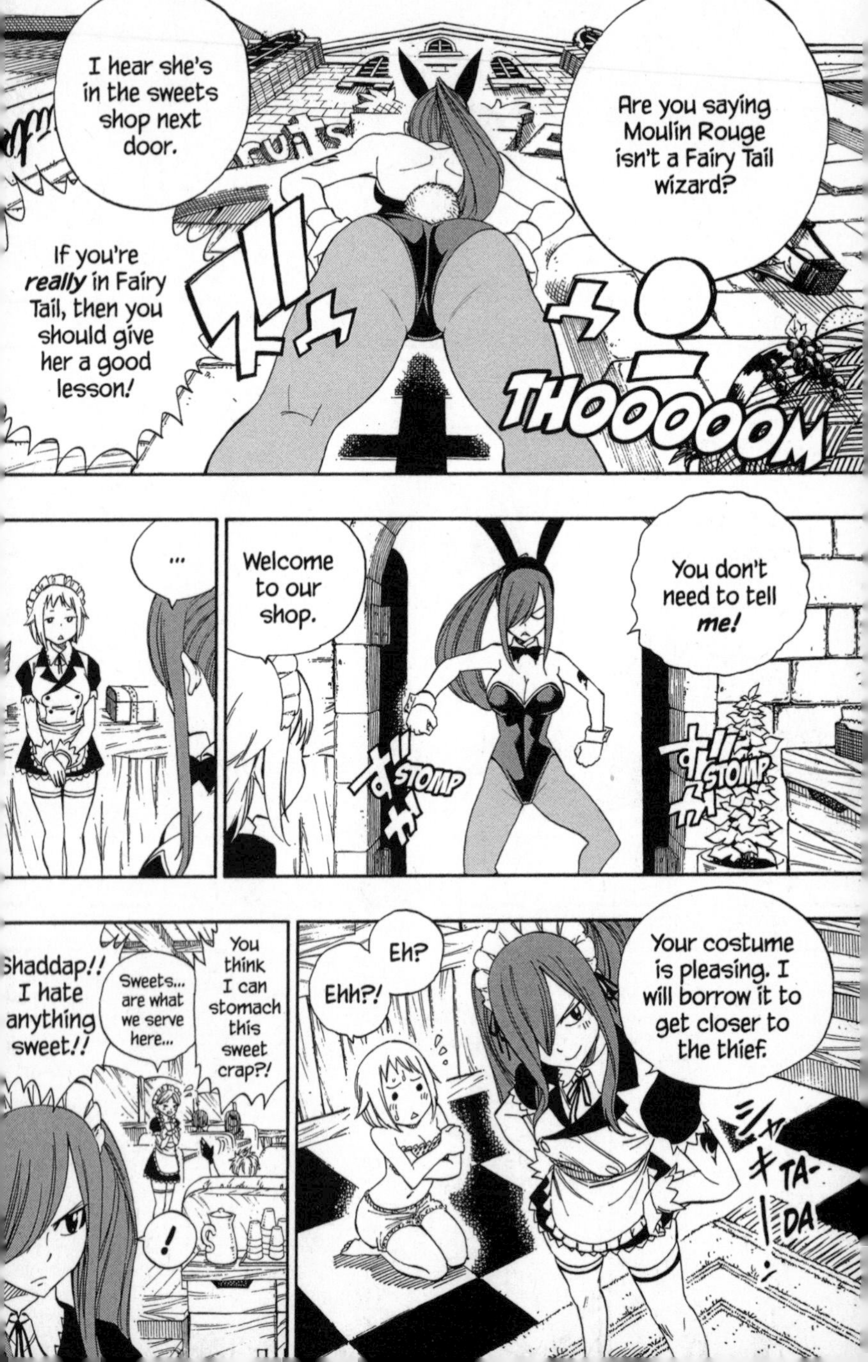
Are you saying Moulin Rouge isn't a Fairy Tail wizard?
I hear she's in the sweets shop next door.
If you're ***really*** in Fairy Tail, then you should give her a good lesson!
THOOOOOM
You don't need to tell ***me!***
STOMP
STOMP
Welcome to our shop.
...
Your costume is pleasing. I will borrow it to get closer to the thief.
TA-DA
Eh?
Ehh?!
You think I can stomach this sweet crap?!
Sweets... are what we serve here...
Shaddap!! I hate anything sweet!!
!

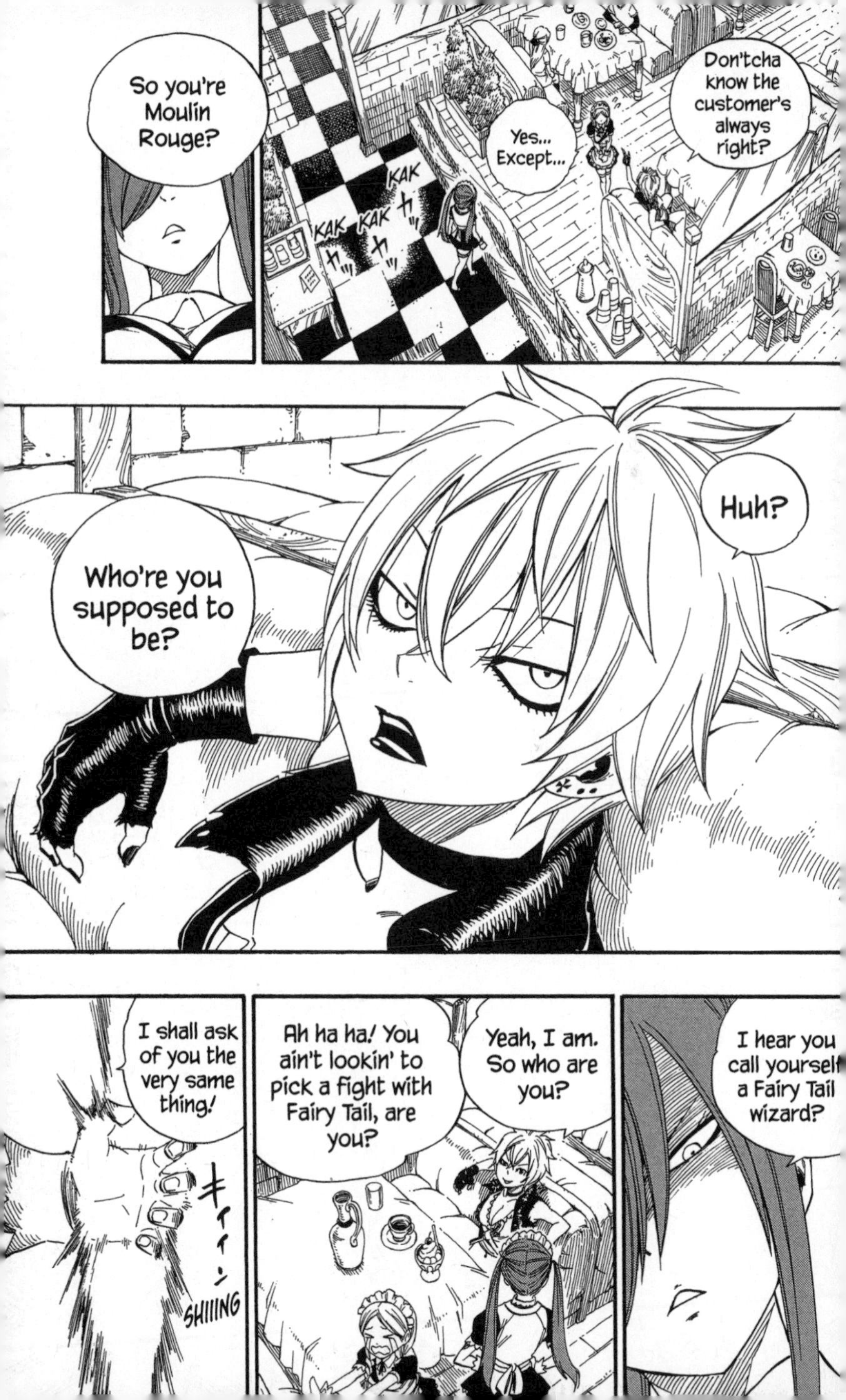
Don'tcha know the customer's always right?
Yes... Except...
KAK
KAK
KAK
So you're Moulin Rouge?
Huh?
Who're you supposed to be?
I hear you call yourself a Fairy Tail wizard?
Yeah, I am. So who are you?
Ah ha ha! You ain't lookin' to pick a fight with Fairy Tail, are you?
I shall ask of you the very same thing!
SHIIING

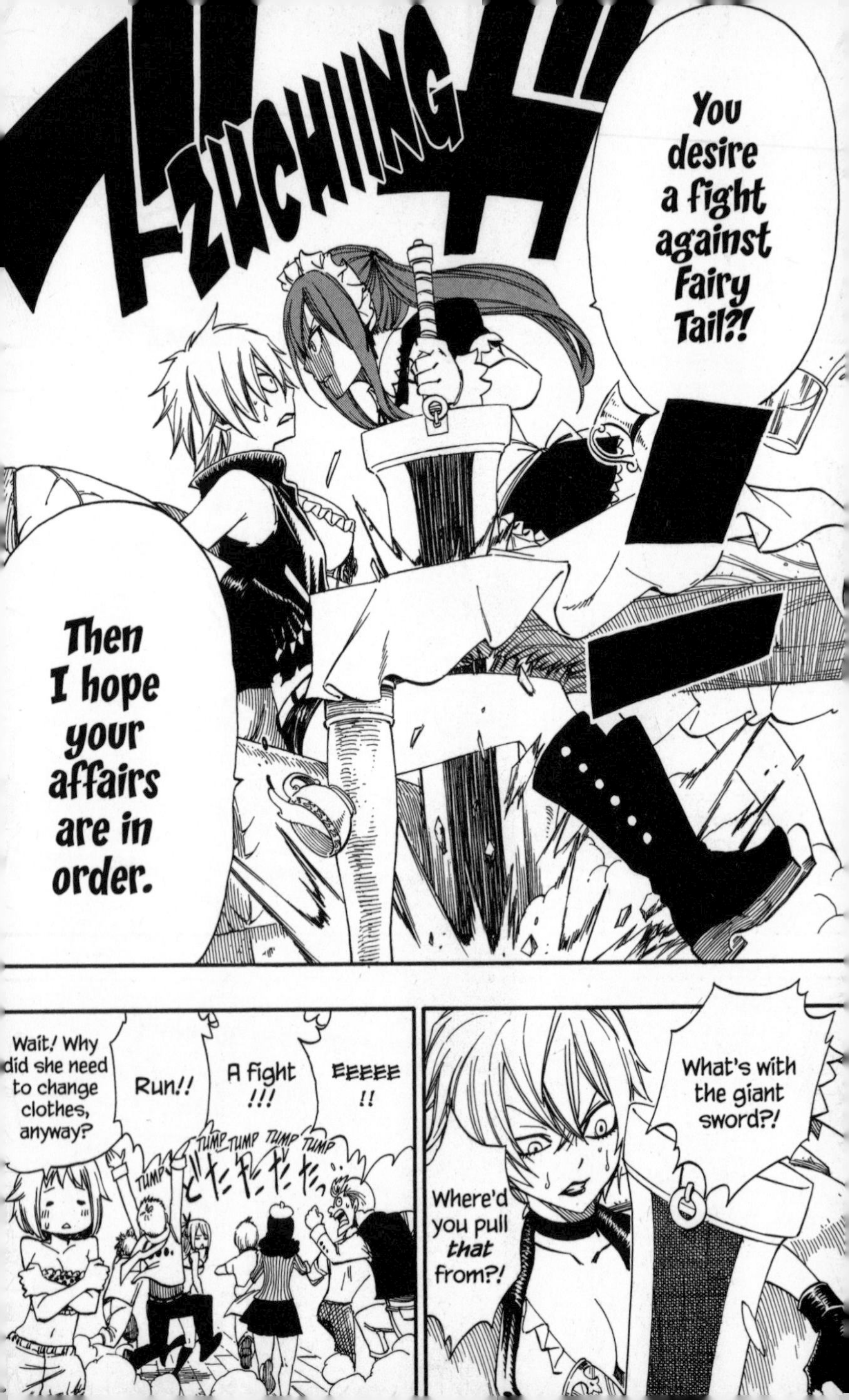
ZUCHIIING
You desire a fight against Fairy Tail?!
Then I hope your affairs are in order.
What's with the giant sword?!
Where'd you pull *that* from?!
EEEEE !!
A fight !!!
Run!!
Wait! Why did she need to change clothes, anyway?
TUMP TUMP TUMP TUMP TUMP

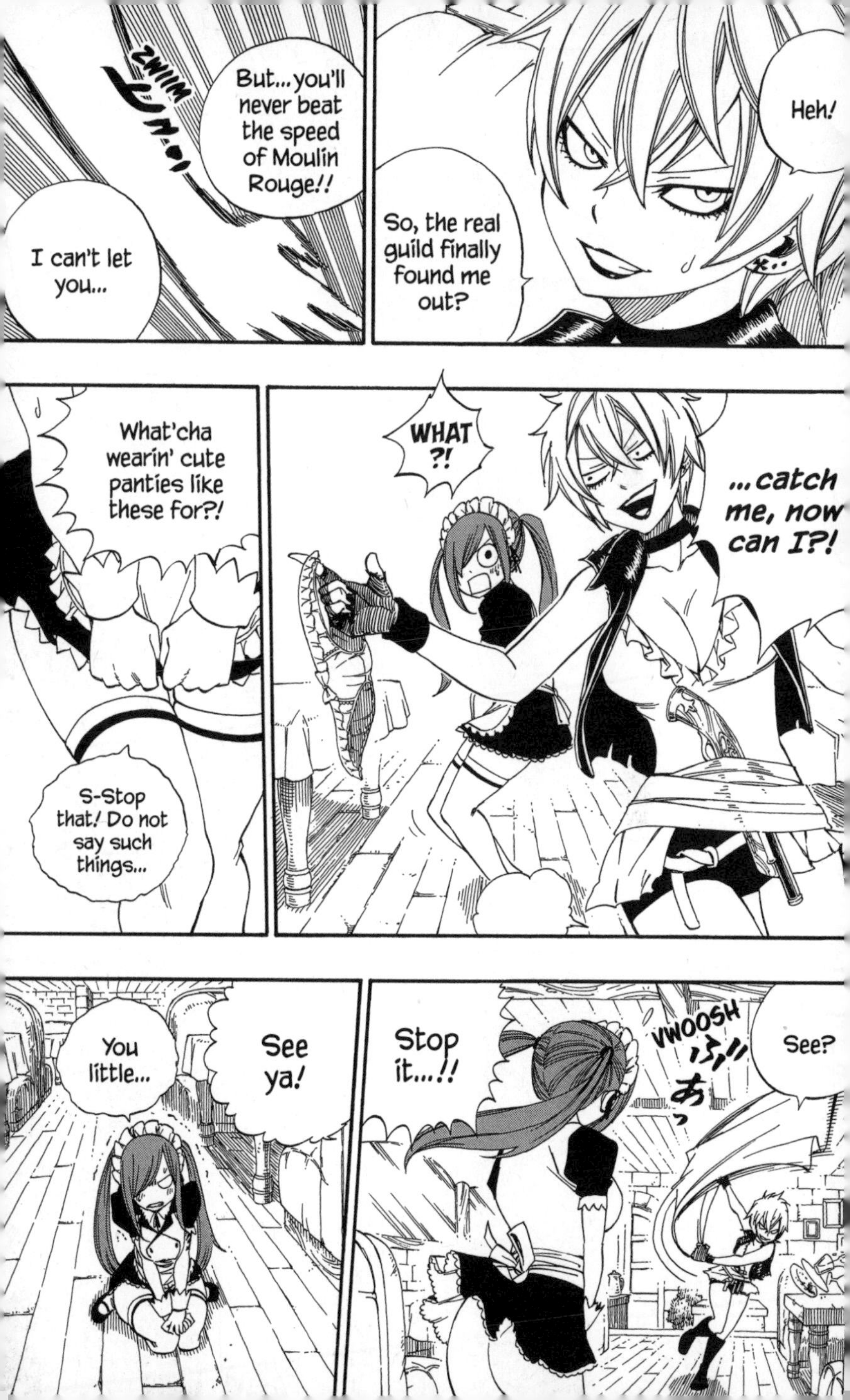
Heh!
So, the real guild finally found me out?
But...you'll never beat the speed of Moulin Rouge!!
I can't let you...
...catch me, now can I?!
WHAT ?!
What'cha wearin' cute panties like these for?!
S-Stop that! Do not say such things...
See?
VWOOSH
Stop it...!!
See ya!
You little...

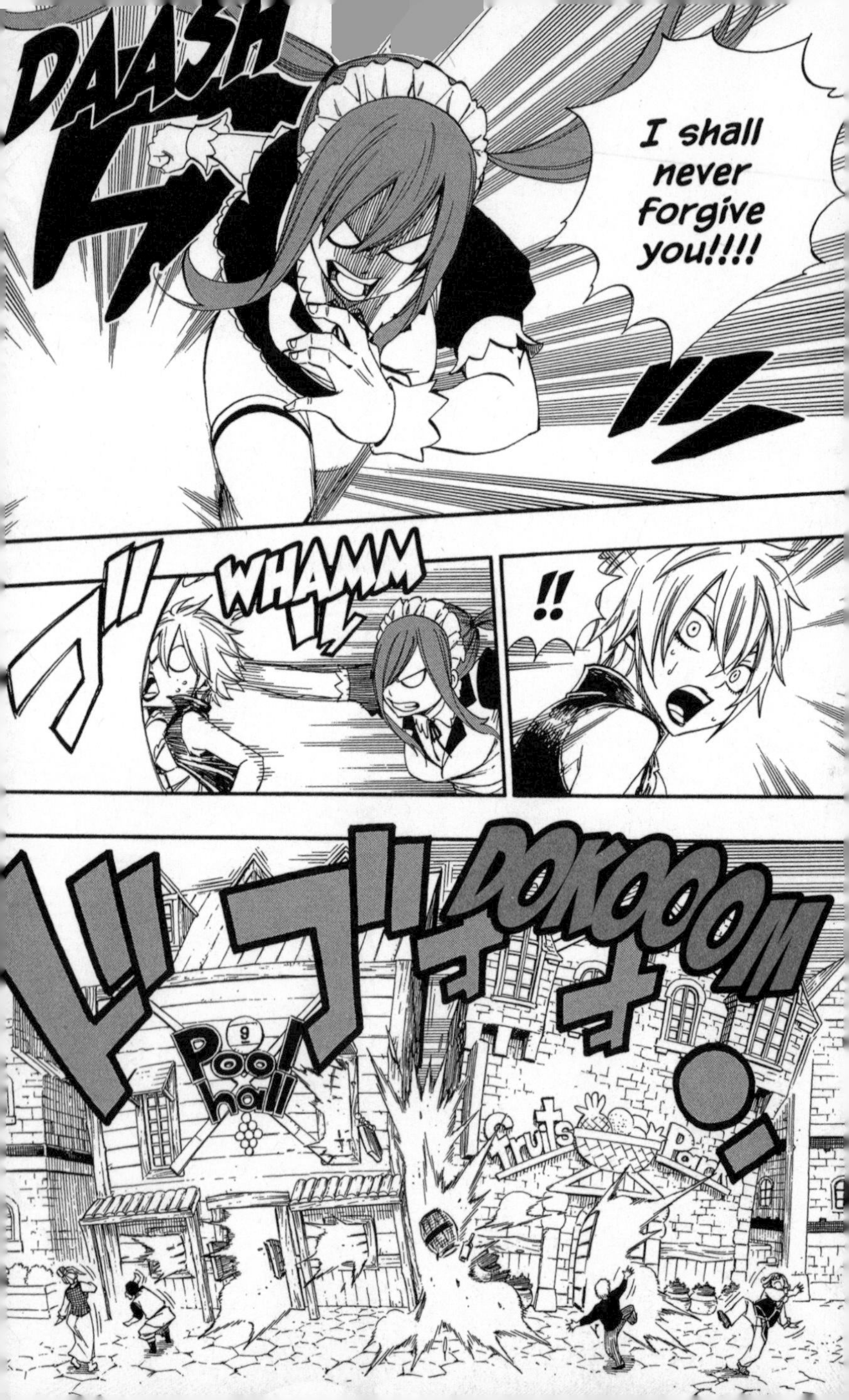
I shall never forgive you!!!!
DA-ASH
!!
WHAMM
DOKOOOM
Pool hall

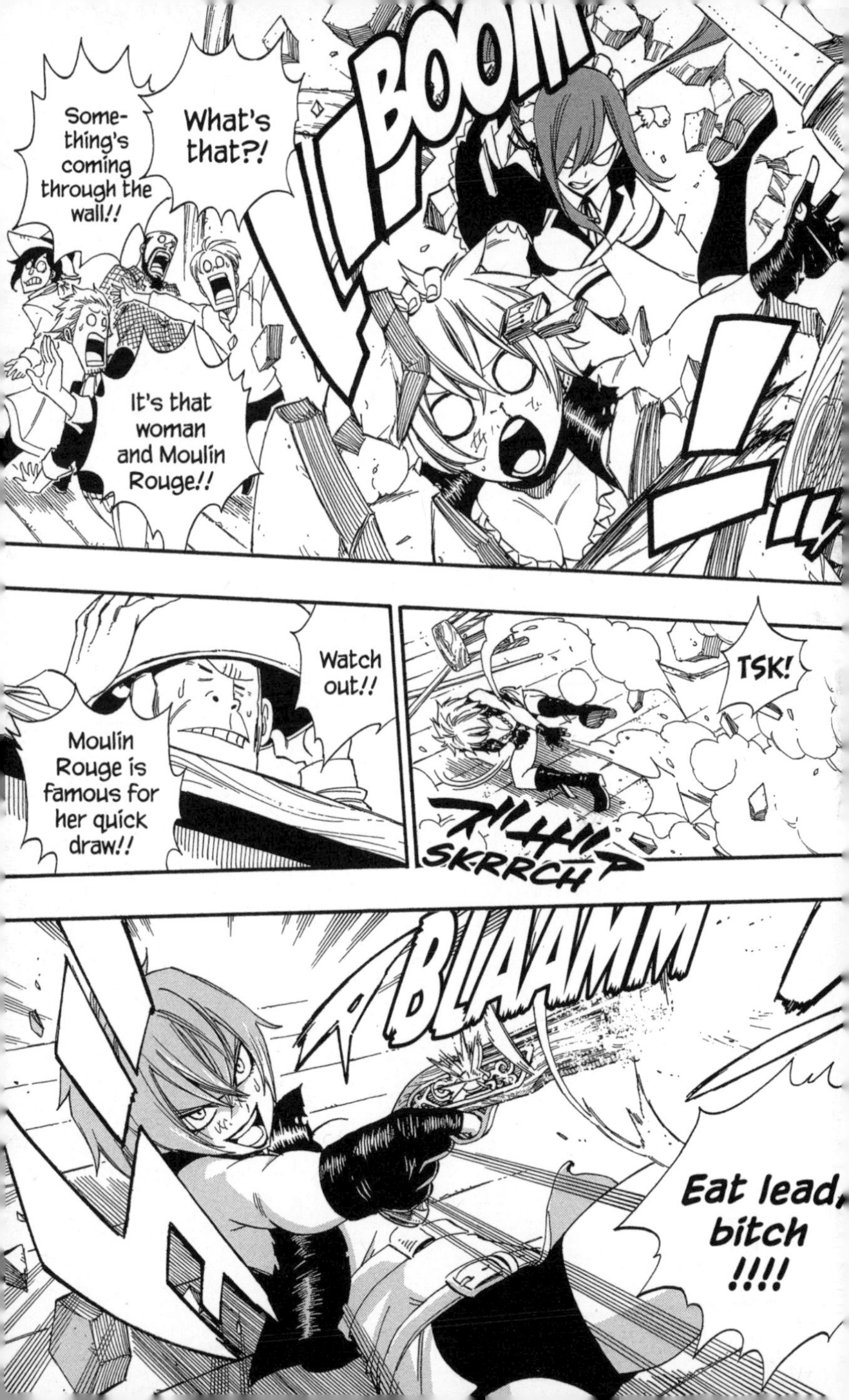
BOOM
What's that?!
Some-thing's coming through the wall!!
It's that woman and Moulin Rouge!!
TSK!
SKRRCH
Watch out!!
Moulin Rouge is famous for her quick draw!!
BLAAMM
Eat lead, bitch !!!!

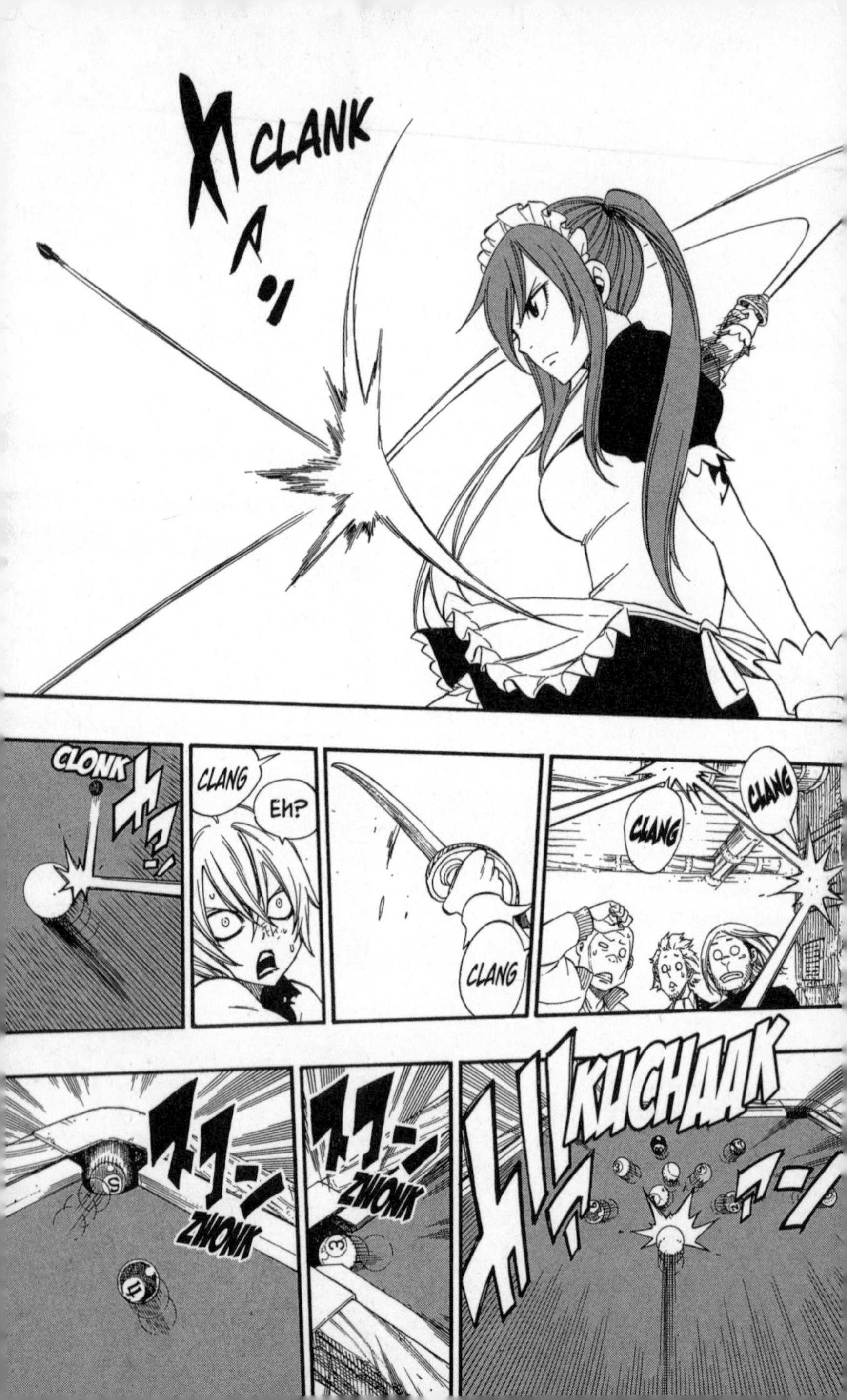
CLANK
CLANG
CLANG
CLANG
CLANG
Eh?
CLONK
KUCHAAK
ZWONK
ZWONK

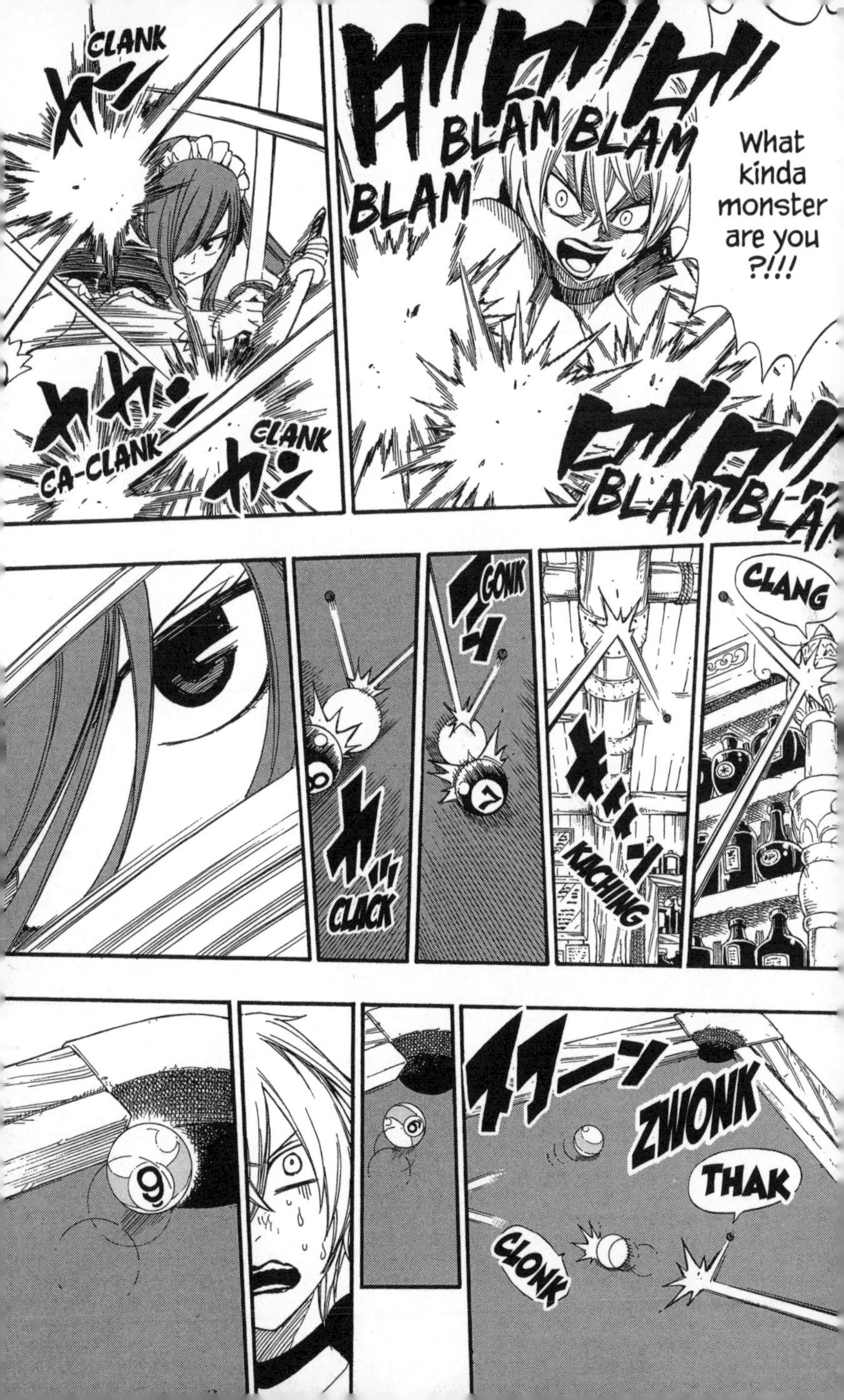
BLAM BLAM
BLAM
What kinda monster are you ?!!!
BLAM BLAM
CLANK
CA-CLANK
CLANK
CLANG
KACHING
GONK
CLACK
ZWONK
THAK
CLONK

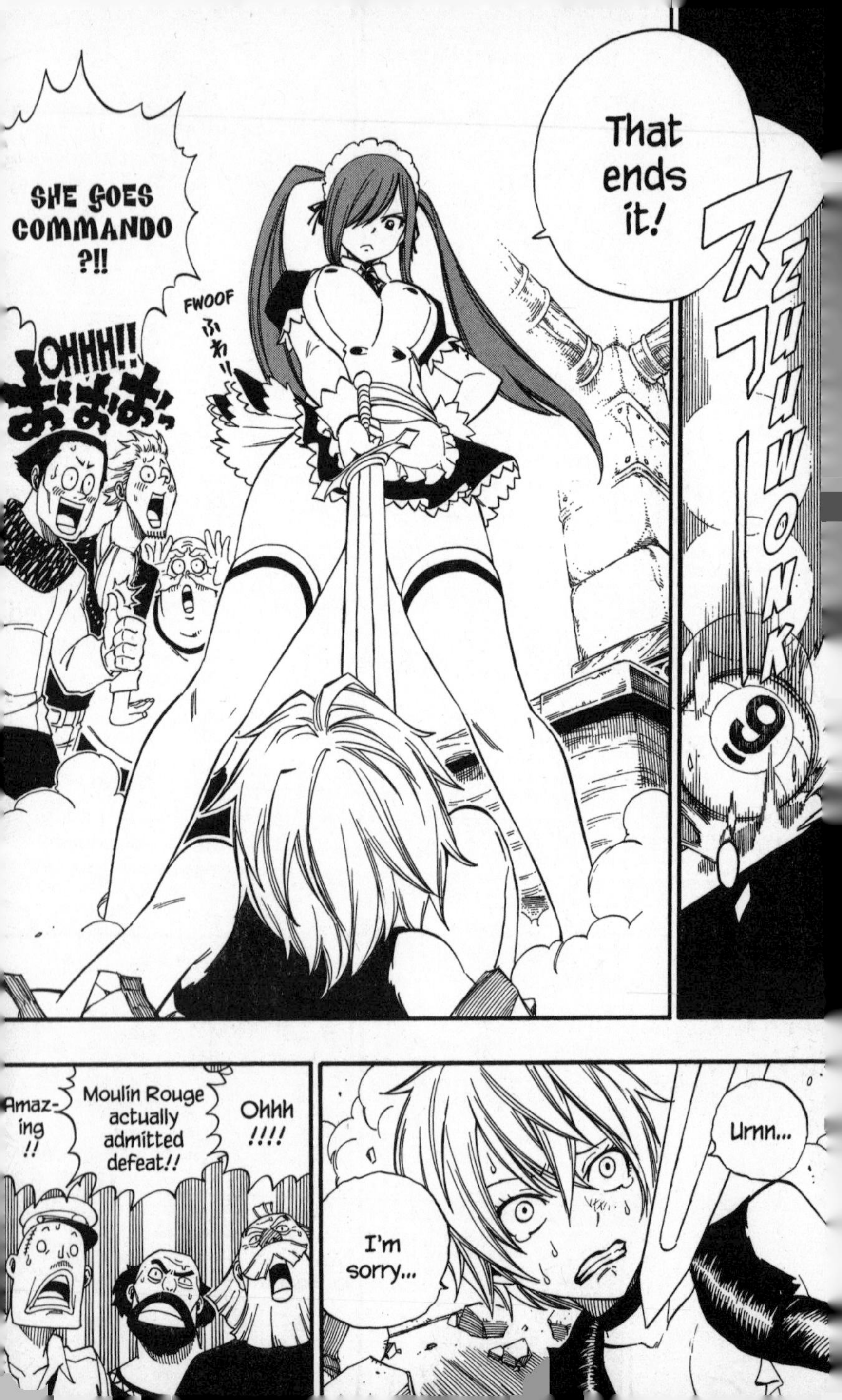
That ends it!
ZUUWONK
スフー
FWOOF
ふわ!!
SHE GOES COMMANDO ?!!
OHHH!!
おおお
Urnn...
I'm sorry...
Ohhh !!!!
Moulin Rouge actually admitted defeat!!
Amaz-ing !!

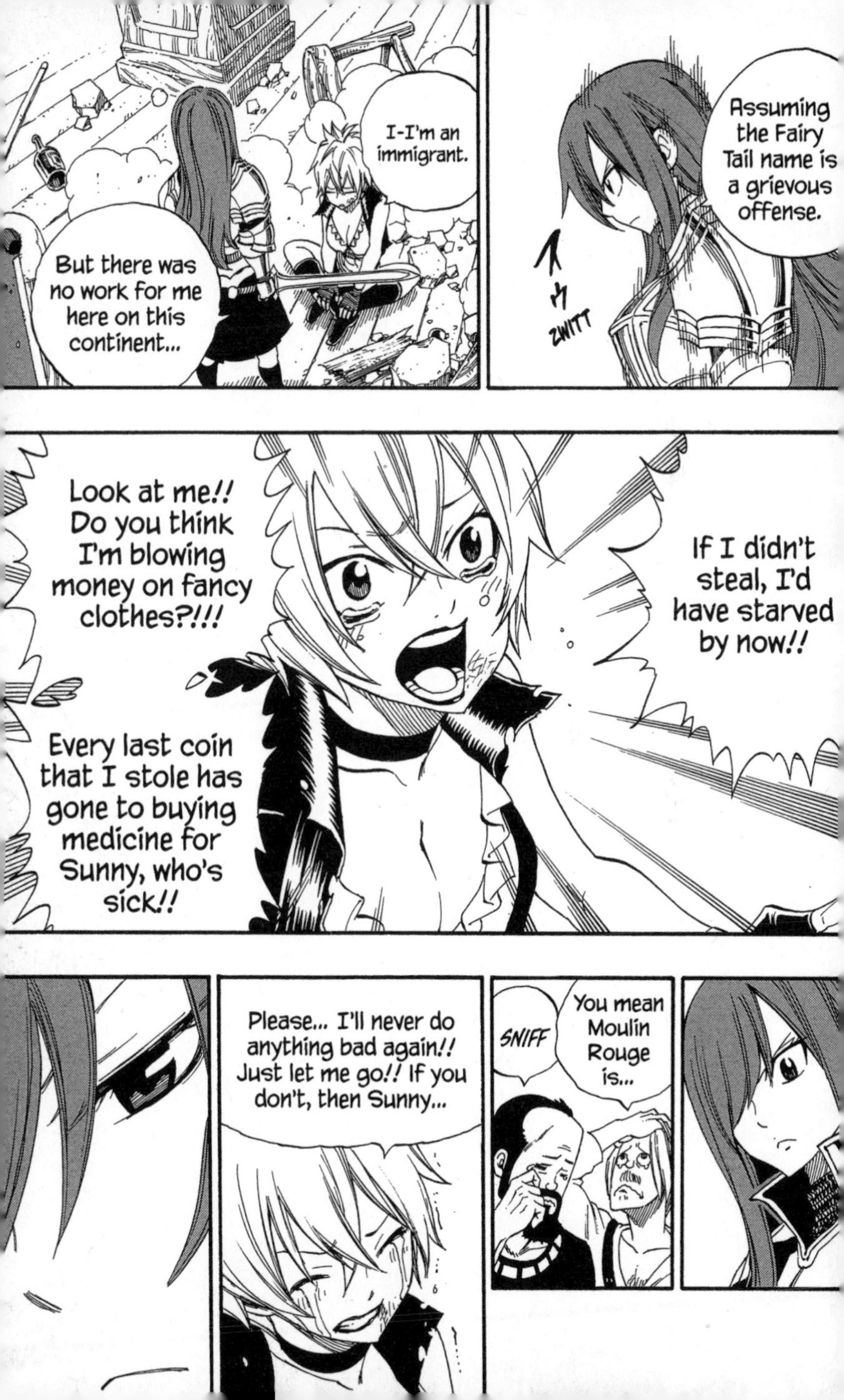
Assuming the Fairy Tail name is a grievous offense.
ZWITT
I-I'm an immigrant.
But there was no work for me here on this continent...
If I didn't steal, I'd have starved by now!!
Look at me!! Do you think I'm blowing money on fancy clothes?!!!
Every last coin that I stole has gone to buying medicine for Sunny, who's sick!!
You mean Moulin Rouge is...
SNIFF
Please... I'll never do anything bad again!! Just let me go!! If you don't, then Sunny...

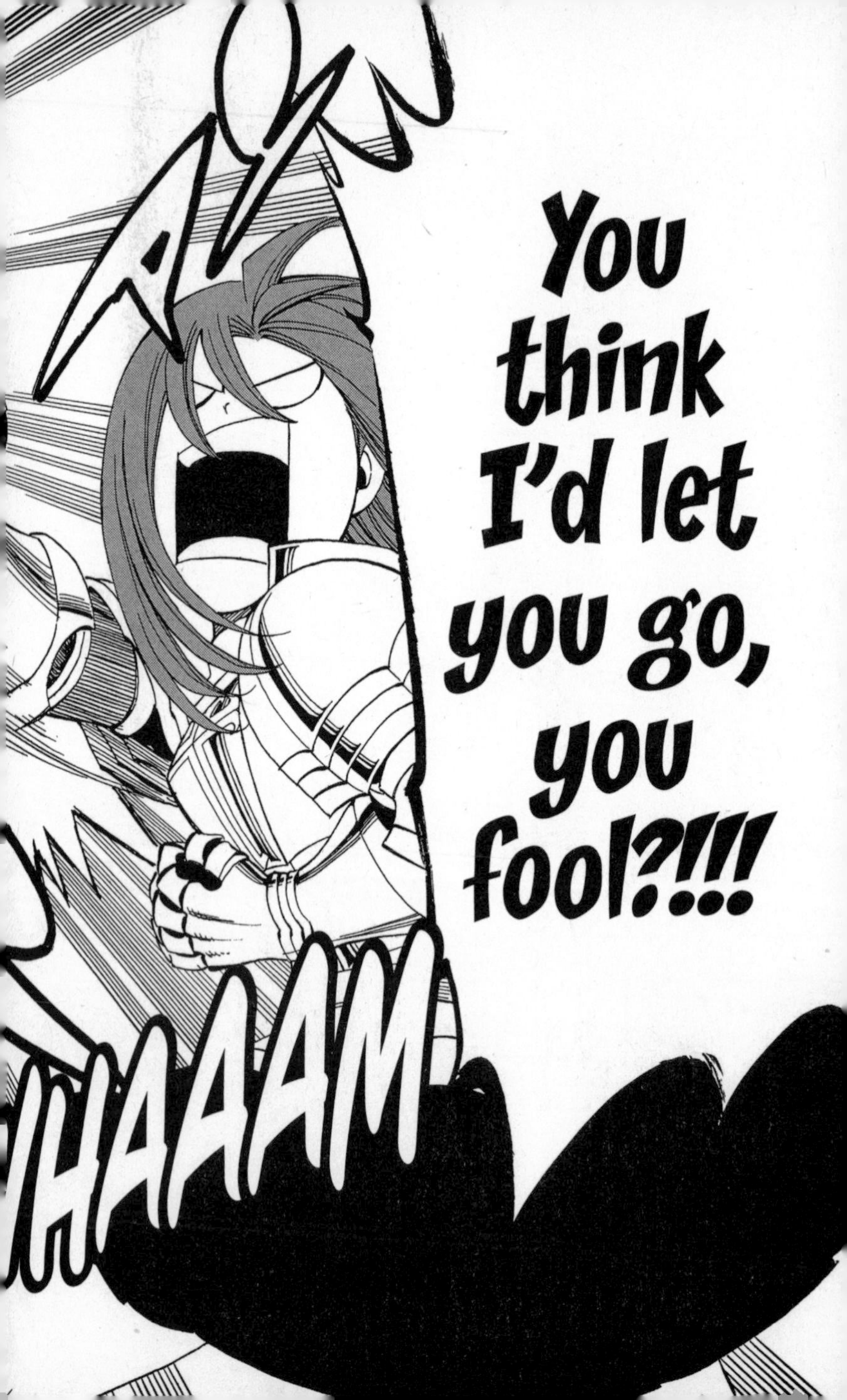
You think I'd let you go, you fool?!!!
HAAAM

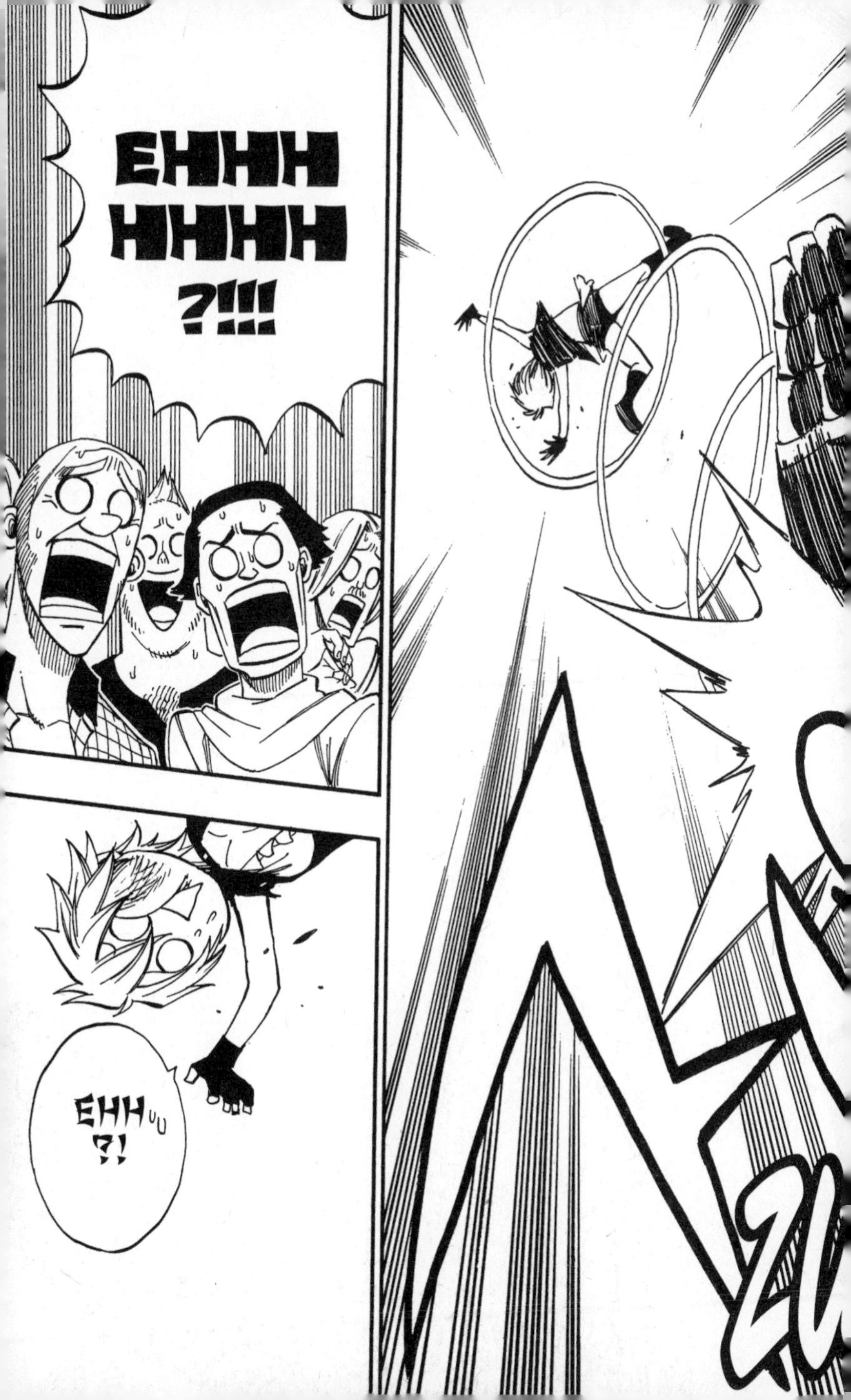
EHHHHHHH?!!!
EHH?!

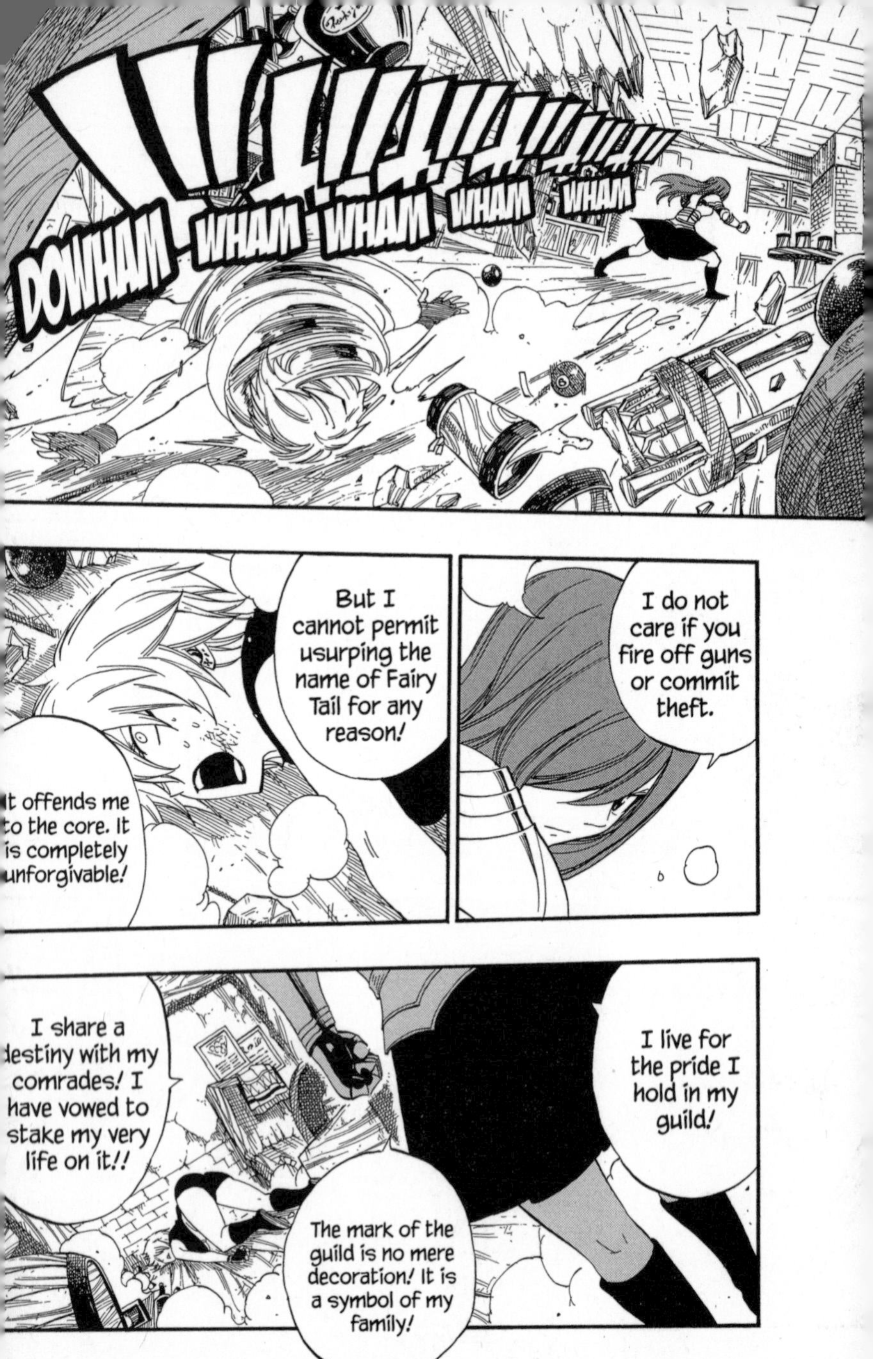
DOWHAM WHAM WHAM WHAM WHAM
I do not care if you fire off guns or commit theft.
But I cannot permit usurping the name of Fairy Tail for any reason!
It offends me to the core. It is completely unforgivable!
I live for the pride I hold in my guild!
The mark of the guild is no mere decoration! It is a symbol of my family!
I share a destiny with my comrades! I have vowed to stake my very life on it!!

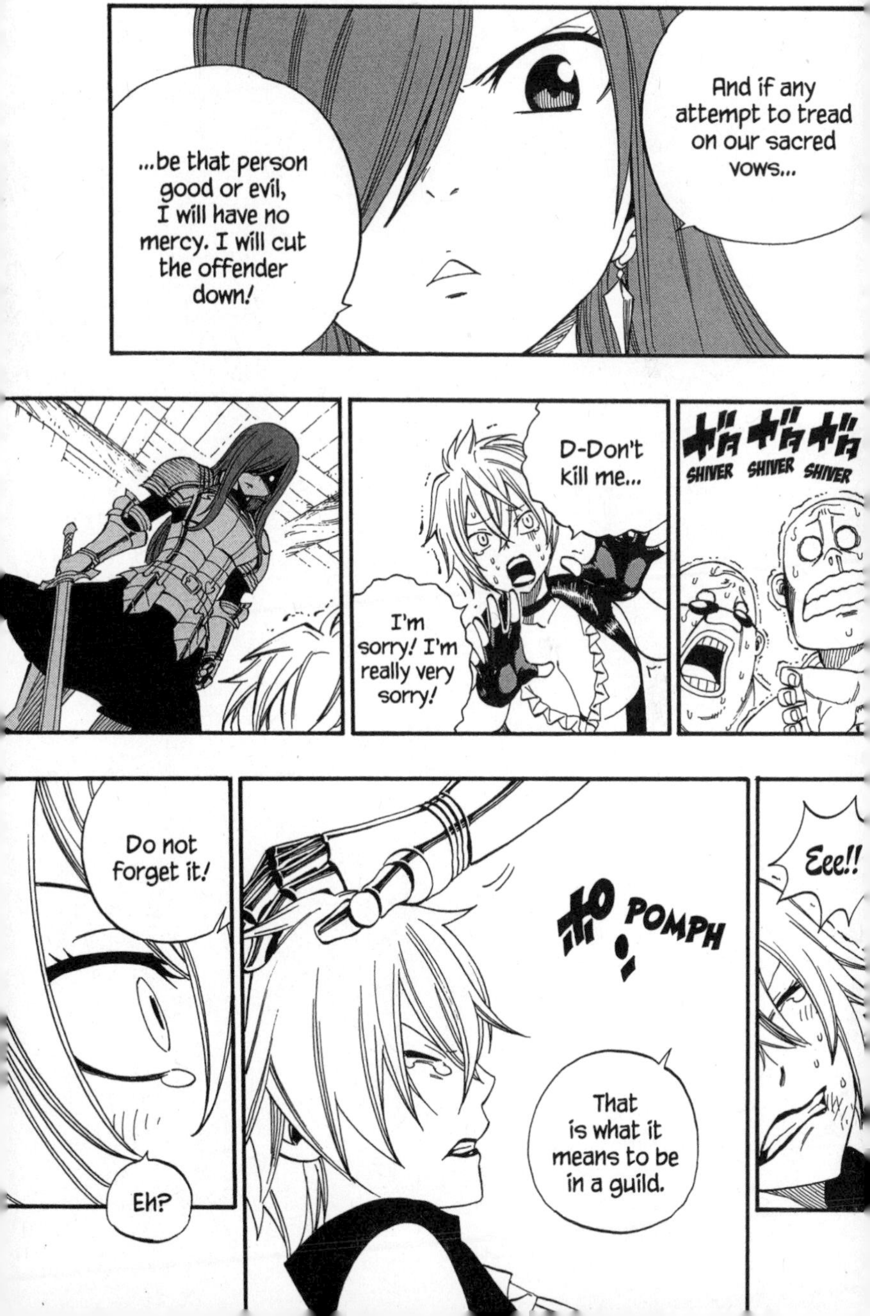
And if any attempt to tread on our sacred vows...
...be that person good or evil, I will have no mercy. I will cut the offender down!
SHIVER SHIVER SHIVER
D-Don't kill me...
I'm sorry! I'm really very sorry!
Eee!!
POMPH
That is what it means to be in a guild.
Do not forget it!
Eh?

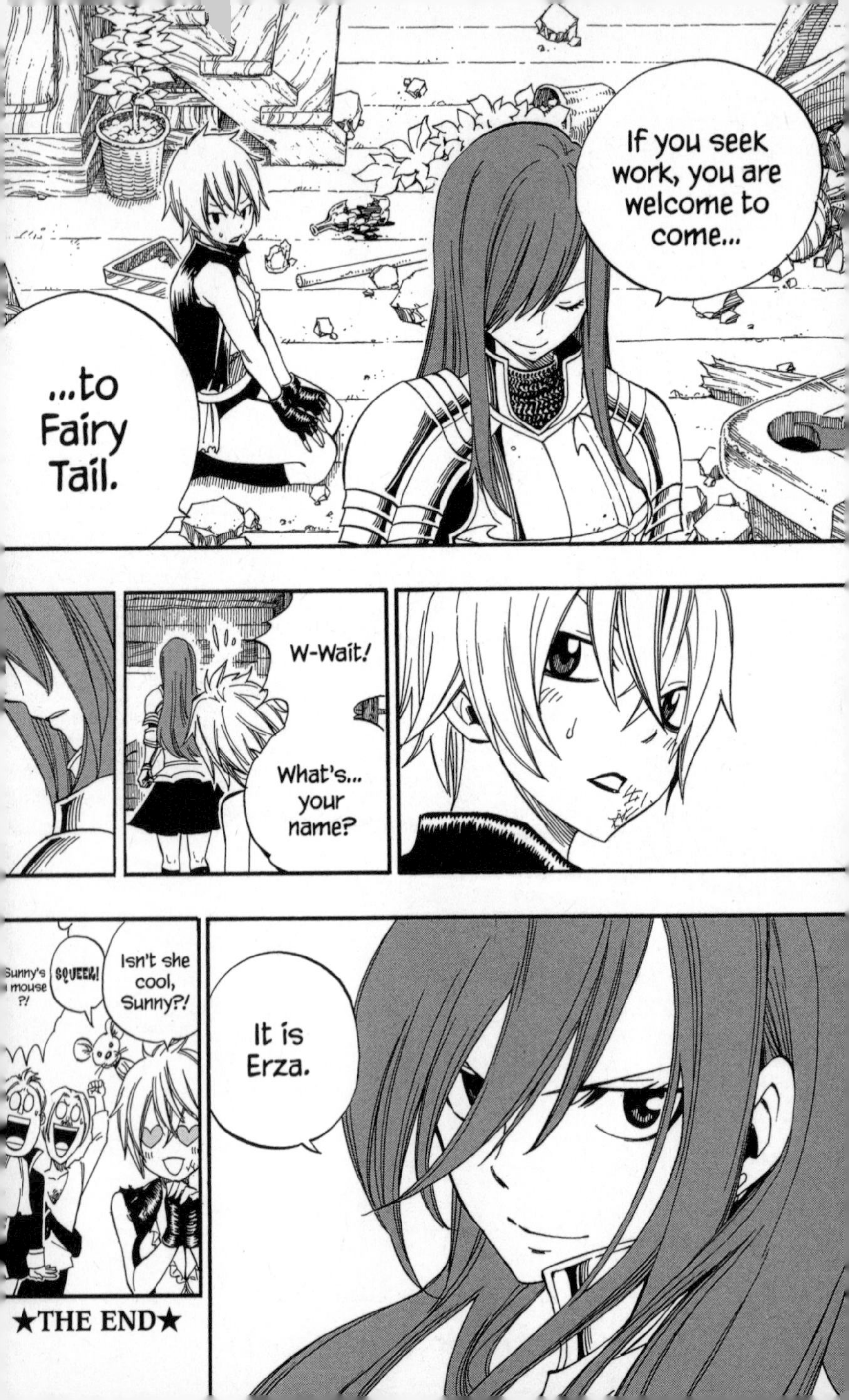
If you seek work, you are welcome to come...
...to Fairy Tail.
W-Wait!
What's... your name?
It is Erza.
Isn't she cool, Sunny?!
SQUEEK!
Sunny's mouse ?!
★THE END★

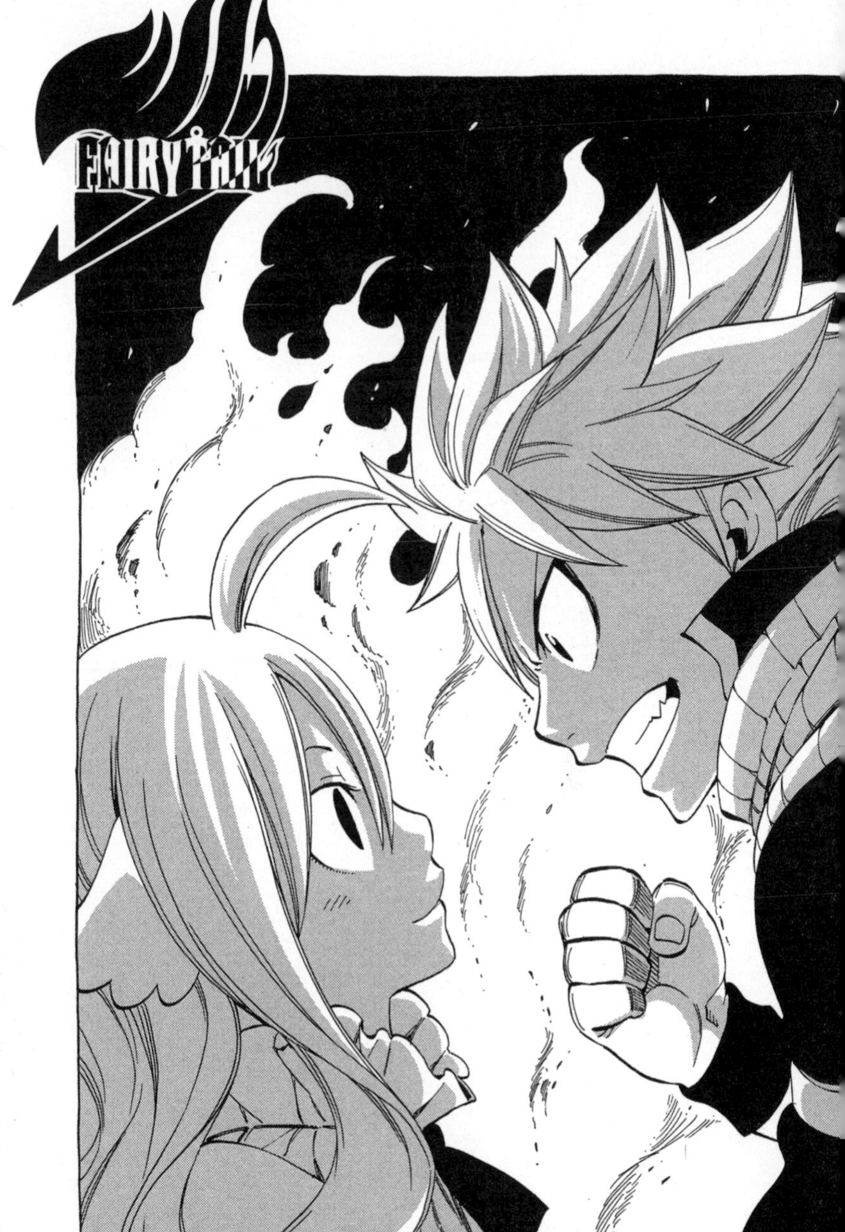
FAIRY TAIL

Natsu vs. Mavis

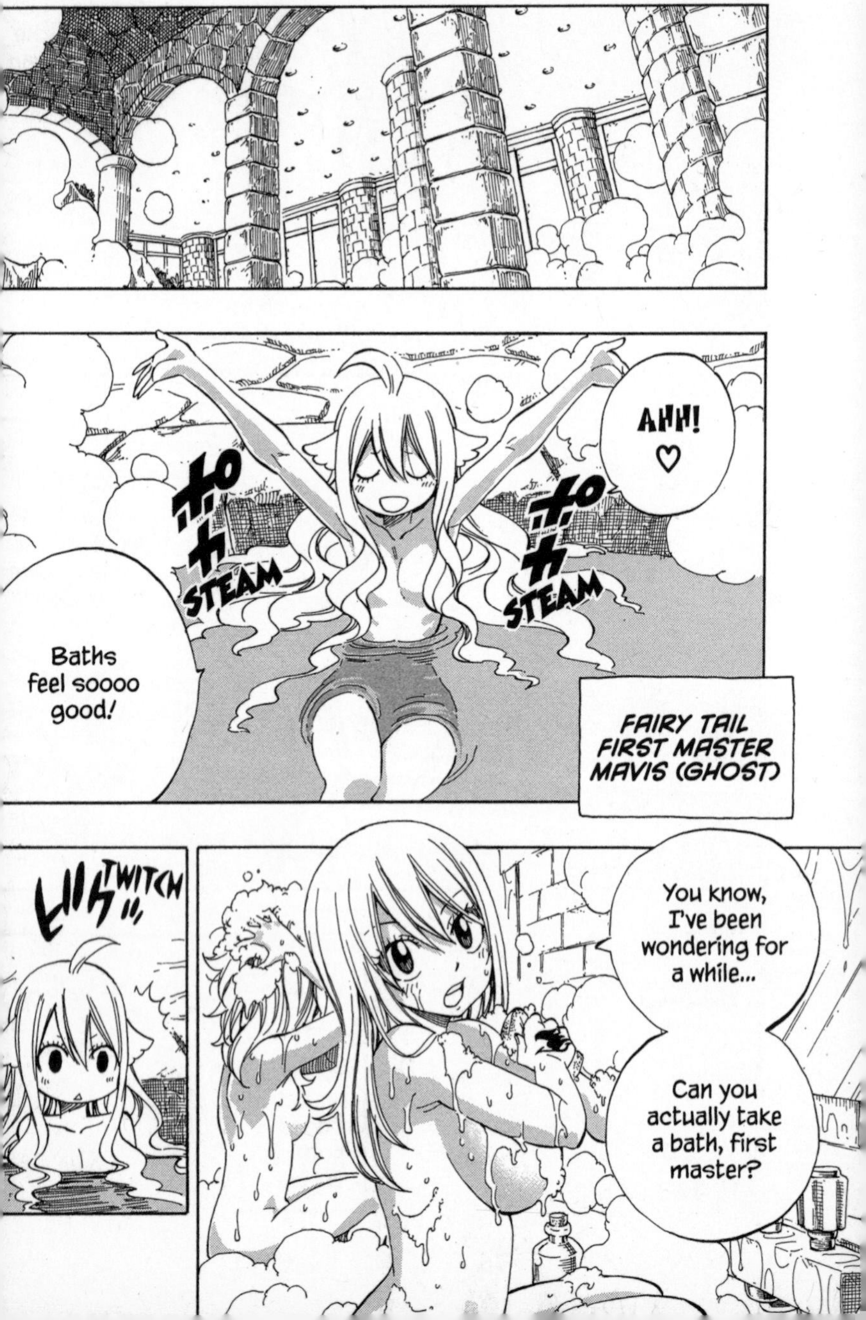
AHH! ♡
STEAM
FAIRY TAIL FIRST MASTER MAVIS (GHOST)
STEAM
Baths feel soooo good!
You know, I've been wondering for a while...
Can you actually take a bath, first master?
TWITCH

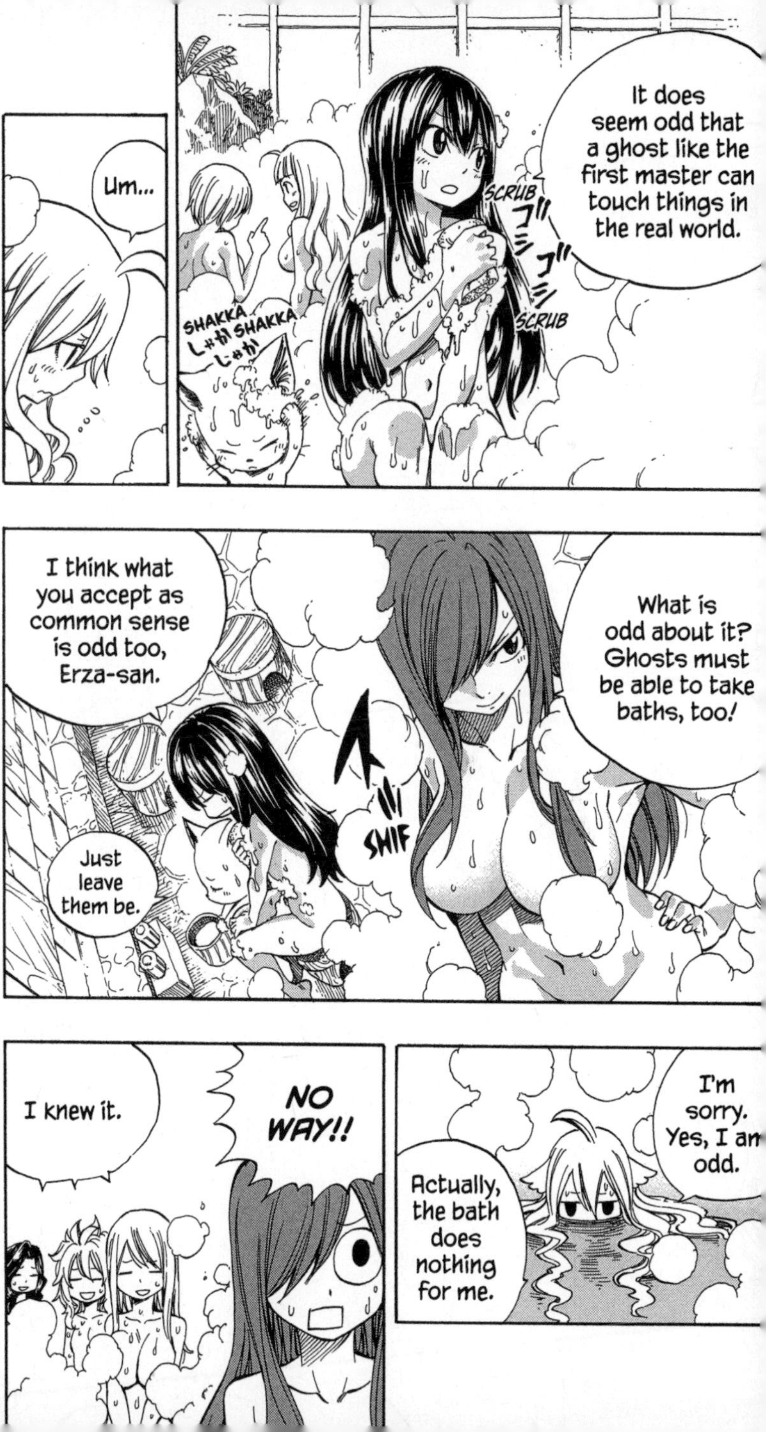
It does seem odd that a ghost like the first master can touch things in the real world.
SCRUB ゴシ
ゴシ SCRUB
SHAKKA しゃか SHAKKA しゃか
Um...
What is odd about it? Ghosts must be able to take baths, too!
SHIF
I think what you accept as common sense is odd too, Erza-san.
Just leave them be.
I'm sorry. Yes, I am odd.
Actually, the bath does nothing for me.
NO WAY!!
I knew it.

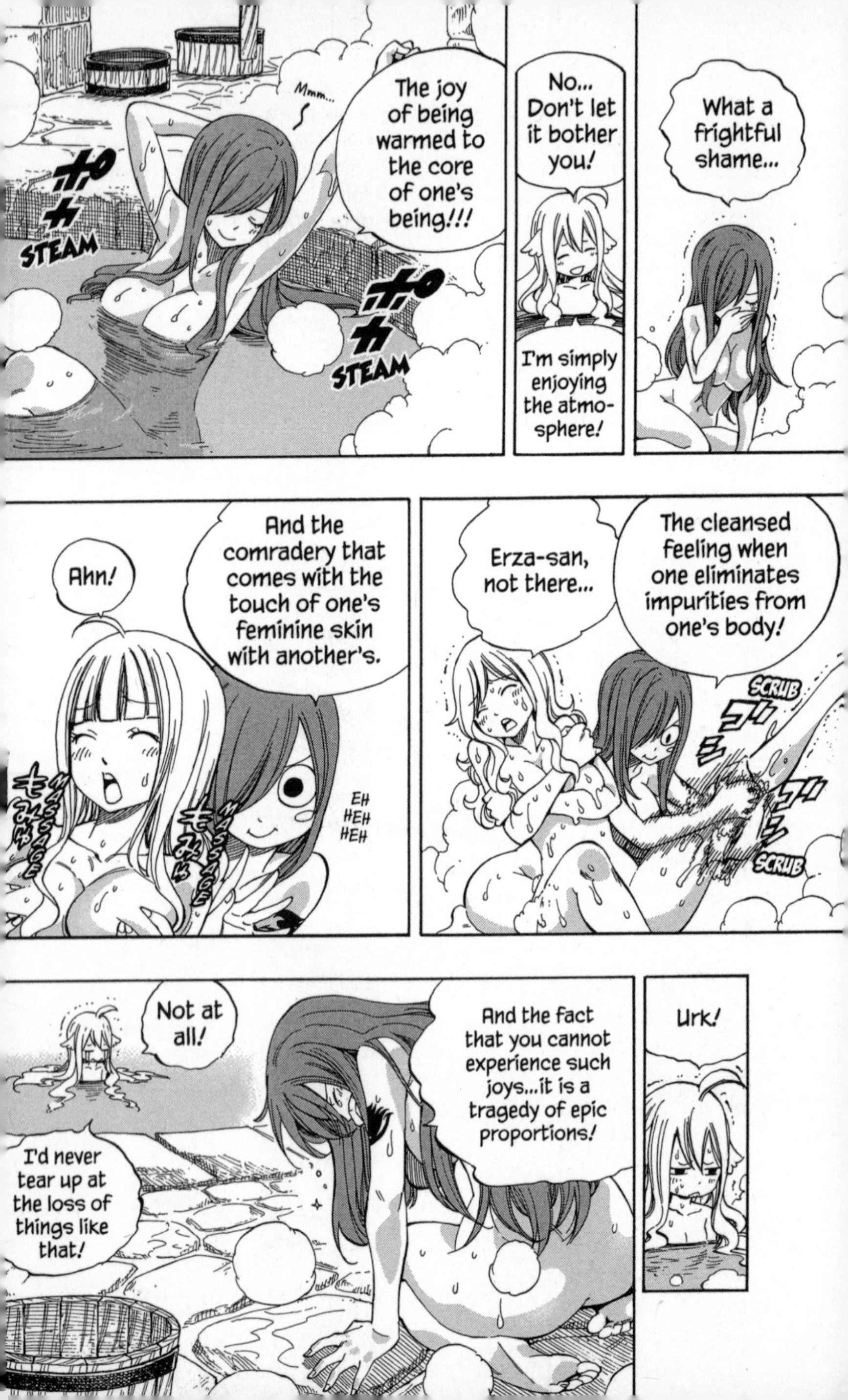
What a frightful shame...
No... Don't let it bother you!
I'm simply enjoying the atmosphere!
Mmm...
The joy of being warmed to the core of one's being!!!
ポカ
STEAM
ポカ
STEAM
The cleansed feeling when one eliminates impurities from one's body!
Erza-san, not there...
ゴシ
SCRUB
ゴシ
SCRUB
And the comradery that comes with the touch of one's feminine skin with another's.
Ahn!
EH HEH HEH
もみ
MASSAGE
もみ
MASSAGE
Urk!
And the fact that you cannot experience such joys...it is a tragedy of epic proportions!
Not at all!
I'd never tear up at the loss of things like that!

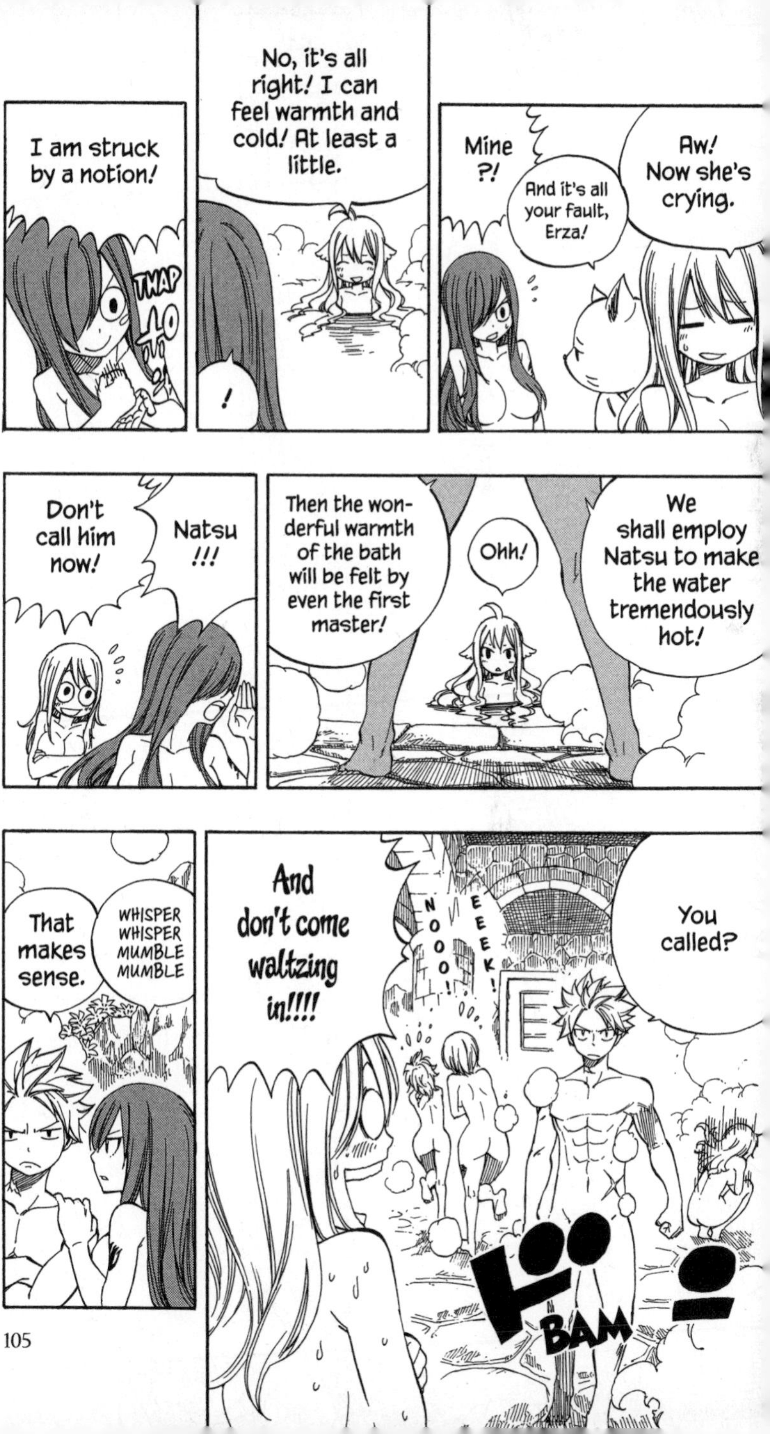
Aw! Now she's crying.
And it's all your fault, Erza!
Mine ?!
No, it's all right! I can feel warmth and cold! At least a little.
!
I am struck by a notion!
THAP
We shall employ Natsu to make the water tremendously hot!
Ohh!
Then the wonderful warmth of the bath will be felt by even the first master!
Natsu !!!
Don't call him now!
You called?
EEEEK!
NOOOO!
And don't come waltzing in!!!!
BAM
WHISPER WHISPER MUMBLE MUMBLE
That makes sense.

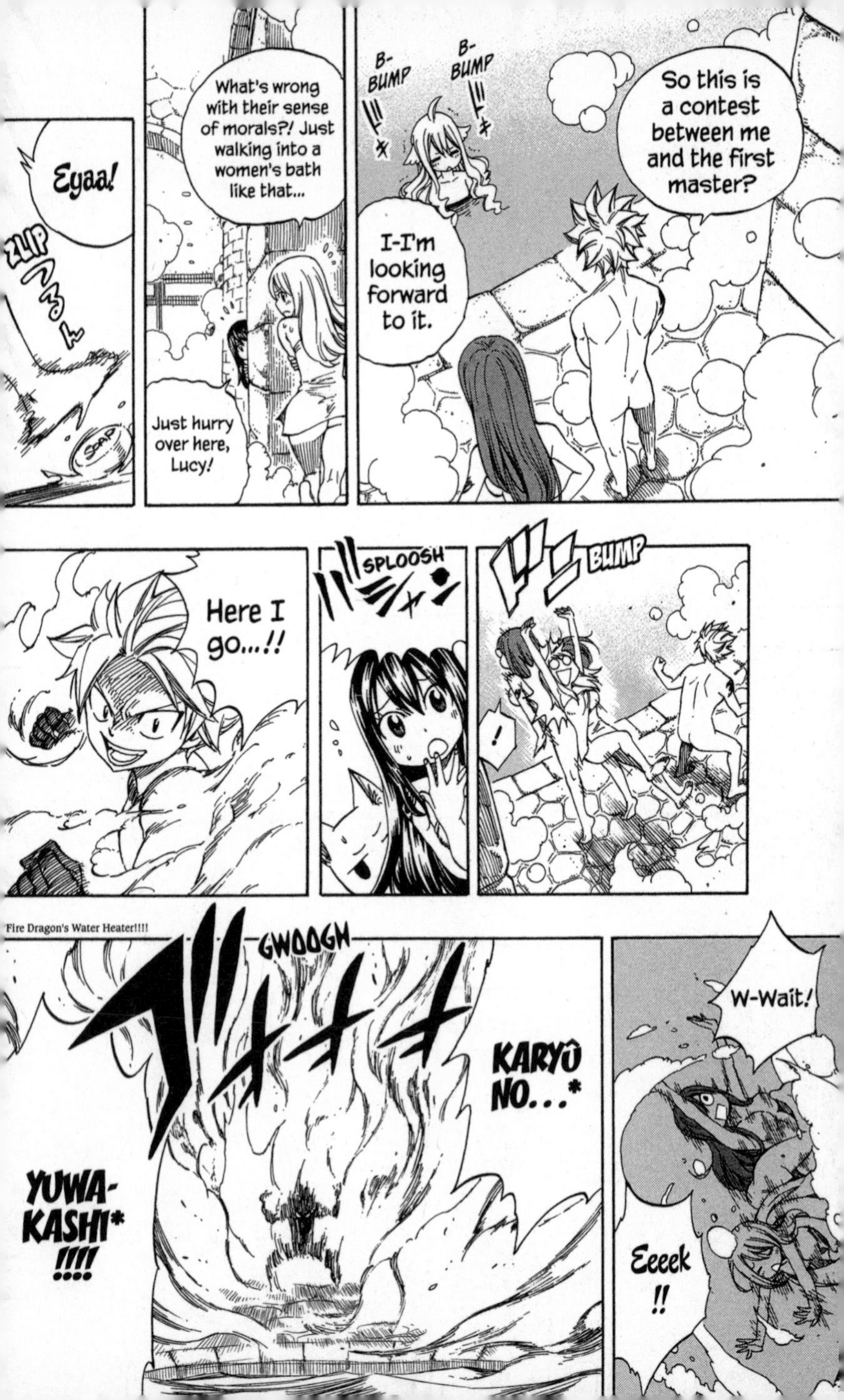
So this is a contest between me and the first master?
B-BUMP
B-BUMP
I-I'm looking forward to it.
What's wrong with their sense of morals?! Just walking into a women's bath like that...
Just hurry over here, Lucy!
Eyaa!
ZLIP
SOAP
BUMP
!
SPLOOSH
Here I go...!!
W-Wait!
Eeeek !!
GWOOGH
KARYÔ NO...*
YUWA-KASHI* !!!!

Fire Dragon's Water Heater!!!!

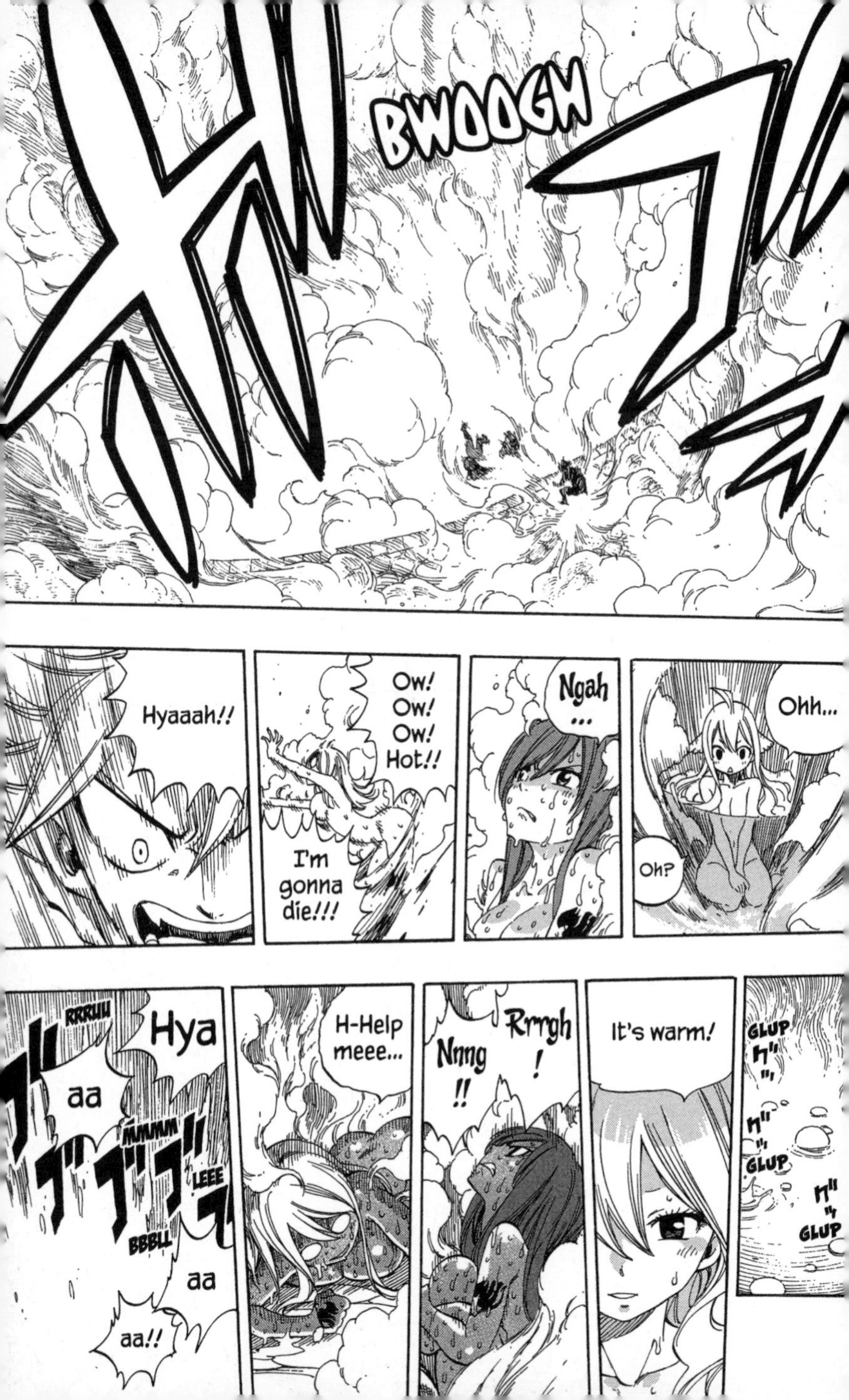
BWOOGH
Ohh...
Oh?
Ngah ...
Ow! Ow! Ow! Hot!!
I'm gonna die!!!
Hyaaah!!
GLUP
GLUP
GLUP
It's warm!
Rrrgh!
Nnng!!
H-Help meee...
RRRUU
Hya
aa
MMMM
LEEE
BBBLL
aa
aa!!

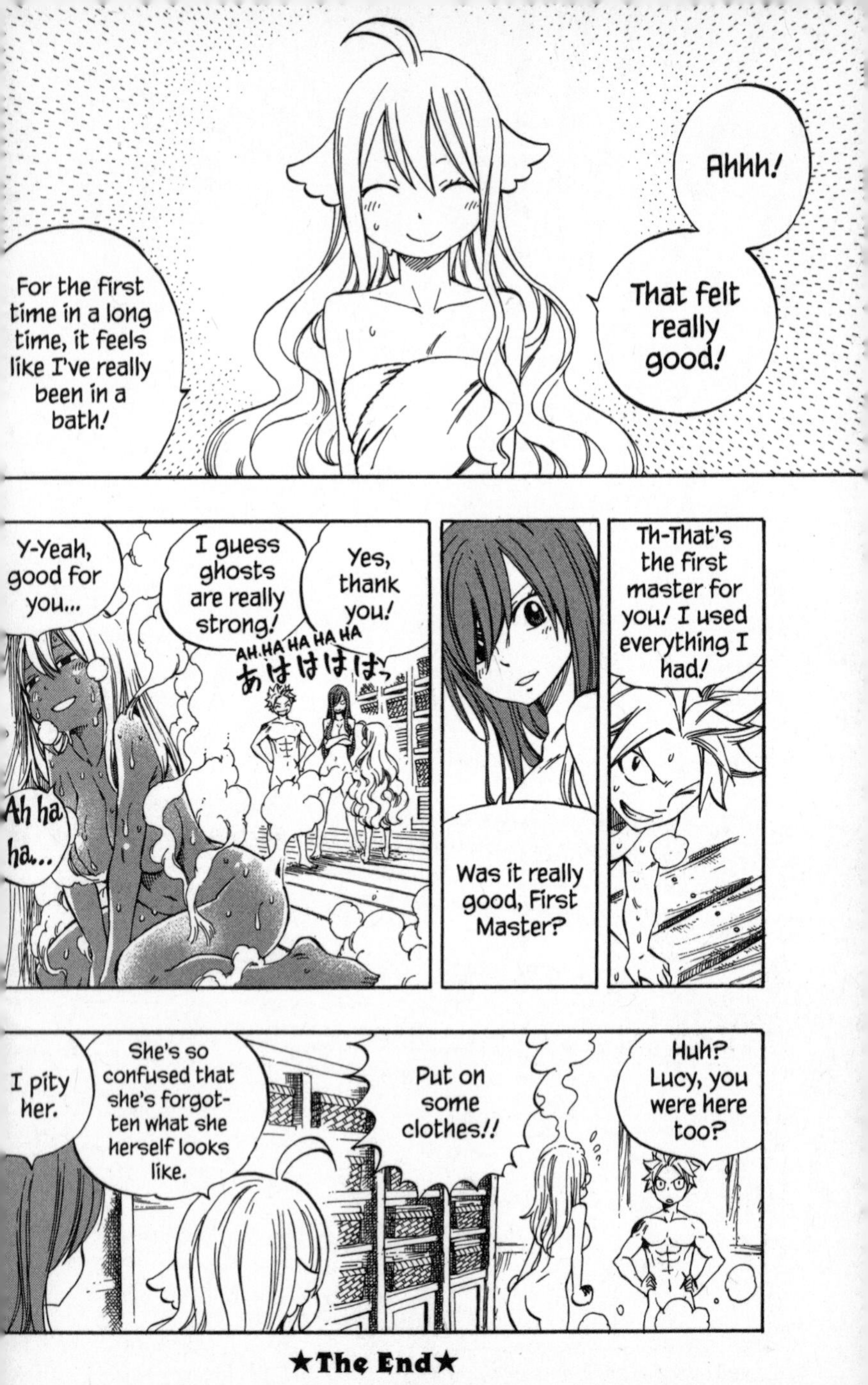
Ahhh!
That felt really good!
For the first time in a long time, it feels like I've really been in a bath!
Th-That's the first master for you! I used everything I had!
Was it really good, First Master?
Yes, thank you!
AH HA HA HA HA
あはははは っ
I guess ghosts are really strong!
Y-Yeah, good for you...
Ah ha ha...
Huh? Lucy, you were here too?
Put on some clothes!!
She's so confused that she's forgot-ten what she herself looks like.
I pity her.

★The End★

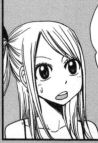

FOUR-PANEL COMICS!

SUBJECT: SWEAT

SALAMANDER'S SWEAT

DRIPPLE
だくん
DRIPPLE
だくん
Sure it's hot, but I've hardly ever seen you in such a sweat!
I wonder who has taken ...
...my strawberry cake?!
I already ate some...
CRAKL CRAKL

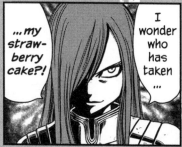

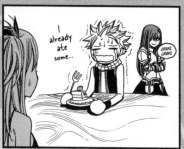

FROM *MAGAZINE SPECIAL*, 2009, ISSUE 7.

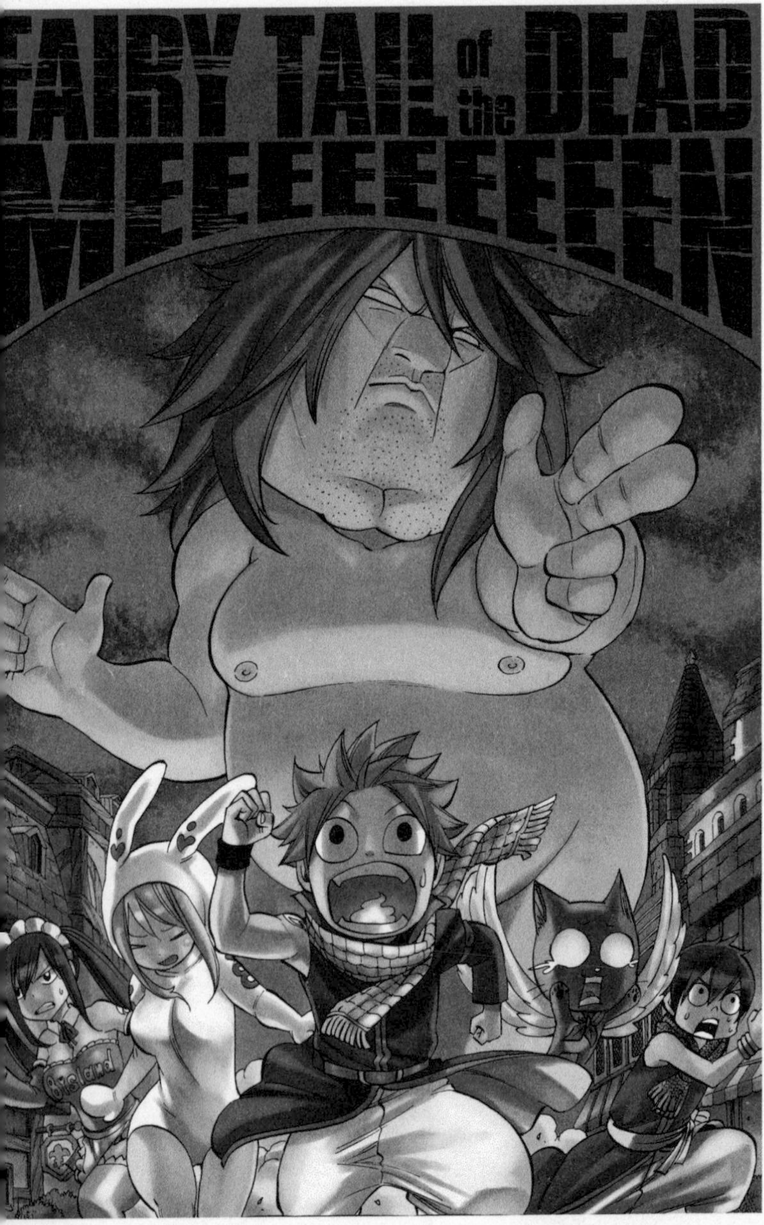
FAIRY TAIL of the DEAD MEEEEEEEEN

AIRY TAIL OF THE DEAD MEEEEEEEEEN

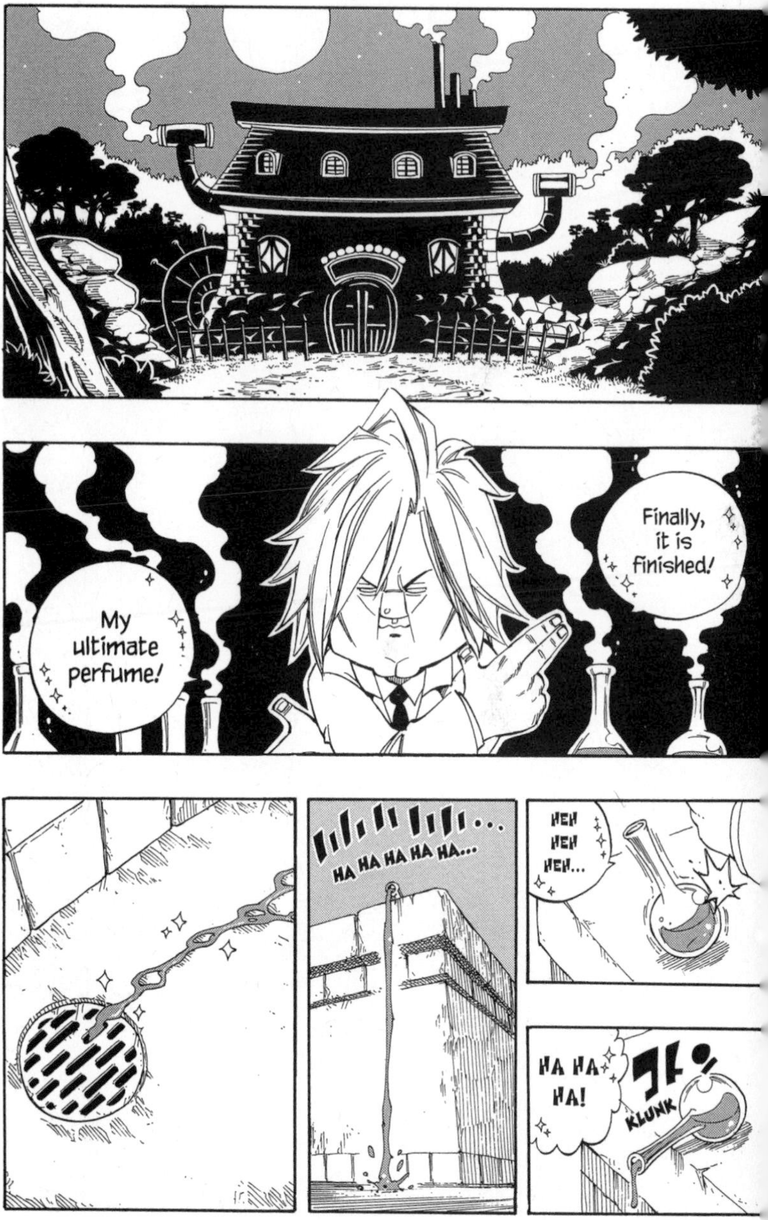
Finally, it is finished!
My ultimate perfume!
HEH HEH HEH...
HA HA HA!
KLUNK
HA HA HA HA HA...

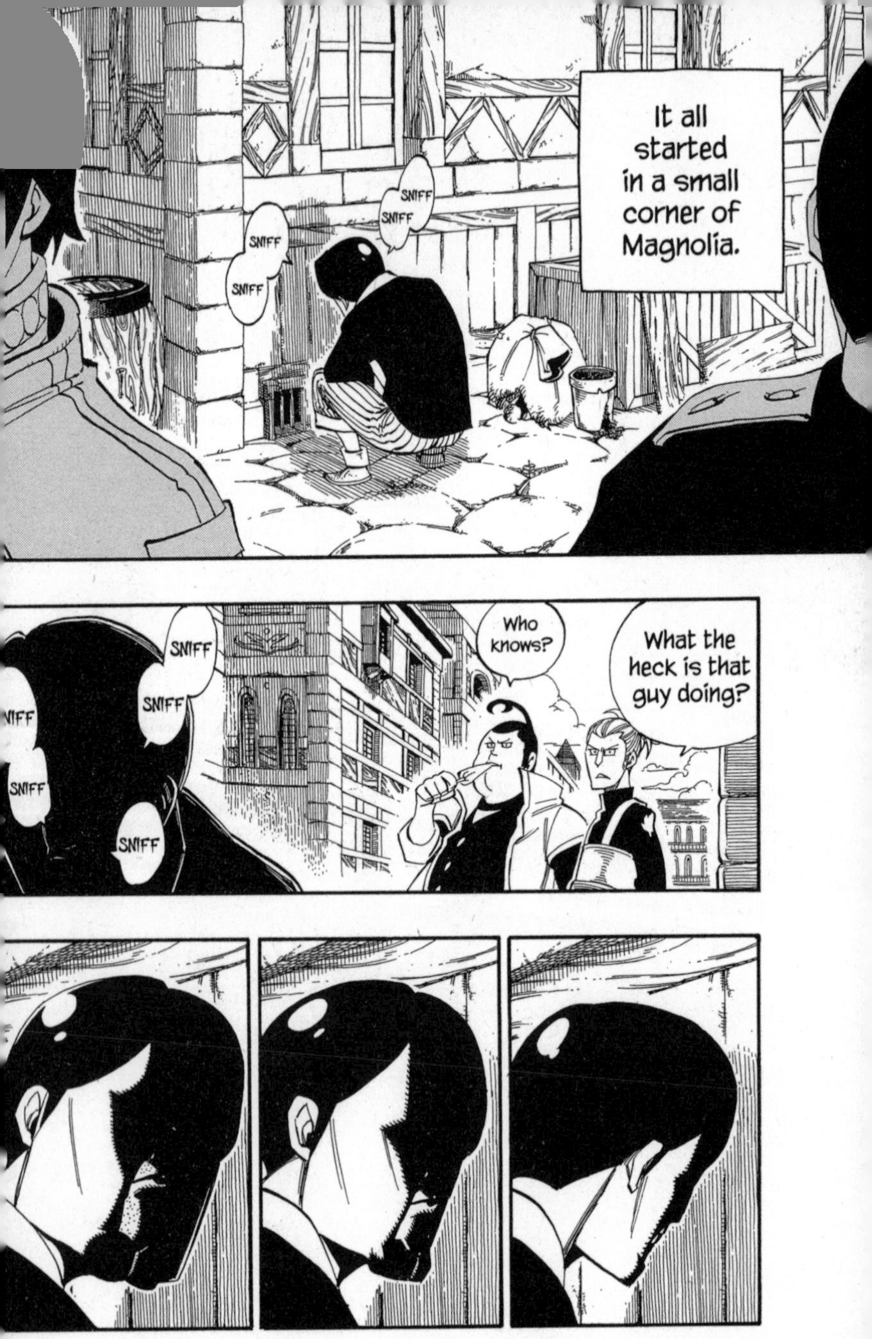
It all started in a small corner of Magnolia.
SNIFF
SNIFF
SNIFF
SNIFF
What the heck is that guy doing?
Who knows?
SNIFF
SNIFF
SNIFF
SNIFF

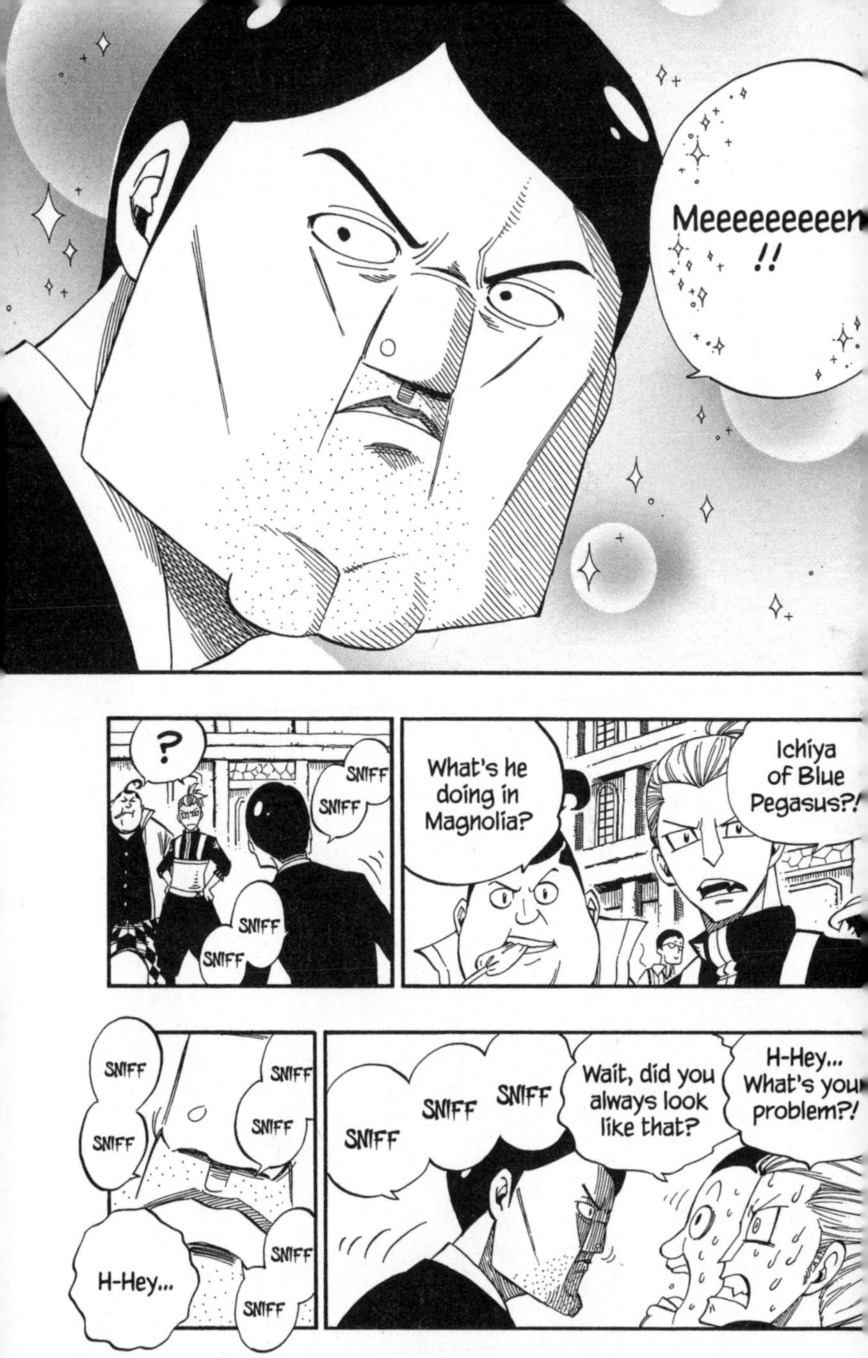
Meeeeeeeeen!!
Ichiya of Blue Pegasus?!
What's he doing in Magnolia?
?
SNIFF
SNIFF
SNIFF
SNIFF
H-Hey... What's your problem?!
Wait, did you always look like that?
SNIFF
SNIFF
SNIFF
SNIFF
SNIFF
SNIFF
SNIFF
SNIFF
SNIFF
H-Hey...

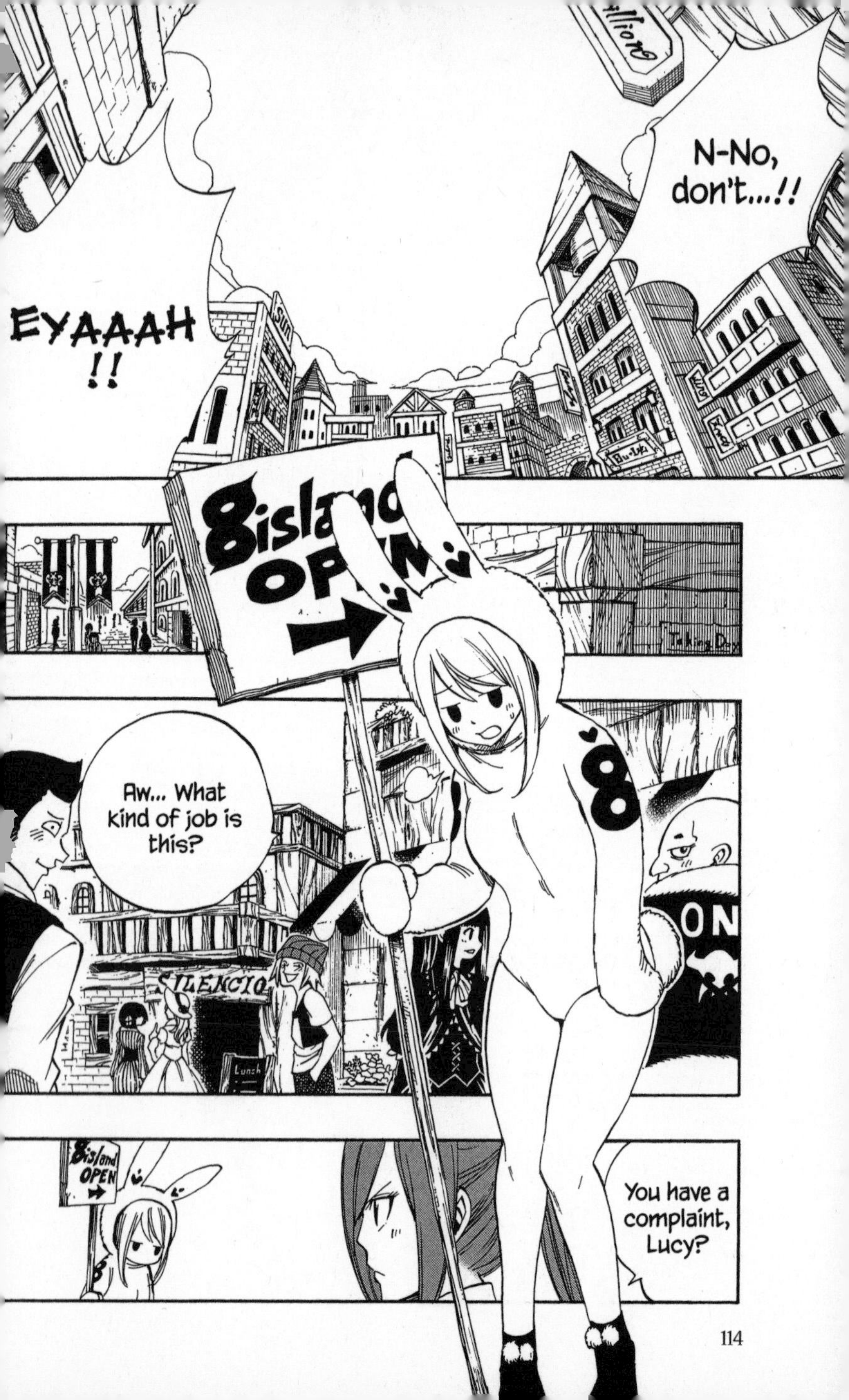
N-No, don't...!!
EYAAAH!!
Aw... What kind of job is this?
You have a complaint, Lucy?
8island OPEN

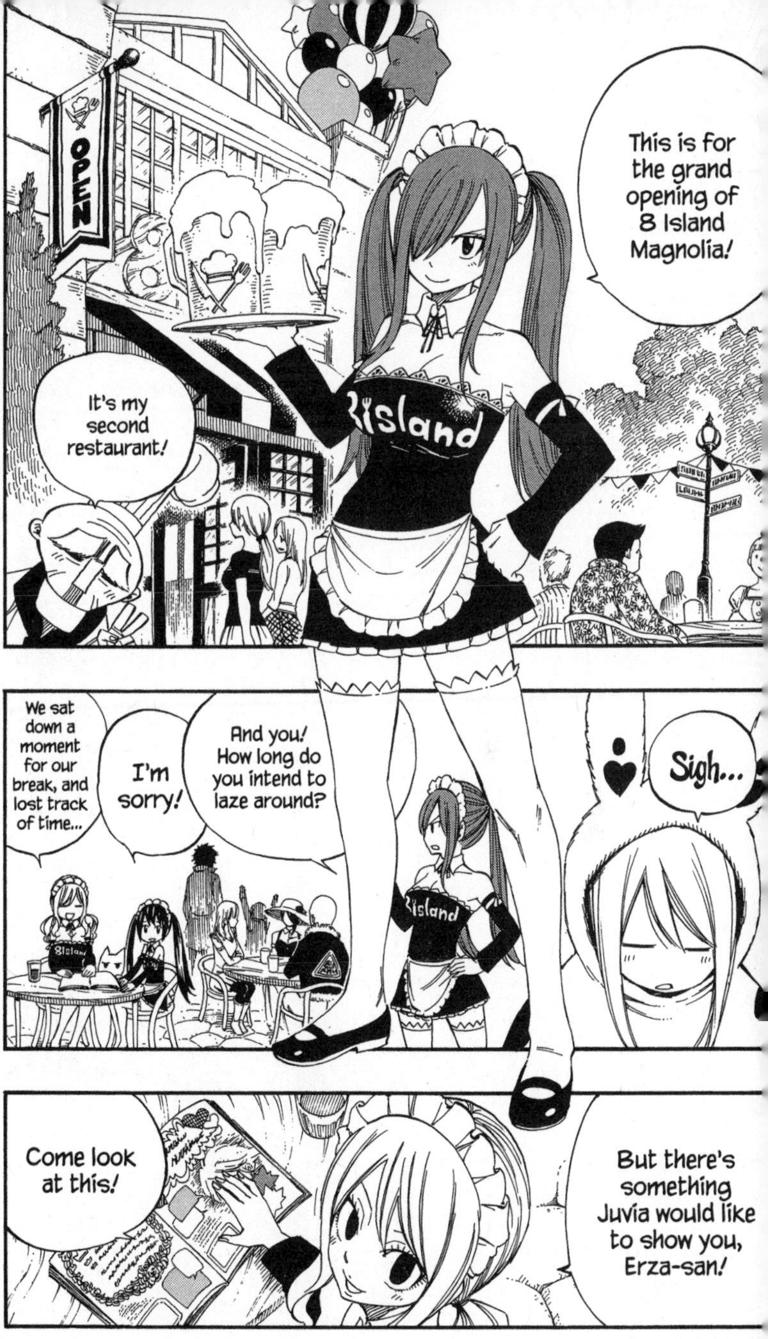
This is for the grand opening of 8 Island Magnolia!
OPEN
It's my second restaurant!
Sigh...
And you! How long do you intend to laze around?
I'm sorry!
We sat down a moment for our break, and lost track of time...
But there's something Juvia would like to show you, Erza-san!
Come look at this!

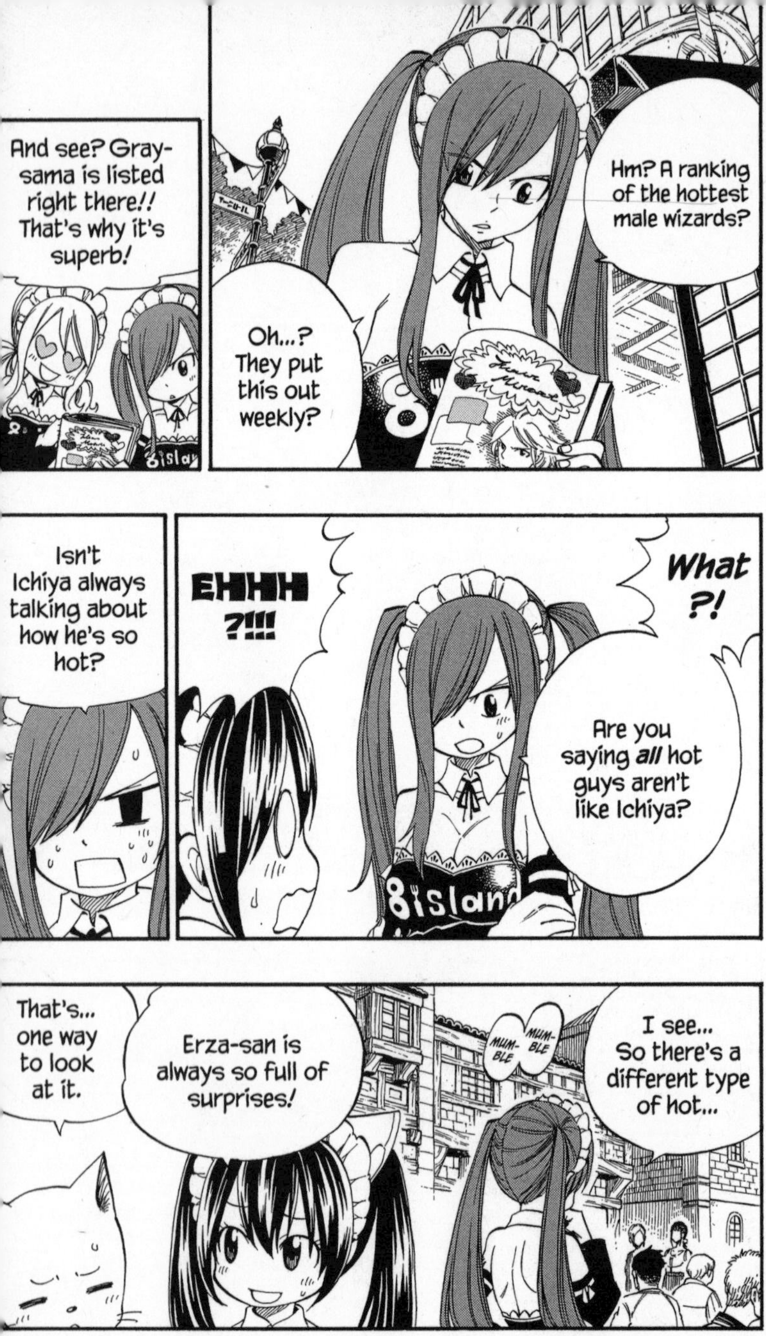
Hm? A ranking of the hottest male wizards?
Oh...? They put this out weekly?
And see? Gray-sama is listed right there!! That's why it's superb!
What?!
EHHH?!!!
Are you saying *all* hot guys aren't like Ichiya?
Isn't Ichiya always talking about how he's so hot?
I see... So there's a different type of hot...
MUMBLE MUMBLE
MUMBLE MUMBLE
Erza-san is always so full of surprises!
That's... one way to look at it.

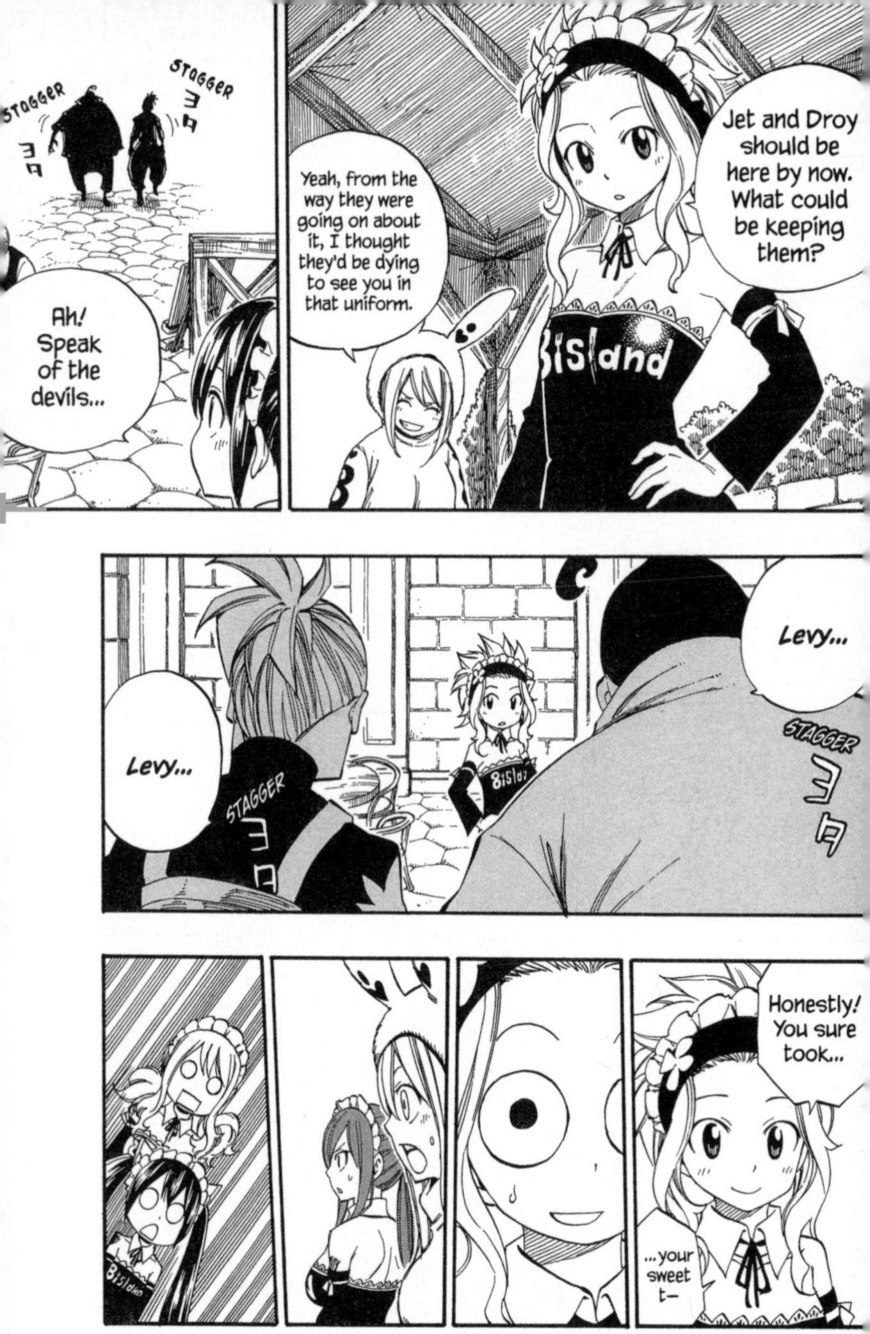
Jet and Droy should be here by now. What could be keeping them?
Yeah, from the way they were going on about it, I thought they'd be dying to see you in that uniform.
Bisland
STAGGER ヨタ
STAGGER ヨタ
Ah! Speak of the devils...
Levy...
STAGGER ヨタ
Levy...
STAGGER ヨタ
Honestly! You sure took...
...your sweet t—

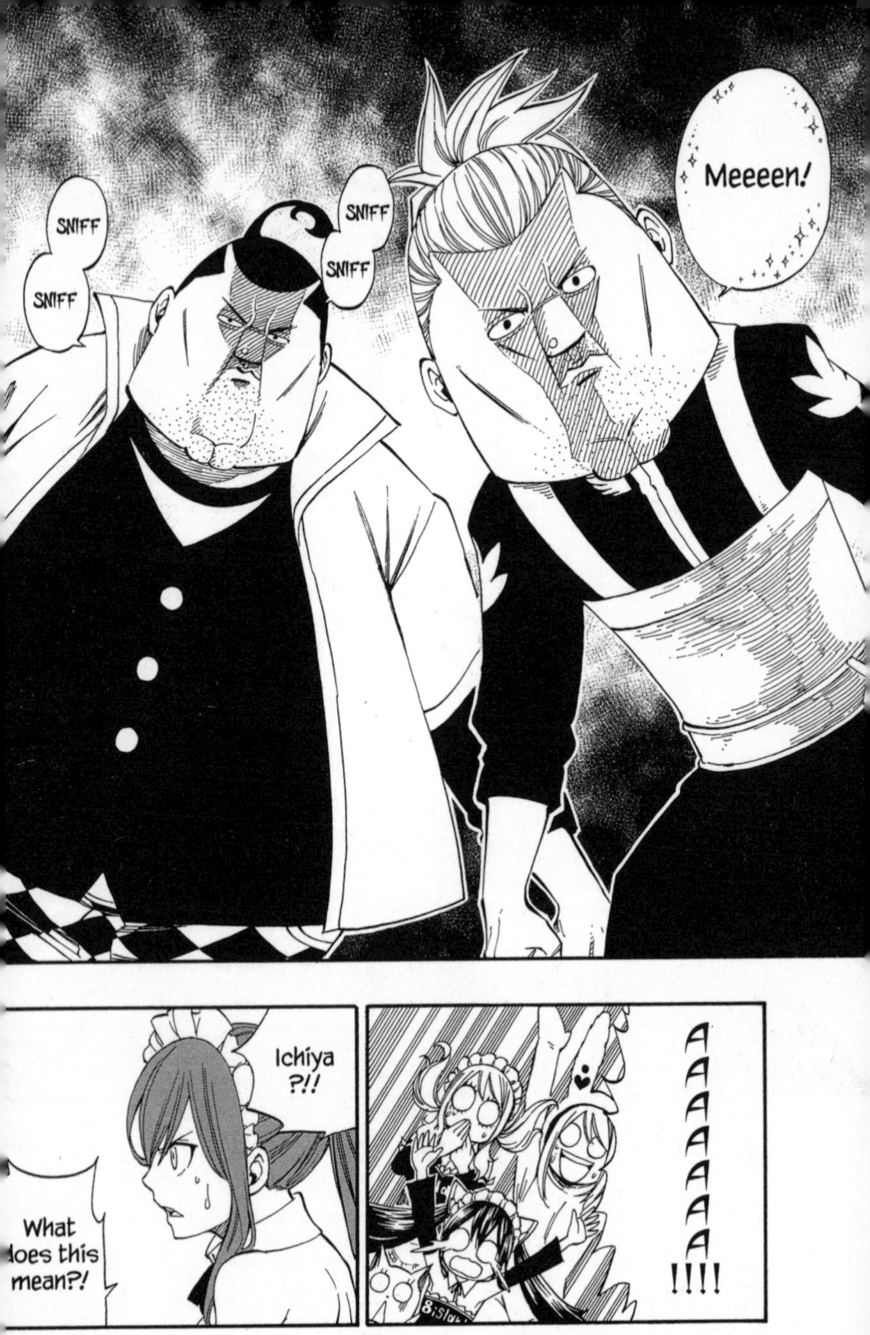
Meeeen!
SNIFF
SNIFF
SNIFF
SNIFF
AAAAAAAA!!!!
Ichiya?!!
What does this mean?!

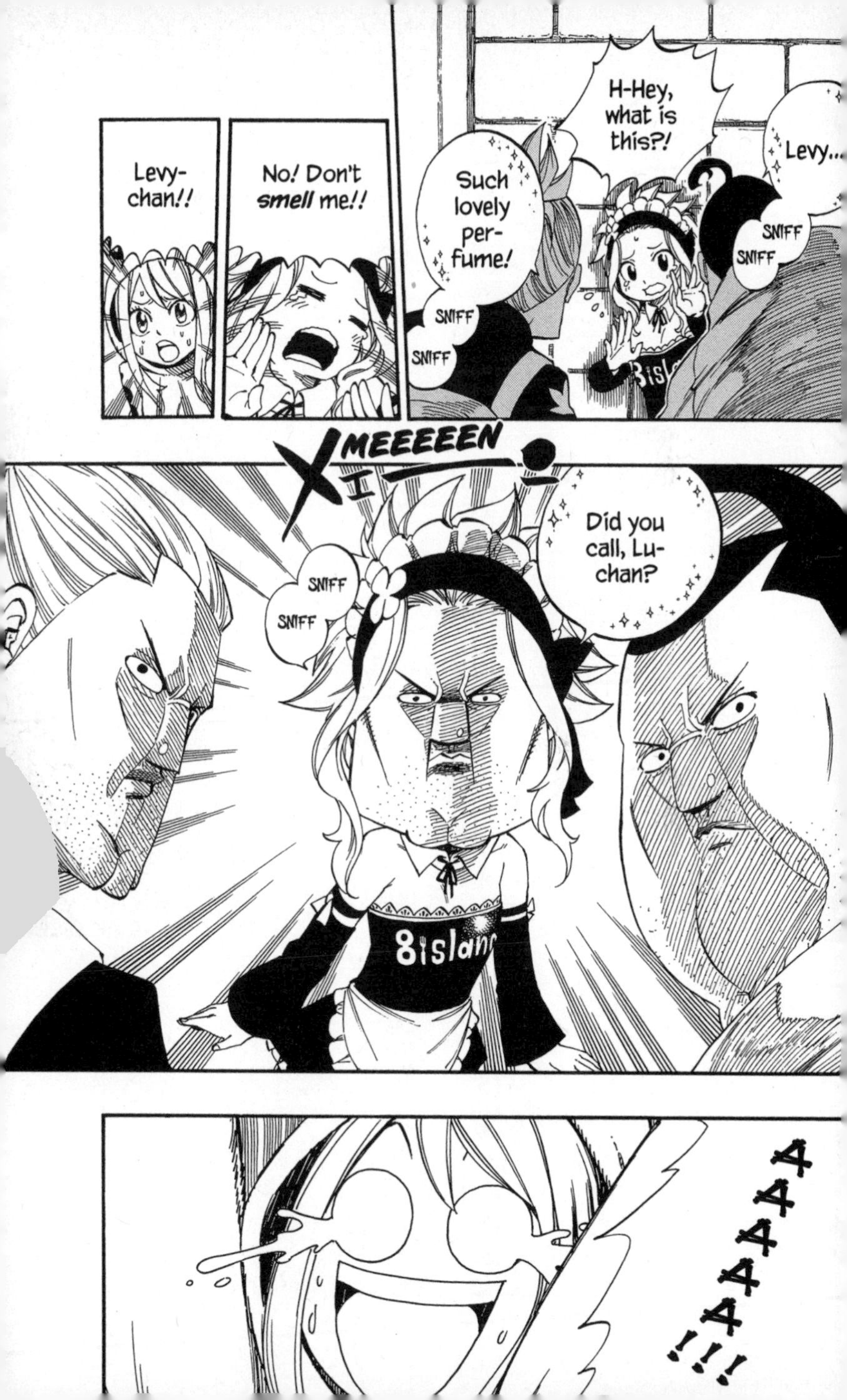
Levy...
H-Hey, what is this?!
SNIFF SNIFF
Such lovely per-fume!
SNIFF SNIFF
No! Don't *smell* me!!
Levy-chan!!
MEEEEEN
Did you call, Lu-chan?
SNIFF SNIFF
AAAAAA!!!

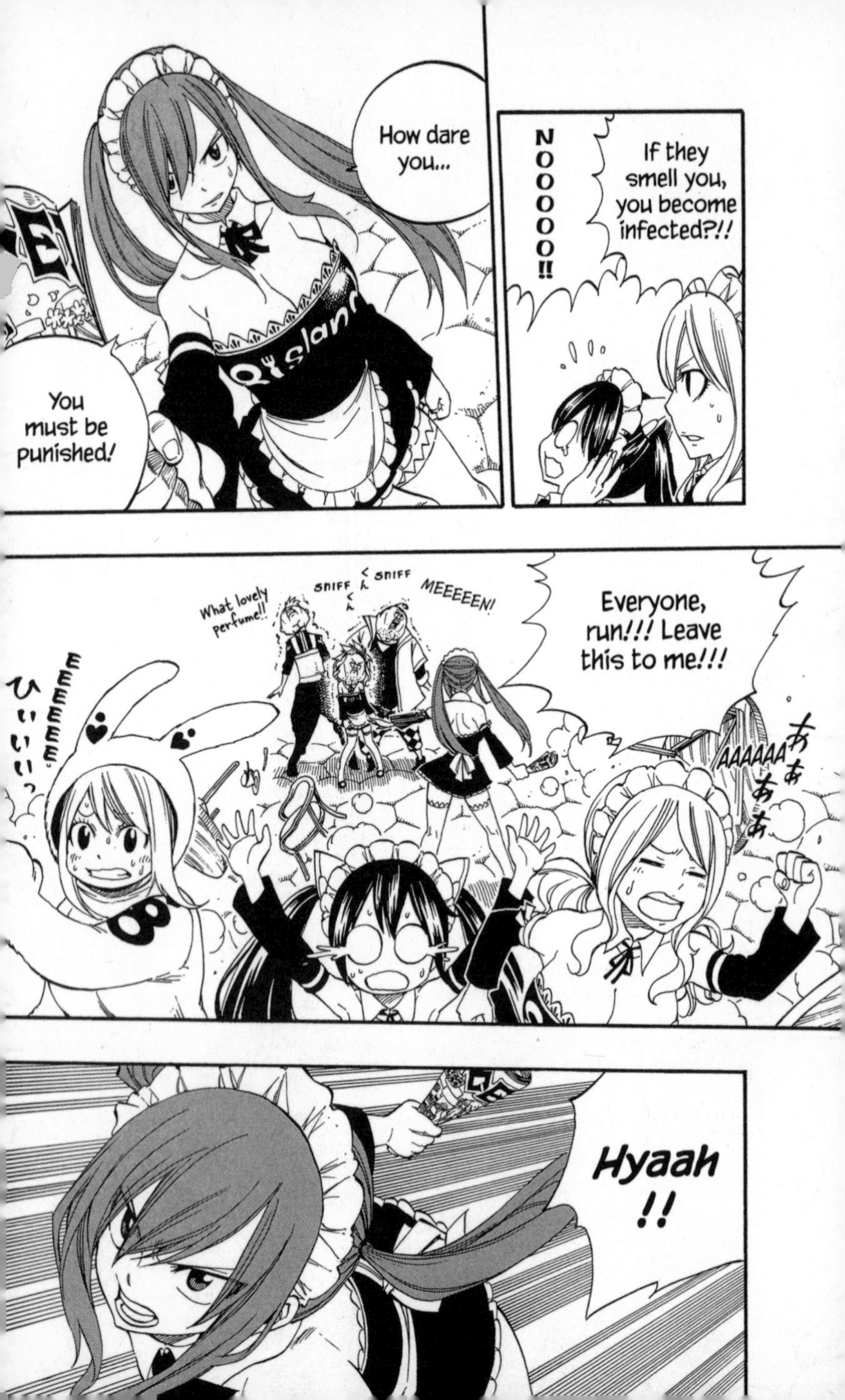
NOOOOOO!!
If they smell you, you become infected?!!
How dare you...
You must be punished!
Everyone, run!!! Leave this to me!!!
AAAAAA
MEEEEEEN!
SNIFF
SNIFF
What lovely perfume!!
EEEEEE
ひぃぃぃっ
Hyaah!!

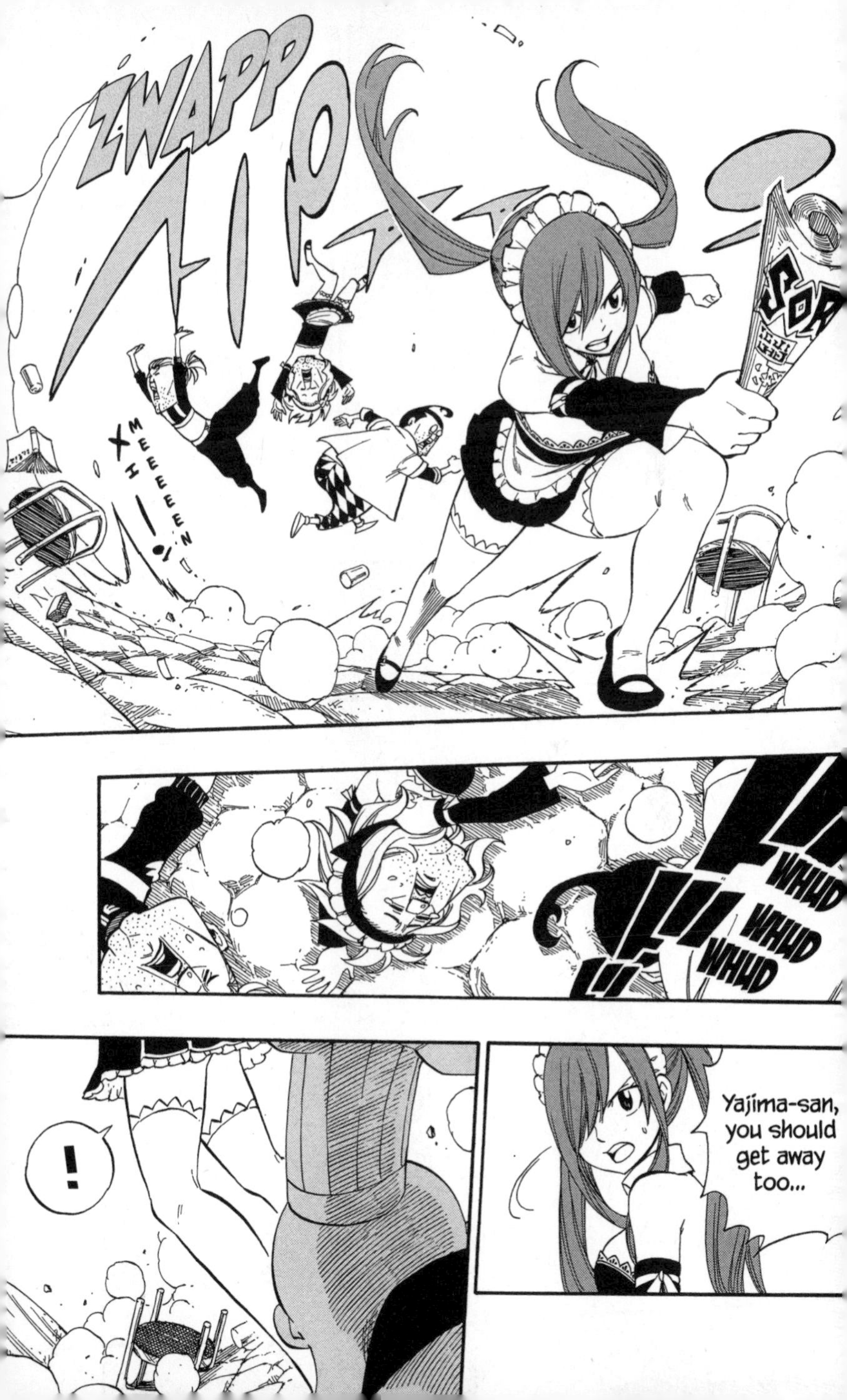
ZWAPP
MEEEEEEN
XI—!
WHUD
WHUD
WHUD
Yajima-san, you should get away too...
!

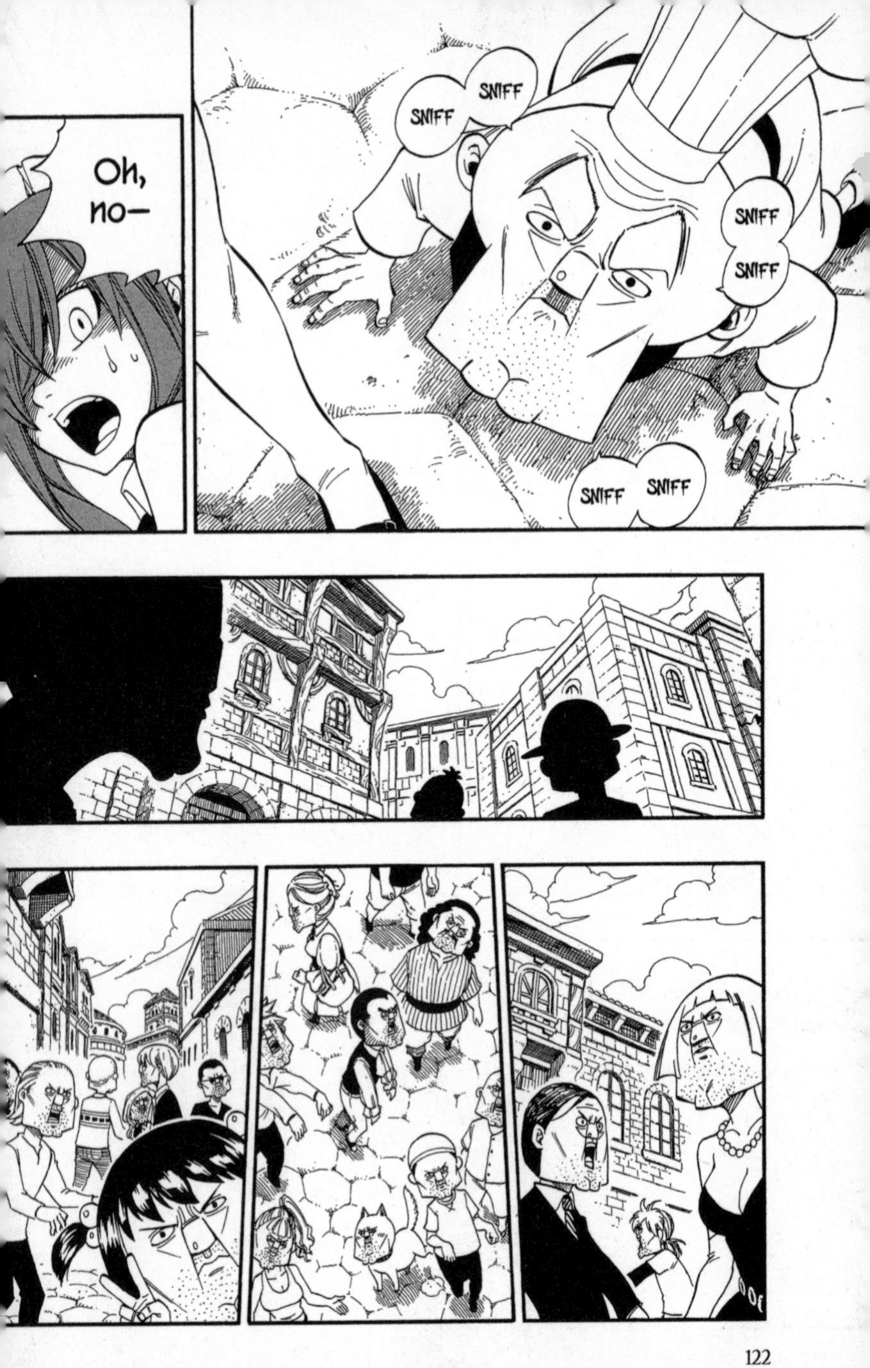
SNIFF
SNIFF
SNIFF
SNIFF
SNIFF
SNIFF
Oh, no—

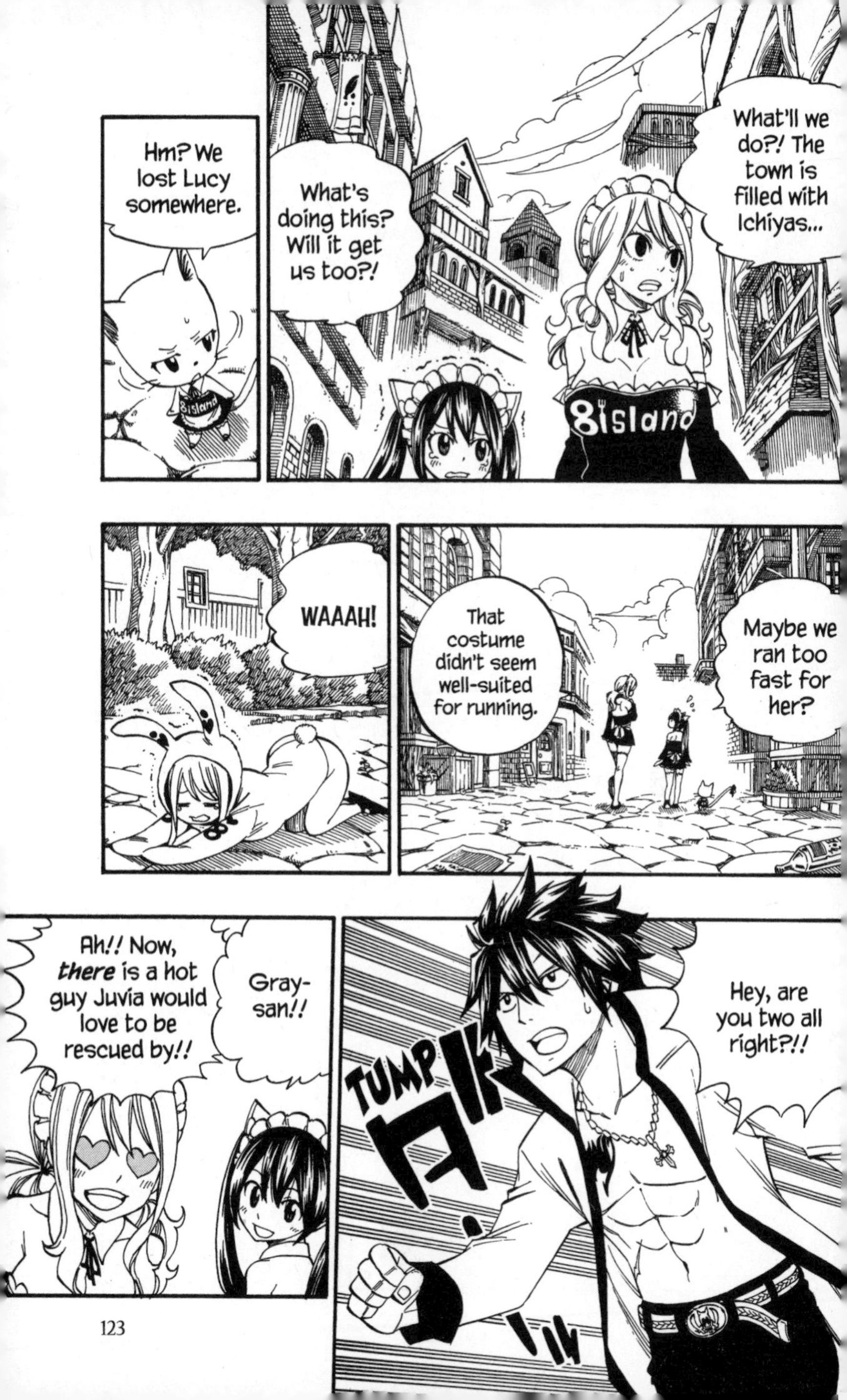
What'll we do?! The town is filled with Ichiyas...
What's doing this? Will it get us too?!
Hm? We lost Lucy somewhere.
8island
8island
Maybe we ran too fast for her?
That costume didn't seem well-suited for running.
WAAAH!
Hey, are you two all right?!!
TUMP
Gray-san!!
Ah!! Now, *there* is a hot guy Juvia would love to be rescued by!!

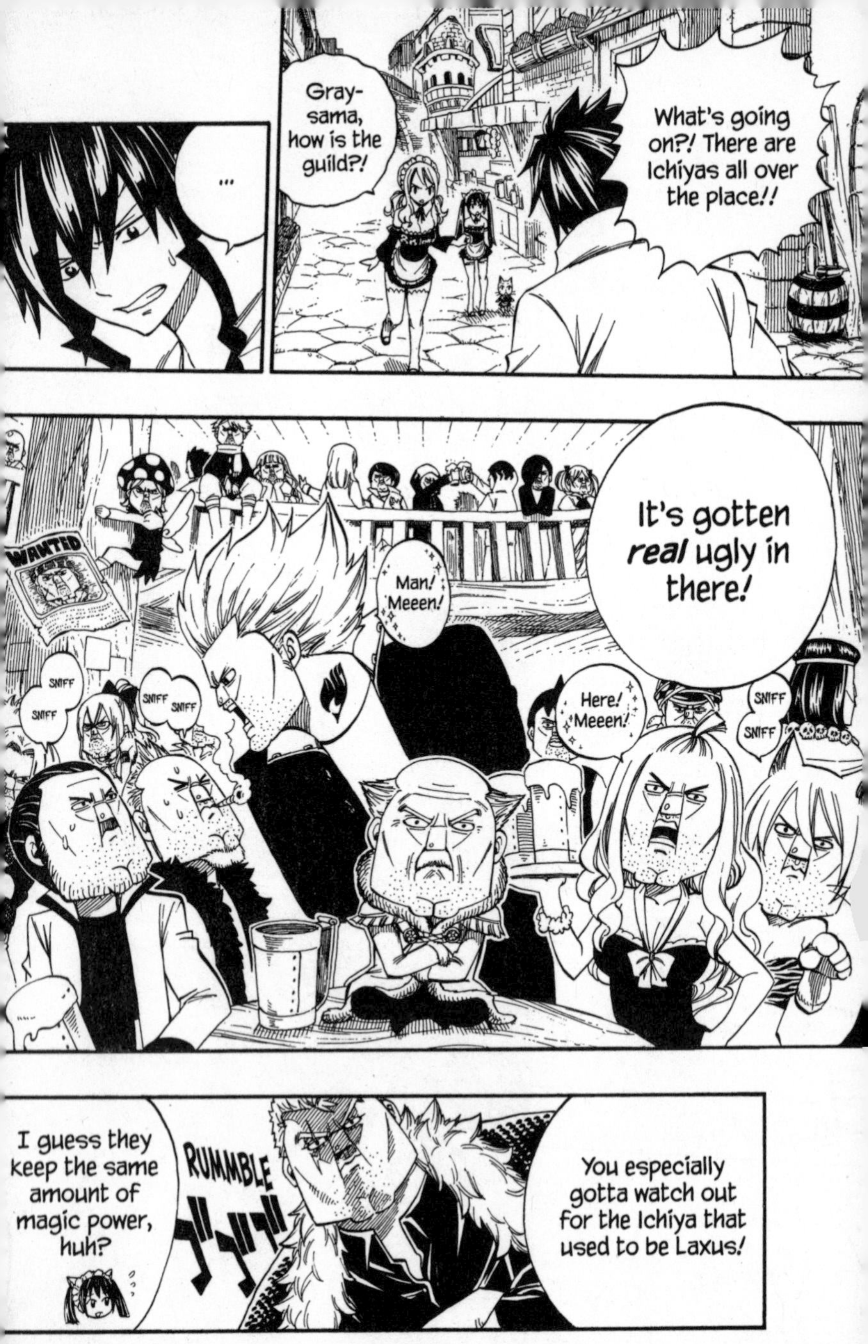
What's going on?! There are Ichiyas all over the place!!
Gray-sama, how is the guild?!
...
It's gotten *real* ugly in there!
SNIFF SNIFF
Here! Meeen!
Man! Meeen!
SNIFF SNIFF
SNIFF SNIFF
You especially gotta watch out for the Ichiya that used to be Laxus!
RUMMBLE
I guess they keep the same amount of magic power, huh?

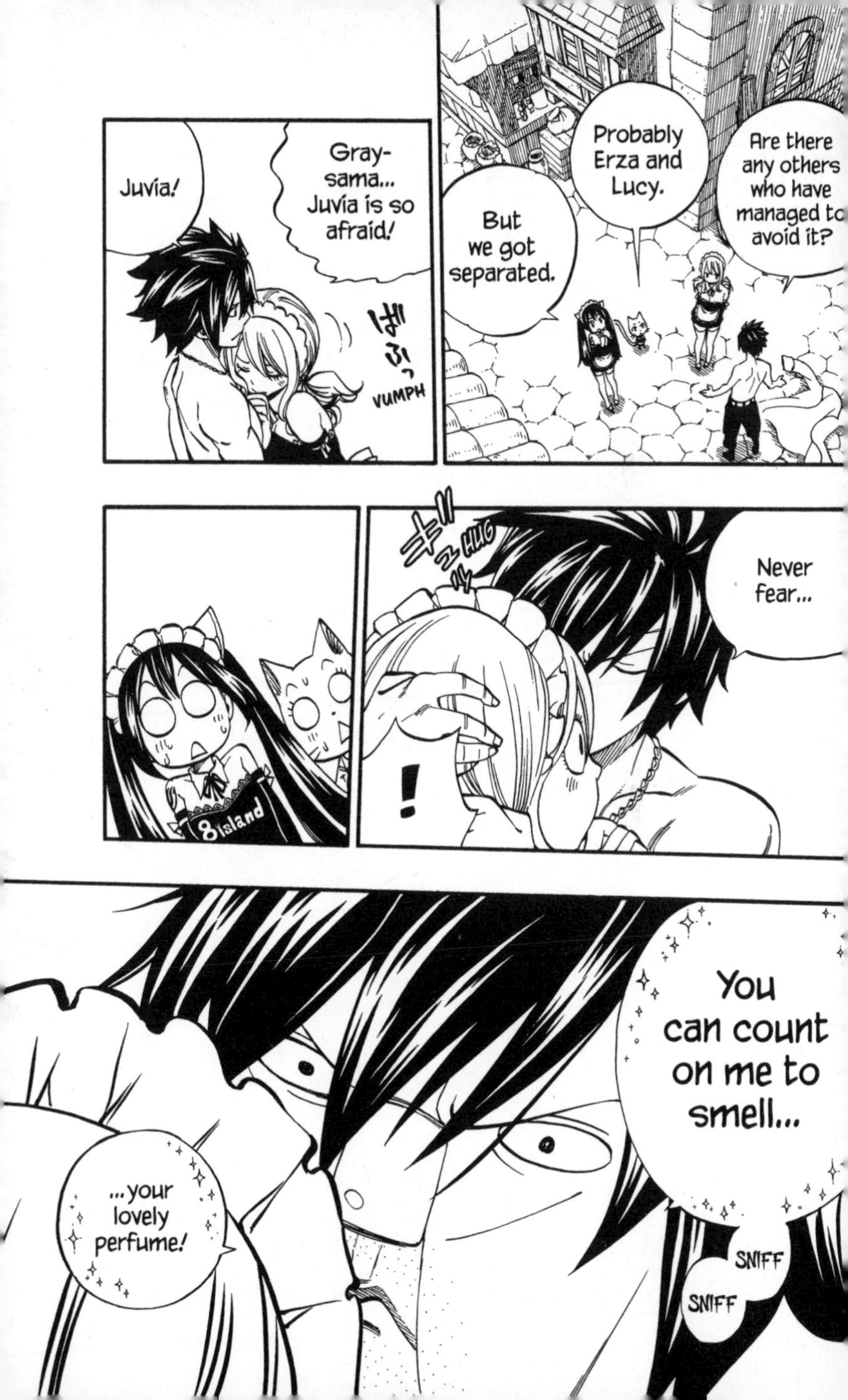
Are there any others who have managed to avoid it?
Probably Erza and Lucy.
But we got separated.
Gray-sama... Juvia is so afraid!
Juvia!
ぼふっ
VUMPH
HUG
Never fear...
!
You can count on me to smell...
...your lovely perfume!
SNIFF
SNIFF

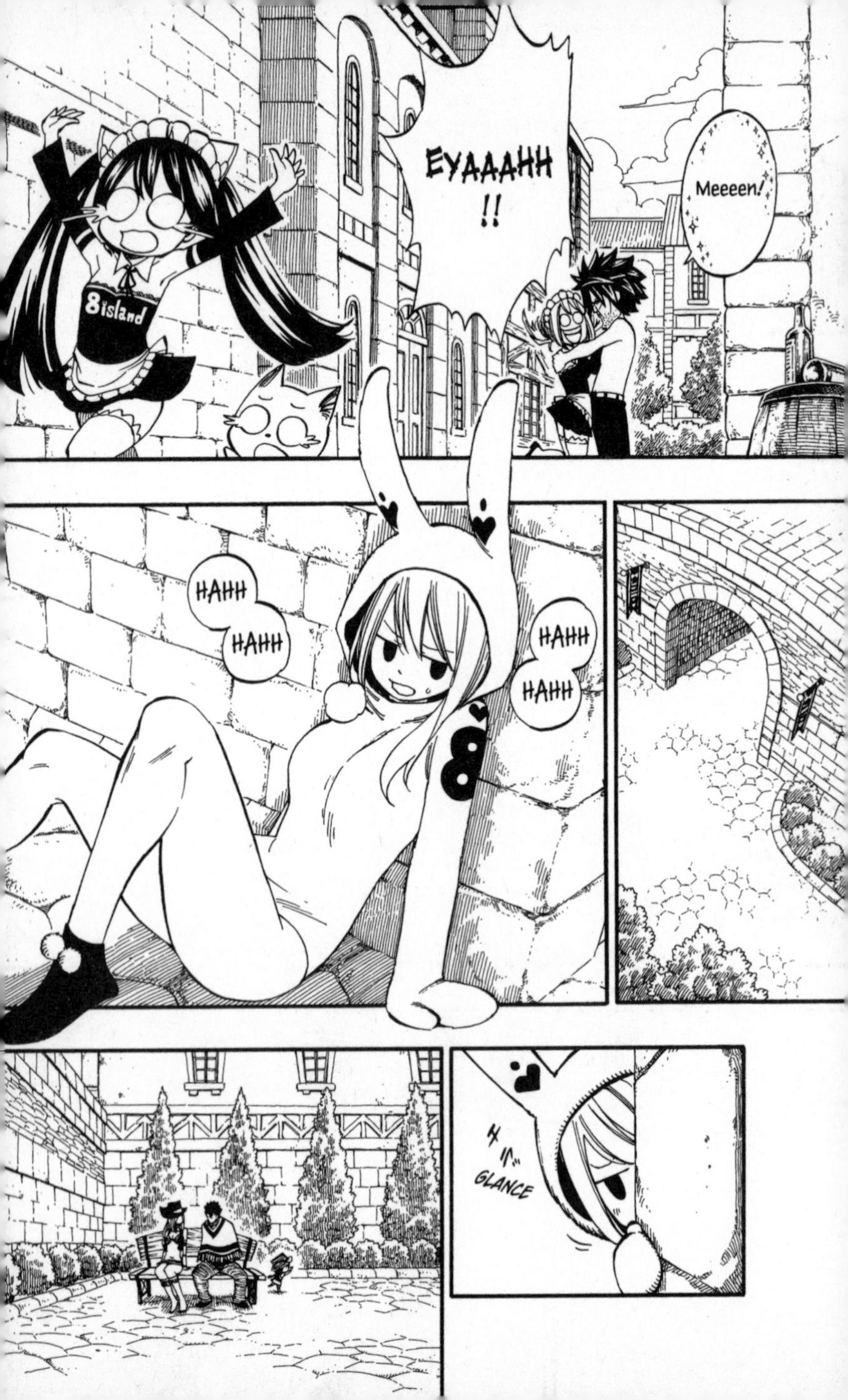
Meeeen!
EYAAAHH !!
HAHH HAHH
HAHH HAHH
GLANCE

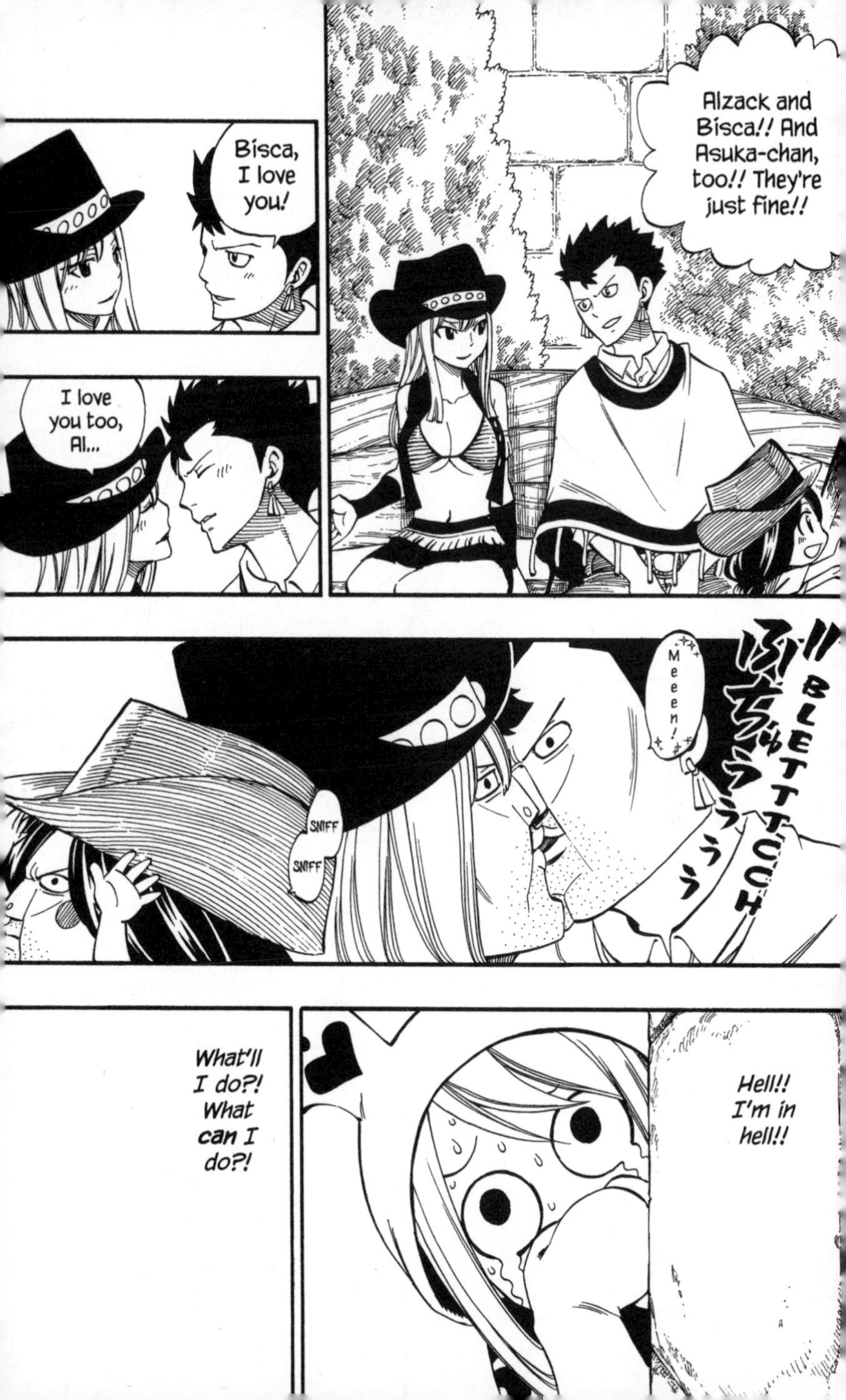

Alzack and Bisca!! And Asuka-chan, too!! They're just fine!!
Bisca, I love you!
I love you too, Al...
BLETTTCCH
Meeen!
SNIFF
SNIFF
Hell!! I'm in hell!!
What'll I do?! What can I do?!

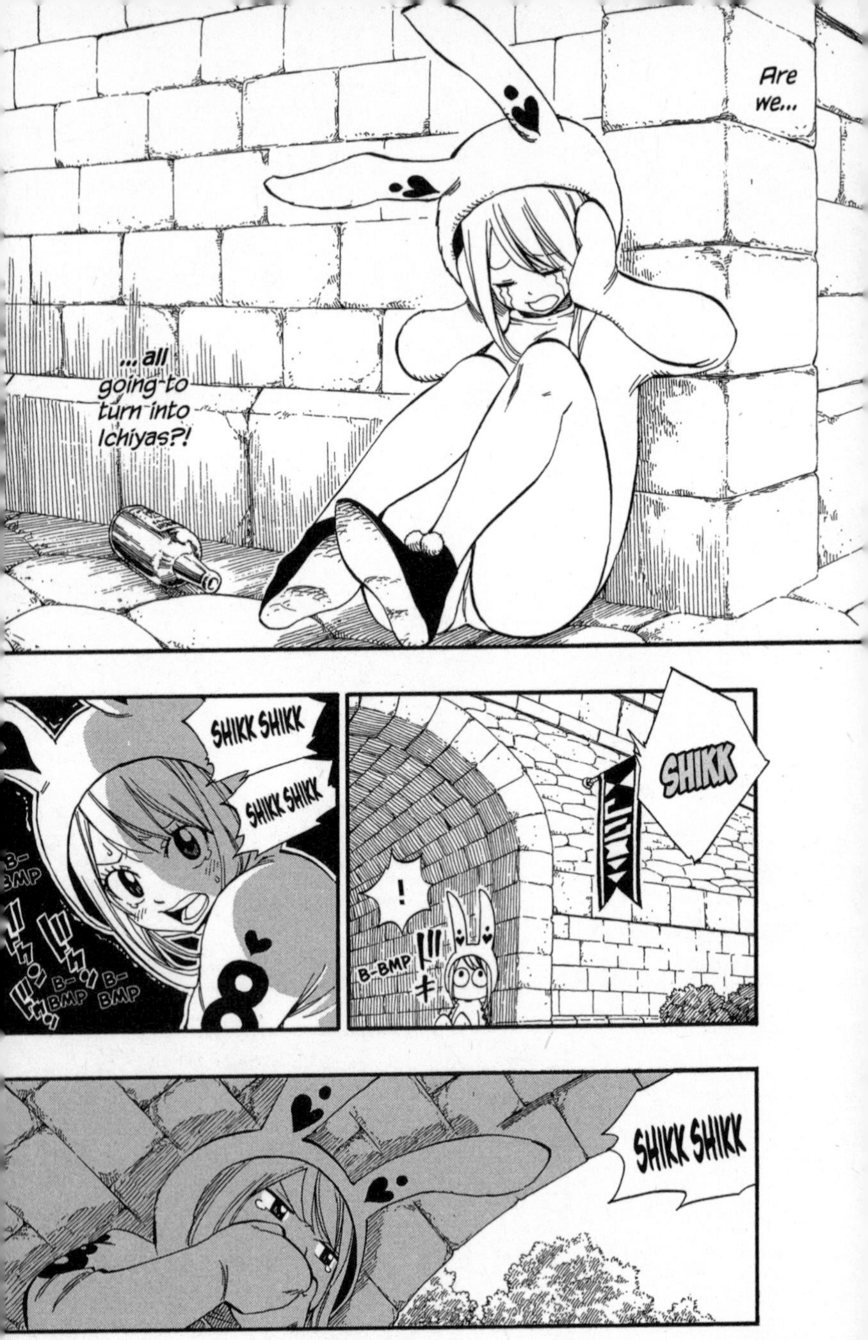
Are we...
...all going to turn into Ichiyas?!
SHIKK
!
B-BMP
SHIKK SHIKK
SHIKK SHIKK
B-BMP
B-BMP
B-BMP
SHIKK SHIKK

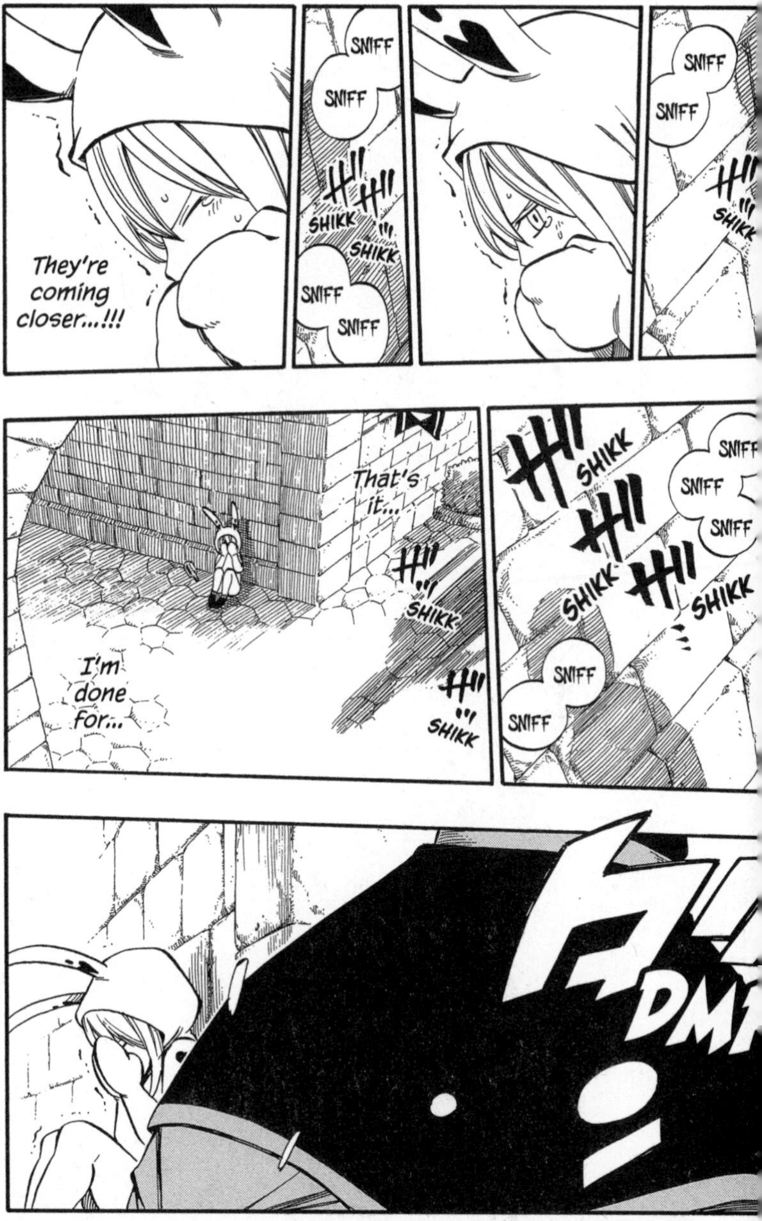
SNIFF
SNIFF
SHIKK
SNIFF
SNIFF
SHIKK
SHIKK
SNIFF
SNIFF
They're coming closer...!!!
SHIKK
SNIFF
SNIFF
SNIFF
SHIKK
SHIKK
SHIKK
SNIFF
SNIFF
That's it...
SHIKK
I'm done for...
SHIKK

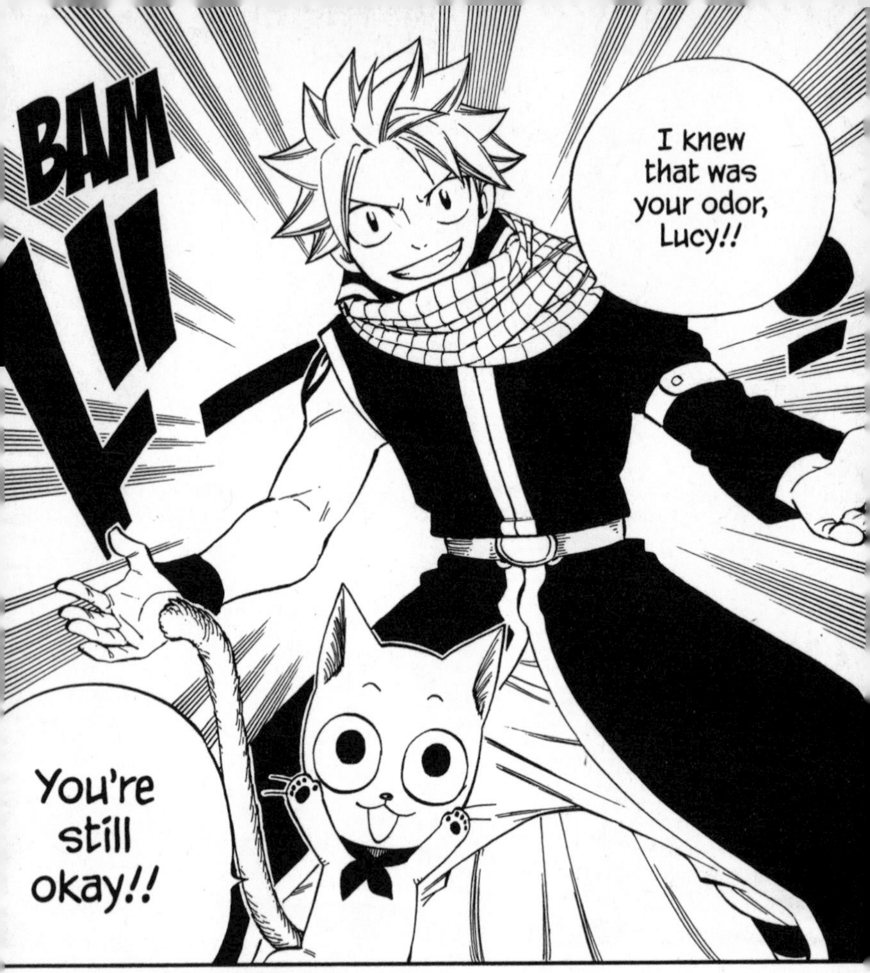
I knew that was your odor, Lucy!!
BAM!!
You're still okay!!
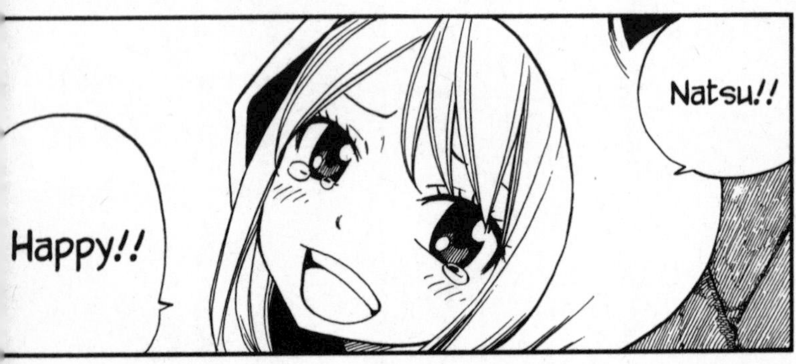
Natsu!!
Happy!!

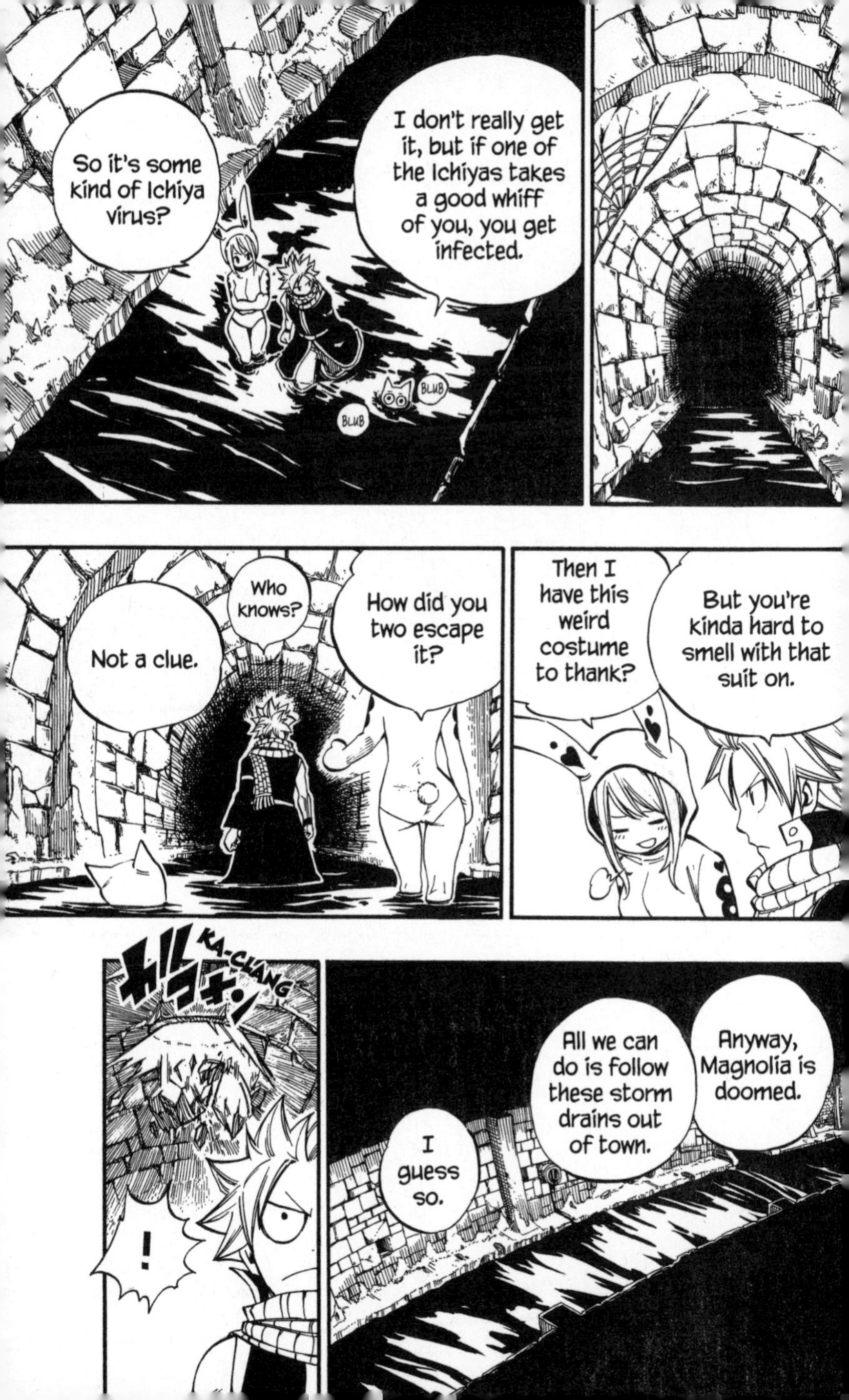
I don't really get it, but if one of the Ichiyas takes a good whiff of you, you get infected.
So it's some kind of Ichiya virus?
BLUB
BLUB
But you're kinda hard to smell with that suit on.
Then I have this weird costume to thank?
How did you two escape it?
Who knows?
Not a clue.
Anyway, Magnolia is doomed.
All we can do is follow these storm drains out of town.
I guess so.
KA-CLANG
!

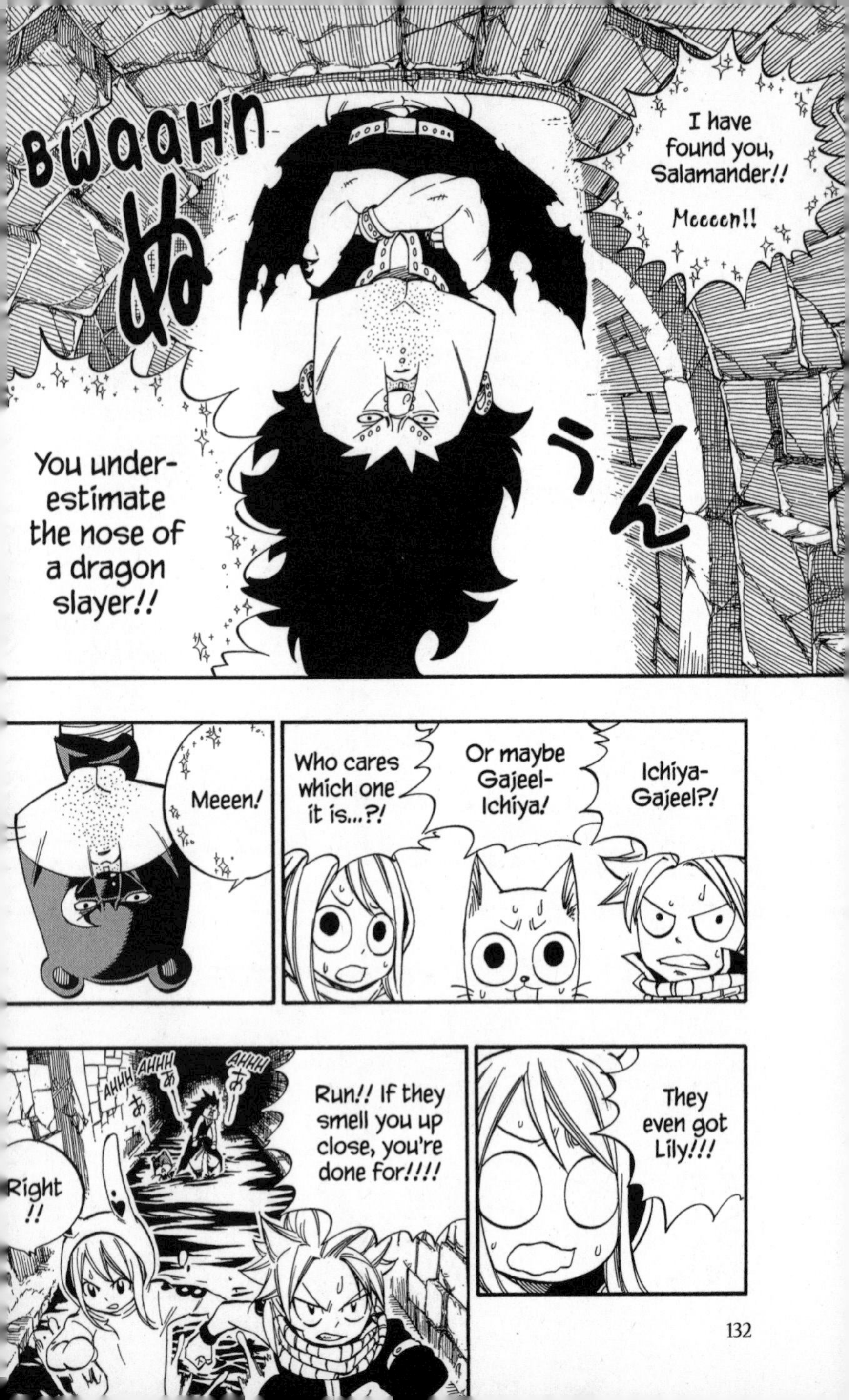
I have found you, Salamander!!
Meeeen!!
BWAAHN
ぬ
うん
You under-estimate the nose of a dragon slayer!!
Ichiya-Gajeel?!
Or maybe Gajeel-Ichiya!
Who cares which one it is...?!
Meeen!
They even got Lily!!!
Run!! If they smell you up close, you're done for!!!!
AHHH あ
AHHH あ
AHHH あ
Right!!

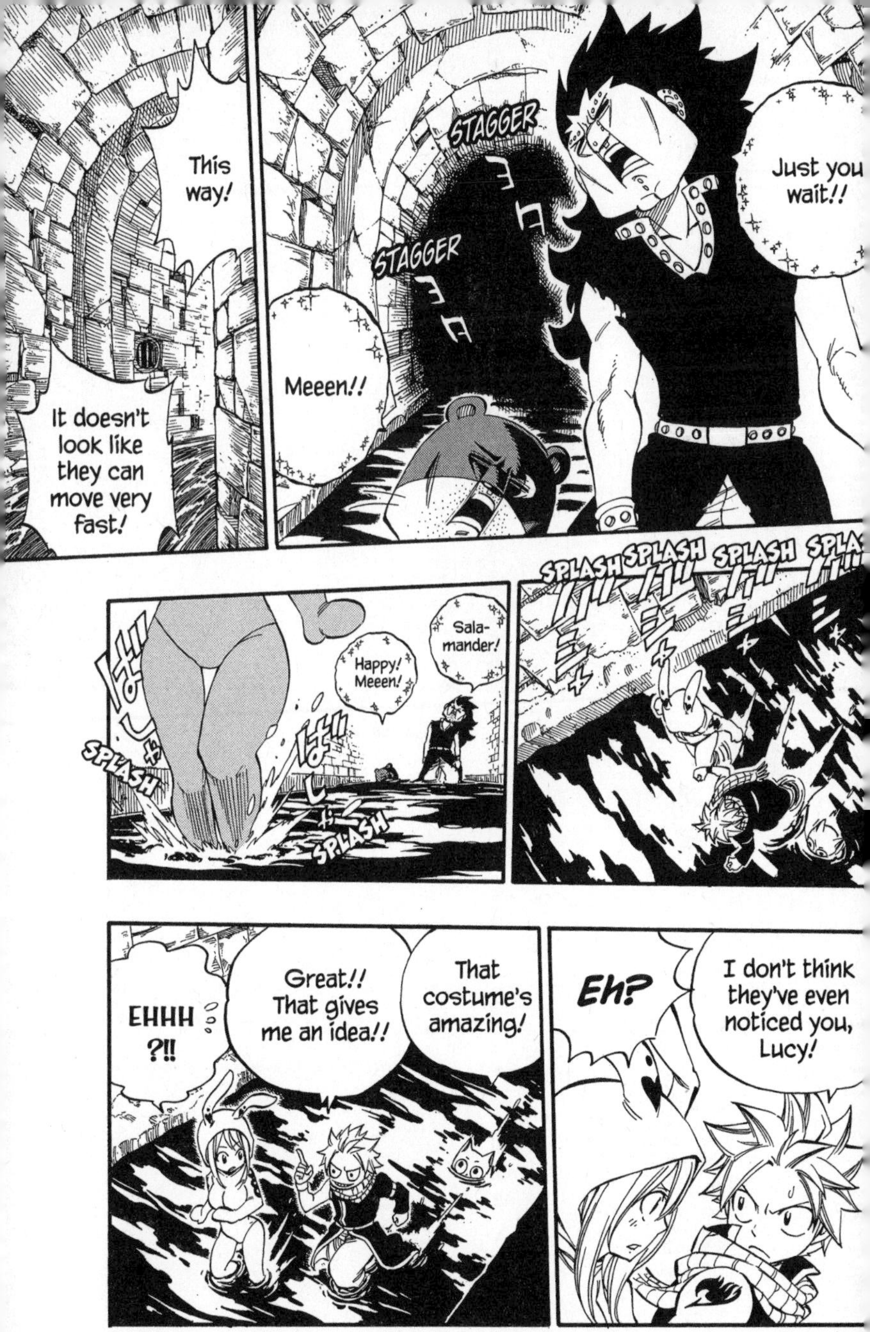
Just you wait!!
STAGGER
STAGGER
Meeen!!
This way!
It doesn't look like they can move very fast!
SPLASH SPLASH SPLASH SPLA
Sala-mander!
Happy! Meeen!
SPLASH
SPLASH
I don't think they've even noticed you, Lucy!
Eh?
That costume's amazing!
Great!! That gives me an idea!!
EHHH ?!!

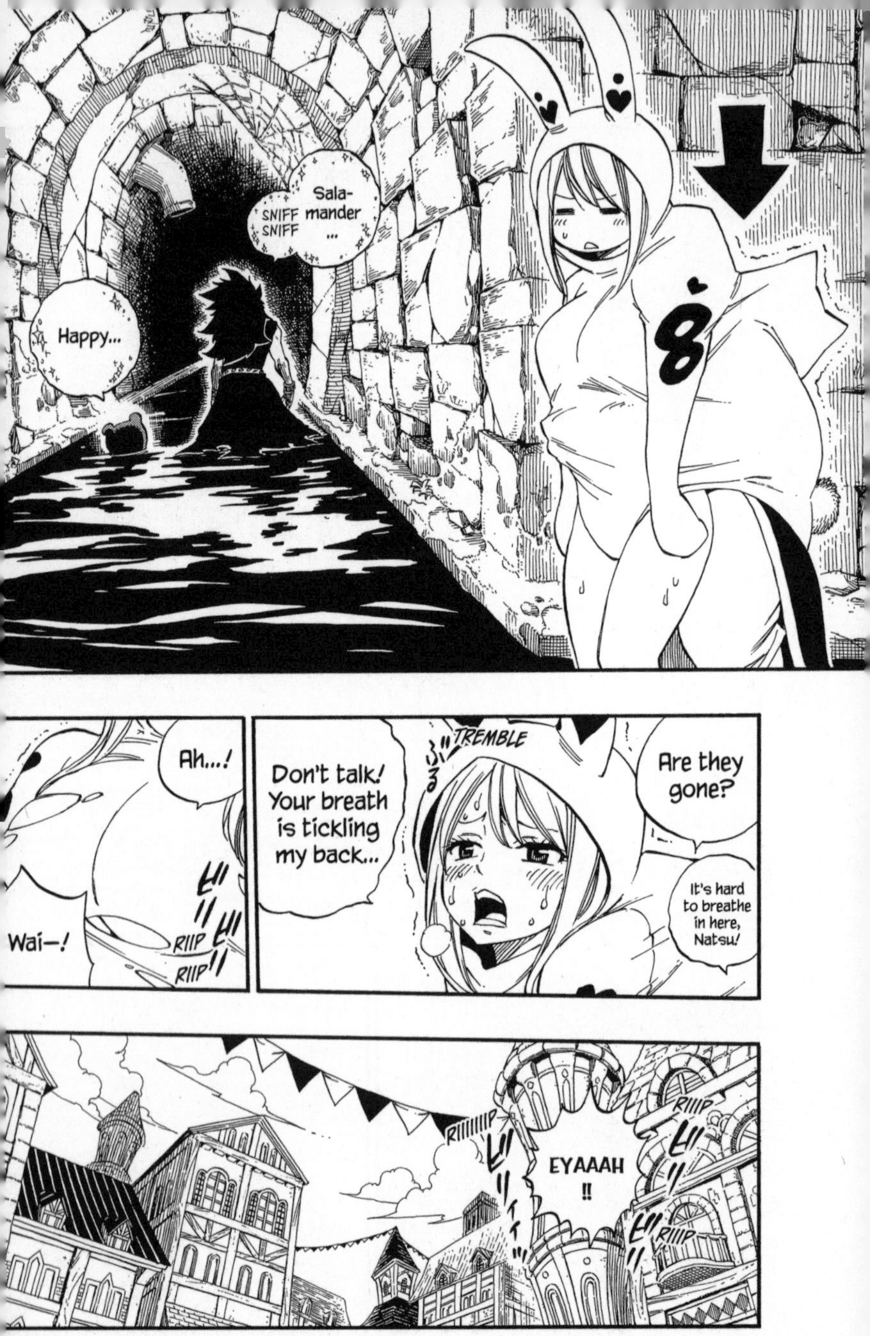
Sala-
mander
...
SNIFF
SNIFF
Happy...
Are they gone?
TREMBLE
It's hard to breathe in here, Natsu!
Don't talk! Your breath is tickling my back...
Ah...!
RIIP
RIIP
Wai–!
RIIIP
RIIIIIIIP
EYAAAH !!
RIIIP

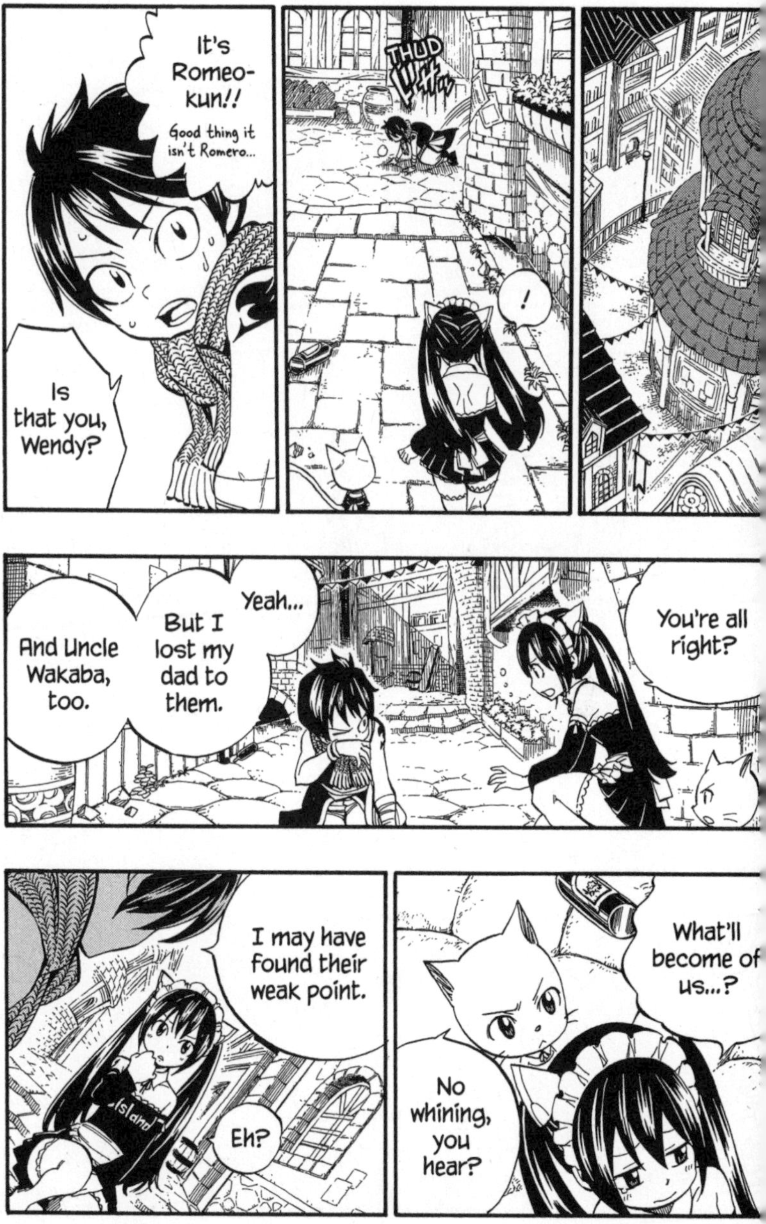
THUD
!
It's Romeo-kun!!
Good thing it isn't Romero...
Is that you, Wendy?
You're all right?
Yeah...
But I lost my dad to them.
And Uncle Wakaba, too.
What'll become of us...?
No whining, you hear?
I may have found their weak point.
Eh?

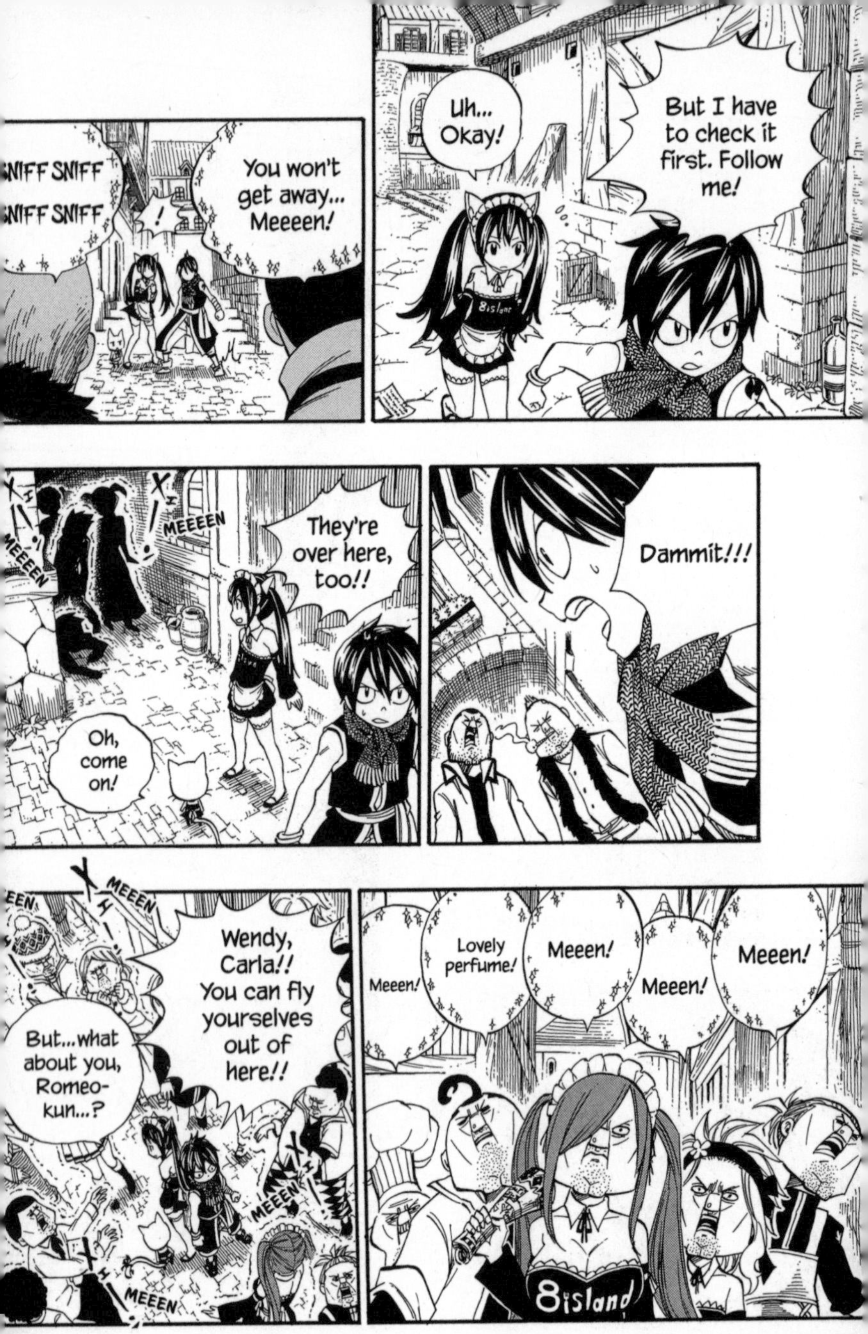

But I have to check it first. Follow me!
Uh... Okay!
You won't get away... Meeeen!
!
SNIFF SNIFF
NIFF SNIFF
Dammit!!!
They're over here, too!!
MEEEEN
MEEEEN
Oh, come on!
Meeen!
Meeen!
Meeen!
Lovely perfume!
Meeen!
MEEEN
Wendy, Carla!! You can fly yourselves out of here!!
EEN
But...what about you, Romeo-kun...?
MEEEN
MEEEN

Wendy, we're going!! I'm sorry, Romeo!!

For Natsu-san? Why?!

Forget about me!! Fly up and look for Natsu!!

I'm sure Natsu can...

Romeo-kun!!

FLAPP

Oh, no...

...Meeeen!!

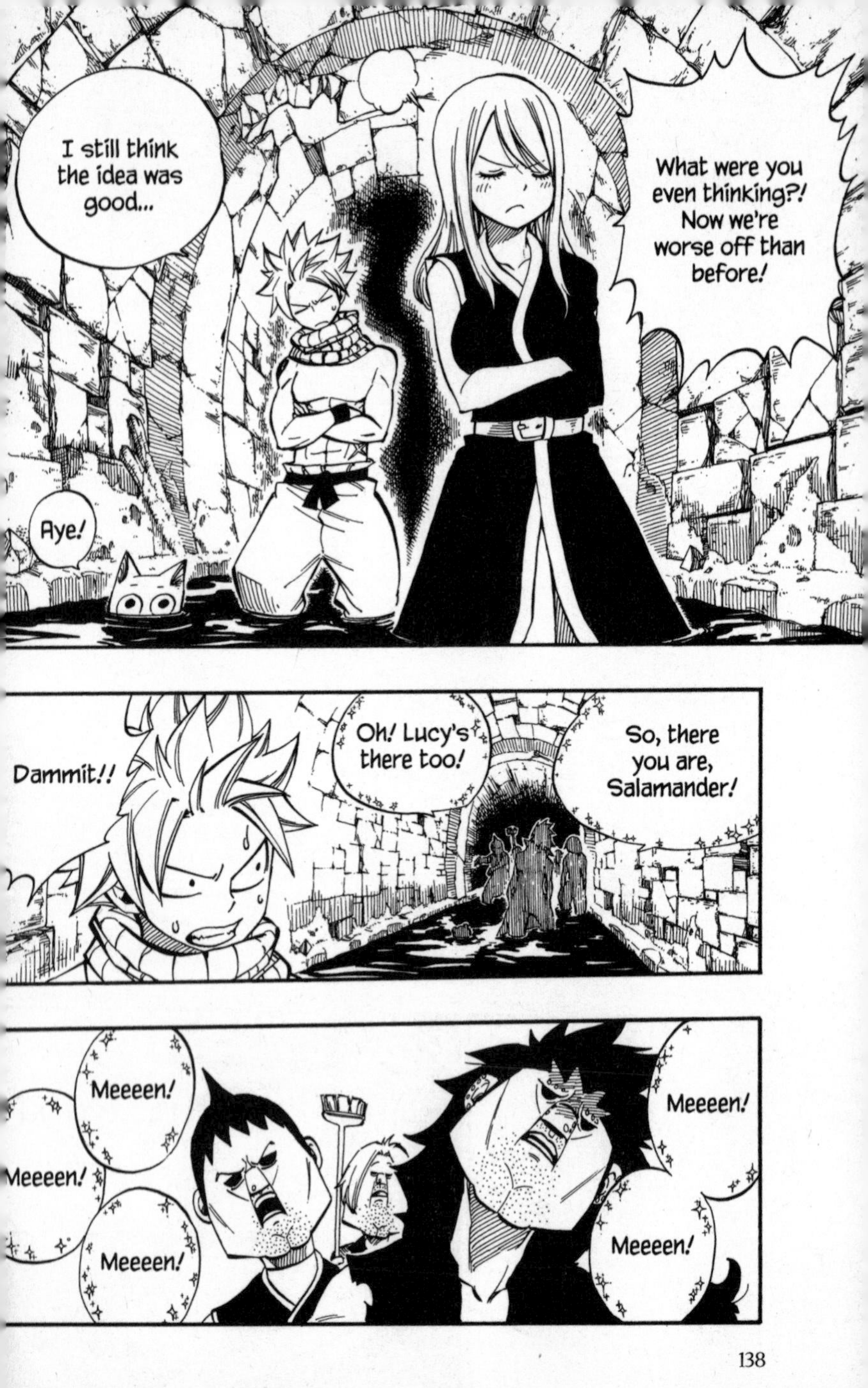
What were you even thinking?! Now we're worse off than before!
I still think the idea was good...
Aye!
So, there you are, Salamander!
Oh! Lucy's there too!
Dammit!!
Meeeen!
Meeeen!
Meeeen!
Meeeen!
Meeeen!

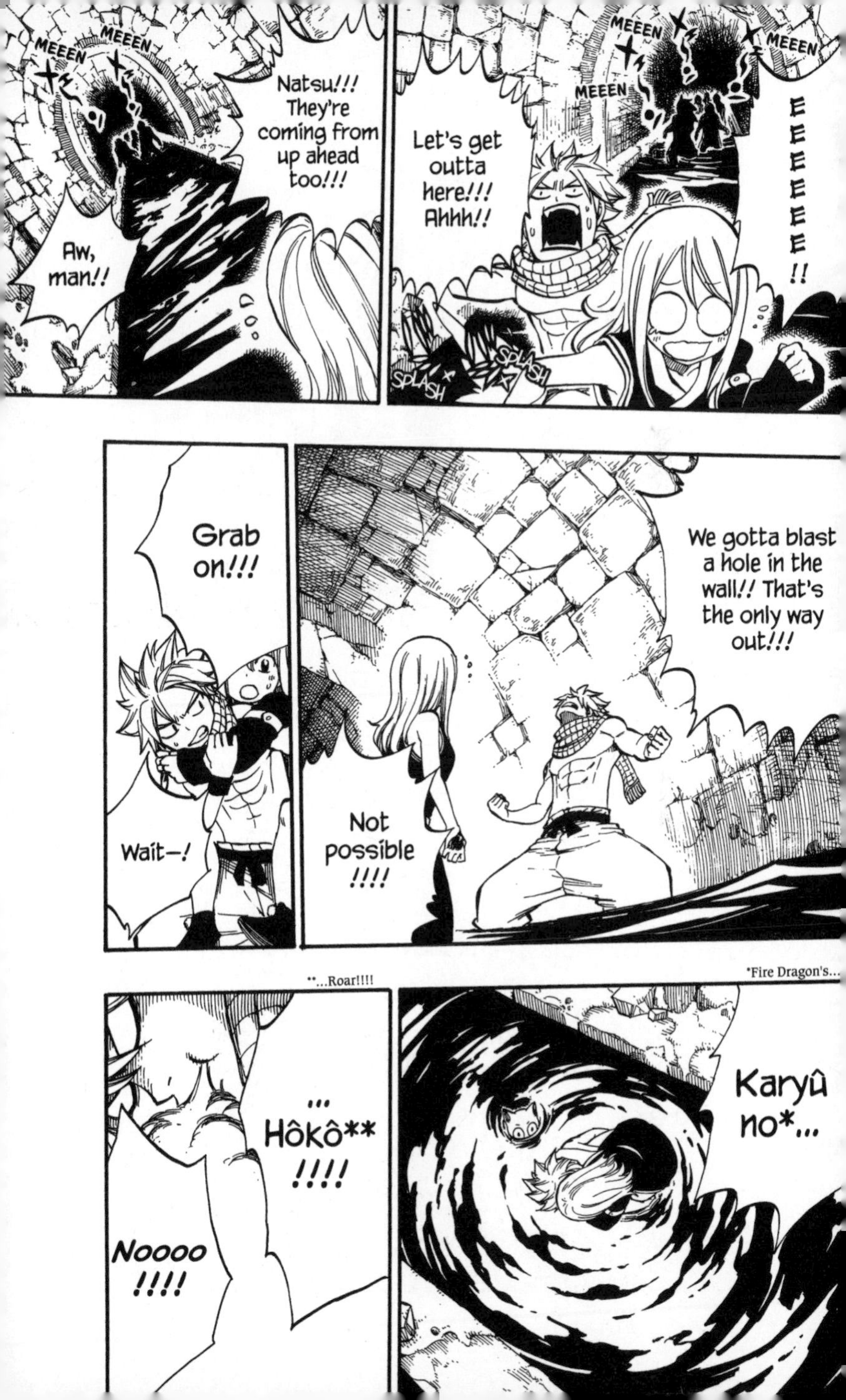
MEEEN
MEEEN
MEEEN
Let's get outta here!!! Ahhh!!
EEEEEEE!!
SPLASH
SPLASH
MEEEN
MEEEN
Natsu!!! They're coming from up ahead too!!!
Aw, man!!
We gotta blast a hole in the wall!! That's the only way out!!!
Not possible!!!!
Grab on!!!
Wait—!
*Fire Dragon's...
Karyû no*...
**...Roar!!!!
... Hôkô** !!!!
Noooo !!!!

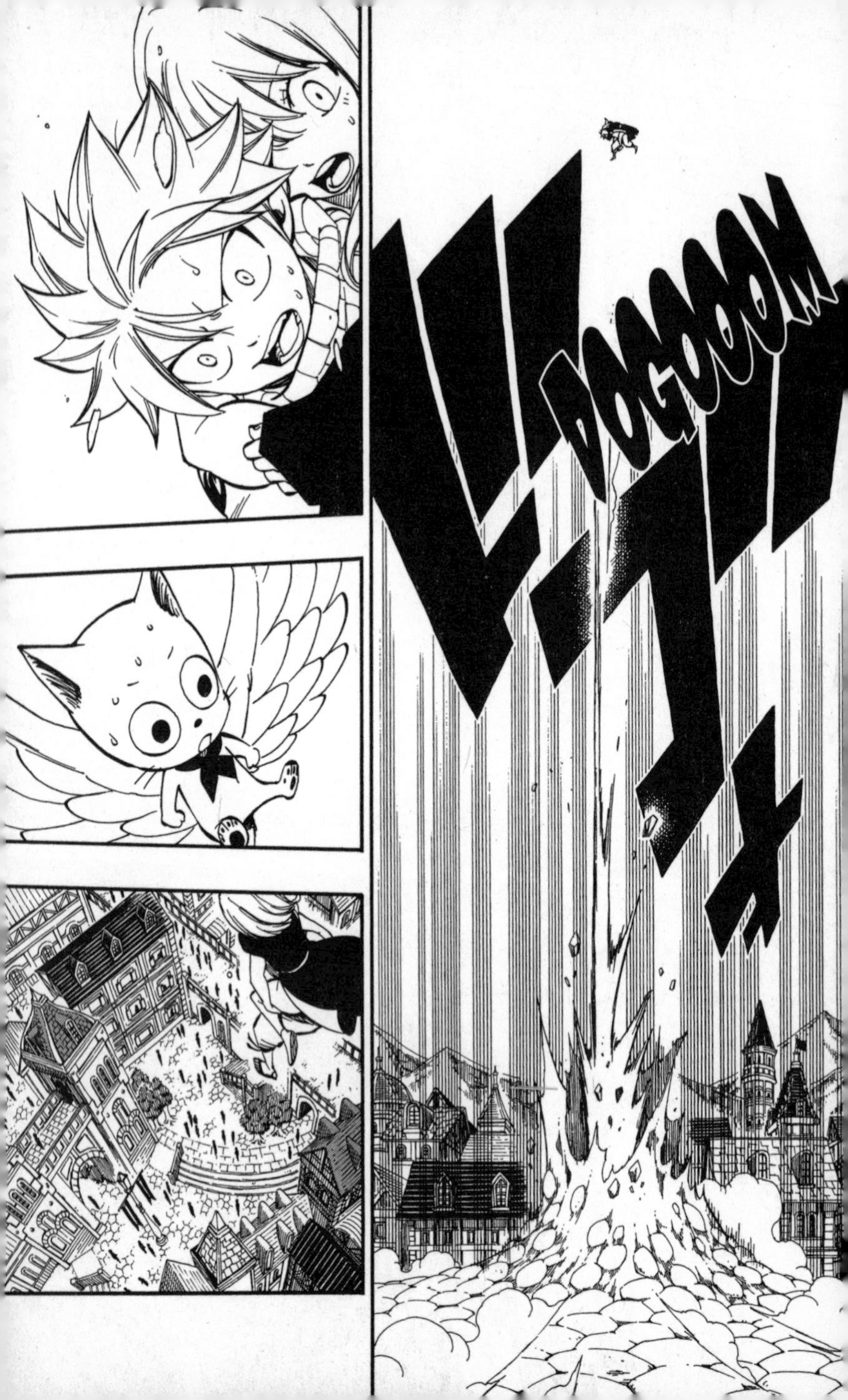
DOGOOOM

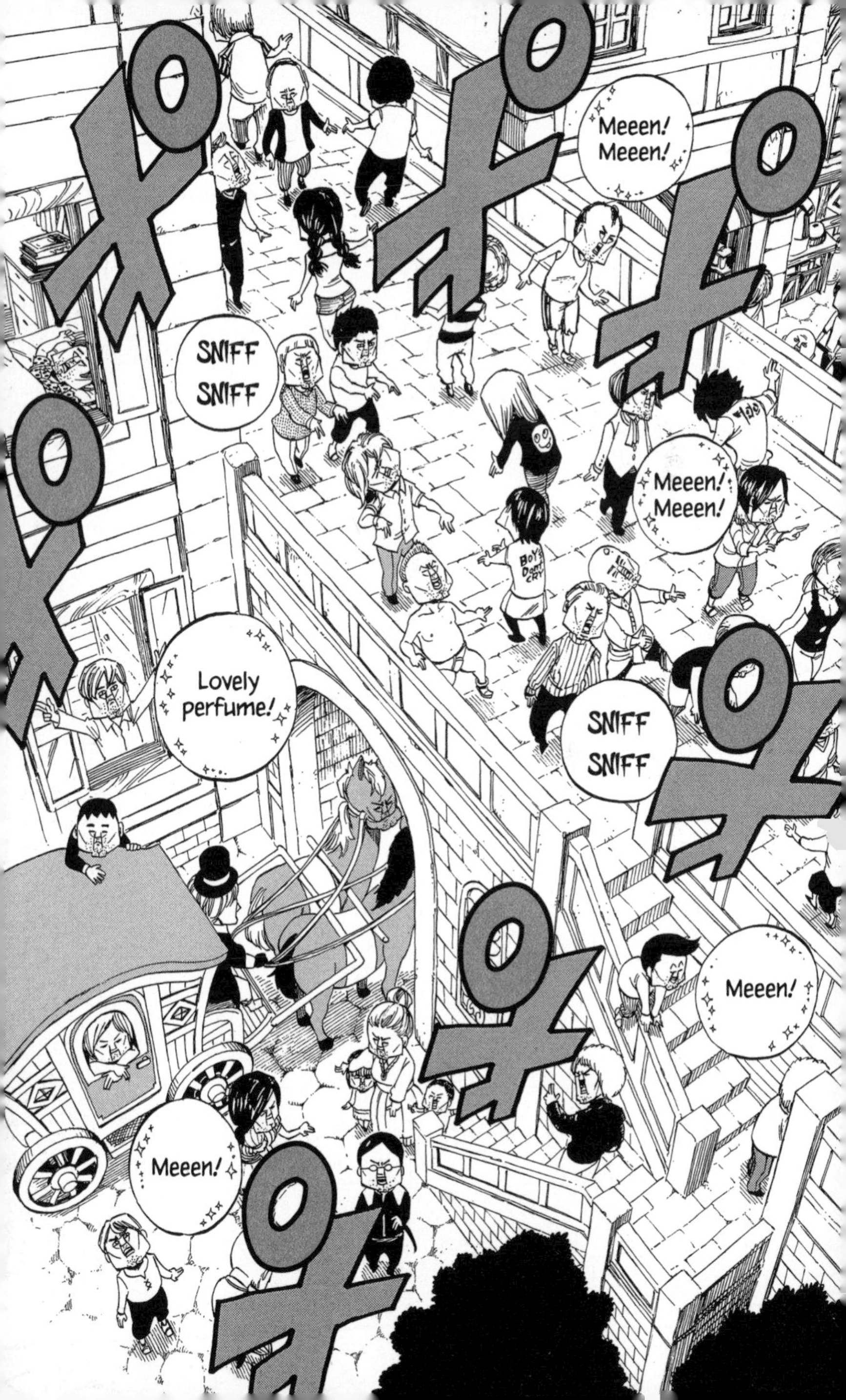
Meeen! Meeen!
SNIFF SNIFF
Meeen! Meeen!
SNIFF SNIFF
Lovely perfume!
Meeen!
Meeen!

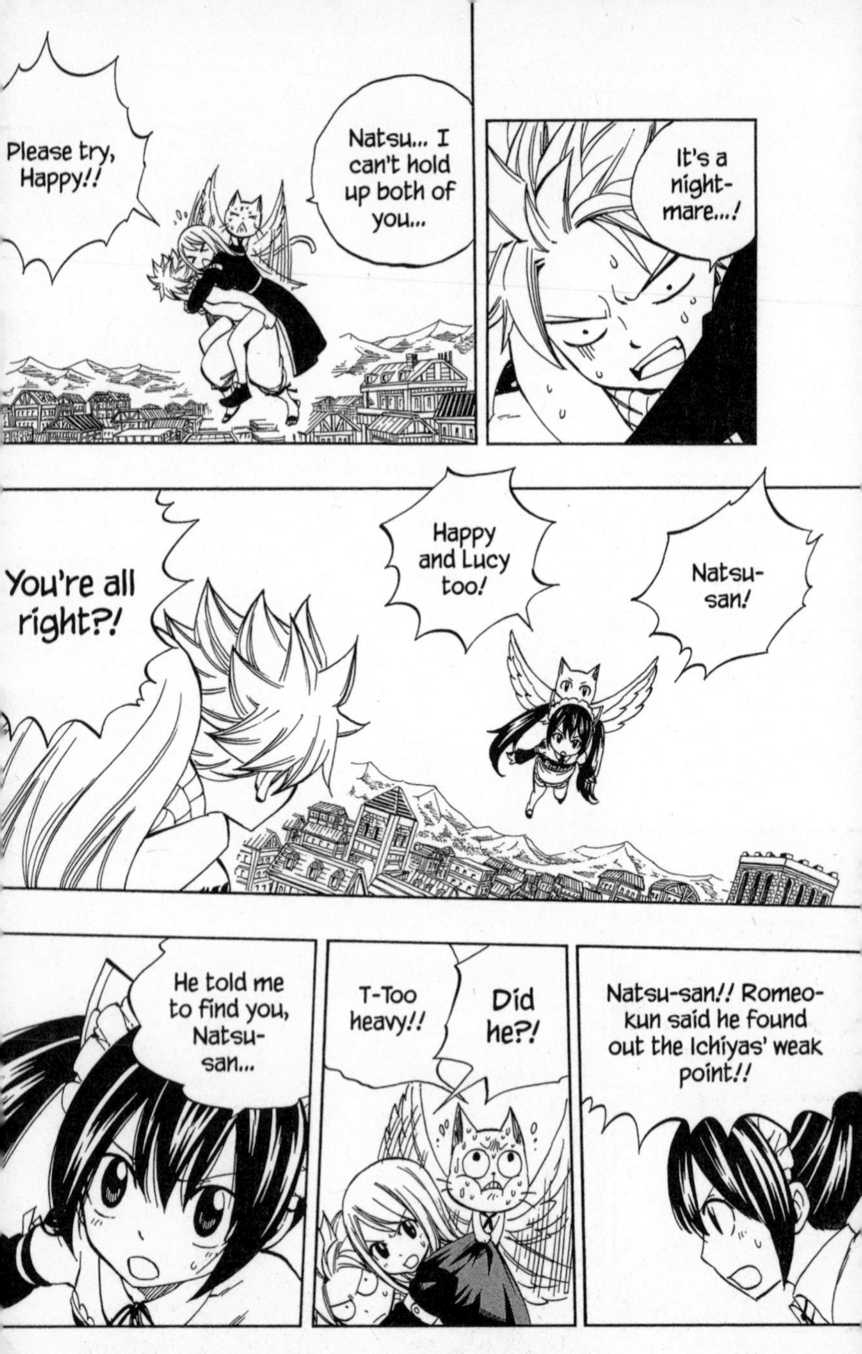
It's a night-mare...!
Natsu... I can't hold up both of you...
Please try, Happy!!
Natsu-san!
Happy and Lucy too!
You're all right?!
Natsu-san!! Romeo-kun said he found out the Ichiyas' weak point!!
Did he?!
T-Too heavy!!
He told me to find you, Natsu-san...

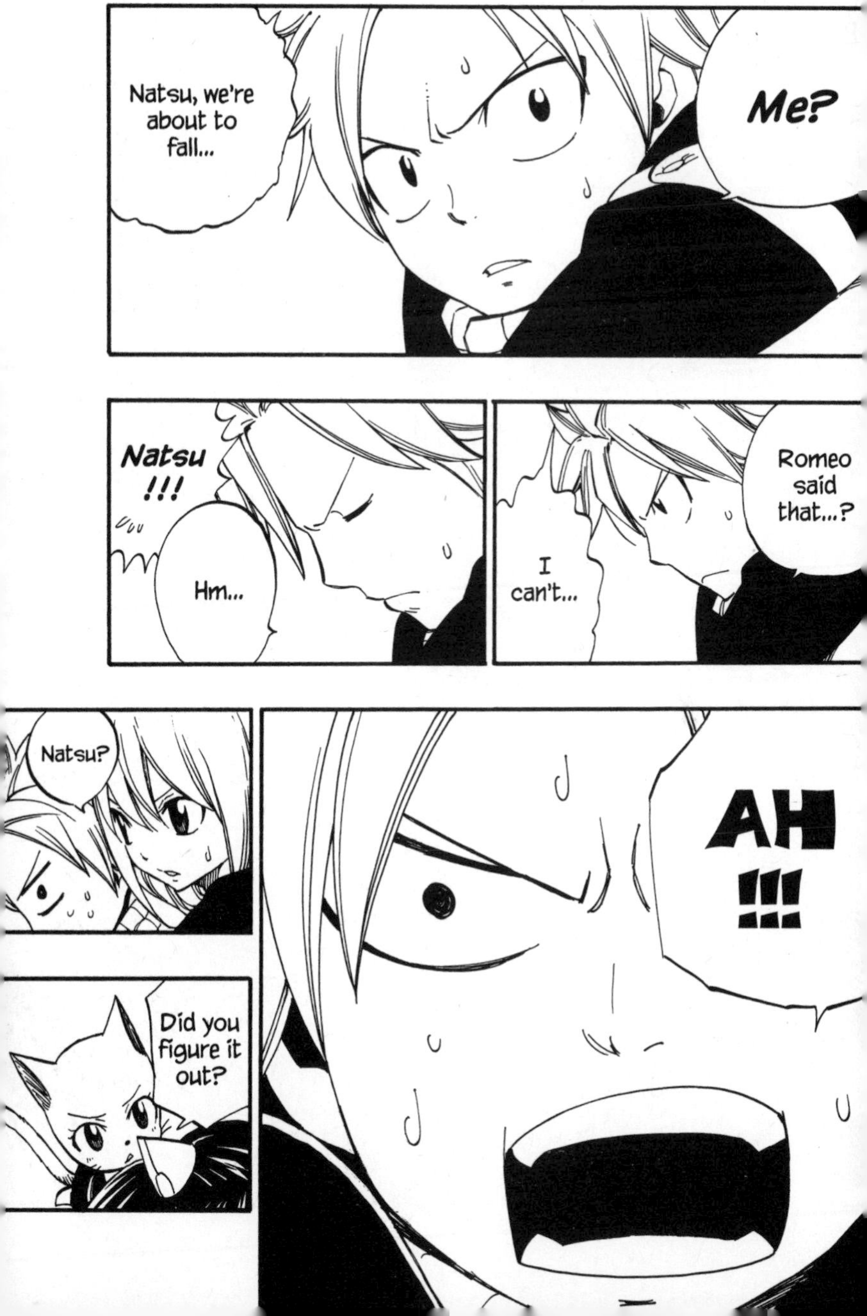
Me?
Natsu, we're about to fall...
Romeo said that...?
I can't...
Natsu !!!
Hm...
AH !!!
Natsu?
Did you figure it out?

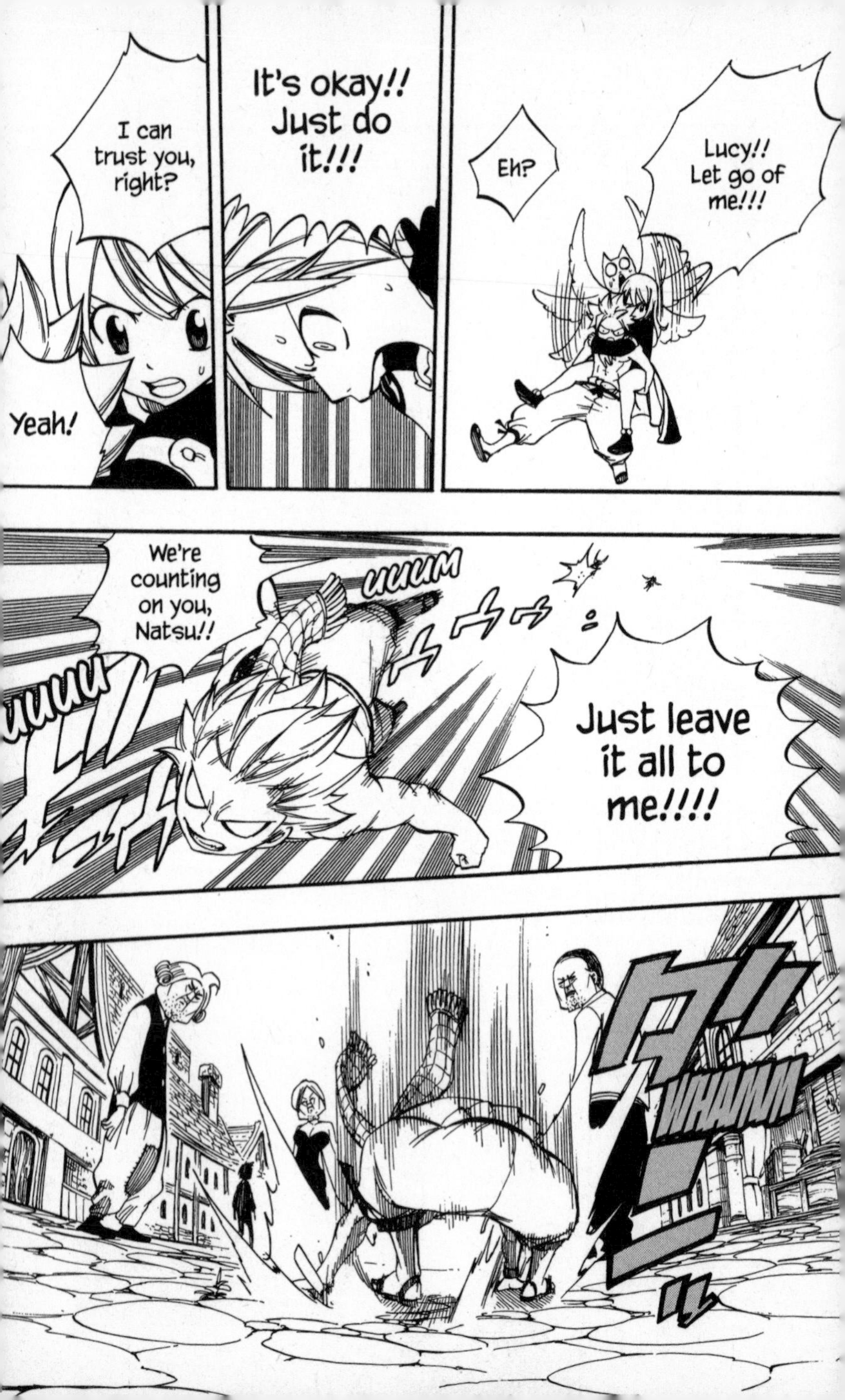
Lucy!! Let go of me!!!
Eh?
It's okay!! Just do it!!!
I can trust you, right?
Yeah!
Just leave it all to me!!!!
UUUM
We're counting on you, Natsu!!
UUUU
WHAMM

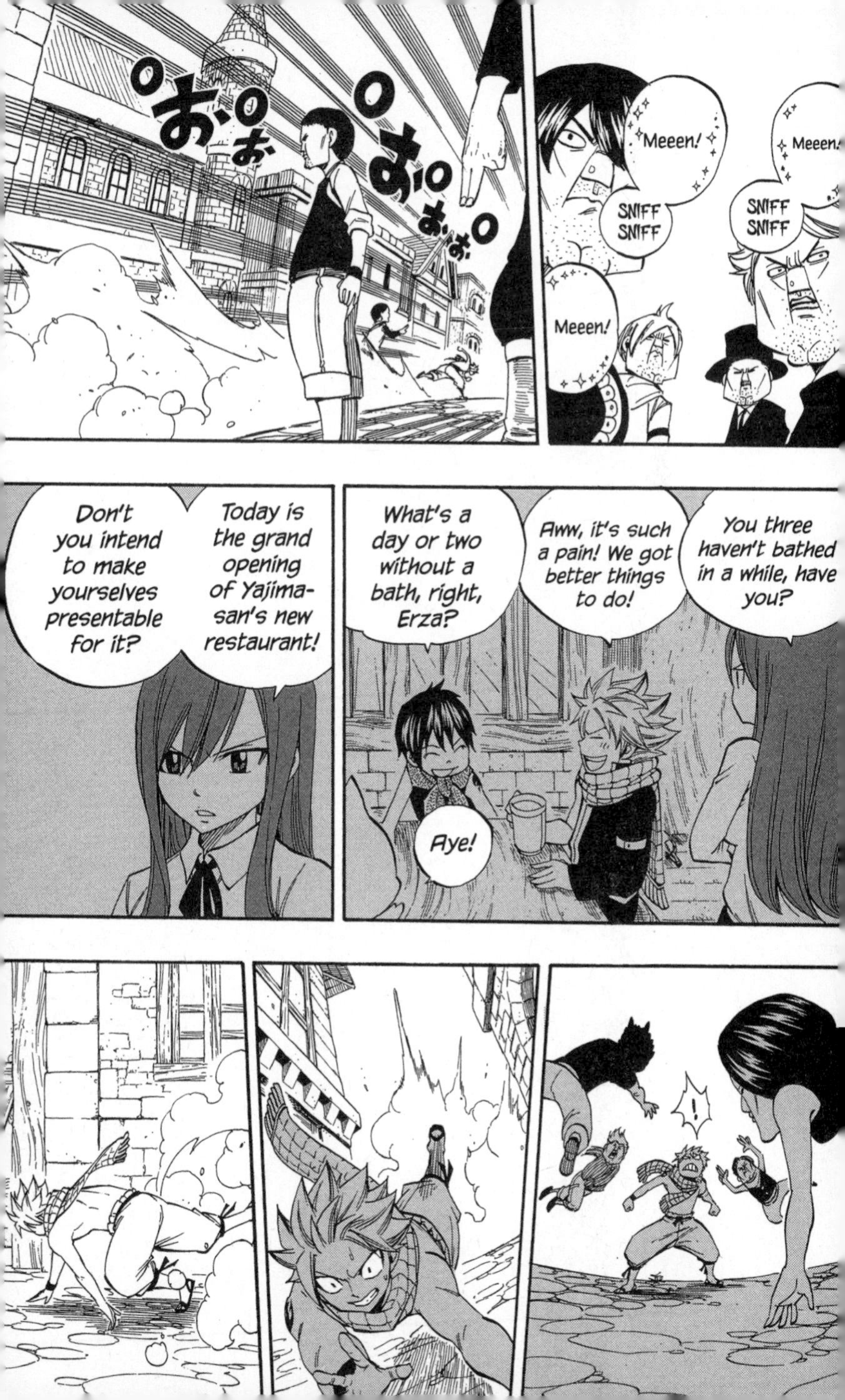
Meeen!
SNIFF SNIFF
Meeen!
SNIFF SNIFF
Meeen!
You three haven't bathed in a while, have you?
Aww, it's such a pain! We got better things to do!
What's a day or two without a bath, right, Erza?
Aye!
Today is the grand opening of Yajima-san's new restaurant!
Don't you intend to make yourselves presentable for it?
!

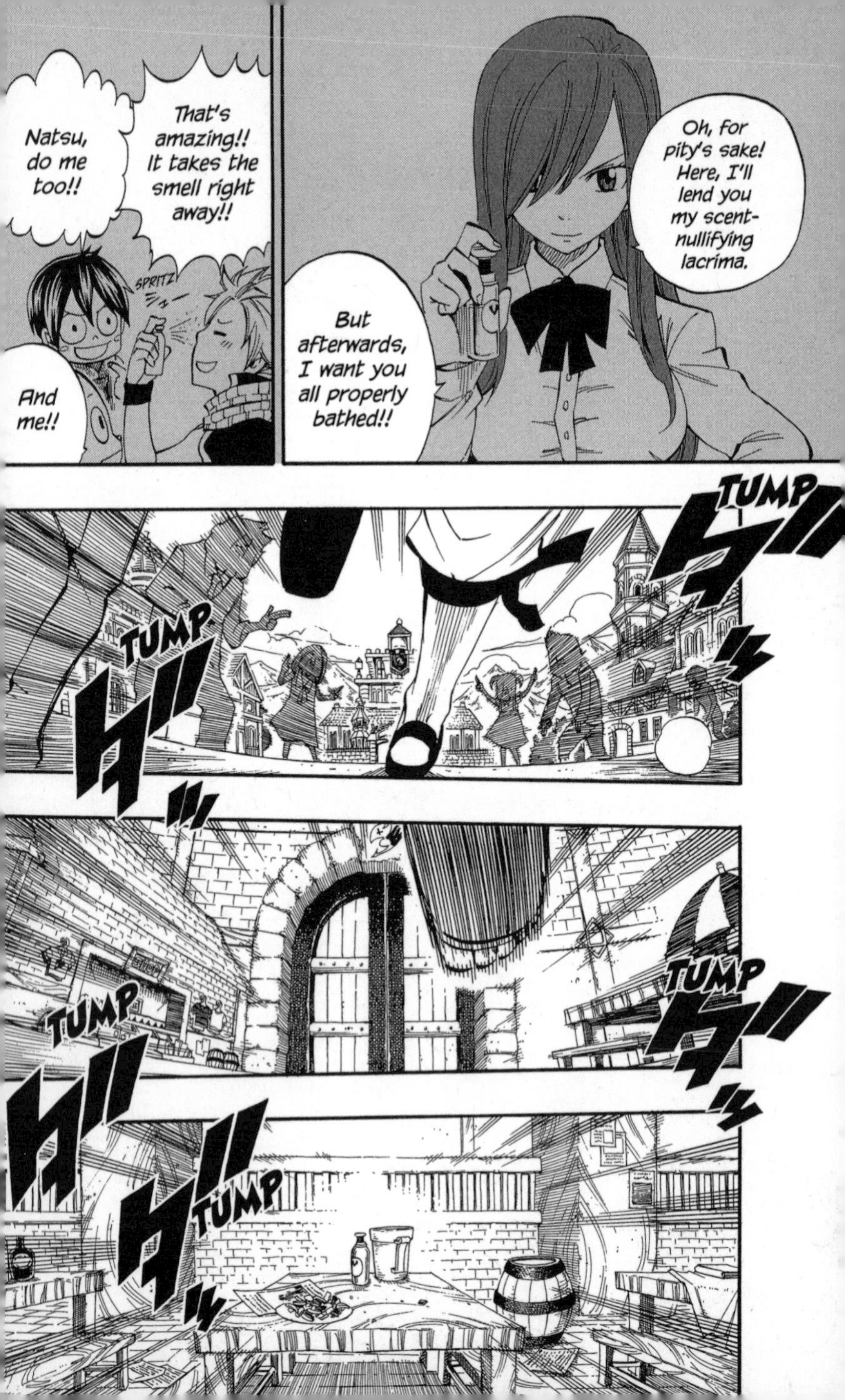
Oh, for pity's sake! Here, I'll lend you my scent-nullifying lacrima.
But afterwards, I want you all properly bathed!!
That's amazing!! It takes the smell right away!!
SPRITZ
Natsu, do me too!!
And me!!
TUMP
TUMP
TUMP
TUMP
TUMP

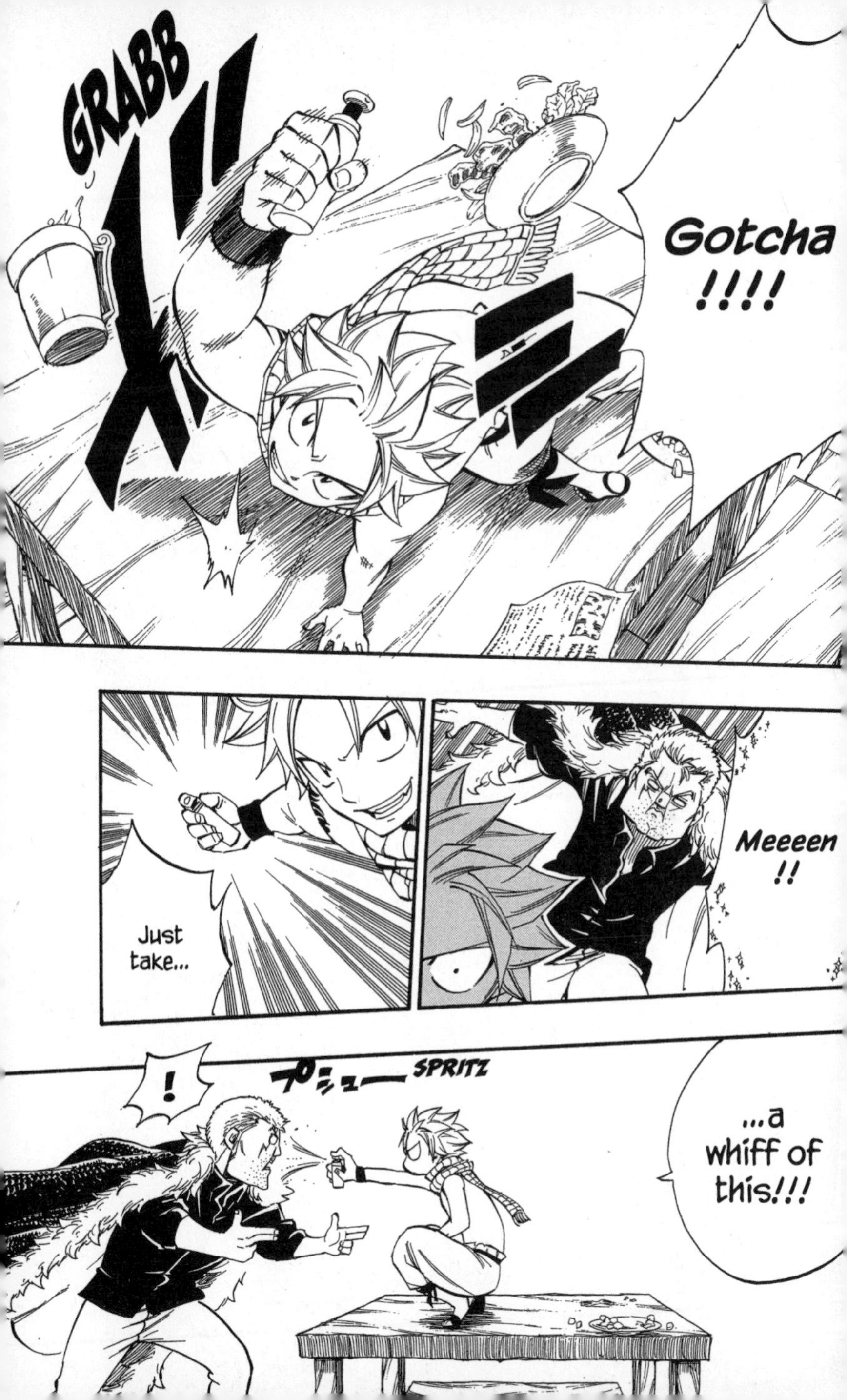
Gotcha !!!!
GRABB
Meeeen !!
Just take...
...a whiff of this!!!
SPRITZ
!

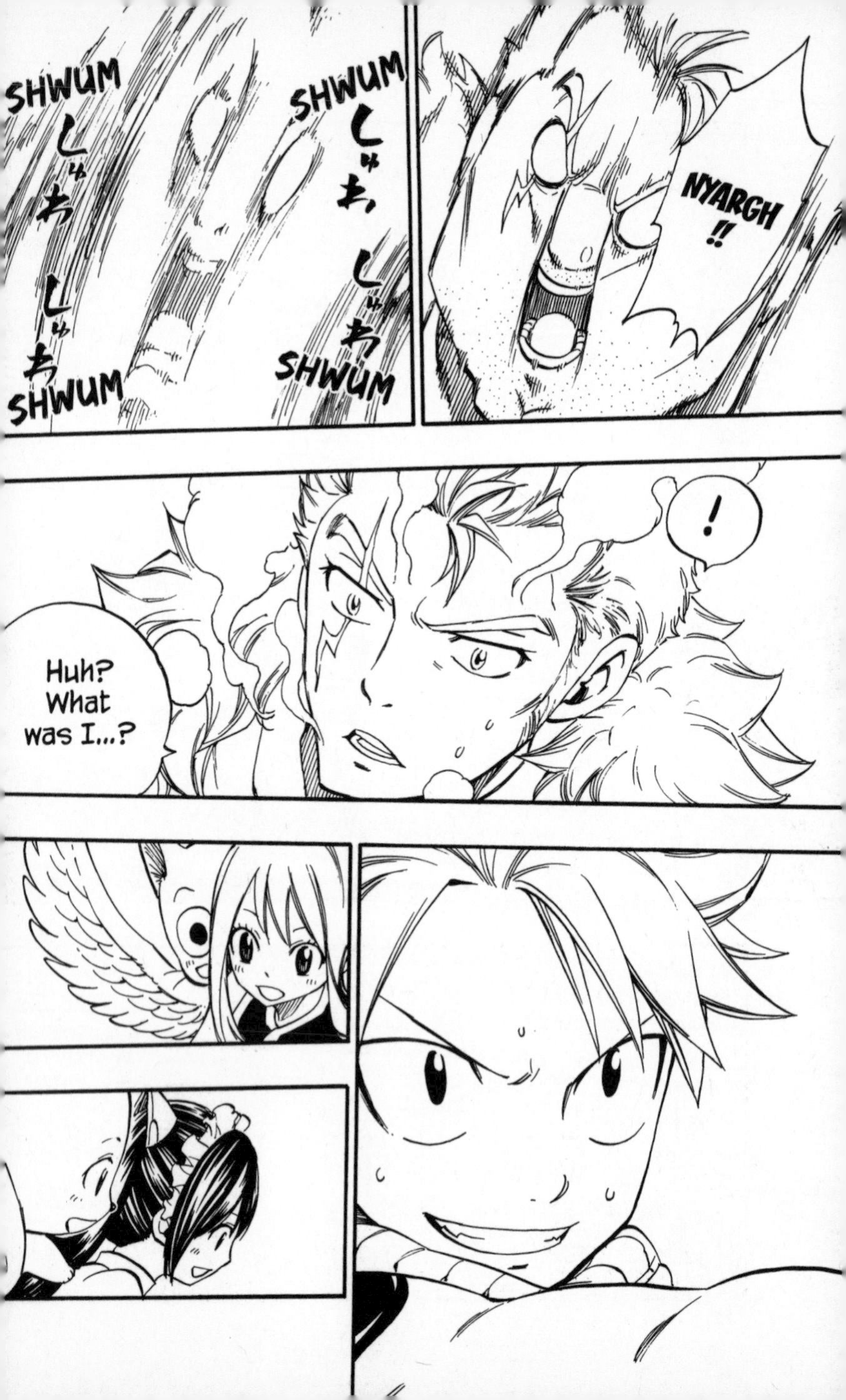
NYARGH!!
SHWUM
しゅわ しゅわ
SHWUM
SHWUM
しゅわ しゅわ
SHWUM
!
Huh? What was I...?

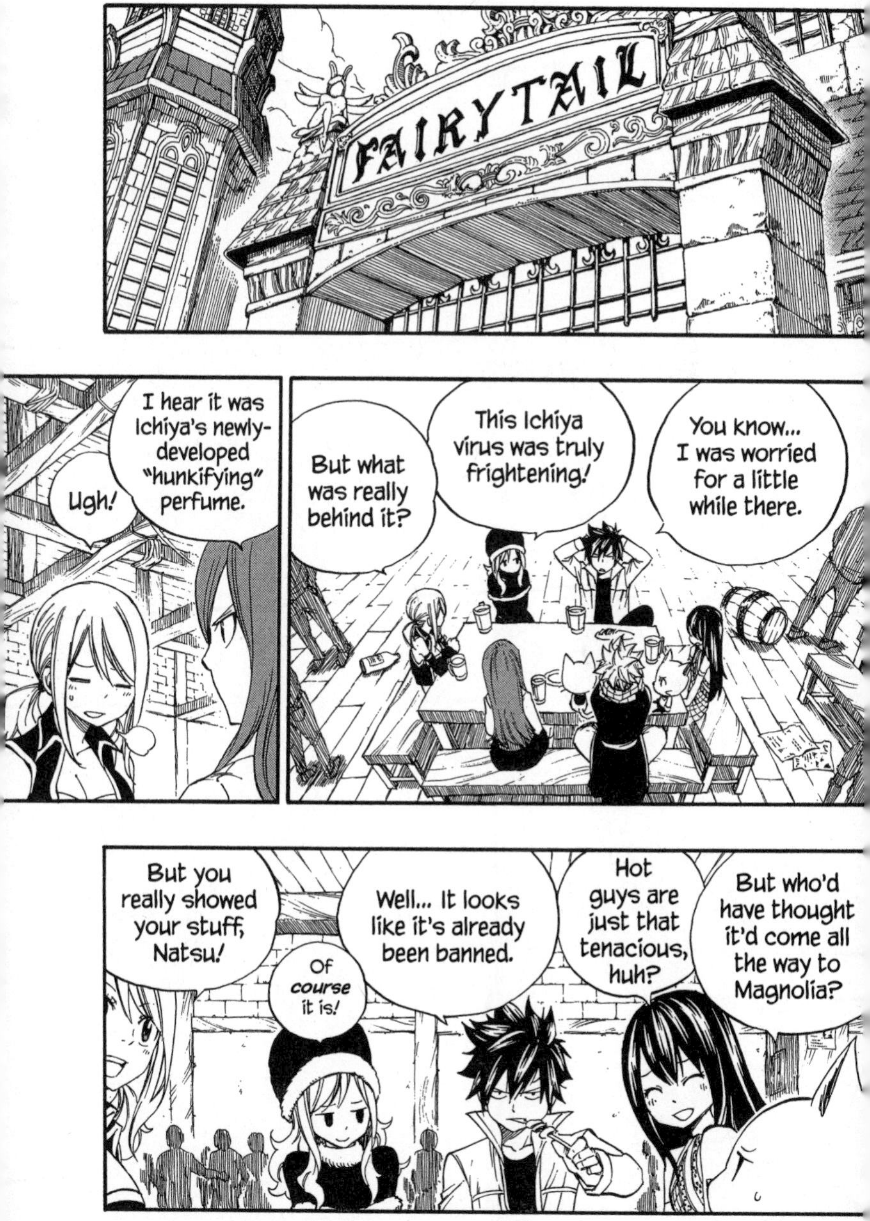
FAIRYTAIL
You know... I was worried for a little while there.
This Ichiya virus was truly frightening!
But what was really behind it?
I hear it was Ichiya's newly-developed "hunkifying" perfume.
Ugh!
But who'd have thought it'd come all the way to Magnolia?
Hot guys are just that tenacious, huh?
Well... It looks like it's already been banned.
Of *course* it is!
But you really showed your stuff, Natsu!

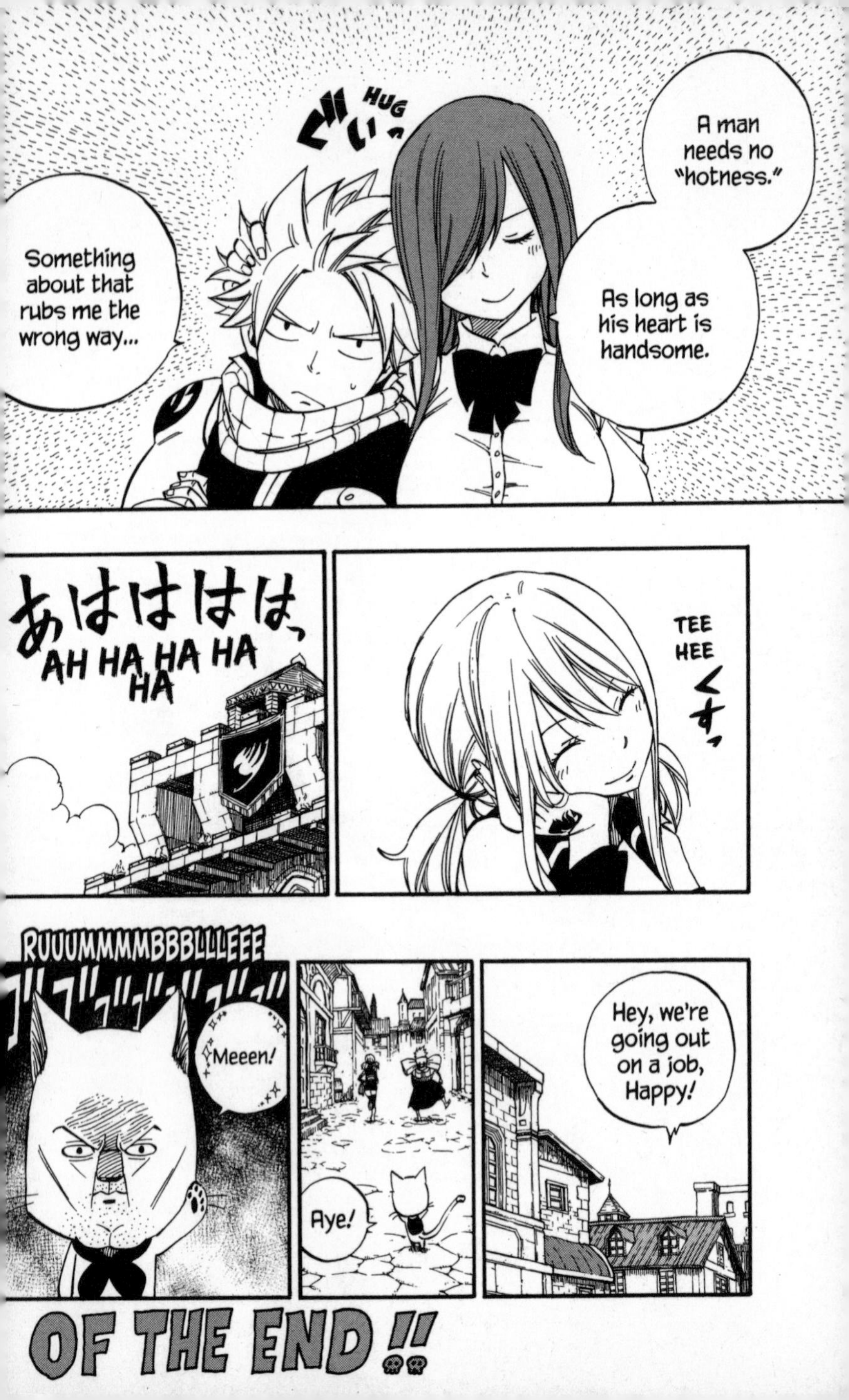
A man needs no "hotness."
As long as his heart is handsome.
HUG
Something about that rubs me the wrong way...
TEE HEE
くすっ
あはははは
AH HA HA HA HA
Hey, we're going out on a job, Happy!
Aye!
Meeen!
RUUUMMMMBBBLLLEEE
OF THE END!!

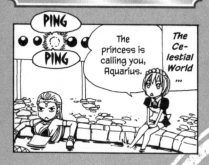

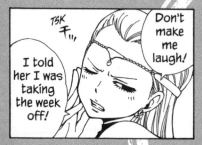

FOUR-PANEL COMICS!

SUBJECT: GOLDEN WEEK

CELESTIAL SPIRIT'S VACATION

The Ce-lestial World ...
The princess is calling you, Aquarius.
PING
PING
Don't make me laugh!
TSK
I told her I was taking the week off!
Why doesn't she come to help?!
BAM
POW
Come on!!
Now she's calling for you.
PING
PING
Even though it's Golden Week...
Right?
Huuuuh?!

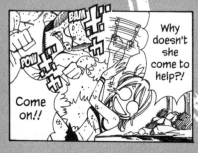

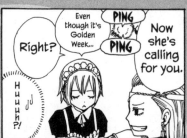

FROM *MAGAZINE SPECIAL*, 2010, ISSUE 5.

FT😺S

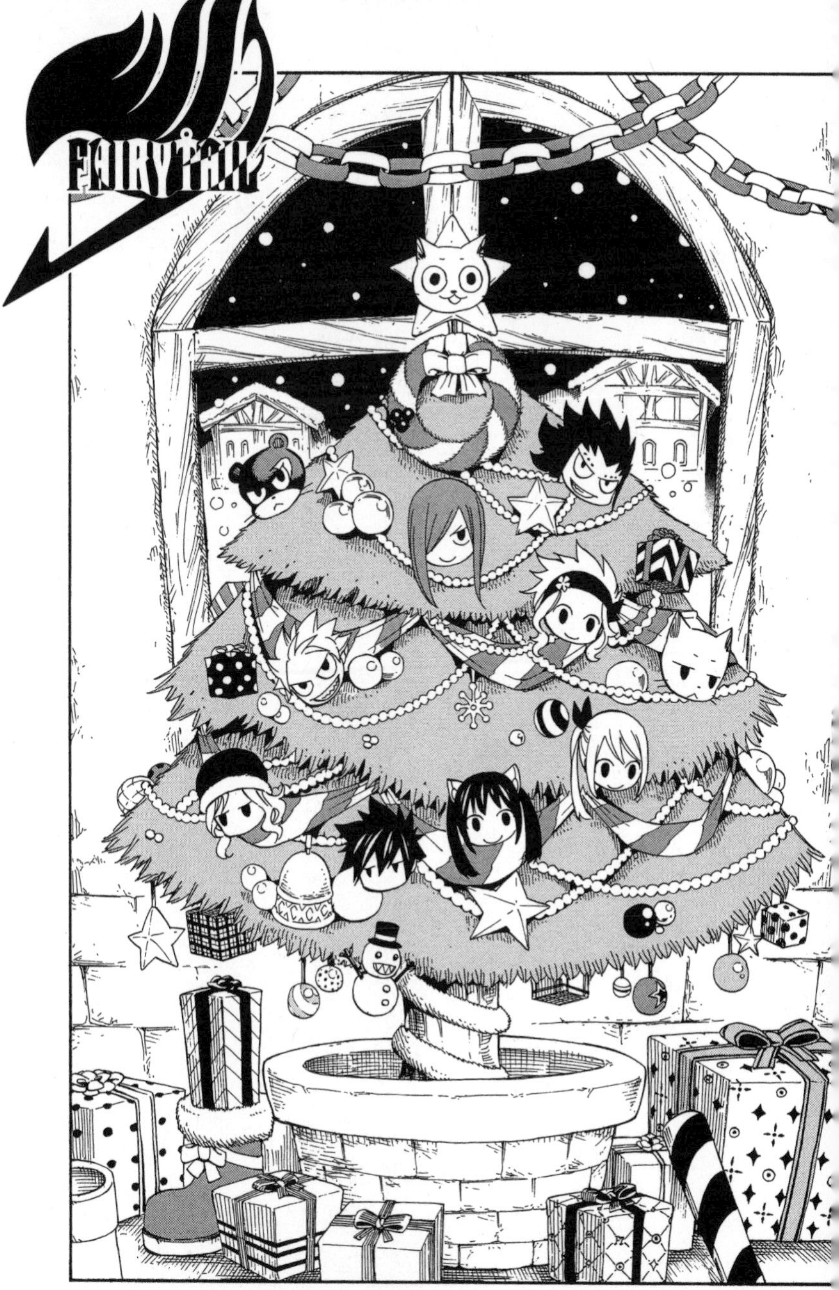
FAIRY TAIL

A Merry, Fairy Christmas

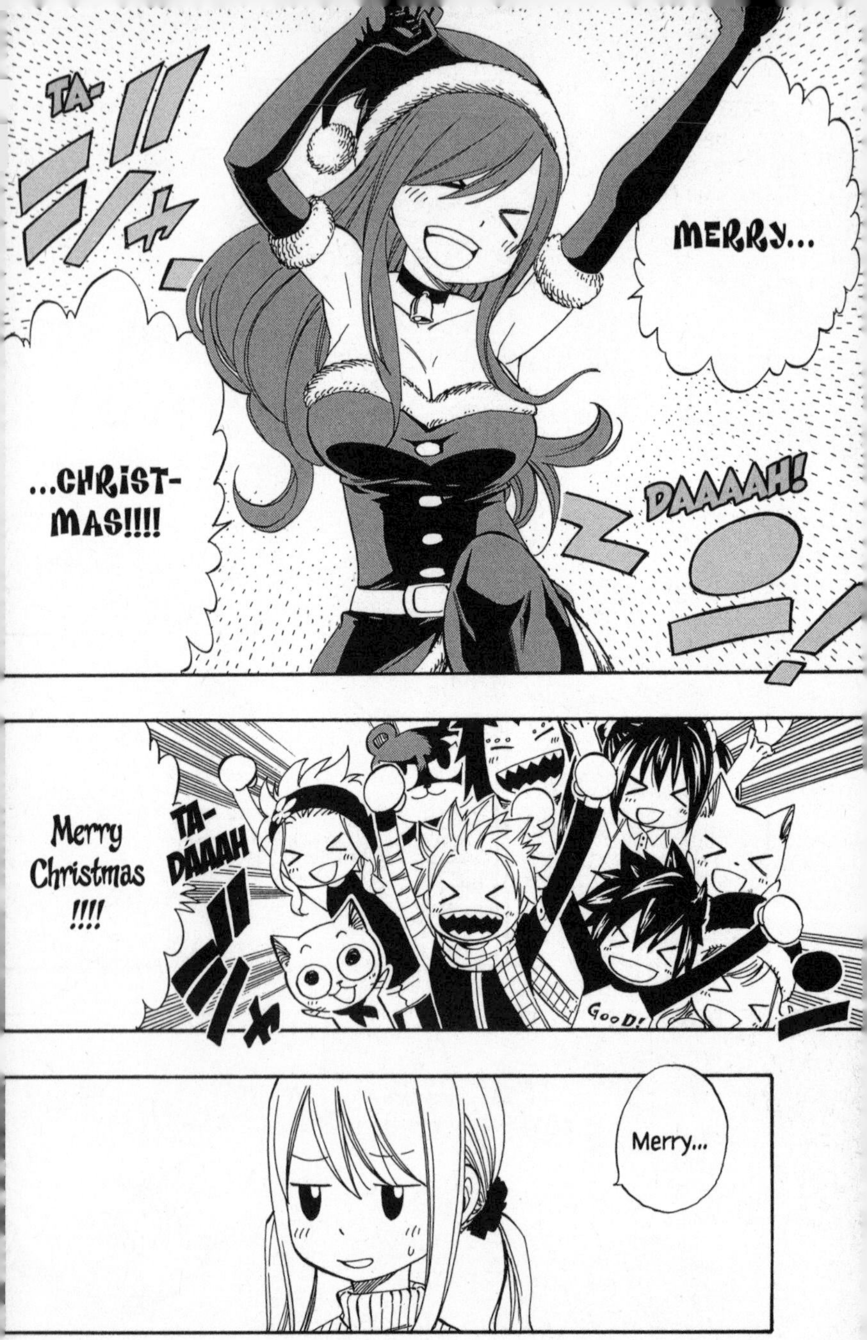
MERRY...
...CHRIST-
MAS!!!!
TA-
DAAAAH!
TA-
DAAAH
Merry
Christmas
!!!!
GOOD!
Merry...

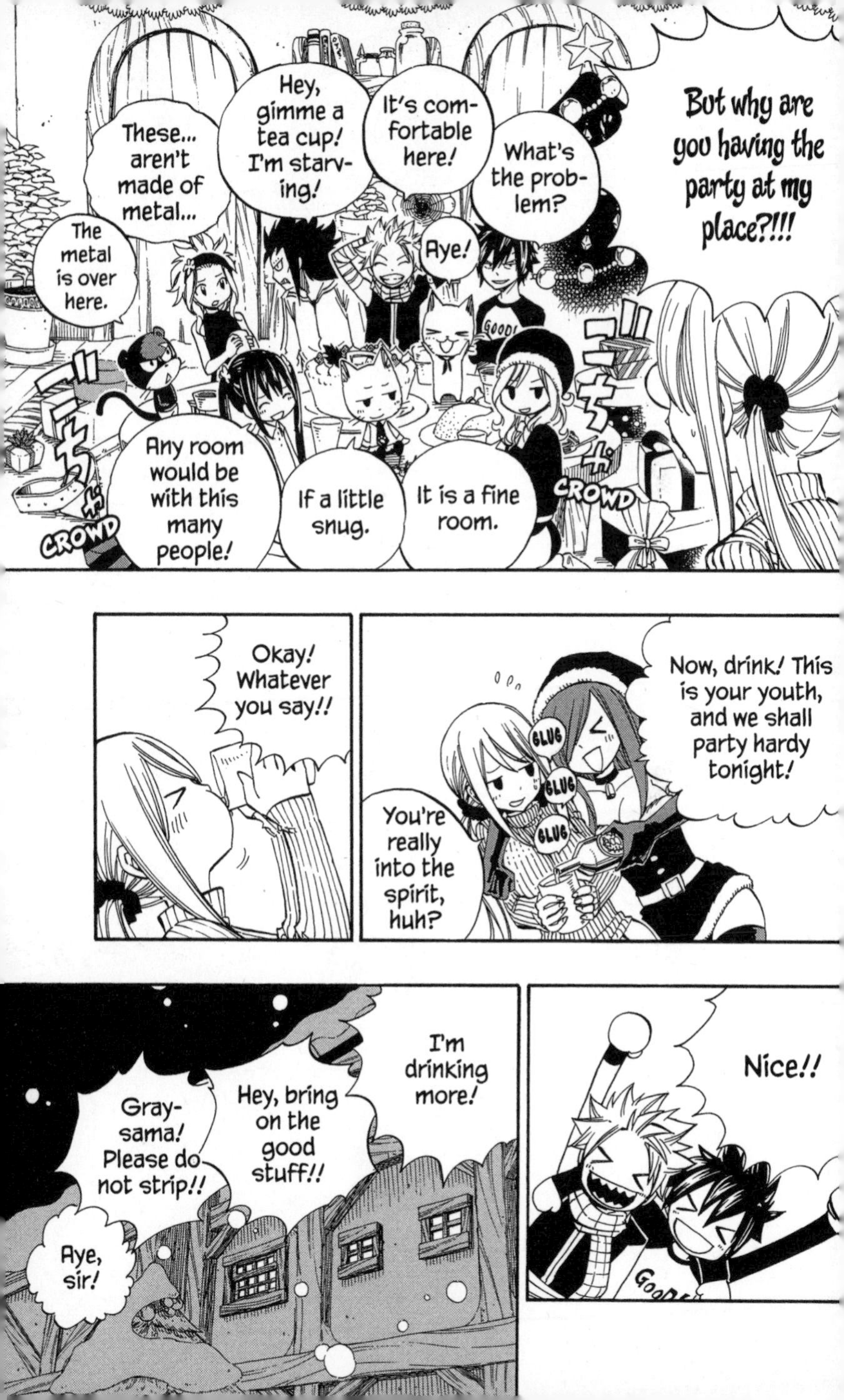

But why are you having the party at my place?!!!
What's the problem?
Aye!
It's comfortable here!
Hey, gimme a tea cup! I'm starving!
These... aren't made of metal...
The metal is over here.
CROWD
It is a fine room.
If a little snug.
Any room would be with this many people!
CROWD
Now, drink! This is your youth, and we shall party hardy tonight!
GLUG
GLUG
GLUG
You're really into the spirit, huh?
Okay! Whatever you say!!
Nice!!
I'm drinking more!
Hey, bring on the good stuff!!
Gray-sama! Please do not strip!!
Aye, sir!

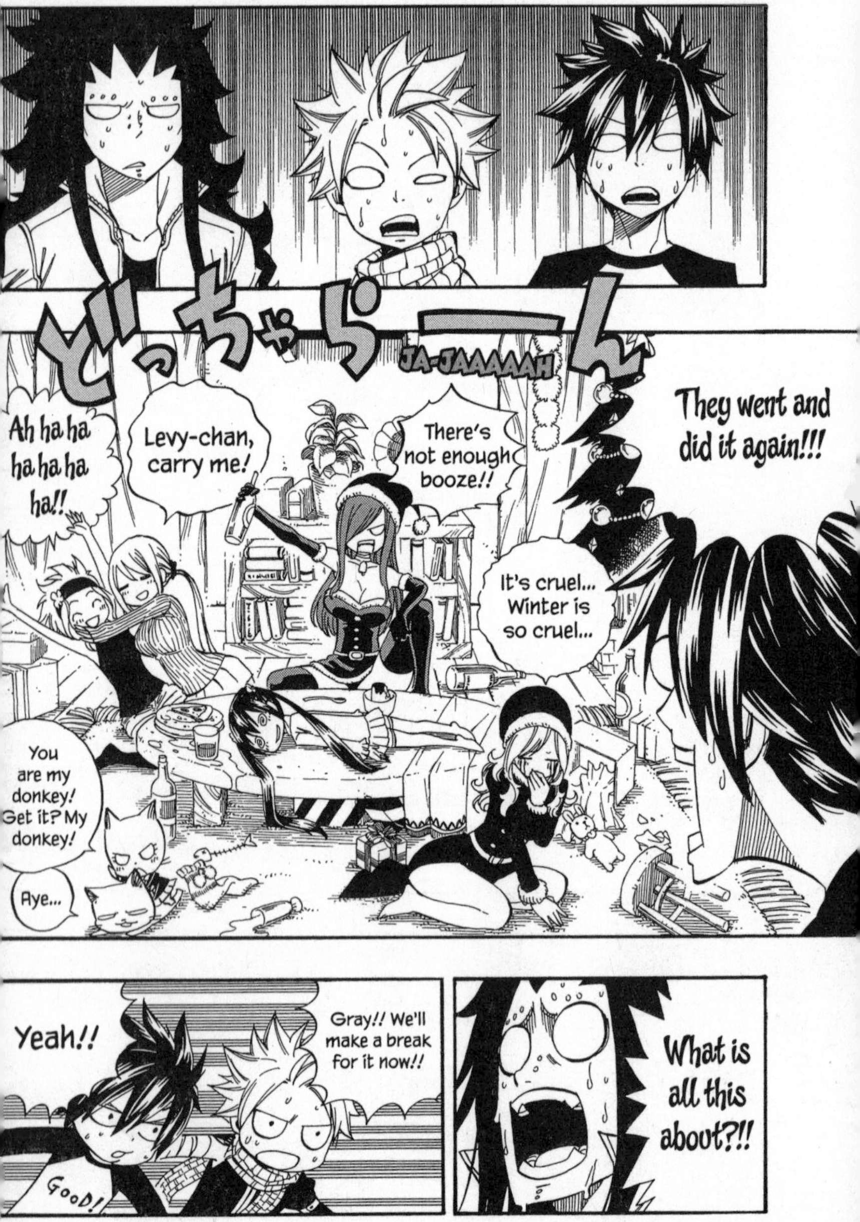
どっちゃらーーん
JA-JAAAAAH
They went and did it again!!!
It's cruel... Winter is so cruel...
There's not enough booze!!
Levy-chan, carry me!
Ah ha ha ha ha ha ha!!
You are my donkey! Get it? My donkey!
Aye...
What is all this about?!!
Gray!! We'll make a break for it now!!
Yeah!!
GOOD!

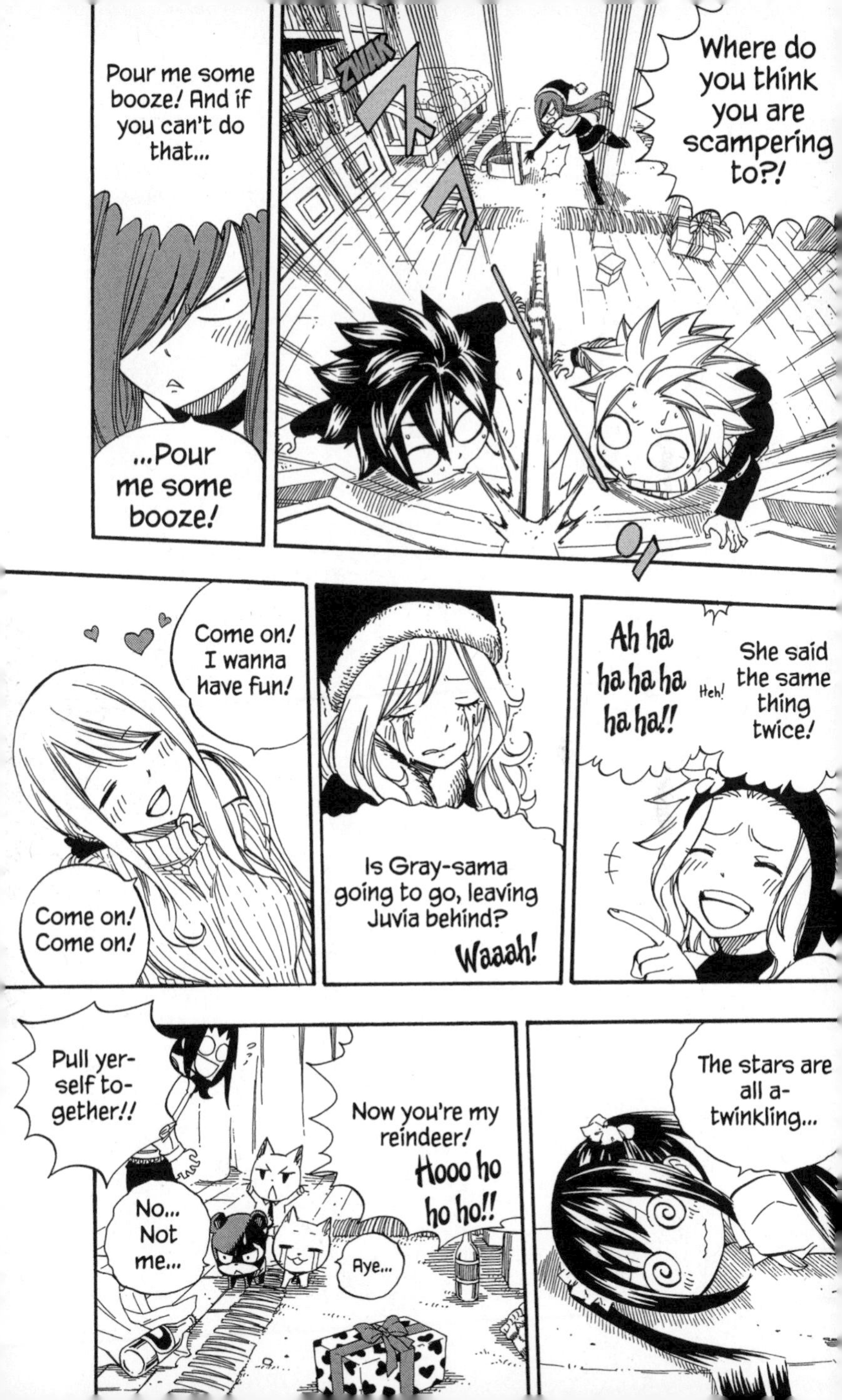
Where do you think you are scampering to?!
ZWAK
Pour me some booze! And if you can't do that...
...Pour me some booze!
She said the same thing twice!
Heh!
Ah ha ha ha ha ha ha!!
Is Gray-sama going to go, leaving Juvia behind?
Waaah!
Come on! I wanna have fun!
Come on! Come on!
The stars are all a-twinkling...
Now you're my reindeer!
Hooo ho ho ho!!
Pull yer-self to-gether!!
Aye...
No... Not me...

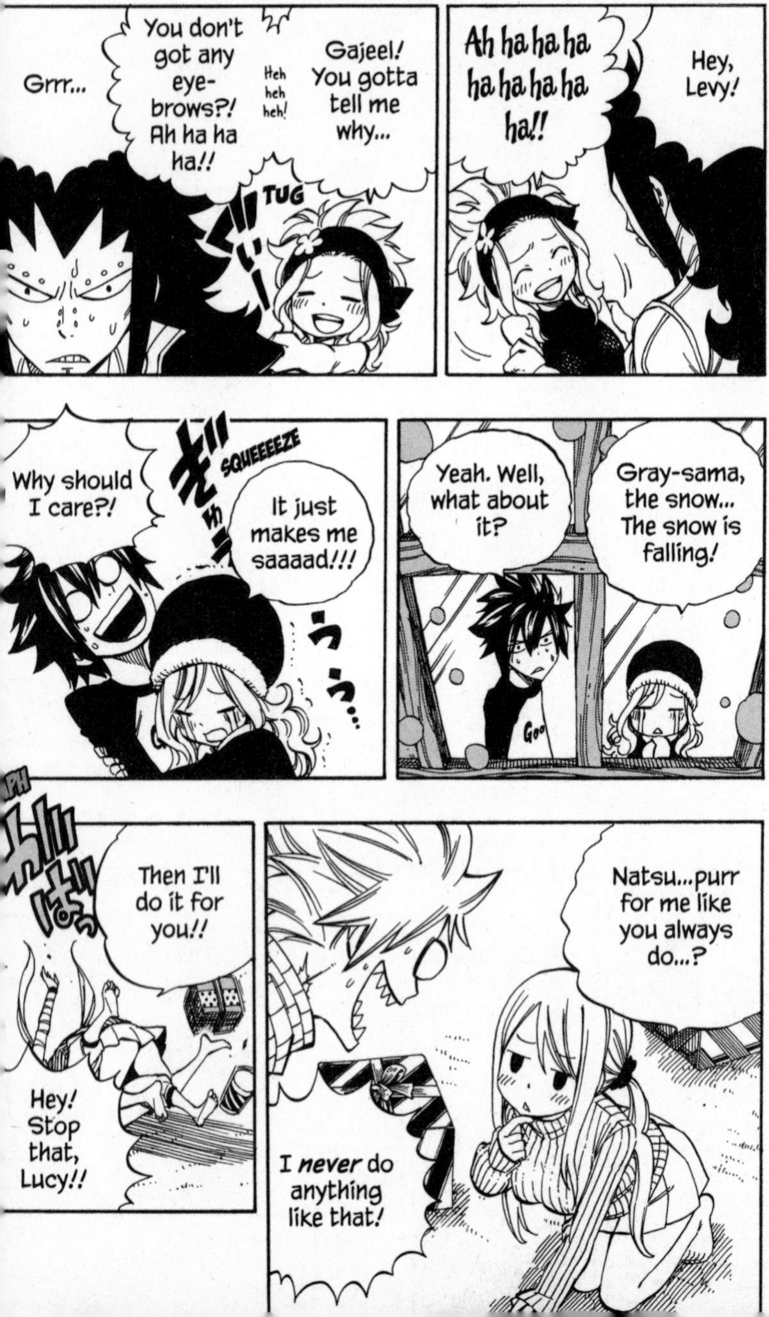
Hey, Levy!
Ah ha ha ha ha ha ha ha ha!!
Gajeel! You gotta tell me why...
Heh heh heh!
You don't got any eyebrows?! Ah ha ha ha!!
TUG
Grrr...
Gray-sama, the snow... The snow is falling!
Yeah. Well, what about it?
It just makes me saaaad!!!
SQUEEEEZE
Why should I care?!
Natsu...purr for me like you always do...?
I *never* do anything like that!
Then I'll do it for you!!
Hey! Stop that, Lucy!!

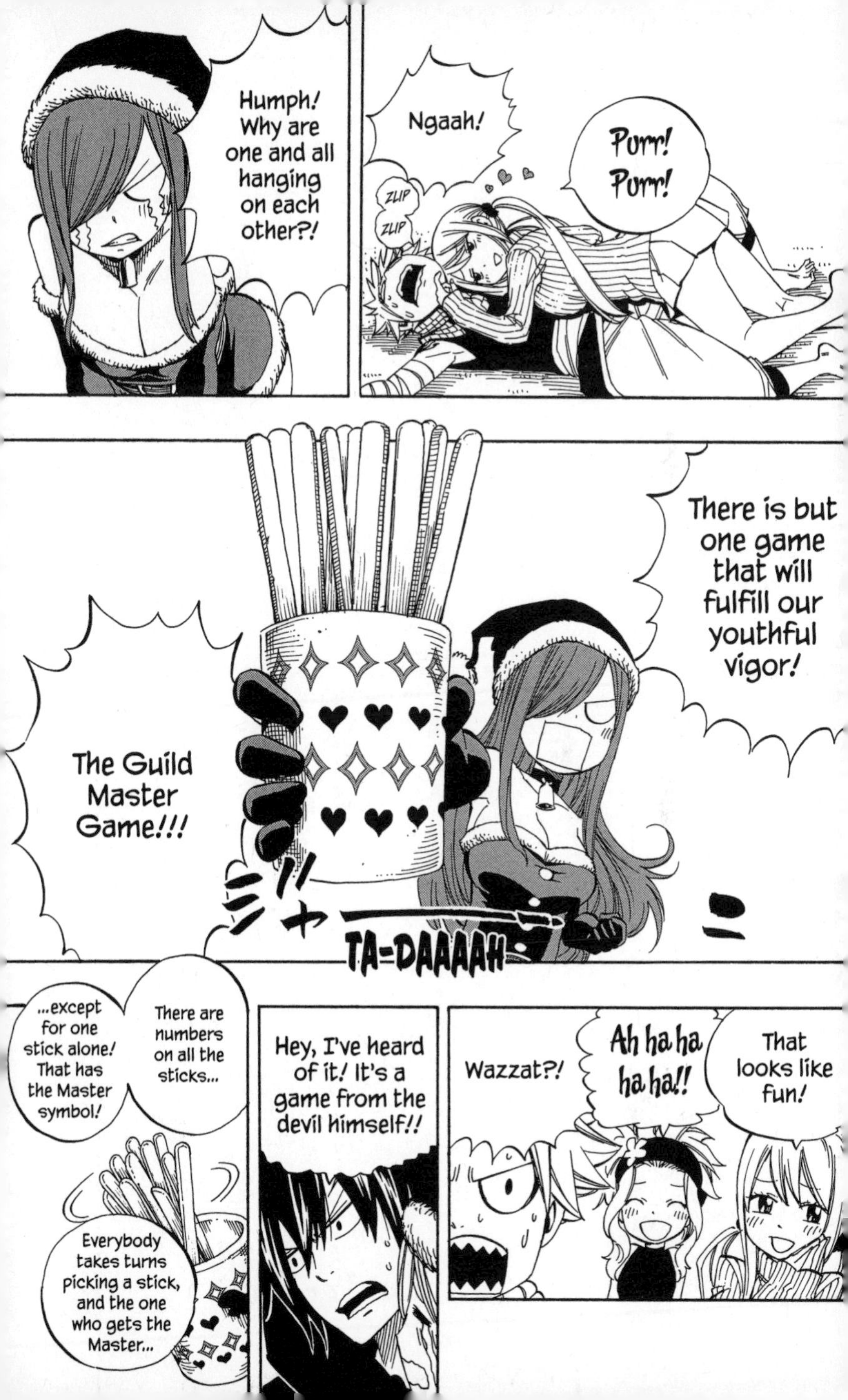
Purr! Purr!
Ngaah!
ZLIP
ZLIP
Humph! Why are one and all hanging on each other?!
There is but one game that will fulfill our youthful vigor!
The Guild Master Game!!!
TA-DAAAH
That looks like fun!
Ah ha ha ha ha!!
Wazzat?!
Hey, I've heard of it! It's a game from the devil himself!!
There are numbers on all the sticks...
...except for one stick alone! That has the Master symbol!
Everybody takes turns picking a stick, and the one who gets the Master...

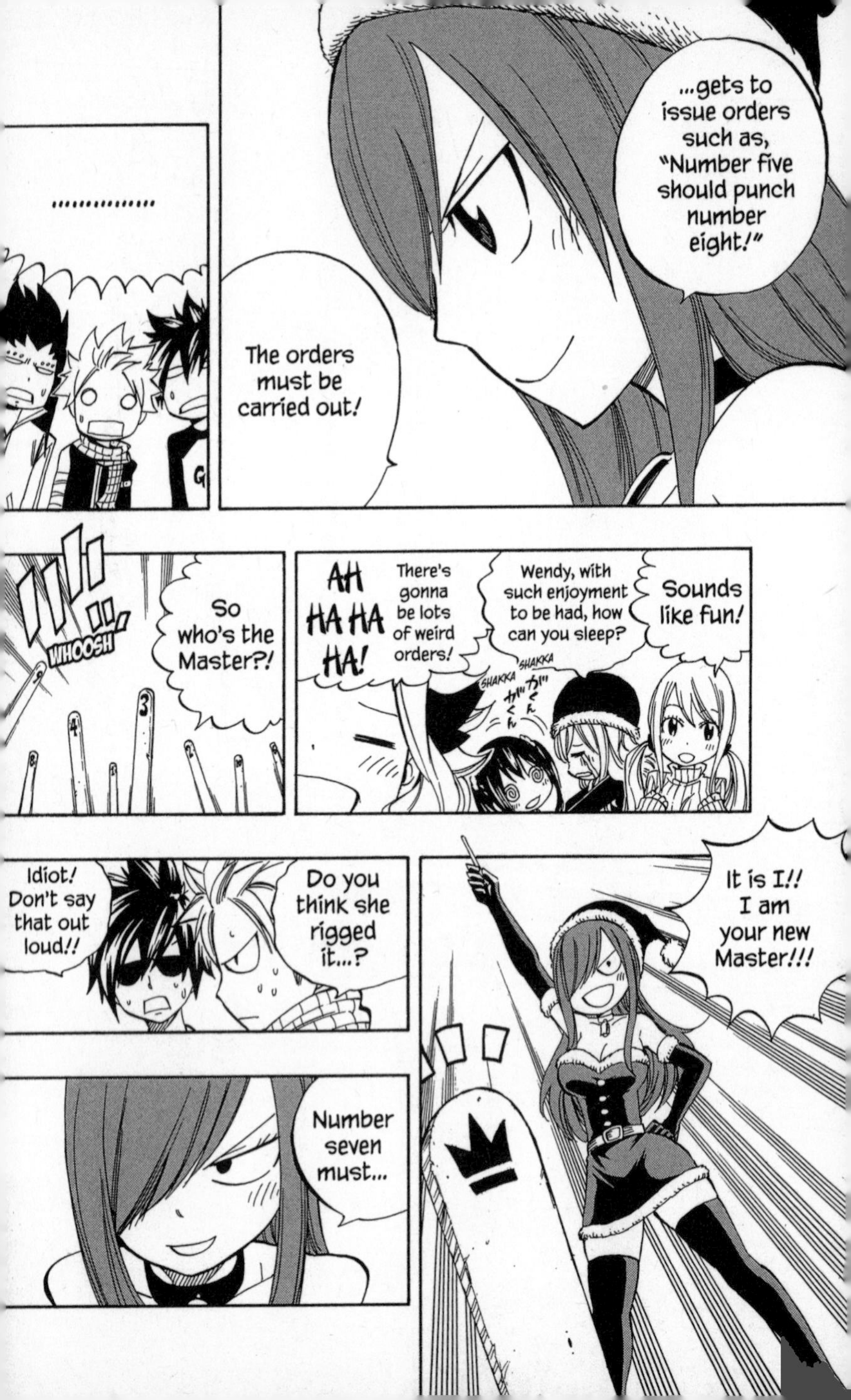
...gets to issue orders such as, "Number five should punch number eight!"
The orders must be carried out!
....
Sounds like fun!
Wendy, with such enjoyment to be had, how can you sleep?
SHAKKA
SHAKKA
There's gonna be lots of weird orders!
AH HA HA HA!
So who's the Master?!
WHOOSH
It is I!! I am your new Master!!!
Do you think she rigged it...?
Idiot! Don't say that out loud!!
Number seven must...

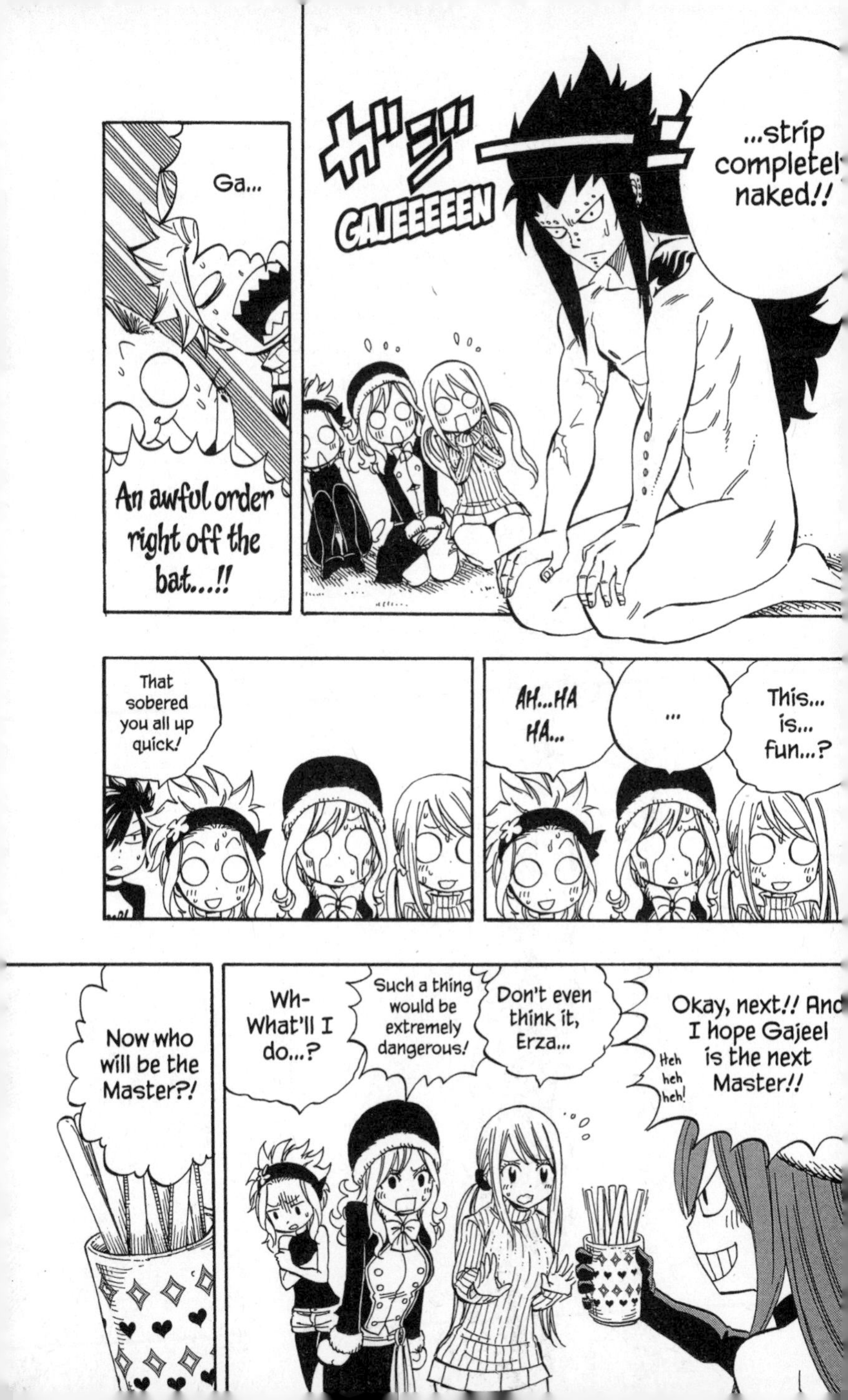
...strip completel naked!!
GAJEEEEEN
Ga...
An awful order right off the bat...!!
This... is... fun...?
...
AH...HA HA...
That sobered you all up quick!
Okay, next!! And I hope Gajeel is the next Master!!
Heh heh heh!
Don't even think it, Erza...
Such a thing would be extremely dangerous!
Wh- What'll I do...?
Now who will be the Master?!

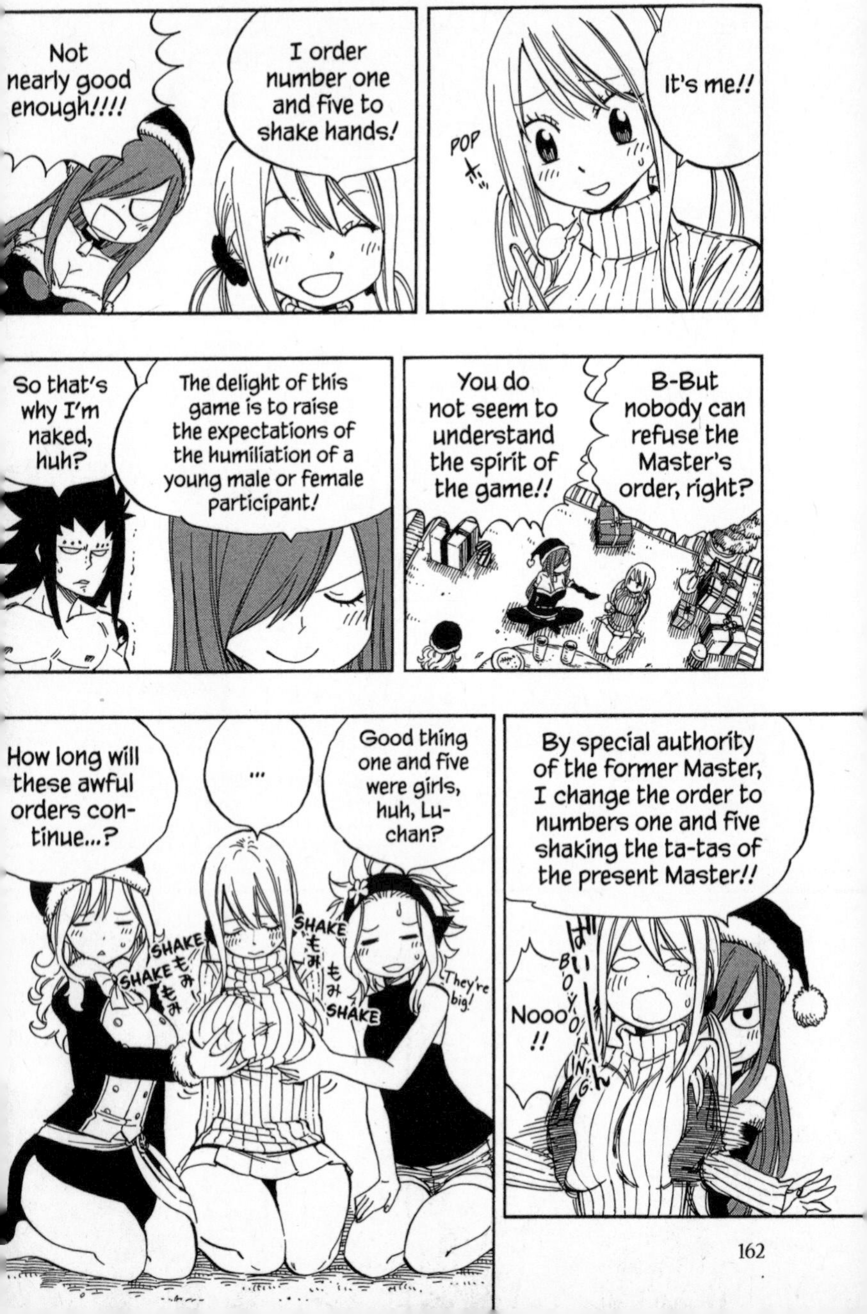
It's me!!
POP
I order number one and five to shake hands!
Not nearly good enough!!!!
B-But nobody can refuse the Master's order, right?
You do not seem to understand the spirit of the game!!
The delight of this game is to raise the expectations of the humiliation of a young male or female participant!
So that's why I'm naked, huh?
By special authority of the former Master, I change the order to numbers one and five shaking the ta-tas of the present Master!!
BOYOING
Nooo!!
Good thing one and five were girls, huh, Lu-chan?
...
How long will these awful orders con-tinue...?
SHAKE もみ
SHAKE もみ
SHAKE もみ
SHAKE もみ
They're big!

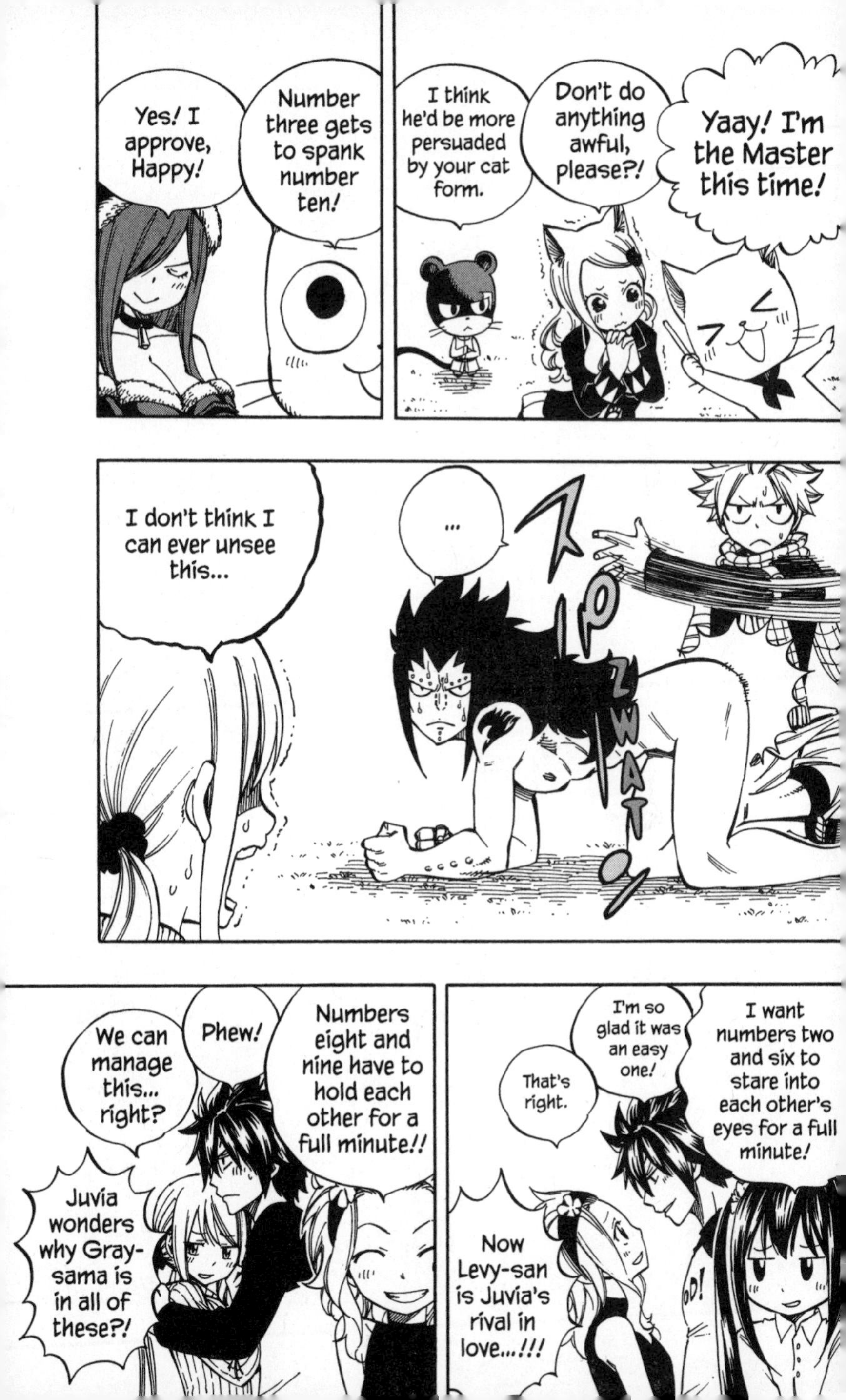

Yaay! I'm the Master this time!
Don't do anything awful, please?!
I think he'd be more persuaded by your cat form.
Number three gets to spank number ten!
Yes! I approve, Happy!
ZWAT
...
I don't think I can ever unsee this...
I want numbers two and six to stare into each other's eyes for a full minute!
I'm so glad it was an easy one!
That's right.
Now Levy-san is Juvia's rival in love...!!!
Numbers eight and nine have to hold each other for a full minute!!
Phew!
We can manage this... right?
Juvia wonders why Gray-sama is in all of these?!

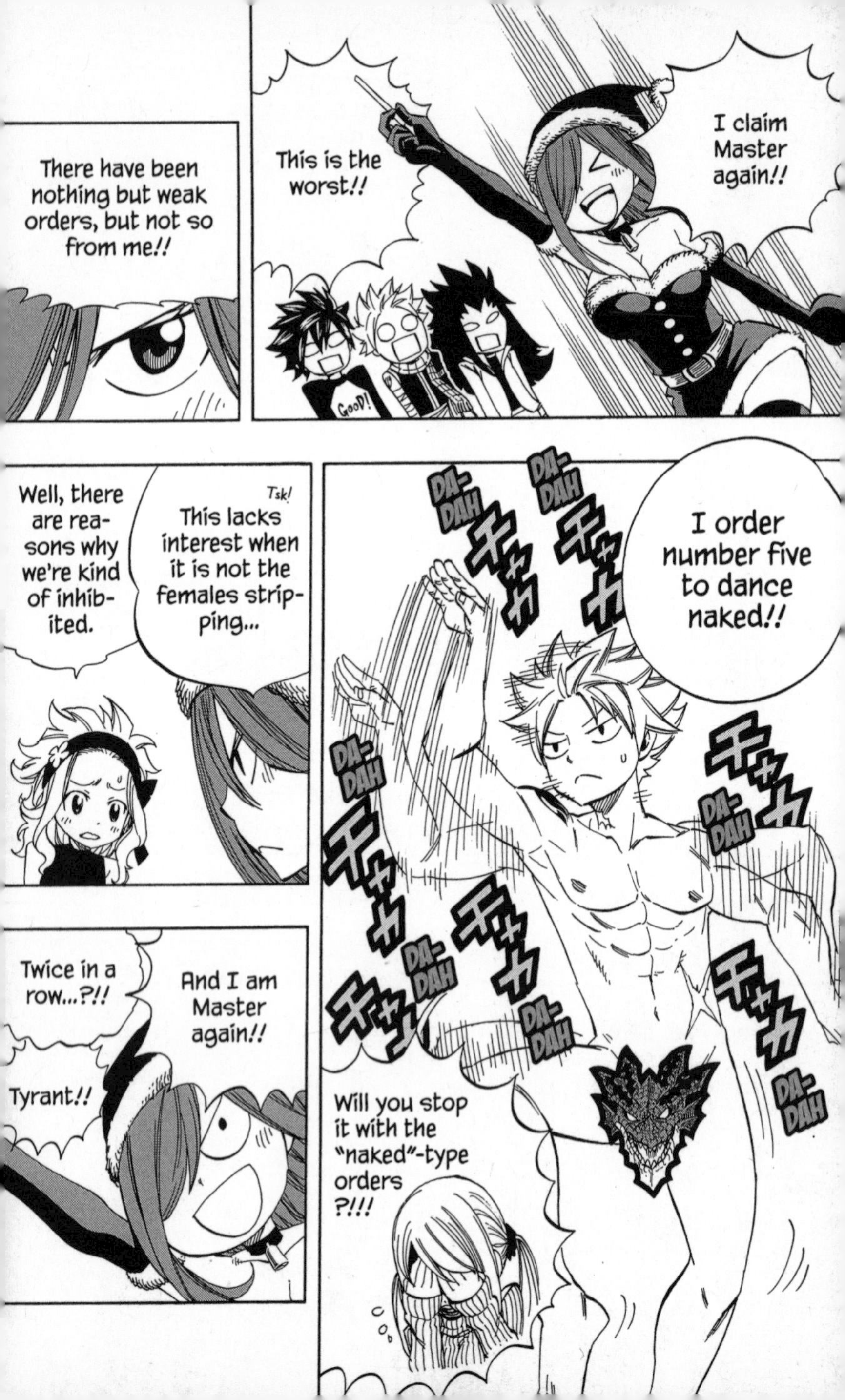
I claim Master again!!
This is the worst!!
GOOD!
There have been nothing but weak orders, but not so from me!!
I order number five to dance naked!!
DA-DAH
DA-DAH
DA-DAH
DA-DAH
DA-DAH
DA-DAH
DA-DAH
Will you stop it with the "naked"-type orders ?!!!
Tsk! This lacks interest when it is not the females stripping...
Well, there are reasons why we're kind of inhibited.
And I am Master again!!
Twice in a row...?!!
Tyrant!!

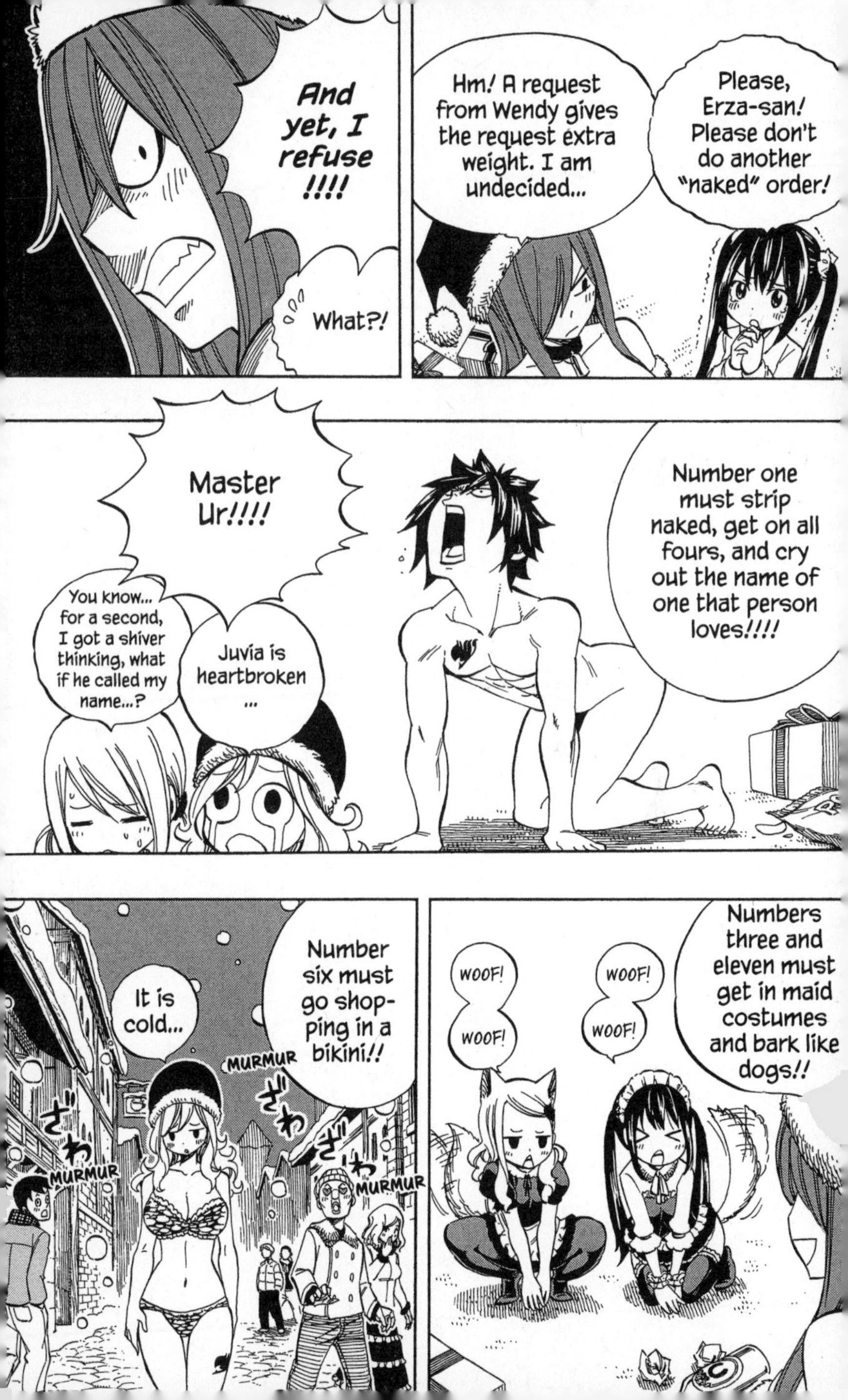
Please, Erza-san! Please don't do another "naked" order!
Hm! A request from Wendy gives the request extra weight. I am undecided...
And yet, I refuse!!!!
What?!
Number one must strip naked, get on all fours, and cry out the name of one that person loves!!!!
Master Ur!!!!
Juvia is heartbroken ...
You know... for a second, I got a shiver thinking, what if he called my name...?
Numbers three and eleven must get in maid costumes and bark like dogs!!
WOOF!
WOOF!
WOOF!
WOOF!
Number six must go shop-ping in a bikini!!
It is cold...
MURMUR
ざわ
MURMUR
ざわ
MURMUR
ざわ
MURMUR

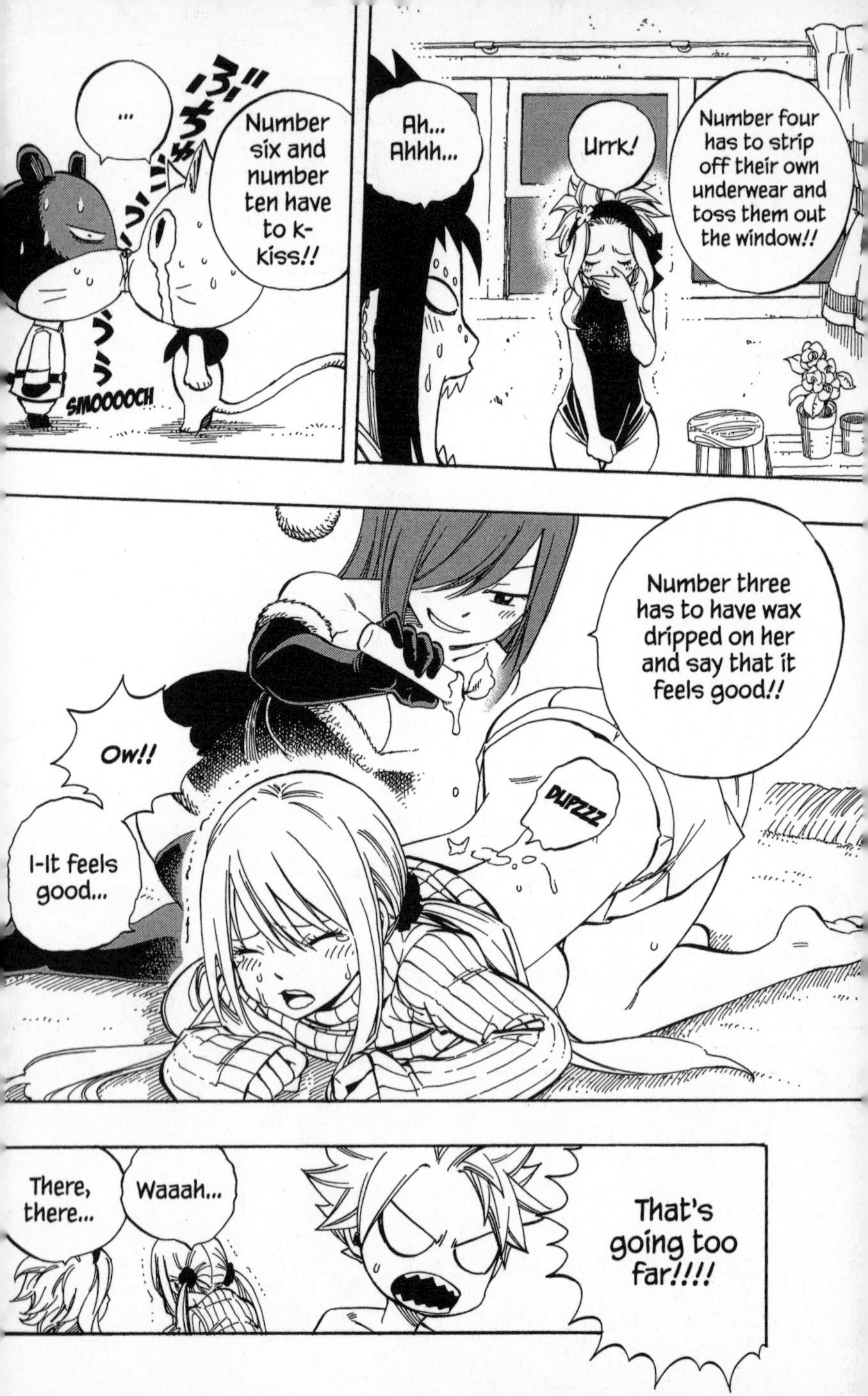
Number four has to strip off their own underwear and toss them out the window!!
Urrk!
Ah... Ahhh...
Number six and number ten have to k-kiss!!
...
SMOOOOOCH
Number three has to have wax dripped on her and say that it feels good!!
DLIPZZZ
Ow!!
I-It feels good...
That's going too far!!!!
Waaah...
There, there...

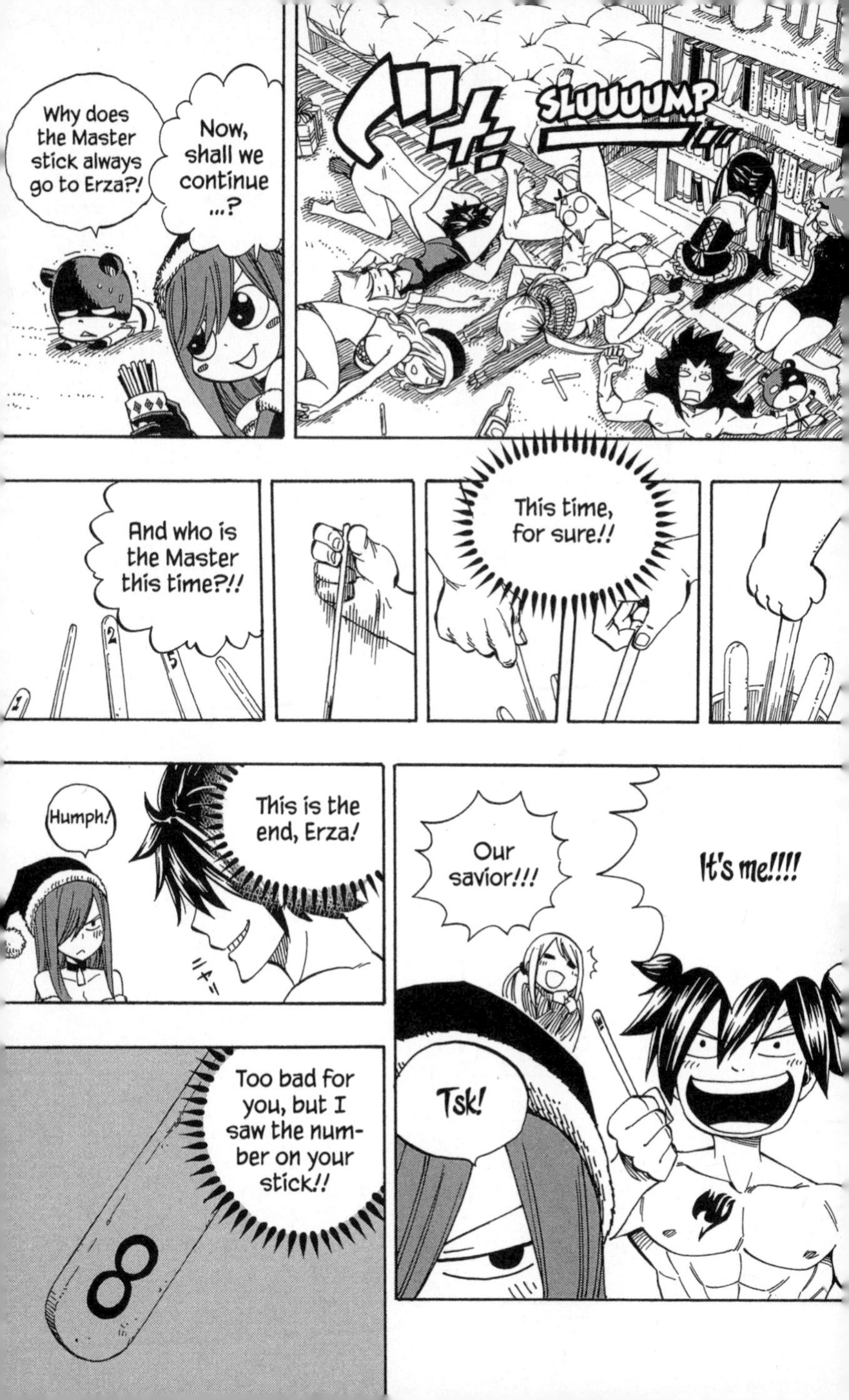

SLUUUUMP
Now, shall we continue ...?
Why does the Master stick always go to Erza?!
This time, for sure!!
And who is the Master this time?!!
It's me!!!!
Our savior!!!
Tsk!
This is the end, Erza!
Humph!
Too bad for you, but I saw the number on your stick!!

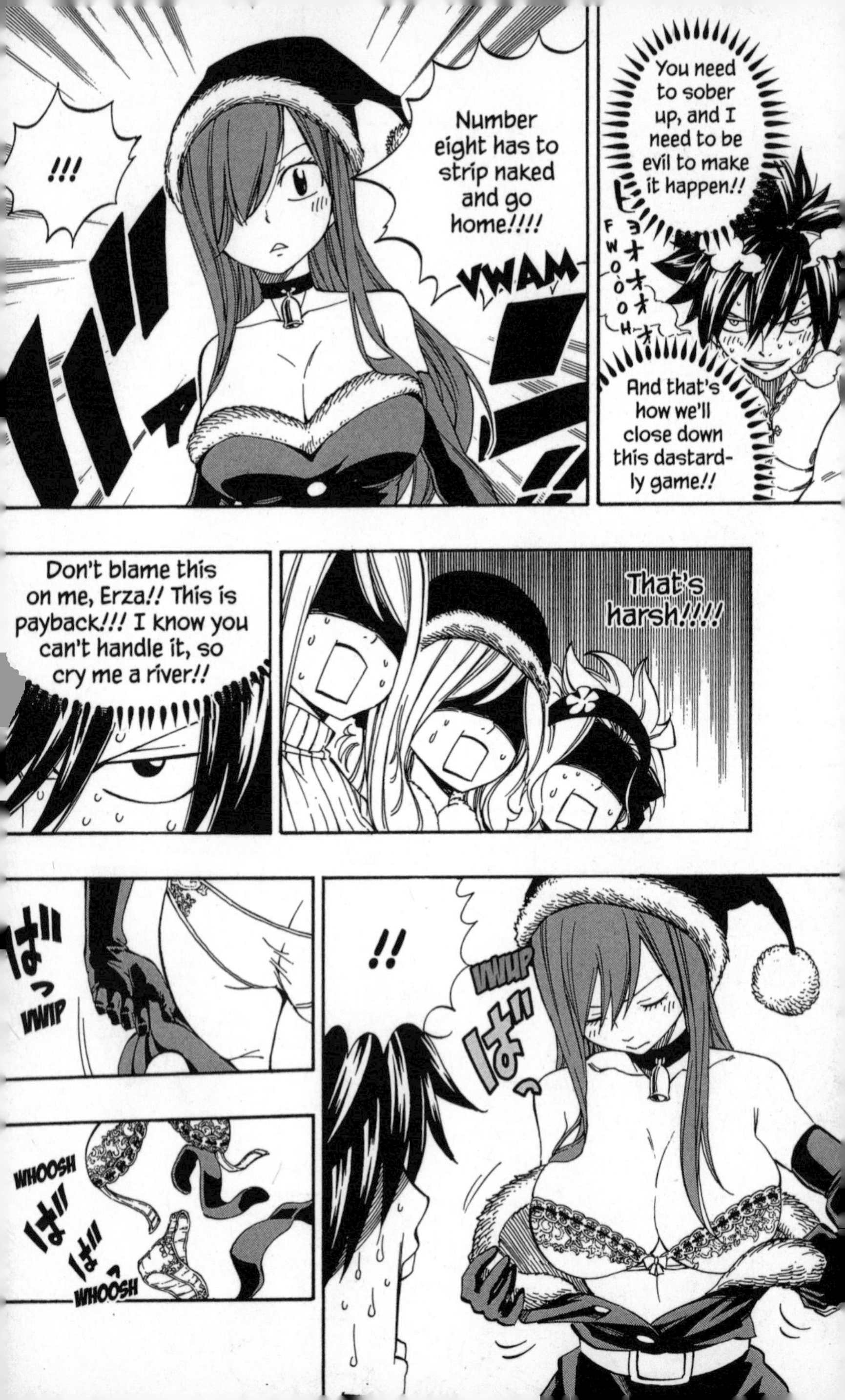
You need to sober up, and I need to be evil to make it happen!!
FWOOOH
And that's how we'll close down this dastardly game!!
Number eight has to strip naked and go home!!!!
VWAM
!!!
That's harsh!!!!
Don't blame this on me, Erza!! This is payback!!! I know you can't handle it, so cry me a river!!
!!
VWUP
VWIP
WHOOSH
WHOOSH

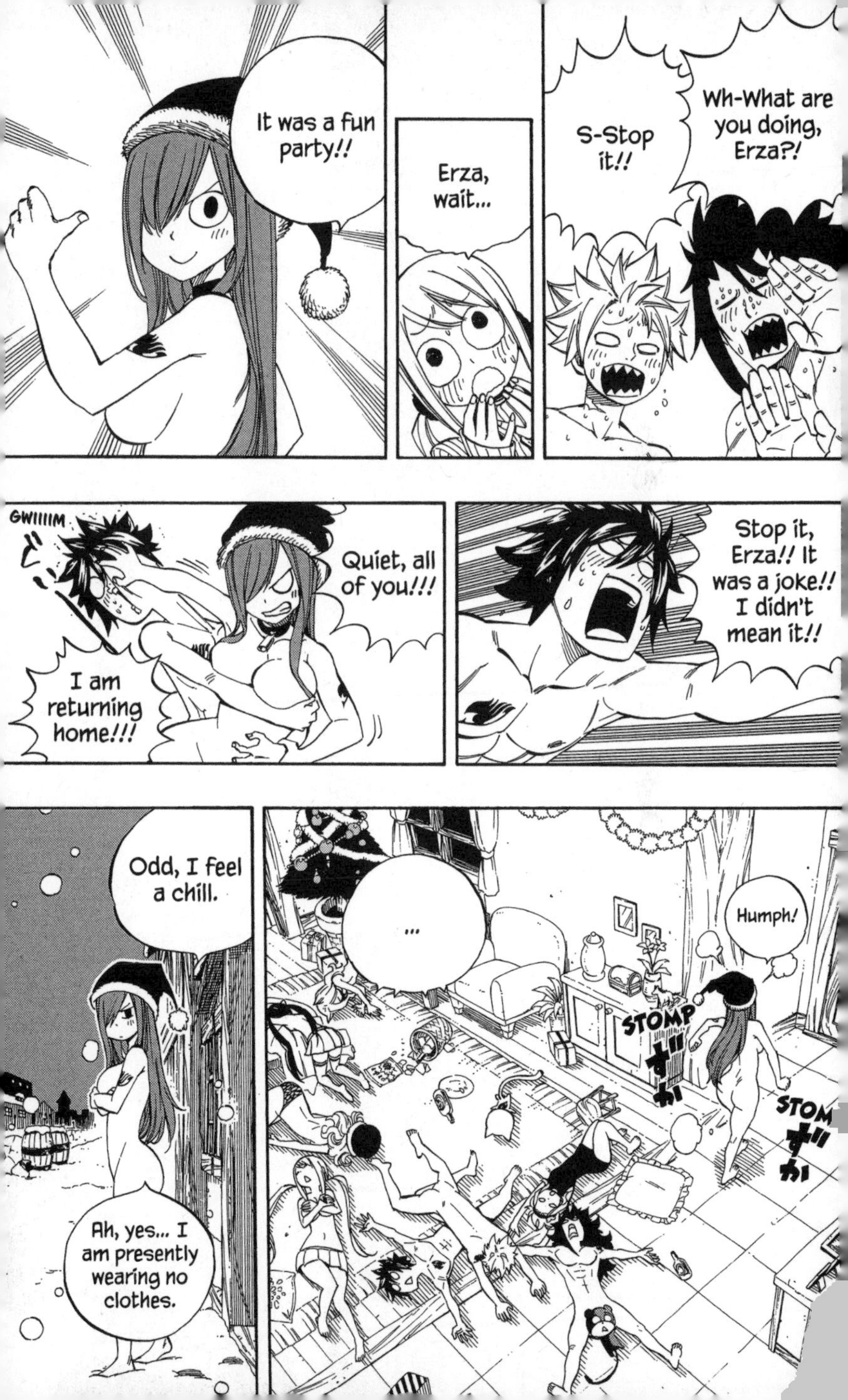
Wh-What are you doing, Erza?!
S-Stop it!!
Erza, wait...
It was a fun party!!
Stop it, Erza!! It was a joke!! I didn't mean it!!
Quiet, all of you!!!
GWIIIIM
I am returning home!!!
Humph!
...
STOMP
STOM
Odd, I feel a chill.
Ah, yes... I am presently wearing no clothes.

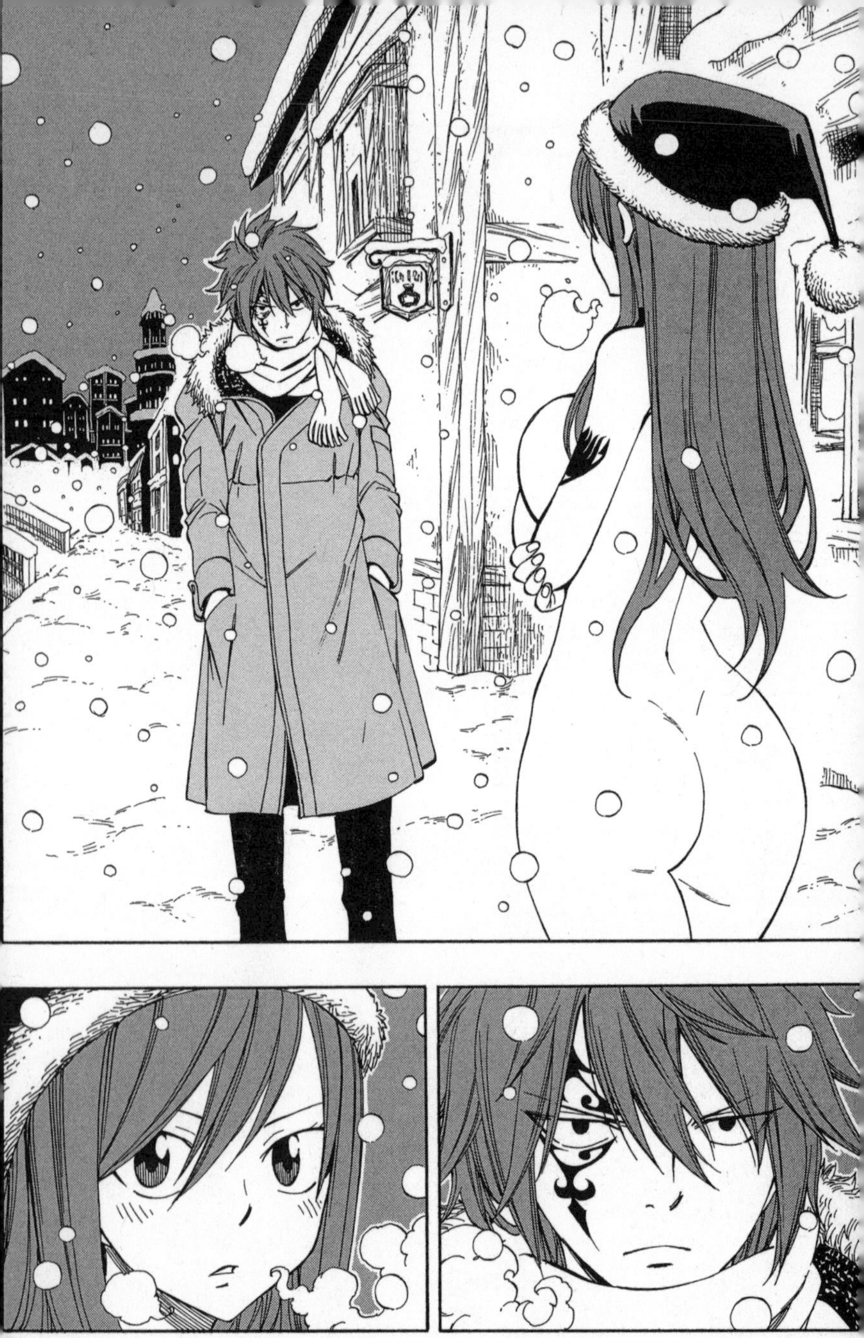

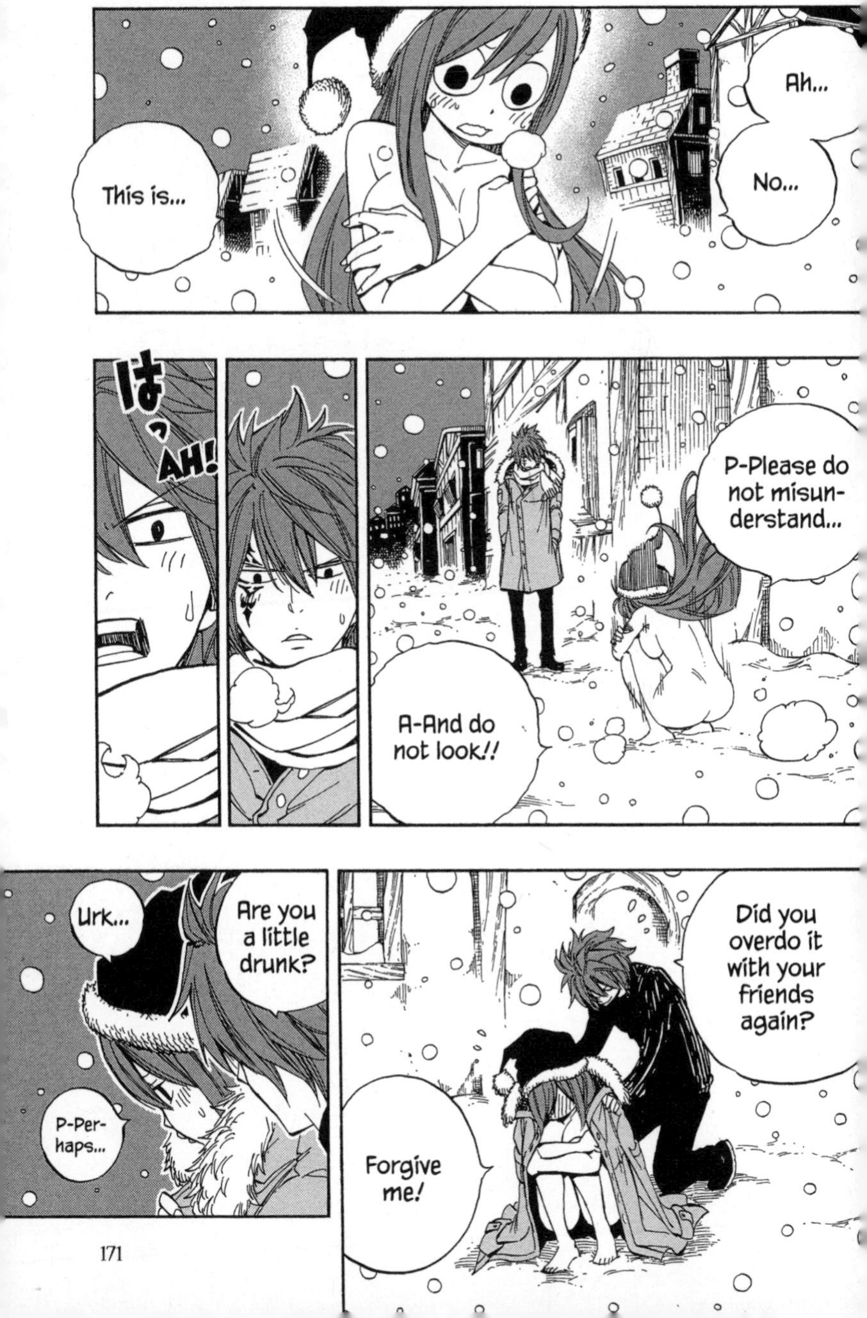
Ah...
No...
This is...
P-Please do not misunderstand...
A-And do not look!!
はっ
AH!
Did you overdo it with your friends again?
Forgive me!
Are you a little drunk?
Urk...
P-Perhaps...

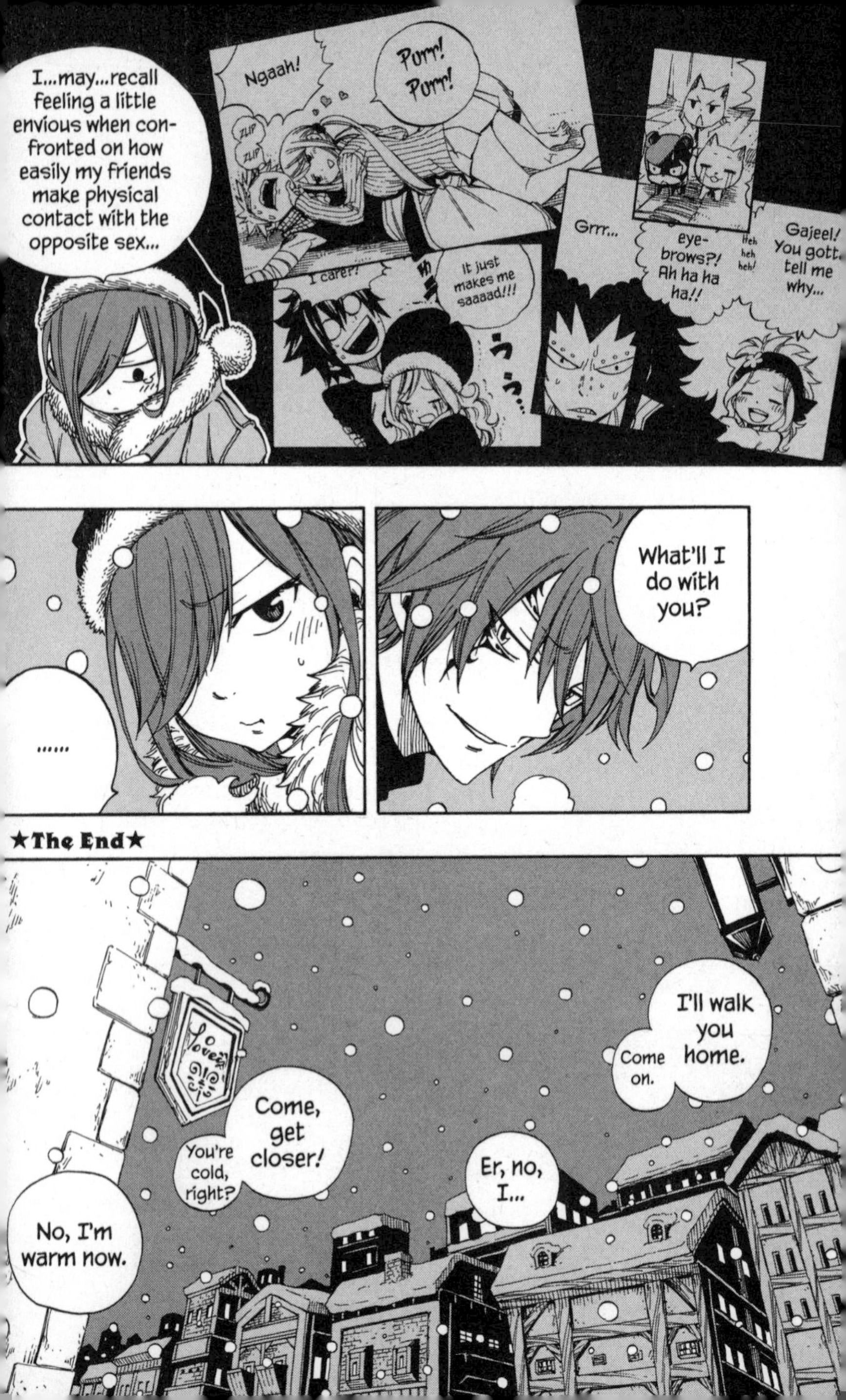
Purr! Purr!
Ngaah!
ZLIP
ZLIP
Gajeel! You gott. tell me why...
Heh heh heh!
eye-brows?! Ah ha ha ha!!
Grrr...
It just makes me saaaad!!!
I care?!
I...may...recall feeling a little envious when con-fronted on how easily my friends make physical contact with the opposite sex...
What'll I do with you?
......
★The End★
I'll walk you home.
Come on.
Er, no, I...
Come, get closer!
You're cold, right?
No, I'm warm now.

FOUR-PANEL COMICS!

SUBJECT: AMBITIONS & DREAMS

WRITER'S NOTEBOOK

Oh, no! I dropped my writer's notebook!
It's filled with ideas that are keys to my dreams and goals!
HEE HEE!
Wa ha ha ha ha!!
Ah!! That's it!!!
But...I don't remember writing anything that funny in it...
Relax! I switched it out for an album of you in your costumes!
What's that sup-posed t'be?!
Hard on the eyes!!
Why can't you just give it back?!

FROM *MAGAZINE SPECIAL*, 2014, ISSUE 1.

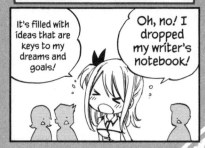

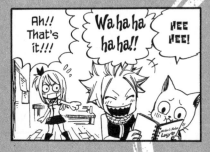

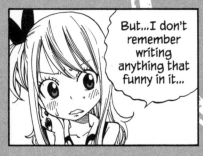

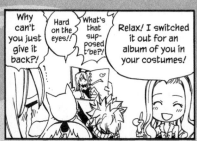

FT☆S

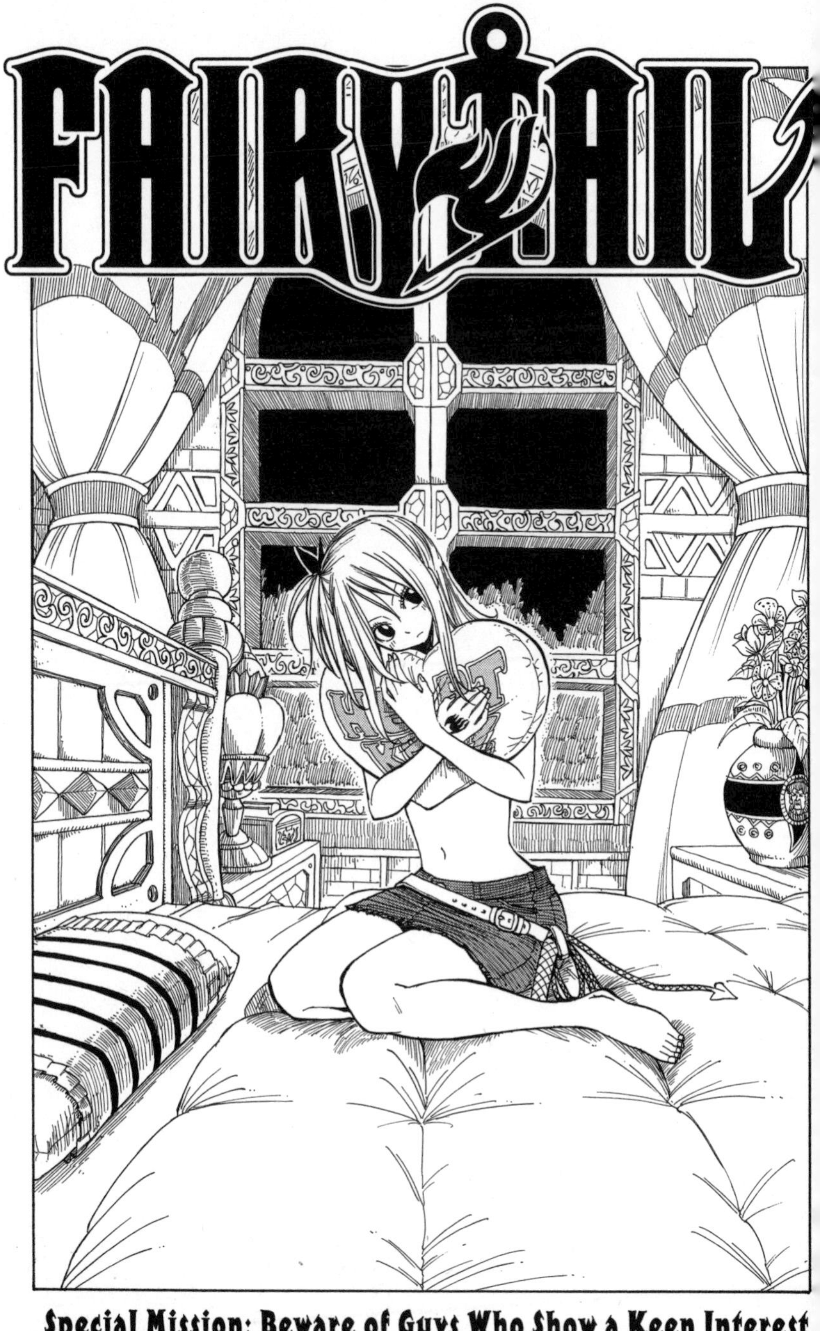
FAIRY TAIL

Special Mission: Beware of Guys Who Show a Keen Interest

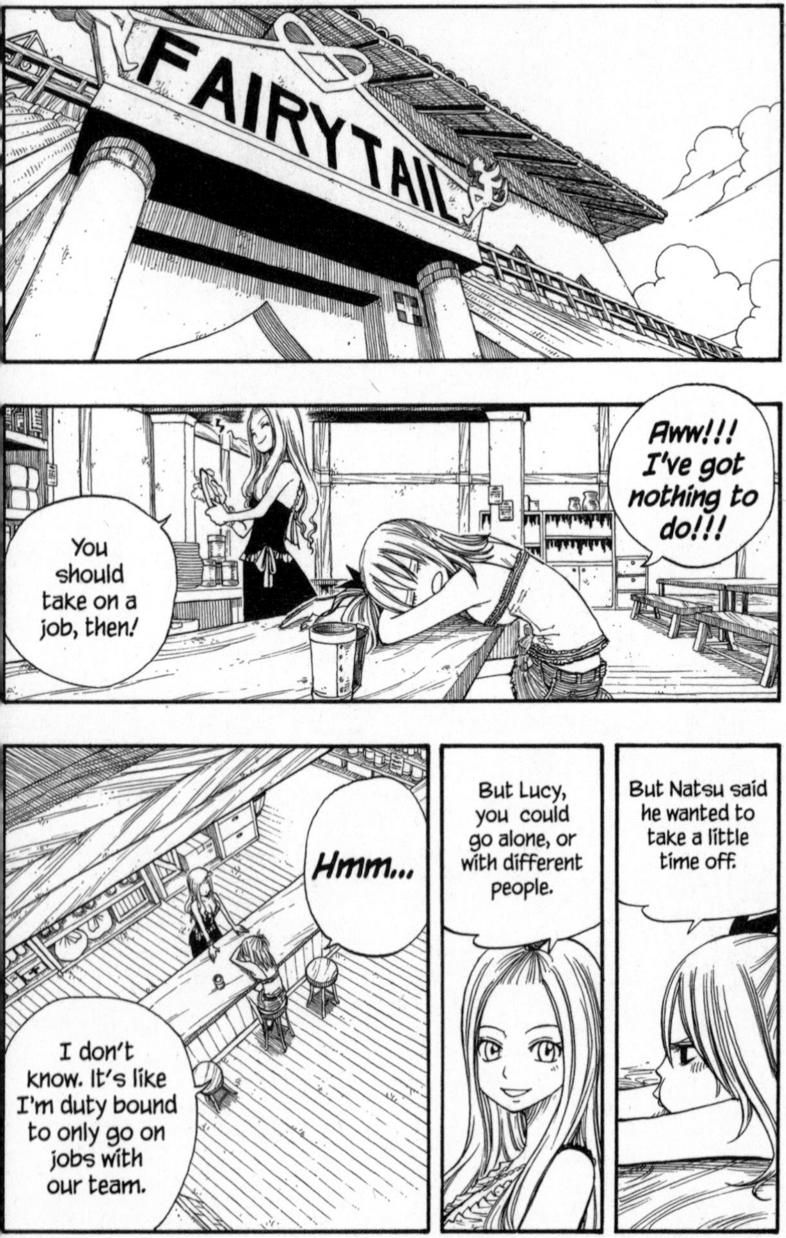
FAIRYTAIL
Aww!!! I've got nothing to do!!!
You should take on a job, then!
But Natsu said he wanted to take a little time off.
But Lucy, you could go alone, or with different people.
Hmm...
I don't know. It's like I'm duty bound to only go on jobs with our team.

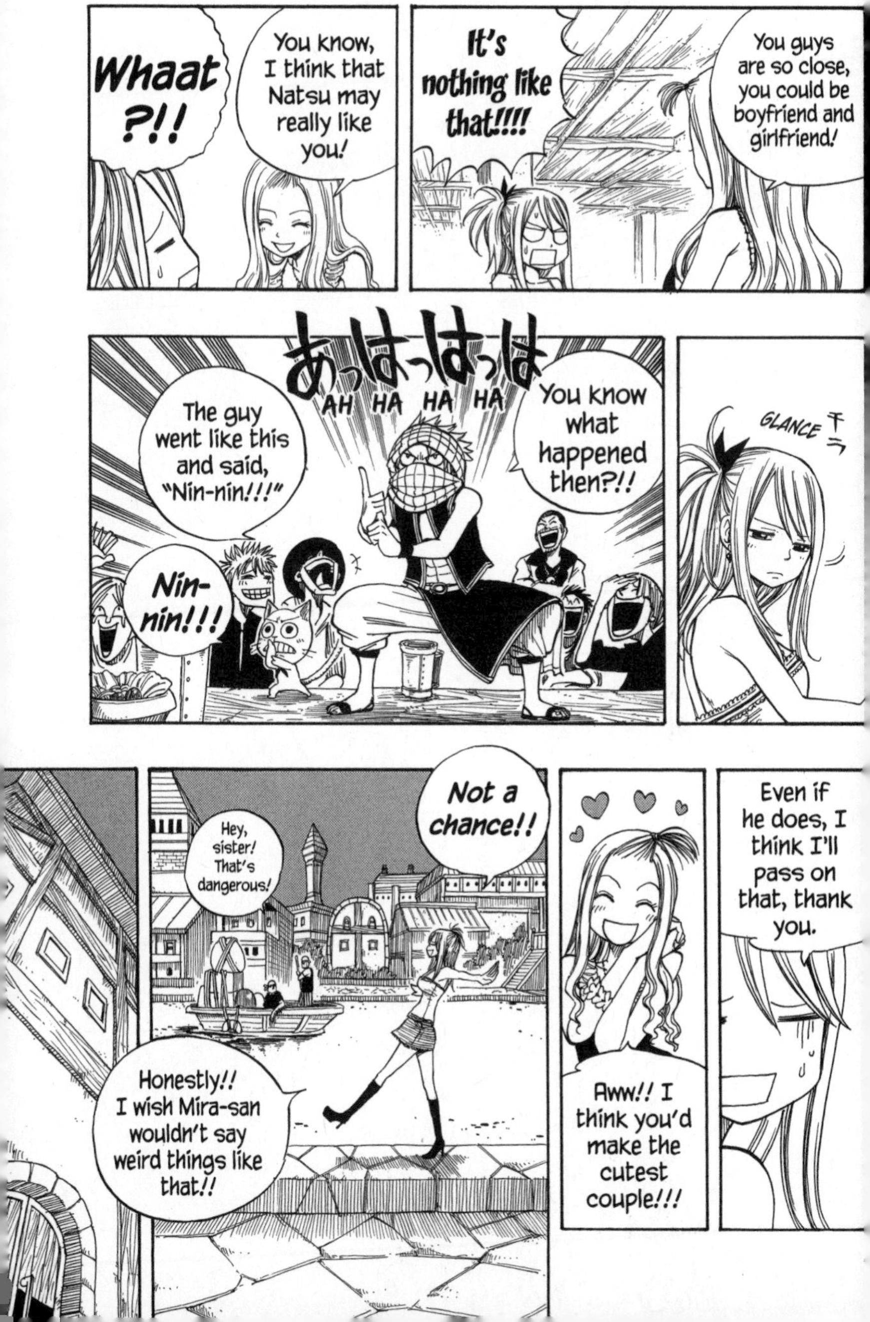
You guys are so close, you could be boyfriend and girlfriend!
It's nothing like that!!!!
You know, I think that Natsu may really like you!
Whaat ?!!
GLANCE チラ
あっはっはっは
AH HA HA HA
You know what happened then?!!
The guy went like this and said, "Nin-nin!!!"
Nin-nin!!!
Even if he does, I think I'll pass on that, thank you.
Aww!! I think you'd make the cutest couple!!!
Not a chance!!
Hey, sister! That's dangerous!
Honestly!! I wish Mira-san wouldn't say weird things like that!!

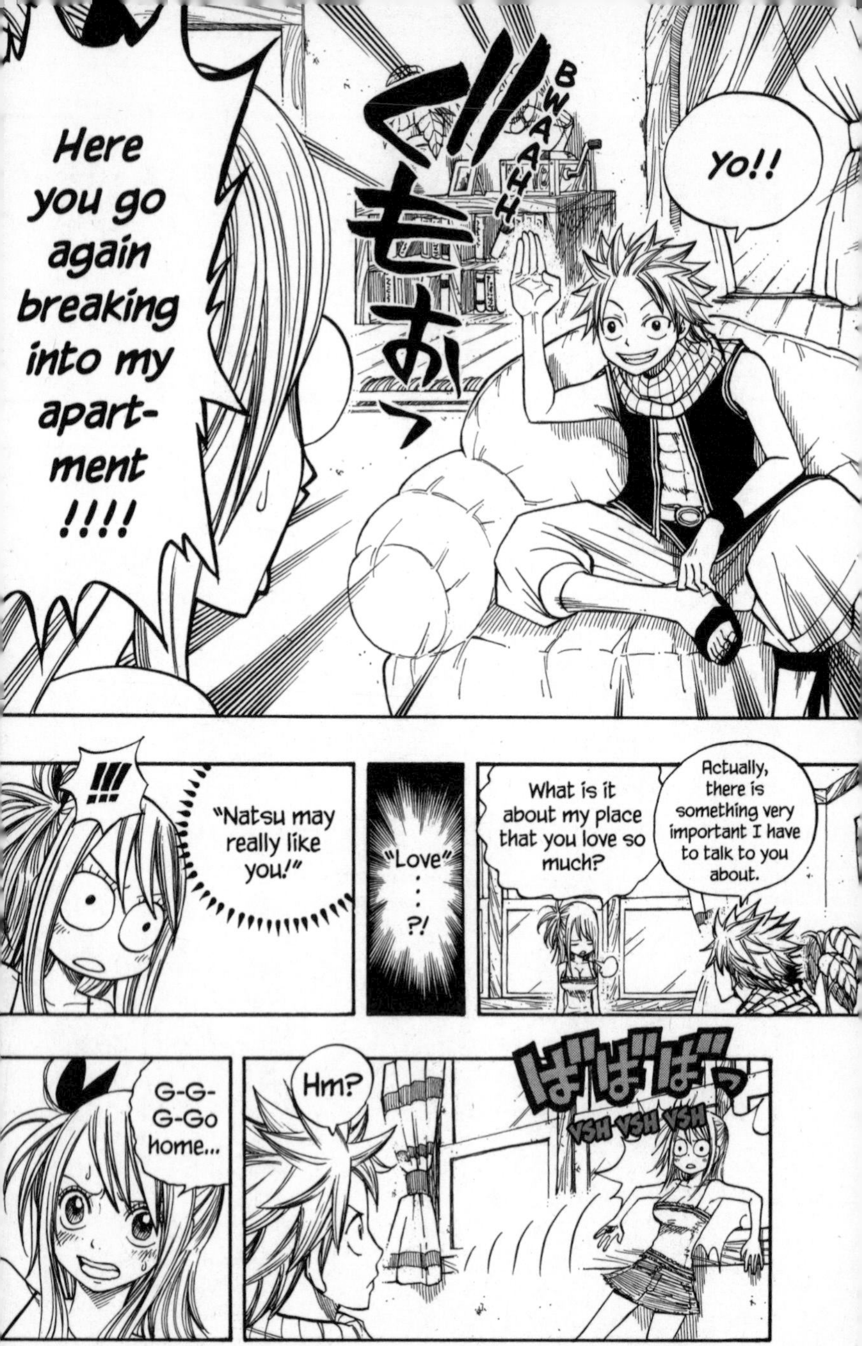
Yo!!
BWAAHH
Here you go again breaking into my apartment!!!!
Actually, there is something very important I have to talk to you about.
What is it about my place that you love so much?
"Love" . . . ?!
"Natsu may really like you!"
!!!
ばばばっ
VSH VSH VSH
Hm?
G-G-G-Go home...

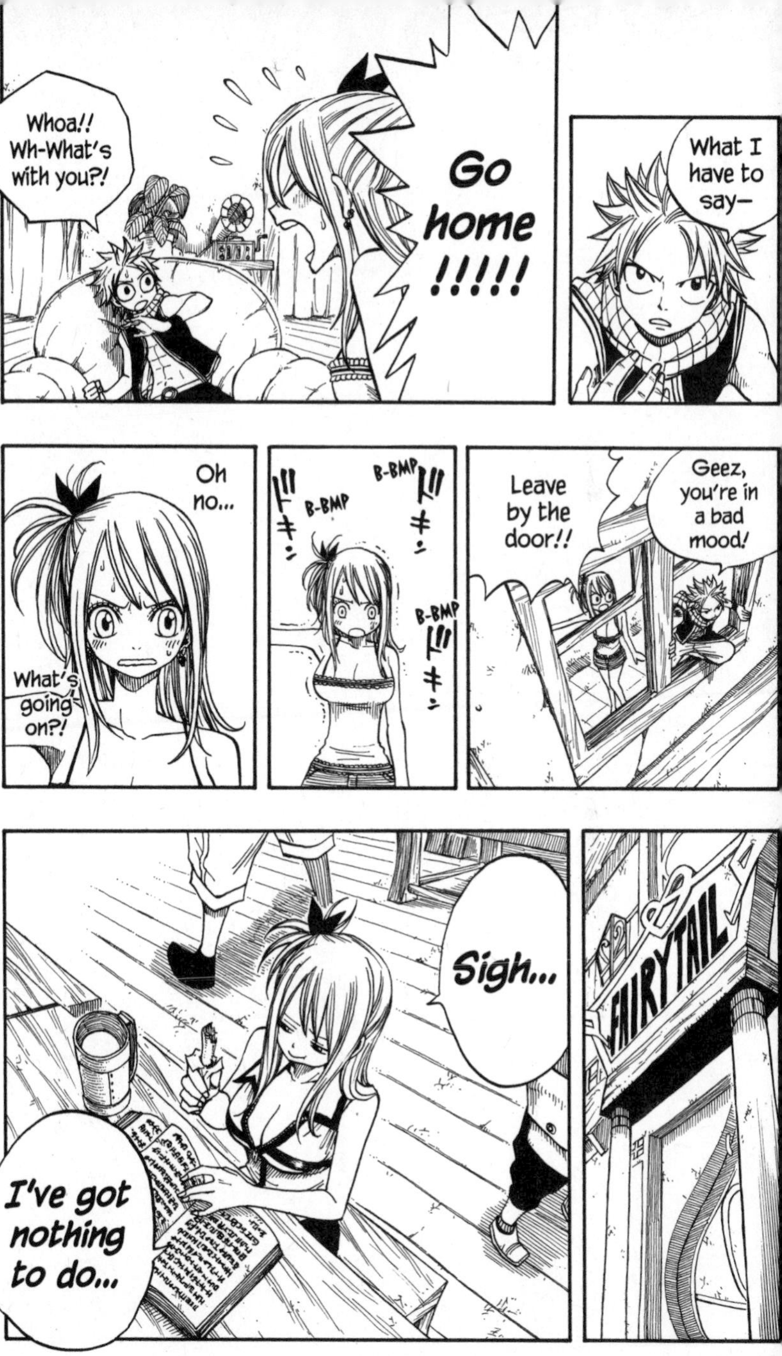
What I have to say—
Go home!!!!!
Whoa!! Wh-What's with you?!
Geez, you're in a bad mood!
Leave by the door!!
B-BMP
ドキン
B-BMP
B-BMP
ドキン
ドキン
Oh no...
What's going on?!
FAIRY TAIL
Sigh...
I've got nothing to do...

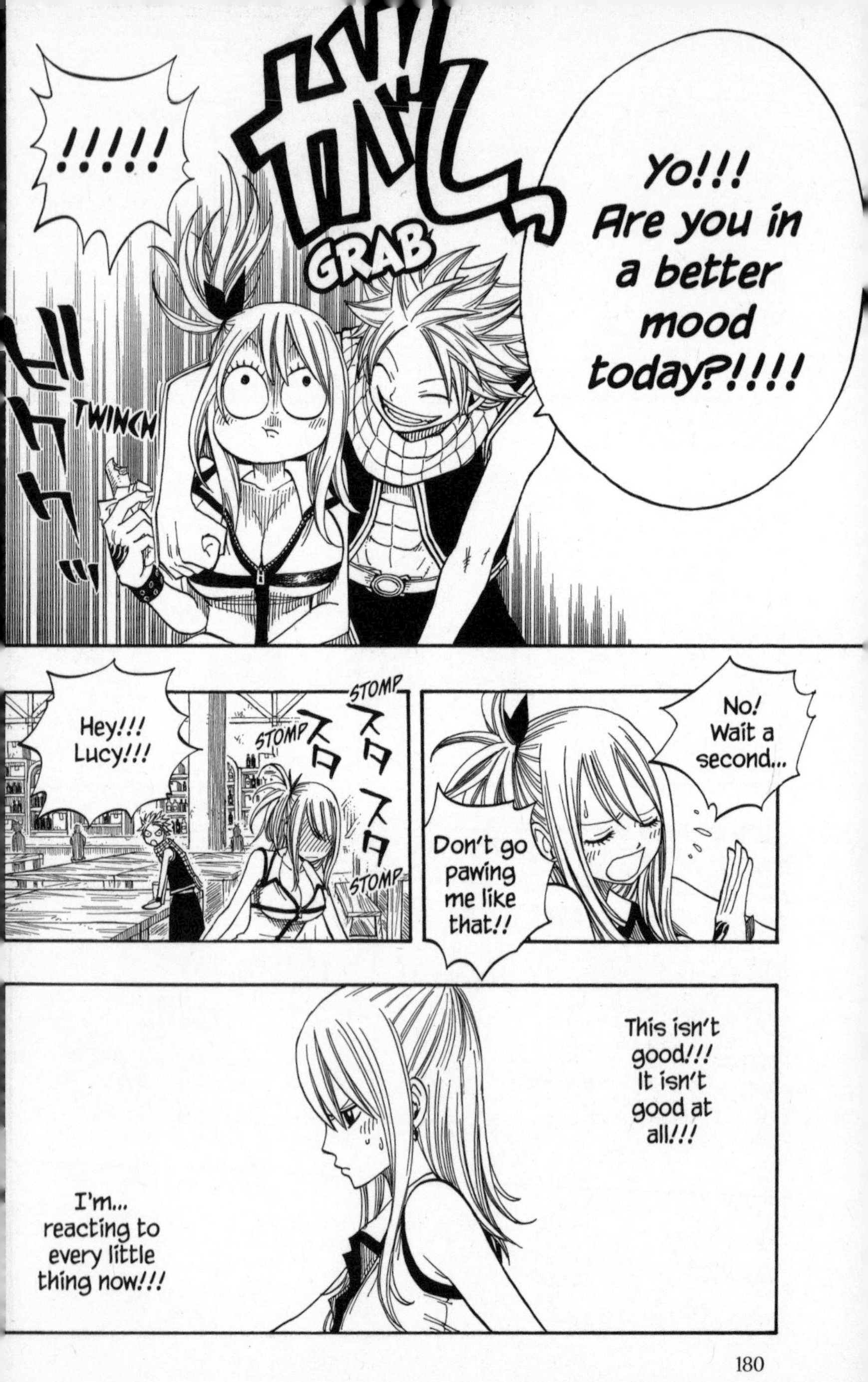
Yo!!! Are you in a better mood today?!!!!
GRAB
!!!!!
TWINCH
No! Wait a second...
Don't go pawing me like that!!
STOMP
STOMP
STOMP
Hey!!! Lucy!!!
This isn't good!!! It isn't good at all!!!
I'm... reacting to every little thing now!!!

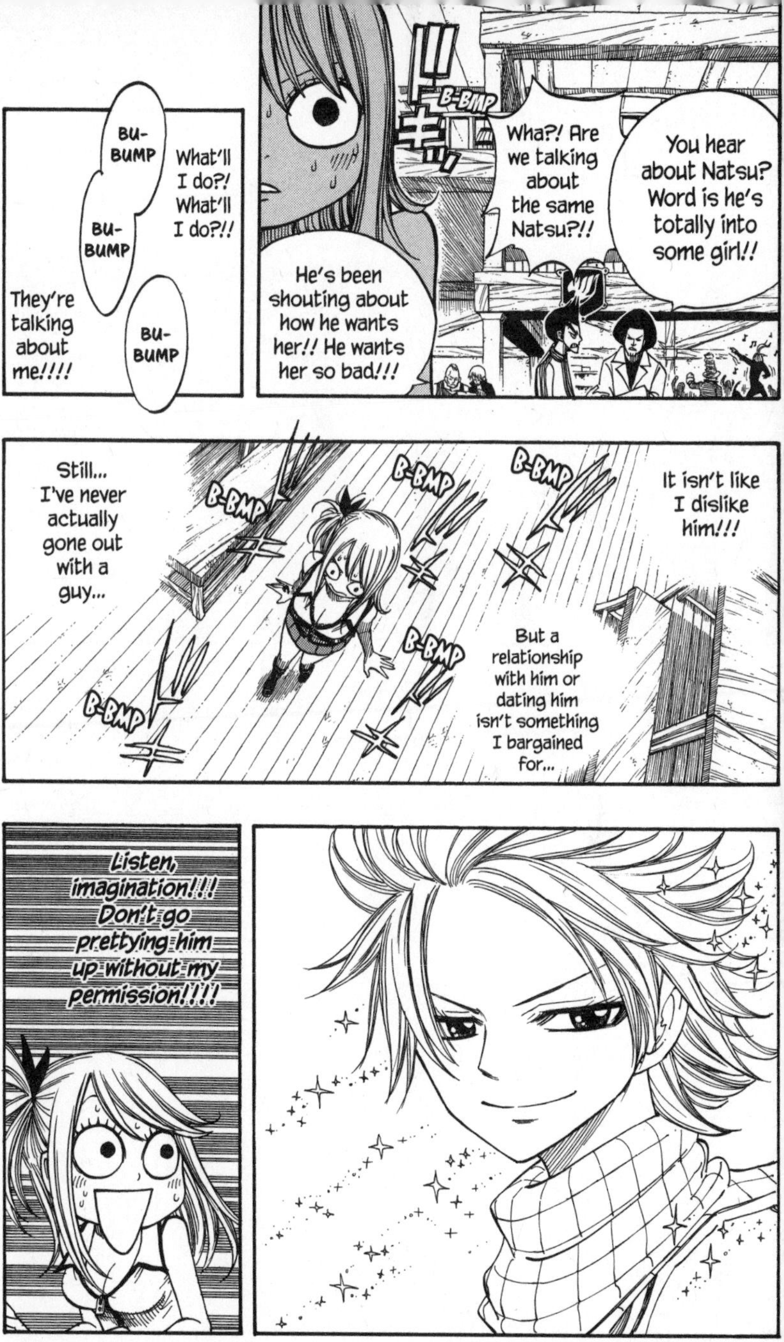
You hear about Natsu? Word is he's totally into some girl!!
Wha?! Are we talking about the same Natsu?!!
B-BMP
He's been shouting about how he wants her!! He wants her so bad!!!
What'll I do?! What'll I do?!!
BU-BUMP
BU-BUMP
BU-BUMP
They're talking about me!!!!
It isn't like I dislike him!!!
B-BMP
B-BMP
B-BMP
But a relationship with him or dating him isn't something I bargained for...
B-BMP
Still... I've never actually gone out with a guy...
B-BMP
Listen, imagination!!! Don't go prettying him up without my permission!!!!

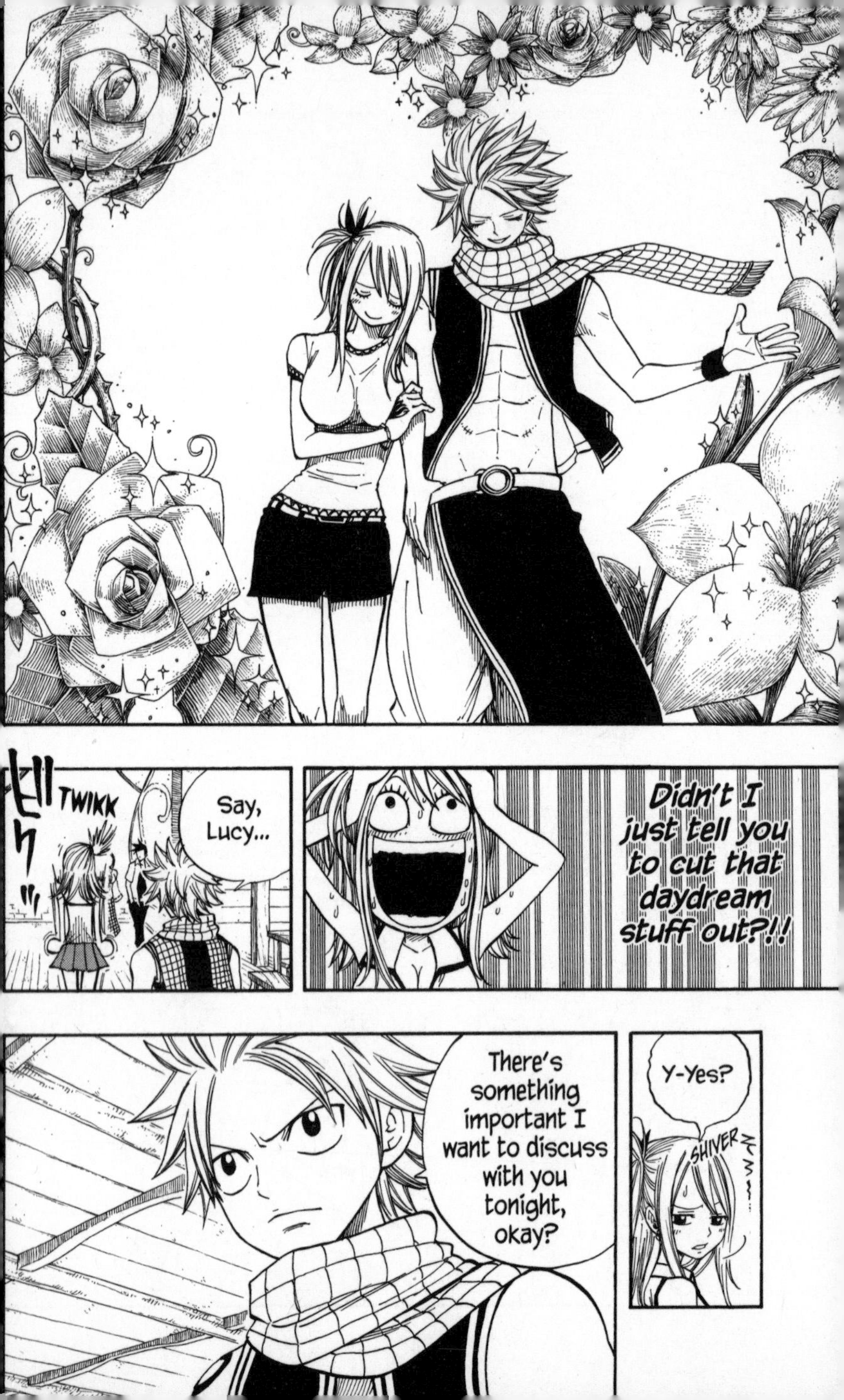

Didn't I just tell you to cut that daydream stuff out?!!
Say, Lucy...
TWIKK
Y-Yes?
SHIVER
There's something important I want to discuss with you tonight, okay?

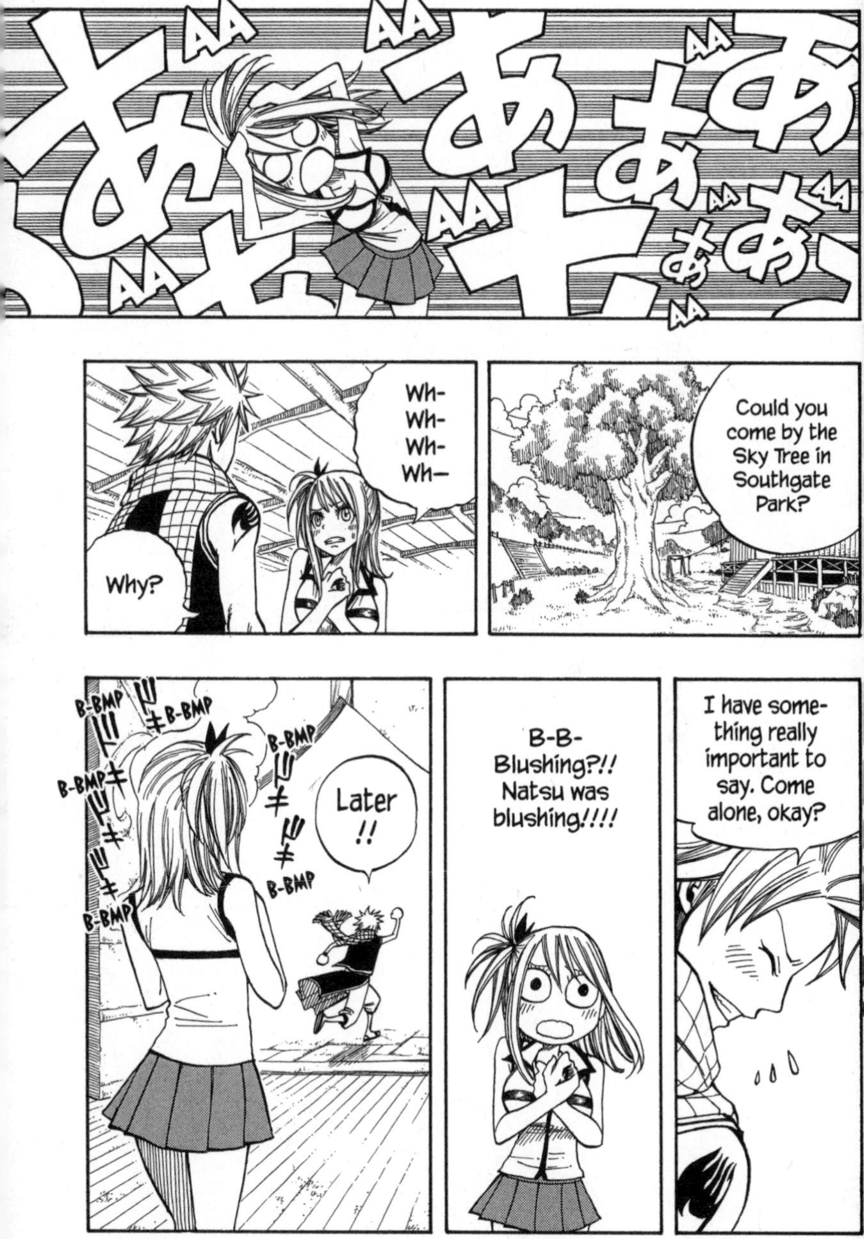
AA AA AA AA AA AA AA AA
あああああ
Could you come by the Sky Tree in Southgate Park?
Wh- Wh- Wh- Wh—
Why?
I have some-thing really important to say. Come alone, okay?
B-B-Blushing?!! Natsu was blushing!!!!
Later !!
B-BMP B-BMP B-BMP B-BMP B-BMP B-BMP

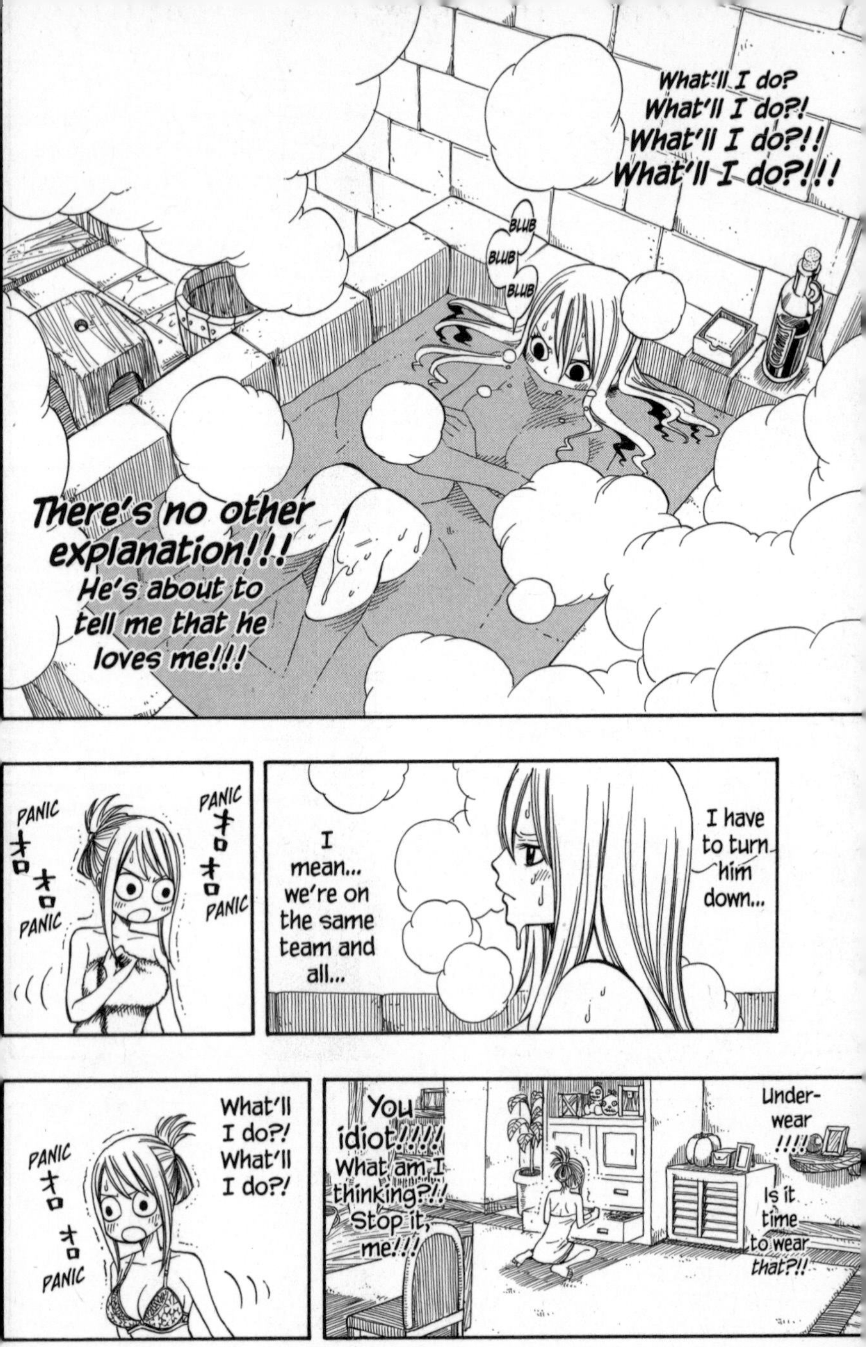
What'll I do? What'll I do?! What'll I do?!! What'll I do?!!!
BLUB BLUB BLUB
There's no other explanation!!! He's about to tell me that he loves me!!!
I have to turn him down...
I mean... we're on the same team and all...
PANIC オロ PANIC オロ
PANIC オロ PANIC オロ
Under-wear!!!!
Is it time to wear that?!!
You idiot!!!! What am I thinking?!! Stop it, me!!!
What'll I do?! What'll I do?!
PANIC オロ オロ PANIC

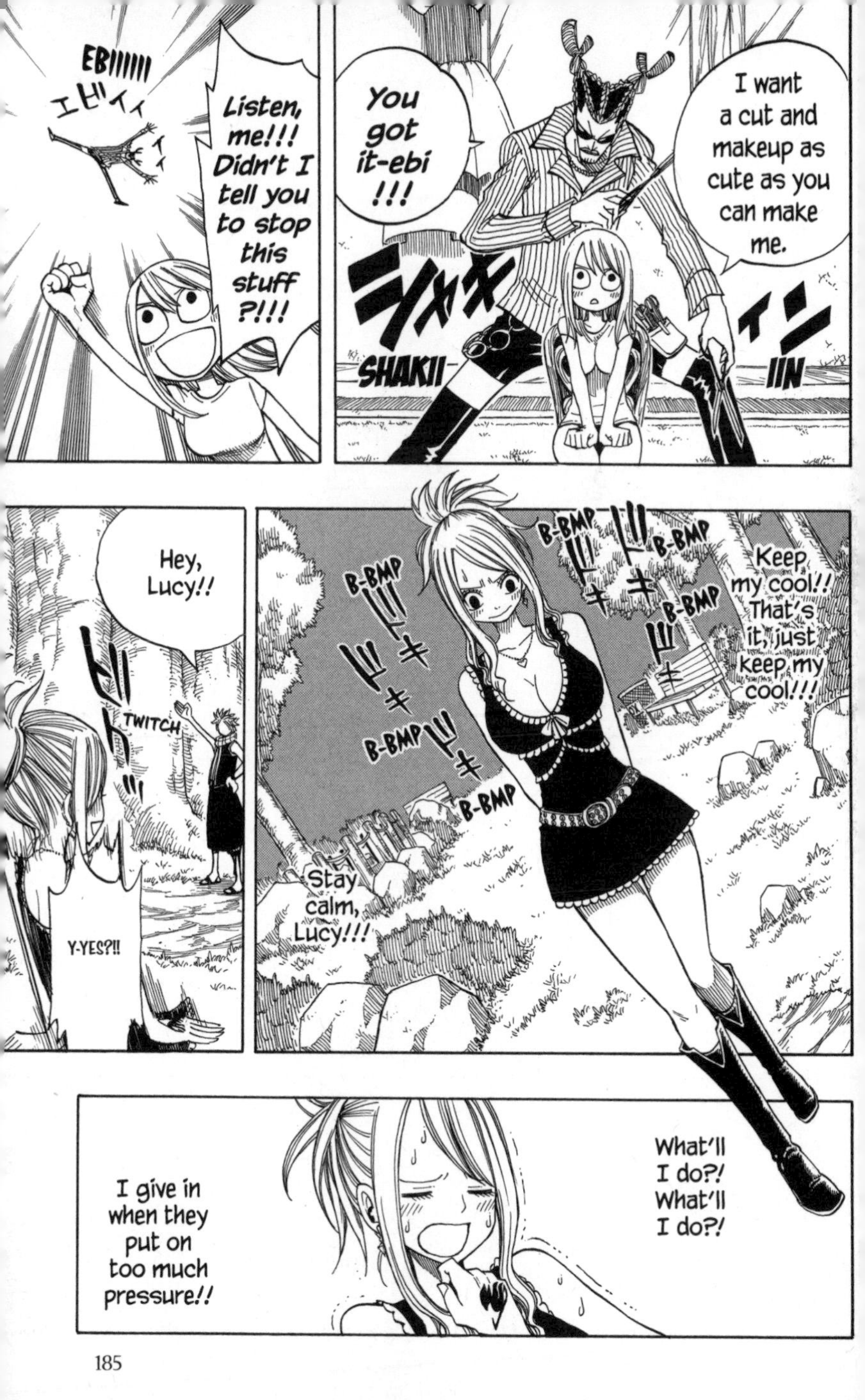
I want a cut and makeup as cute as you can make me.
You got it-ebi!!!
SHAKII
IIN
Listen, me!!! Didn't I tell you to stop this stuff?!!!
EBI!!!!!!
エビイィイイ
Keep my cool!! That's it, just keep my cool!!!
B-BMP
B-BMP
B-BMP
B-BMP
B-BMP
B-BMP
Stay calm, Lucy!!!
Hey, Lucy!!
TWITCH
Y-YES?!!
What'll I do?! What'll I do?!
I give in when they put on too much pressure!!

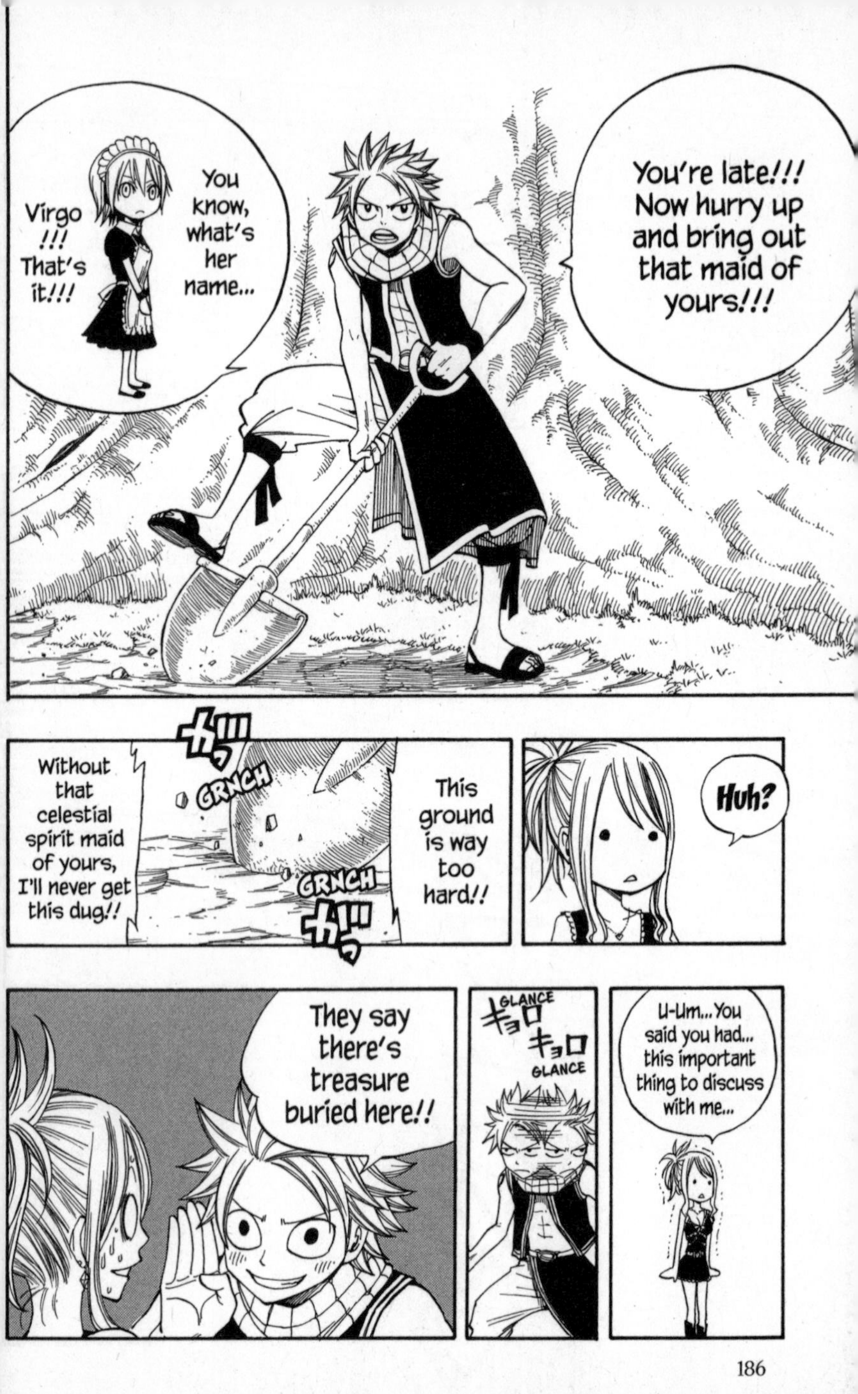

You're late!!! Now hurry up and bring out that maid of yours!!!
You know, what's her name...
Virgo!!! That's it!!!
Huh?
This ground is way too hard!!
GRNCH
GRNCH
Without that celestial spirit maid of yours, I'll never get this dug!!
U-Um...You said you had... this important thing to discuss with me...
キョロ GLANCE
キョロ GLANCE
They say there's treasure buried here!!

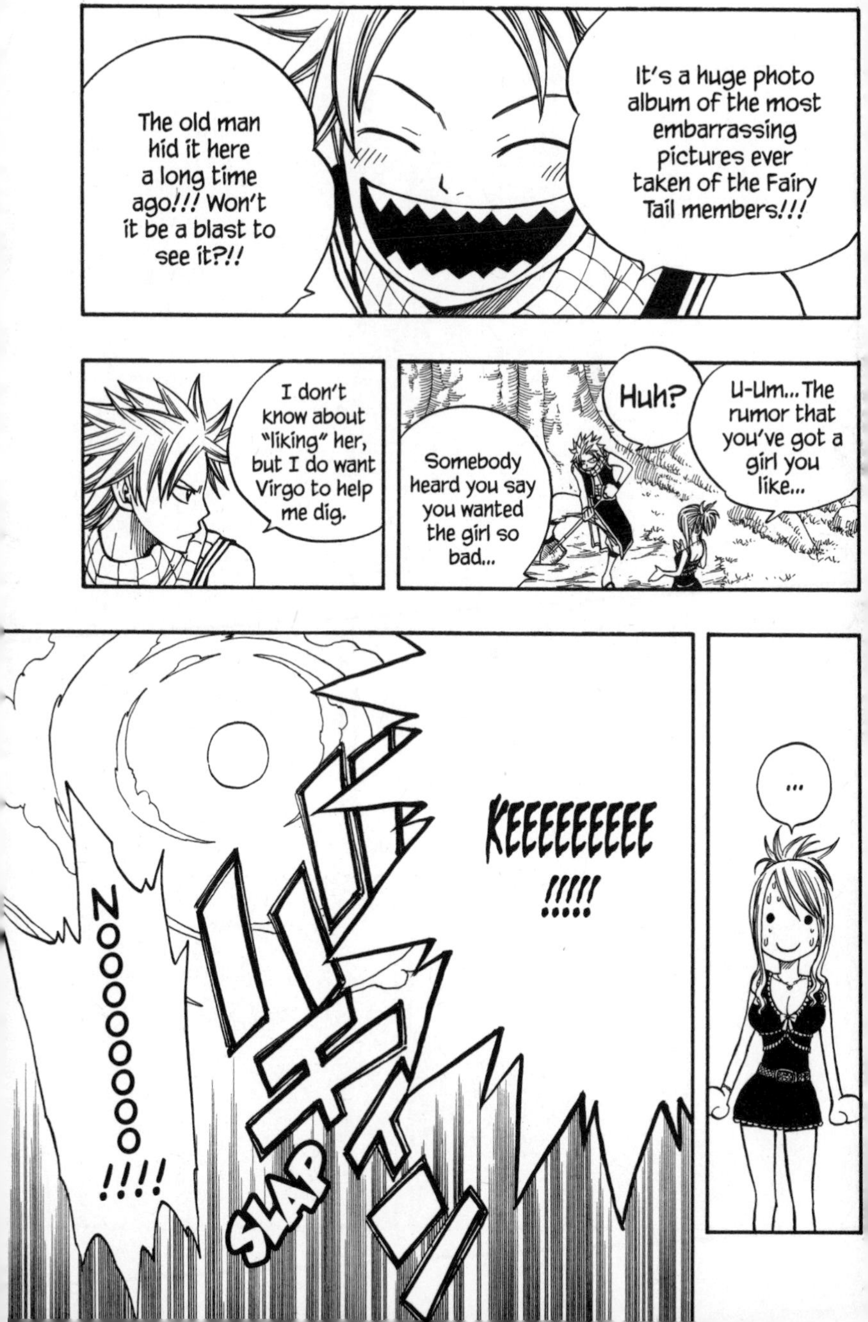
It's a huge photo album of the most embarrassing pictures ever taken of the Fairy Tail members!!!
The old man hid it here a long time ago!!! Won't it be a blast to see it?!!
Huh?
U-Um... The rumor that you've got a girl you like...
Somebody heard you say you wanted the girl so bad...
I don't know about "liking" her, but I do want Virgo to help me dig.
...
KEEEEEEEEEE !!!!!
NOOOOOOOOO !!!!
SLAP

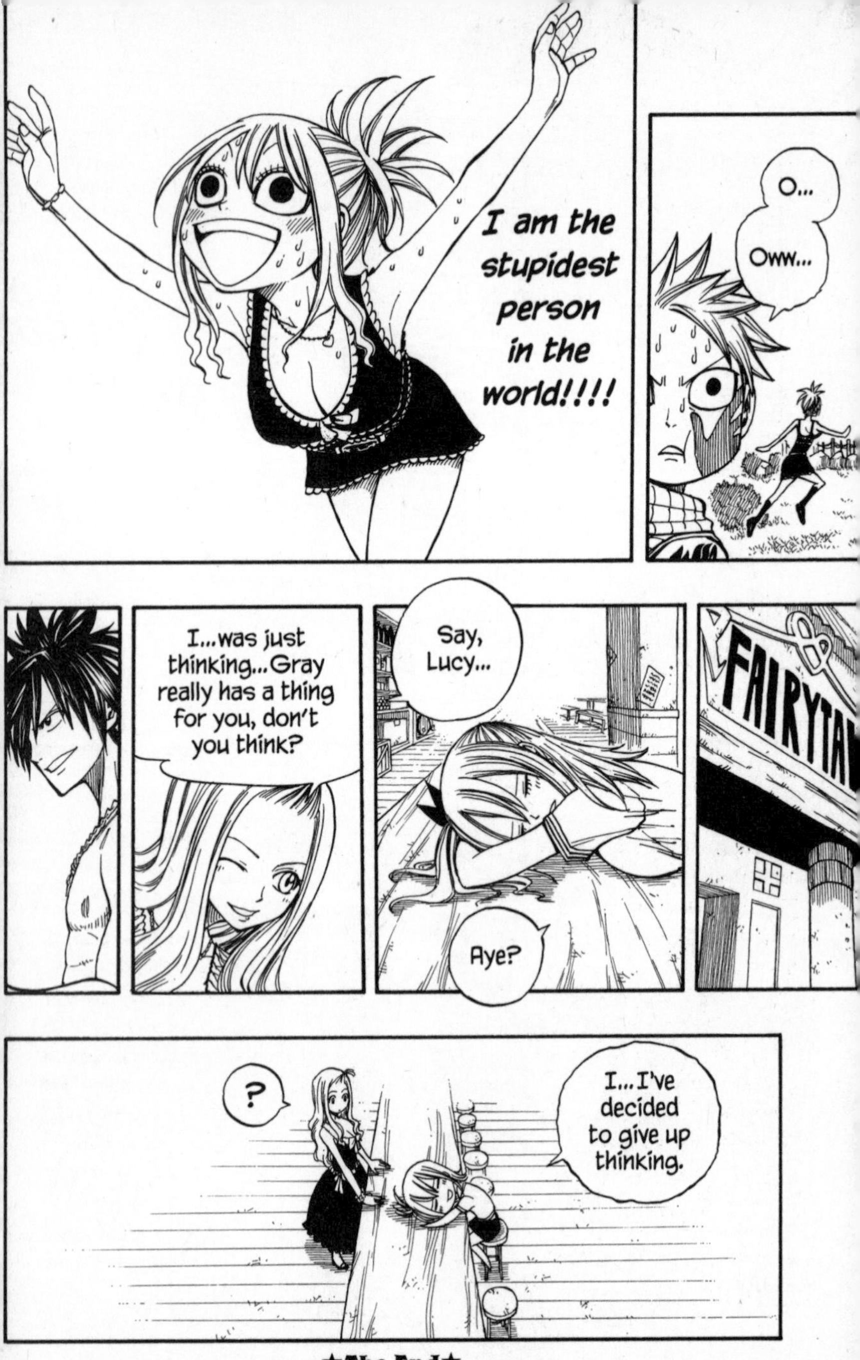
O...
Oww...
I am the stupidest person in the world!!!!
Say, Lucy...
Aye?
I...was just thinking...Gray really has a thing for you, don't you think?
I...I've decided to give up thinking.
?

★The End★

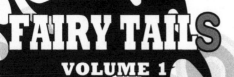

FAIRY TAILS VOLUME 1 EXPLANATION & AFTERWORD by HIRO MASHIMA

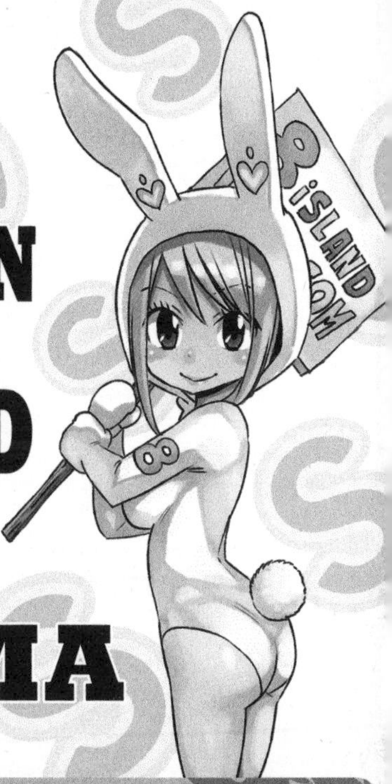
iSLAND

THE FAIRIES' BOOBY PRIZES

Since I wrote things like these explanations and afterwords for this story twice already, I figured that I really didn't have anything more to say about it. But then I remembered something.
I vaguely remember at the *name* (a rough version of the comic for editing purposes) stage, I tried to draw Mira's punishment of Erza as being more erotic, but my editor stopped me.
Wait... Maybe it was him trying to get me to make it more erotic, and I stopped him...
Sorry! I told you the memory was vague.

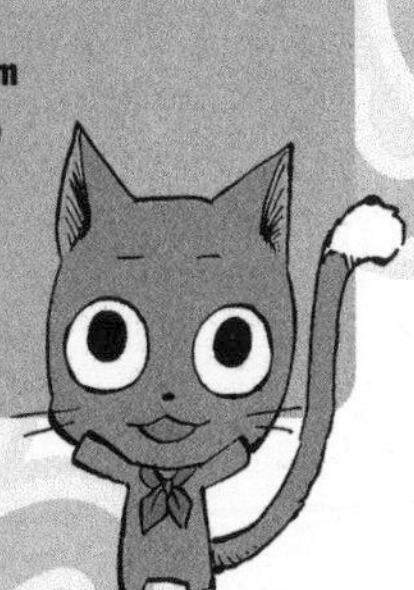

HAPPY THE BLUE CAT

I drew this less as a short story, and more in the style of a picture book.
In it, Happy is wondering about his what makes him happy, but to tell you the truth, I was also wondering about this same subject quite a lot at the time. It's his name, so no matter how much trouble he may be in or how sad he might be, he can still always be called, "Happy." I kept thinking about how weird that was...but when it came time to draw this, I was forced to reconsider, and I came to the conclusion that Happy is really a good name. All the weird feelings I had when I was drawing a character who was both in trouble and Happy were blown away with the wind.

413 DAYS

This is a Juvia story. It's probably from a time when I was sort of in a Gray & Juvia obsession phase. So I'll take this space to let you know about a difficulty with Gray as a character. Gray fans can be separated into five different general categories.

1. These people just want Gray to be happy. Anything that leads to that goal is fine with them.
2. These people want Gray to end up with Juvia.
3. These people want Gray to end up with Lucy.
4. These people want Gray to end up without a romantic relationship at all.
5. These people don't care about Gray's love life. They just want to see him in great battles.

Now I've clearly decided what the future holds for Gray, and even if a clear majority of fans felt one way or the other, I can state definitively that it won't change how I wrap up the story. But as a creator, it would make me happiest if most people were in Category 1.

WELCOME HOME, FROSCH

This was a short story that ran in *Bessatsu Shonen Magazine,* wasn't it? I have this personal impression that the fan base of *Bessatsu Shonen Magazine* includes a lot of girls (it's nothing more than a personal impression, though), so I thought that it'd be good to have the two good-looking guys, Sting and Rogue, have an buddy-style adventure. But before I knew it, the story was all about Frosch. I have to say that personally, I really love this short story.
As a side note, while I was drawing the scene where Frosch meets up with Gray and Juvia, members of my staff asked me if it was a parody of a certain famous anime. I never even noticed until they mentioned it. Of course, it was never my intention to parody anything, but it turned into a scene that recalls a famous anime. If you want to know what it's from, ask someone who knows a lot of anime.

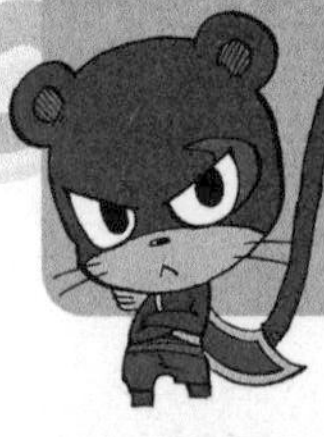

THAT WOMAN, ERZA

This was a short story that was published in the *seinen* (older men's) manga magazine, *Young Magazine.* I approached it as if there were no one reading the magazine who knew about *Fairy Tail,* so I tried my best to make it as easy for new readers to get into it as possible. Actually, this was the first thing I ever had published in a *seinen* magazine, and I was pretty unsure of myself. But it seems that a lot of the magazine's readers liked it, so that made me very happy. After that, the Moulin Rouge that appeared in the short story became a part of the main *Fairy Tail* story. Actually, I had a character named Bisca Moulin from the very start.

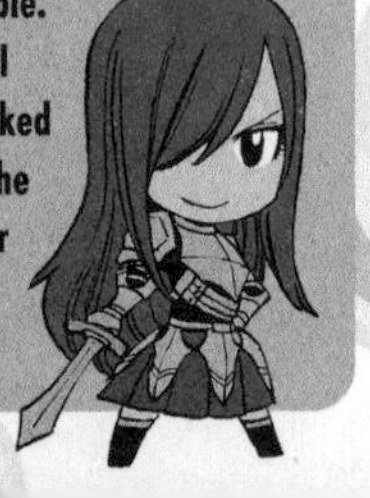

A MERRY, FAIRY CHRISTMAS

This is the "King's Game," right? The dream of every boy everywhere. But this is the story of the girl Erza getting too carried away with the game and going on a rampage. It had lots of nude guys and girls in erotic situations, so it turned out to be a pretty cruel story to its characters.
But I really only hope that after this one scene, the episode at the end with Erza and Jellal, the reader was able to settle down again.
As a side note, just a month earlier in the same monthly magazine as this ran in, there was another manga that used the "King's Game" as the driving force in the chapter, so it seemed like I was copying it. It was actually an extremely rare coincidence.

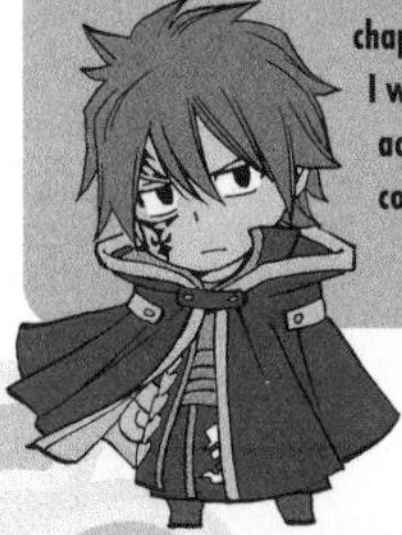

SPECIAL MISSION: BEWARE OF GUYS WHO SHOW A KEEN INTEREST!

This is a kind of cute little story from the very early days of the series about how Lucy gets some heart palpitations when it comes to Natsu.
I had absolutely no intention of putting Natsu and Lucy in any kind of romantic relationship, but the fan base took it in entirely the opposite way. Let's not discuss the future of their relationship, but up to now, I've been drawing their relationship as greater than just friends, but less than lovers. I actually may kind of like that kind of relationship. I think it's really cute how Lucy's imagination runs away with her in this short story.

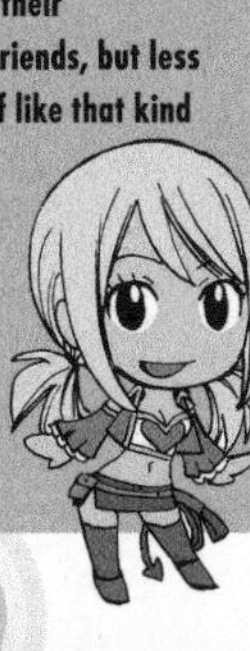

NATSU VS. MAVIS

I think I wrote this in an afterword or explanation recently, but for this story, I had only a small number of pages, so I tried to cram in as much fan service as I possibly could.
I really liked the look on Erza's face as she is trying to endure the boiling water. I also like poor Lucy afterwards. But it was about this time that I started to get messages from Lucy fans to please stop putting her into those awful situations. Sorry, but that's just the kind of character Lucy is...

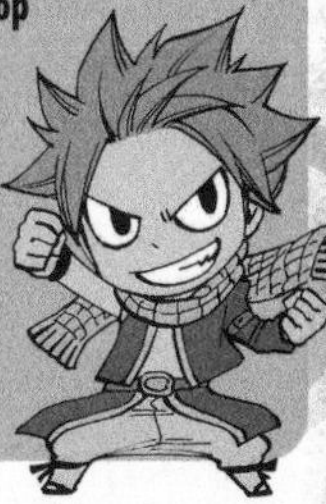

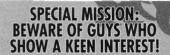

FAIRY TAIL OF THE DEAD MEEEEEEEEN

From the start, this story was linked to an anime version. A very long time ago, I heard that the director of the TV series who also did most of the series planning, Mr. Ishihira, was a big fan of zombie shows. So I thought that if I wrote something like a zombie(?) story, that Mr. Ishihira could bake it into a really interesting show.
This whole production was pretty chaotic, but with a lot of help from everyone connected with the animation, we managed to put the episode on the air during the same week that the manga was published in *Weekly Shonen Magazine.* It probably goes without saying, but I really love the character of Ichiya-san, so drawing this manga was a real joy. I distinctly remember worrying over whether to Ichiya-fy Wendy or not.

Translation Notes:

Page 35, Originally About Curry

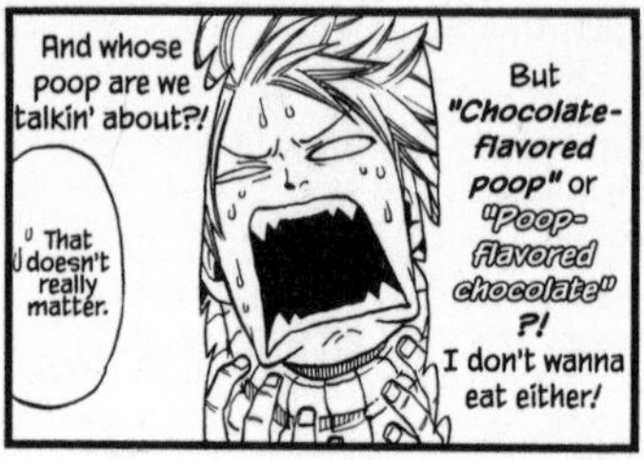
And whose poop are we talkin' about?!
That doesn't really matter.
But "Chocolate-flavored poop" or "Poop-flavored chocolate"?! I don't wanna eat either!

This is an old schoolyard "terrible choice" game that kids play in Japan. The original is, "would you choose the curry (spicy)-flavored chocolate (sweet), or chocolate-flavored curry? Would you rather expect sweet and get spicy, or expect spice and get sweet? The "poop" angle is Happy's own.

Page 39, Brain Buster

The Brain Buster is a wrestling move by which one lifts one's opponent into the air until the opponent is almost upside down, then slams the opponent back into the ground either on his/her head or back.

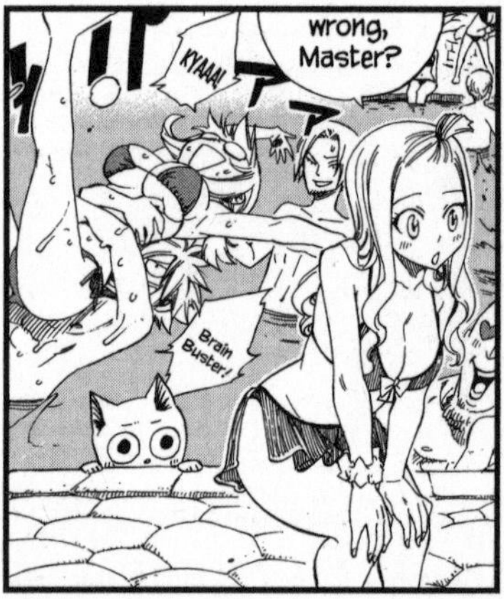
wrong, Master?
KYAAA!
Brain Buster!

Page 53, Child's First Shopping Trip

There used to be a popular TV program called *Hajimete no Otsukai* (loosely translates to "Child's First Shopping Trip") that films a small child of about three or four years old who is told to go alone from their home to the store to buy one or two grocery items. Children at that age are easily distracted and quickly get lost, so every program was something of a small-scale adventure. Although the series has gone off the air, *Child's First Shopping Trip* specials still air occasionally on Japanese TV.

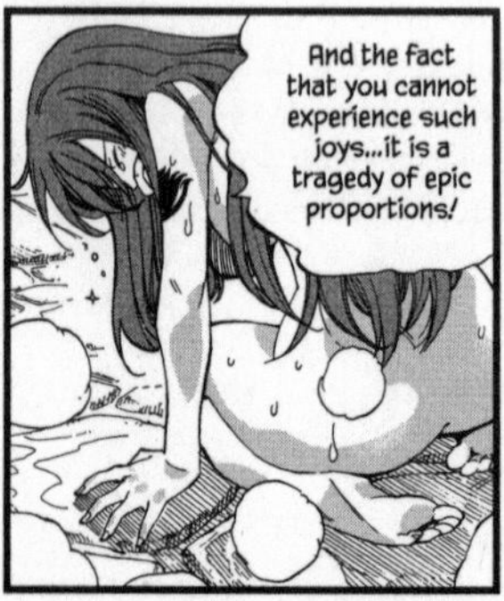
And the fact that you cannot experience such joys...it is a tragedy of epic proportions!

Page 104, Baths

These are common "joys" of the Japanese *ofuro* baths, although the skin-touching-skin thing is taken way too far. Most Japanese really enjoy the warmed-though-to-the-core feeling of soaking in a hot bath for a while, and the refreshing feeling of being clean. Also, a good, long bath is considered to be a refreshing end to a long day of work, reviving one's energy.

Page 155, Christmas Party

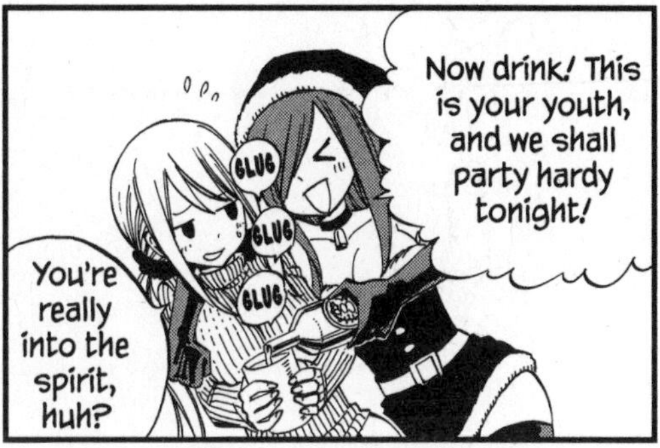
Now drink! This is your youth, and we shall party hardy tonight!
GLUG
GLUG
GLUG
You're really into the spirit, huh?

Aside from some of the trappings of Christmas, such as presents and Santa Claus costumes, the way Christmas and New Years are celebrated in Japan is pretty much the reverse of the way it's celebrated in the US. In Japan, Christmas is a night when you're out with your date, and it includes raucous parties with lots of alcohol, while New Years is a quiet time meant to be spent with the family. Most Japanese don't realize that Christmas in the west is not celebrated the way that they celebrate it.

Page 173, Writer's Notebook

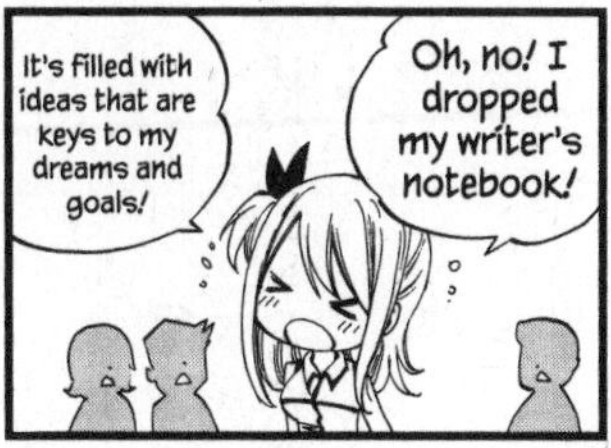
Oh, no! I dropped my writer's notebook!
It's filled with ideas that are keys to my dreams and goals!

In Japan, it's popular for writers and manga authors to keep a little notebook where they jot down story ideas. Usually the entries consist of details they saw during the day, or ideas that struck them out of the blue, and for manga artists, they may include little situations they can make a four-panel strip or comic element out of. In Japanese, plots are called *neta*, and these notebooks are called *neta-chô* (with *chô* meaning "notebook").

Page 190, That Anime

Though Mashima-sensei remains vague, the anime in question here appears to be *Clannad*. The main male and female characters are played by the voice actors for Gray and Juvia, and the two main character's daughter is played by the same voice actor as the person who plays Frosch.

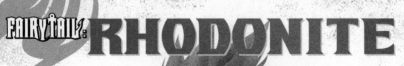

FAIRY TAIL: RHODONITE

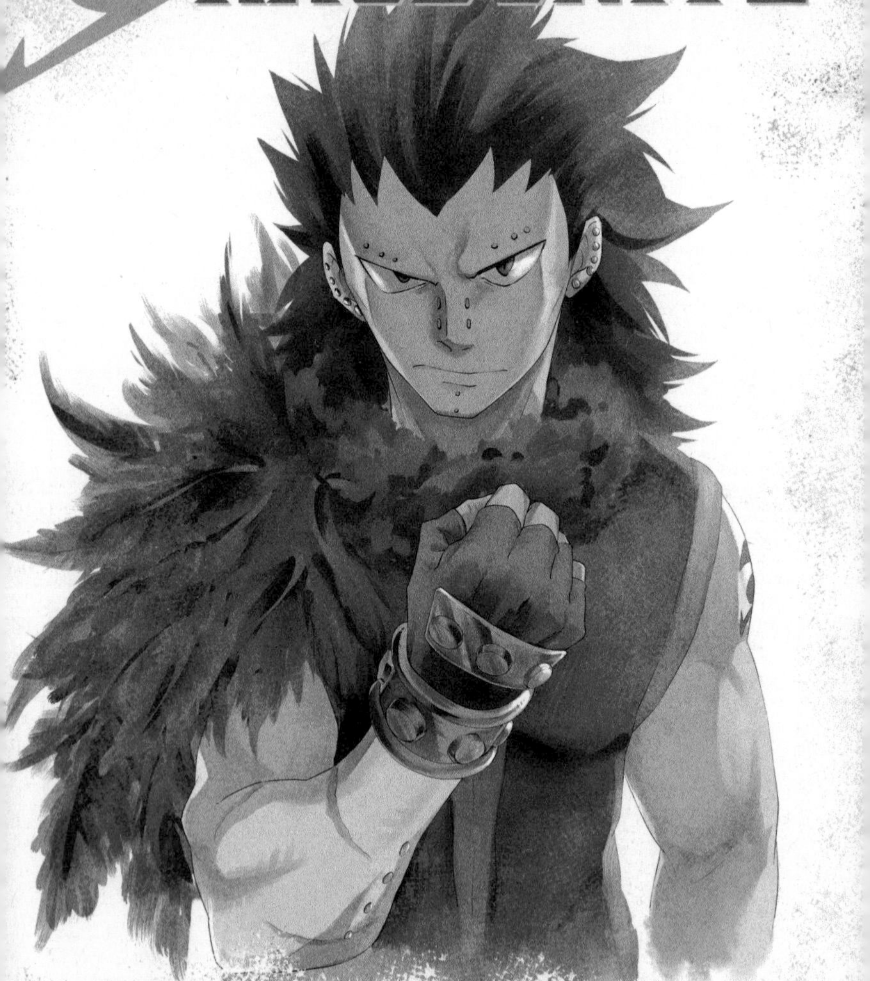

The iron dragon slayer, Gajeel Redfox, has lived his life in the shadows. Even in the motley crew of Fairy Tail, he didn't always fit in. When Gajeel gets news of an escaped prisoner he may be connected to, he must leave on a journey to confront his past. Will he stand strong with his new family in Fairy Tail, or will old forces pull him back into the darkness? Discover Gajeel's story in this official *Fairy Tail* spinoff!

We're pleased to present you with a preview of *Fairy Tail: Rhodonite* – available now!

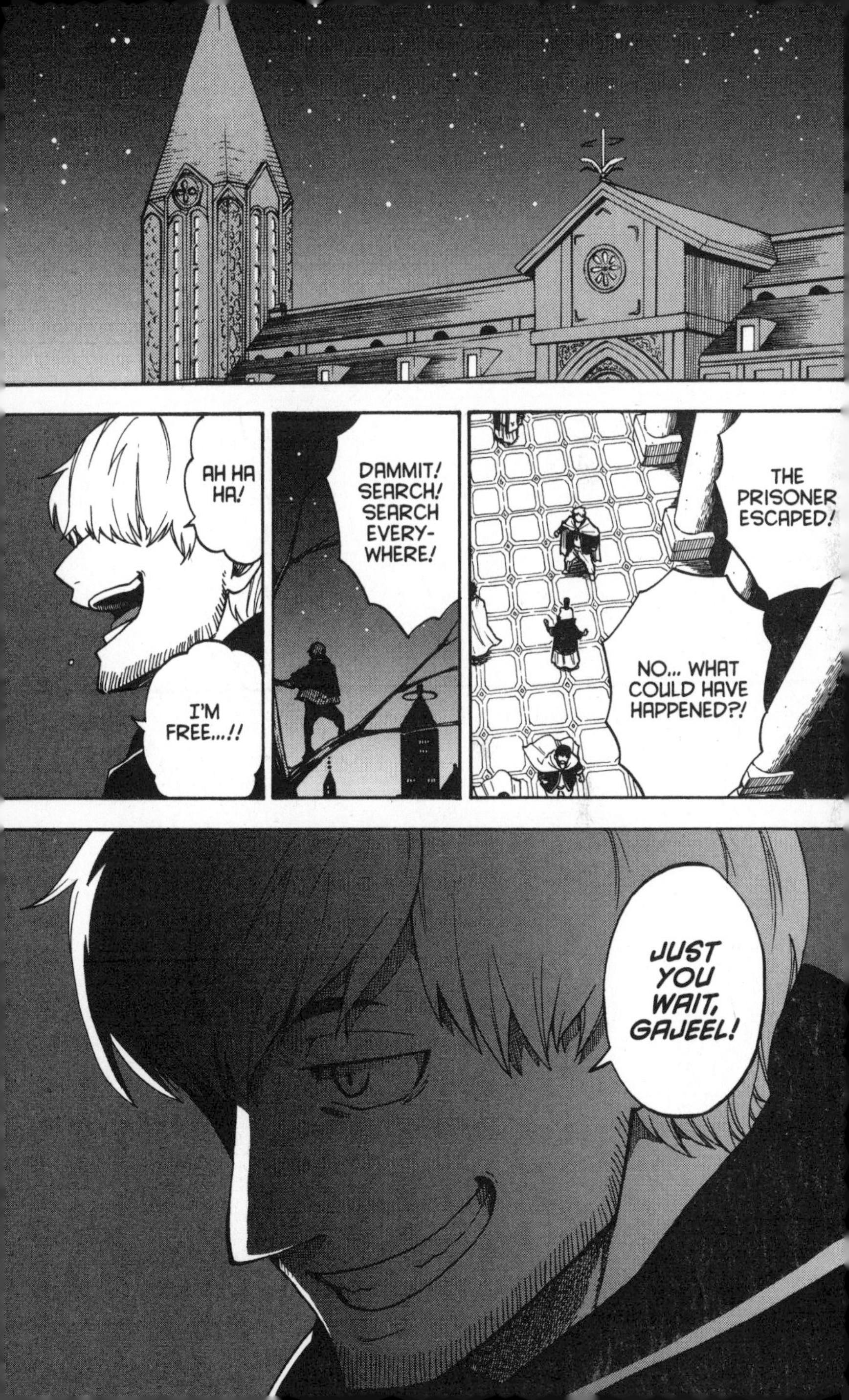
THE PRISONER ESCAPED!
NO... WHAT COULD HAVE HAPPENED?!
DAMMIT! SEARCH! SEARCH EVERYWHERE!
AH HA HA!
I'M FREE...!!
JUST YOU WAIT, GAJEEL!

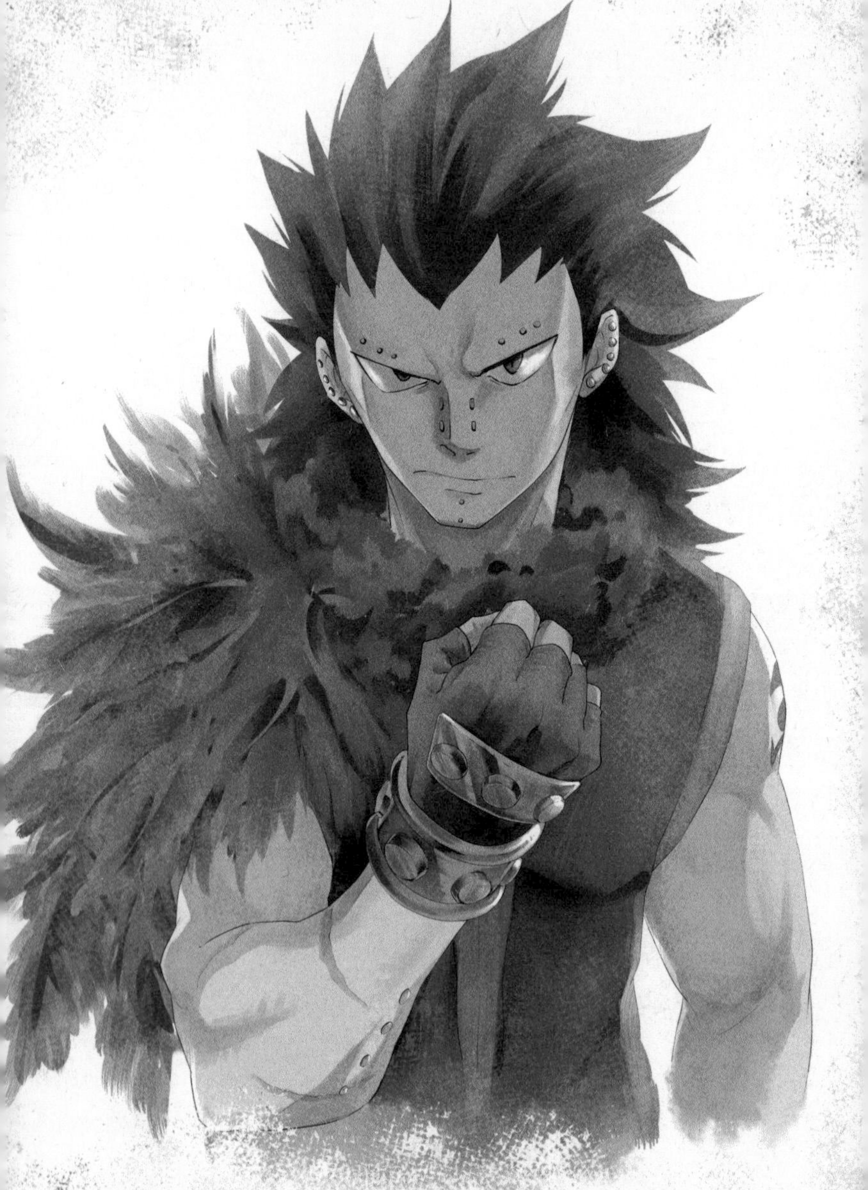

Chapter 1: Where is Gajeel?

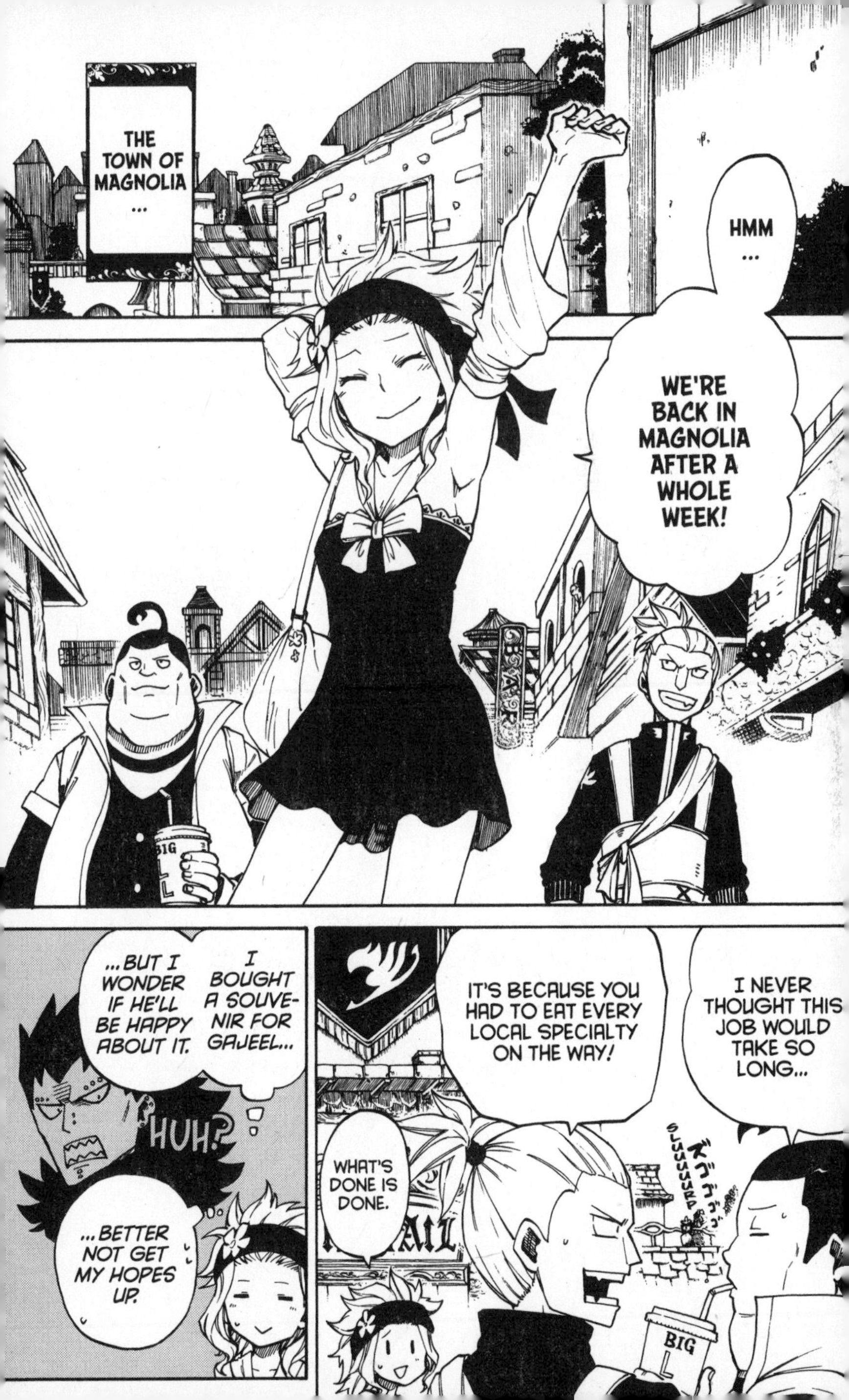
THE TOWN OF MAGNOLIA ...
HMM ...
WE'RE BACK IN MAGNOLIA AFTER A WHOLE WEEK!
I NEVER THOUGHT THIS JOB WOULD TAKE SO LONG...
IT'S BECAUSE YOU HAD TO EAT EVERY LOCAL SPECIALTY ON THE WAY!
SLUUUUURP
WHAT'S DONE IS DONE.
I BOUGHT A SOUVENIR FOR GAJEEL...
...BUT I WONDER IF HE'LL BE HAPPY ABOUT IT.
HUH?
...BETTER NOT GET MY HOPES UP.

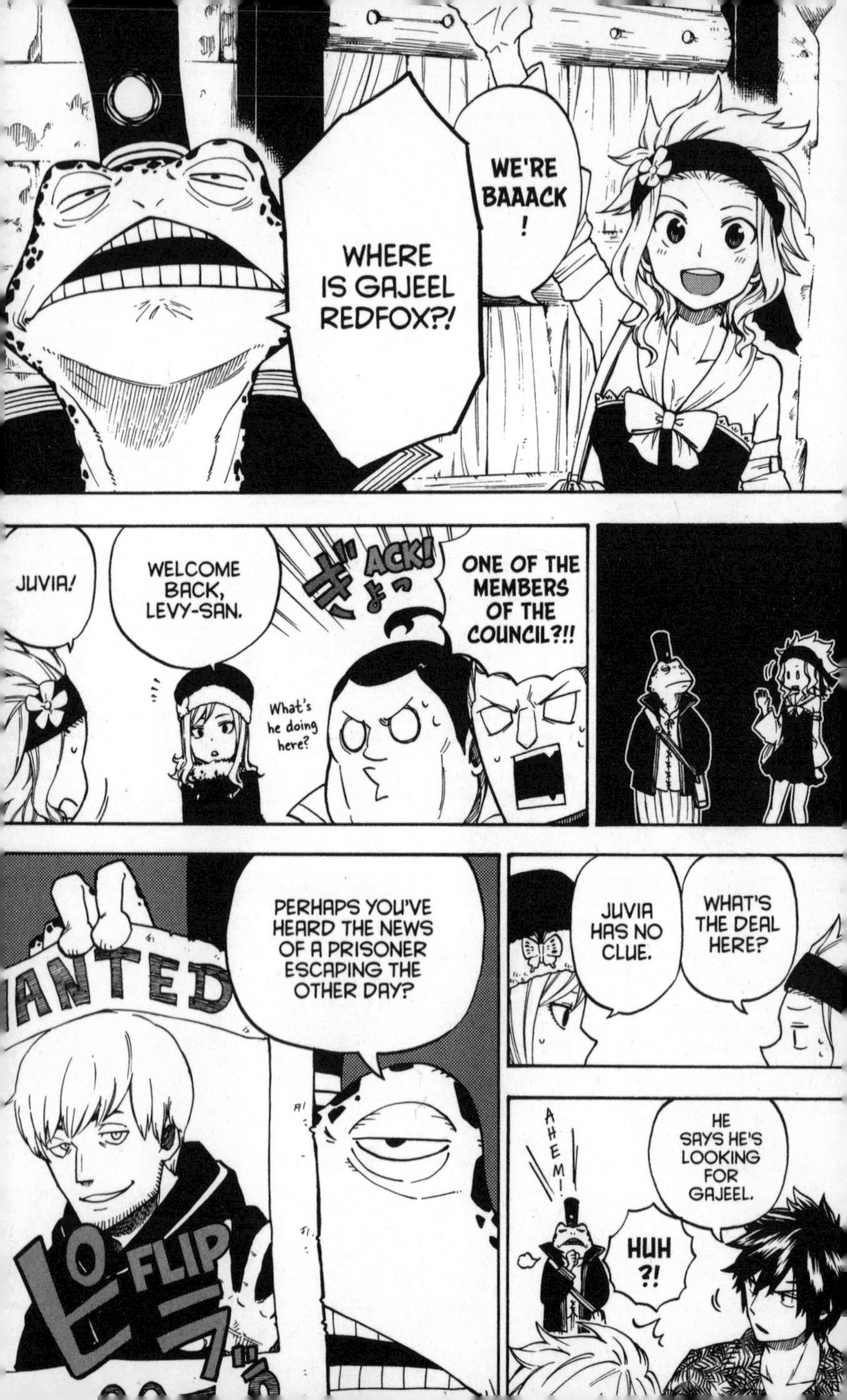
WE'RE BAAACK!
WHERE IS GAJEEL REDFOX?!
ONE OF THE MEMBERS OF THE COUNCIL?!!
ACK!
What's he doing here?
WELCOME BACK, LEVY-SAN.
JUVIA!
WHAT'S THE DEAL HERE?
JUVIA HAS NO CLUE.
HE SAYS HE'S LOOKING FOR GAJEEL.
HUH ?!
AHEM!
PERHAPS YOU'VE HEARD THE NEWS OF A PRISONER ESCAPING THE OTHER DAY?
FLIP

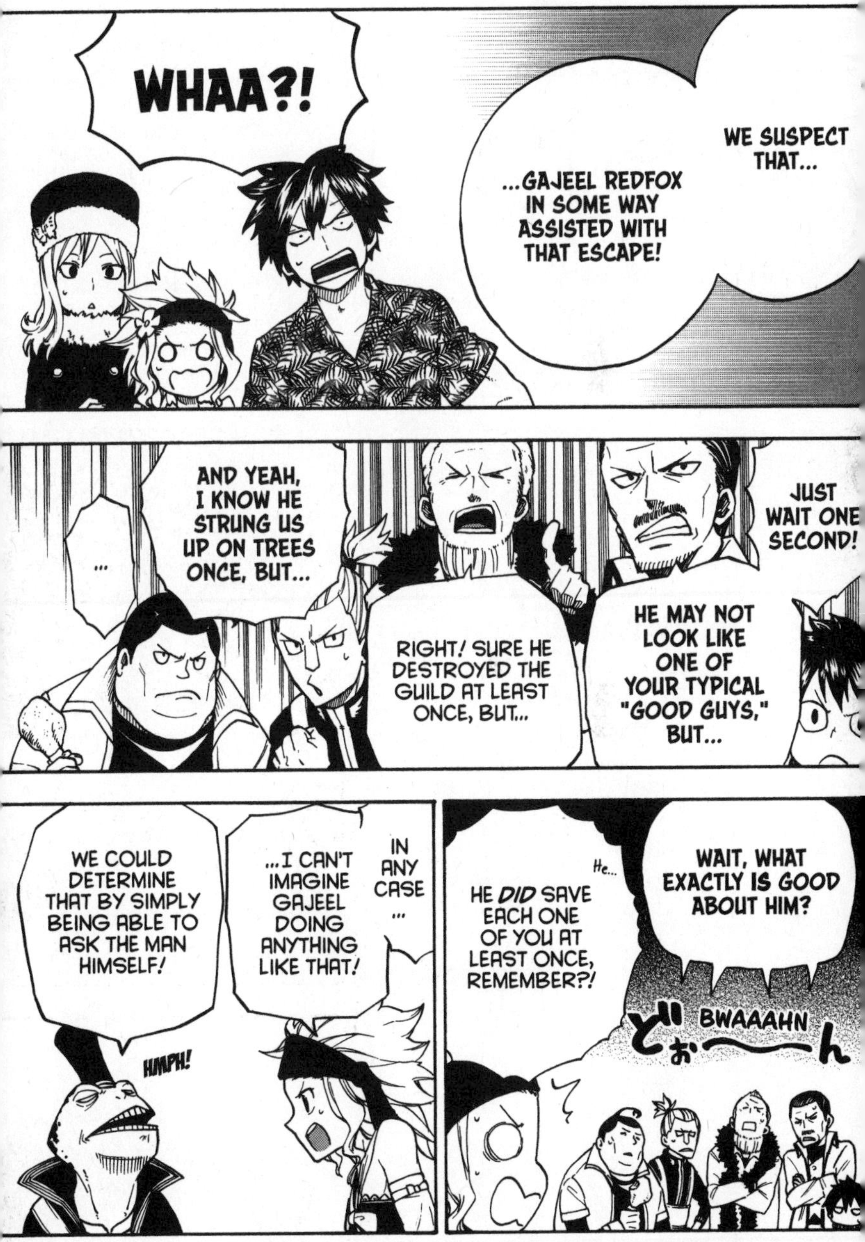
WE SUSPECT THAT...
...GAJEEL REDFOX IN SOME WAY ASSISTED WITH THAT ESCAPE!
WHAA?!
JUST WAIT ONE SECOND!
HE MAY NOT LOOK LIKE ONE OF YOUR TYPICAL "GOOD GUYS," BUT...
RIGHT! SURE HE DESTROYED THE GUILD AT LEAST ONCE, BUT...
AND YEAH, I KNOW HE STRUNG US UP ON TREES ONCE, BUT...
...
He...
HE *DID* SAVE EACH ONE OF YOU AT LEAST ONCE, REMEMBER?!
WAIT, WHAT EXACTLY IS GOOD ABOUT HIM?
どぉ〜〜ん BWAAAHN
IN ANY CASE...
...I CAN'T IMAGINE GAJEEL DOING ANYTHING LIKE THAT!
WE COULD DETERMINE THAT BY SIMPLY BEING ABLE TO ASK THE MAN HIMSELF!
HMPH!

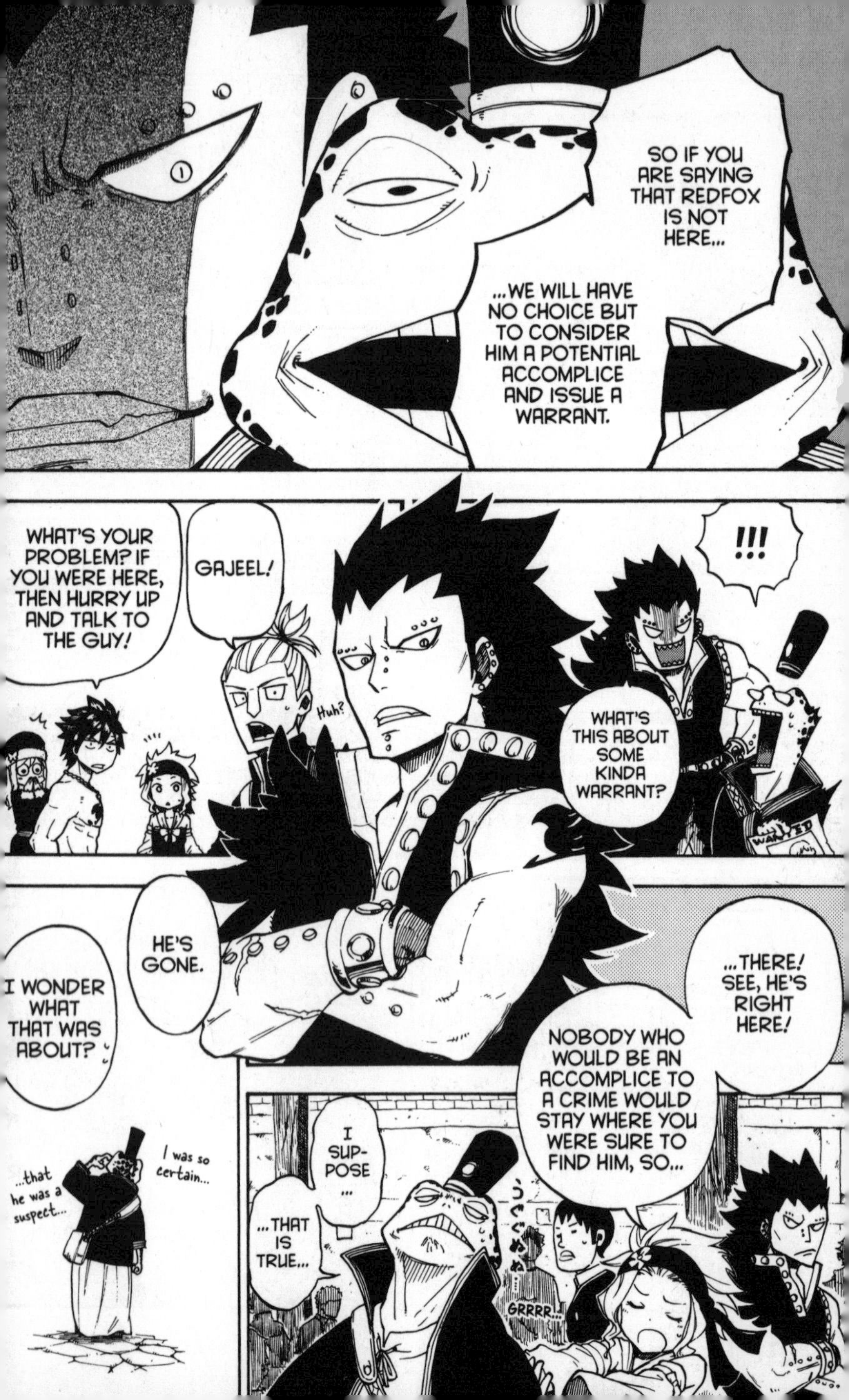
SO IF YOU ARE SAYING THAT REDFOX IS NOT HERE...
...WE WILL HAVE NO CHOICE BUT TO CONSIDER HIM A POTENTIAL ACCOMPLICE AND ISSUE A WARRANT.
!!!
WHAT'S THIS ABOUT SOME KINDA WARRANT?
GAJEEL!
Huh?
WHAT'S YOUR PROBLEM? IF YOU WERE HERE, THEN HURRY UP AND TALK TO THE GUY!
...THERE! SEE, HE'S RIGHT HERE!
NOBODY WHO WOULD BE AN ACCOMPLICE TO A CRIME WOULD STAY WHERE YOU WERE SURE TO FIND HIM, SO...
GRRRR...
I SUPPOSE...
...THAT IS TRUE...
HE'S GONE.
I WONDER WHAT THAT WAS ABOUT?
I was so certain...
...that he was a suspect...

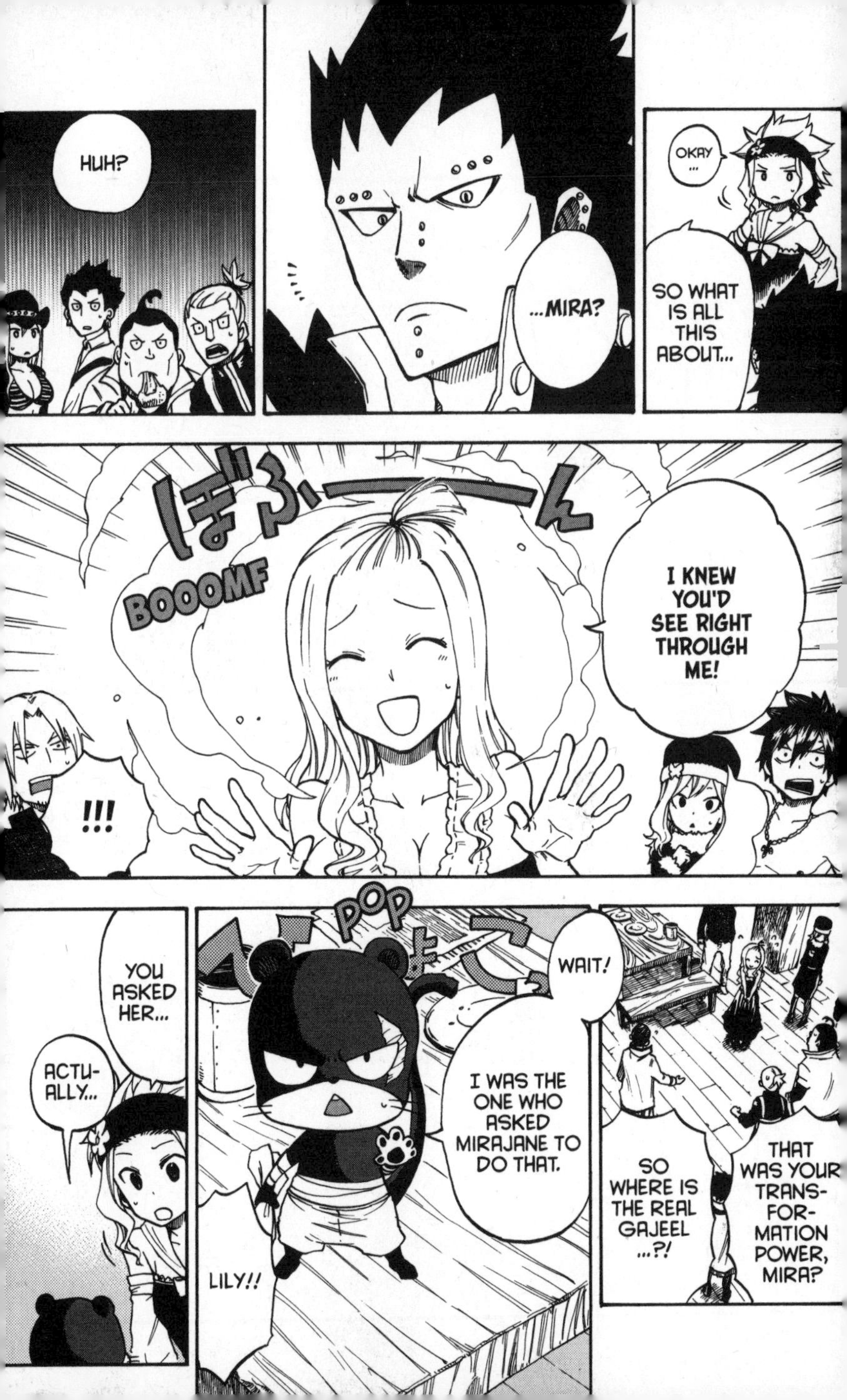
OKAY ...
SO WHAT IS ALL THIS ABOUT...
...MIRA?
HUH?
ぼふーーーん
BOOOMF
I KNEW YOU'D SEE RIGHT THROUGH ME!
!!!
THAT WAS YOUR TRANS-FOR-MATION POWER, MIRA?
SO WHERE IS THE REAL GAJEEL ...?!
POP
WAIT!
I WAS THE ONE WHO ASKED MIRAJANE TO DO THAT.
LILY!!
YOU ASKED HER...
ACTU-ALLY...

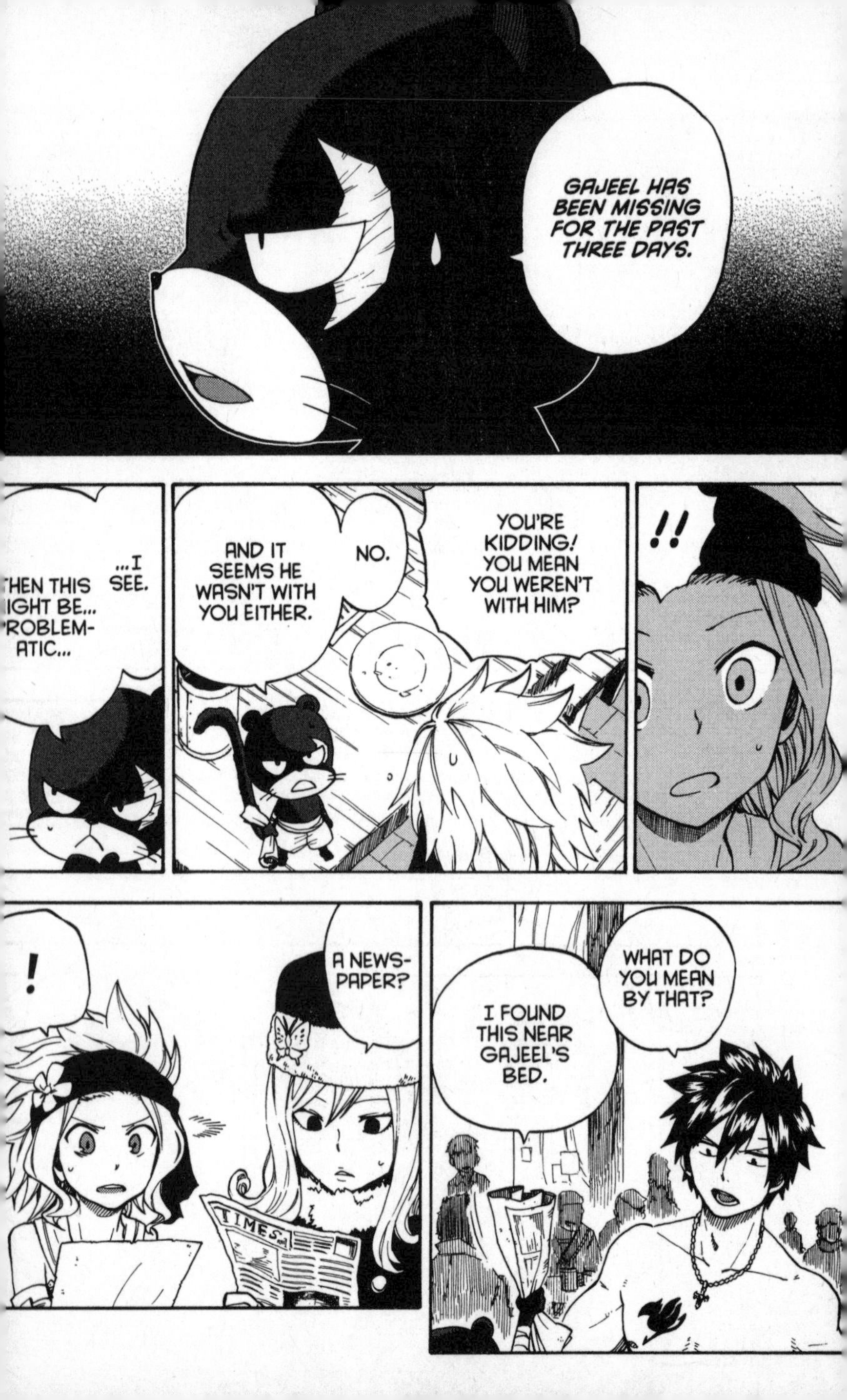
GAJEEL HAS BEEN MISSING FOR THE PAST THREE DAYS.
!!
YOU'RE KIDDING! YOU MEAN YOU WEREN'T WITH HIM?
NO.
AND IT SEEMS HE WASN'T WITH YOU EITHER.
...I SEE.
THEN THIS MIGHT BE... PROBLEM-ATIC...
WHAT DO YOU MEAN BY THAT?
I FOUND THIS NEAR GAJEEL'S BED.
A NEWS-PAPER?
!
TIMES

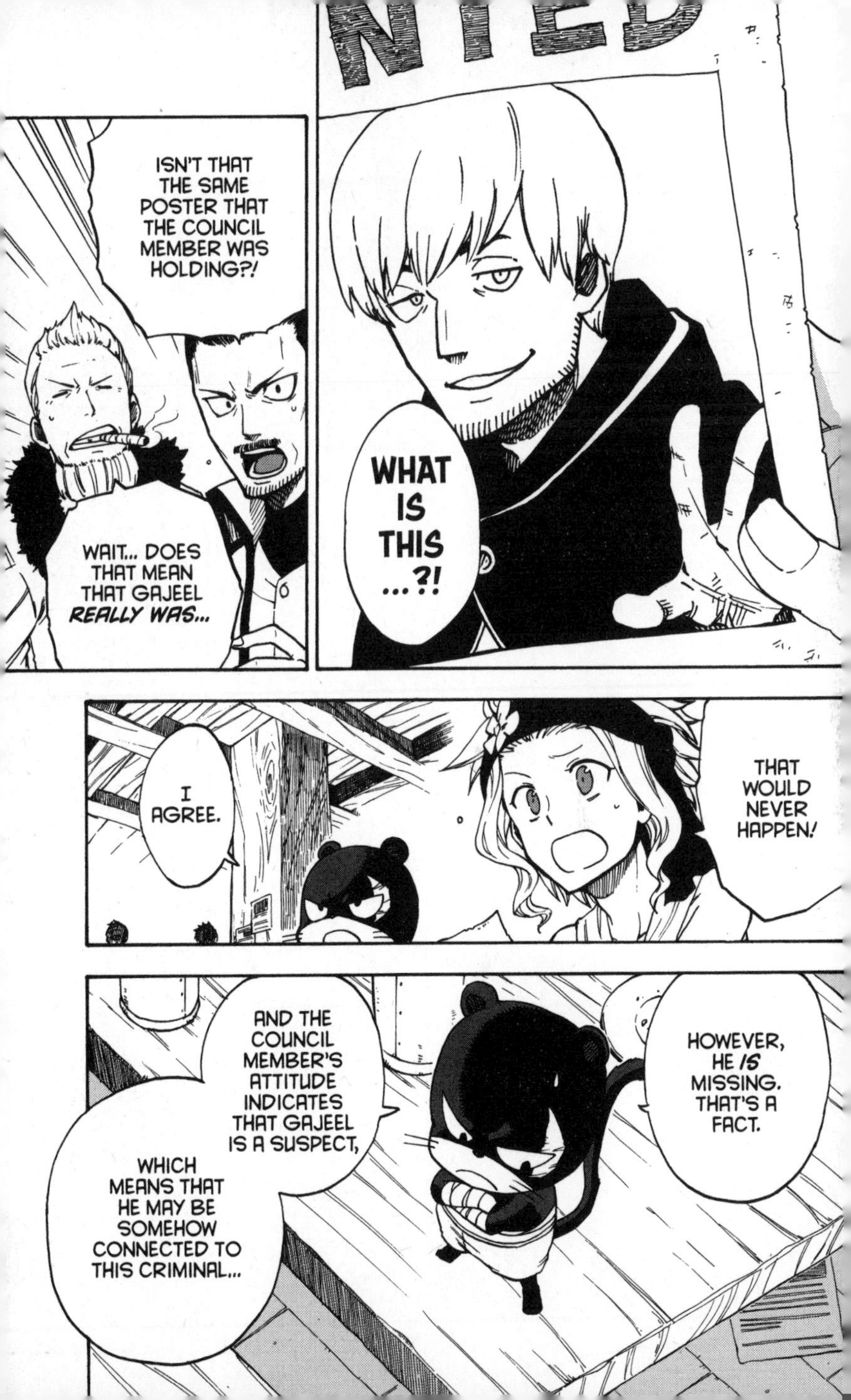
WHAT IS THIS ...?!
ISN'T THAT THE SAME POSTER THAT THE COUNCIL MEMBER WAS HOLDING?!
WAIT... DOES THAT MEAN THAT GAJEEL *REALLY WAS...*
THAT WOULD NEVER HAPPEN!
I AGREE.
HOWEVER, HE *IS* MISSING. THAT'S A FACT.
AND THE COUNCIL MEMBER'S ATTITUDE INDICATES THAT GAJEEL IS A SUSPECT,
WHICH MEANS THAT HE MAY BE SOMEHOW CONNECTED TO THIS CRIMINAL...

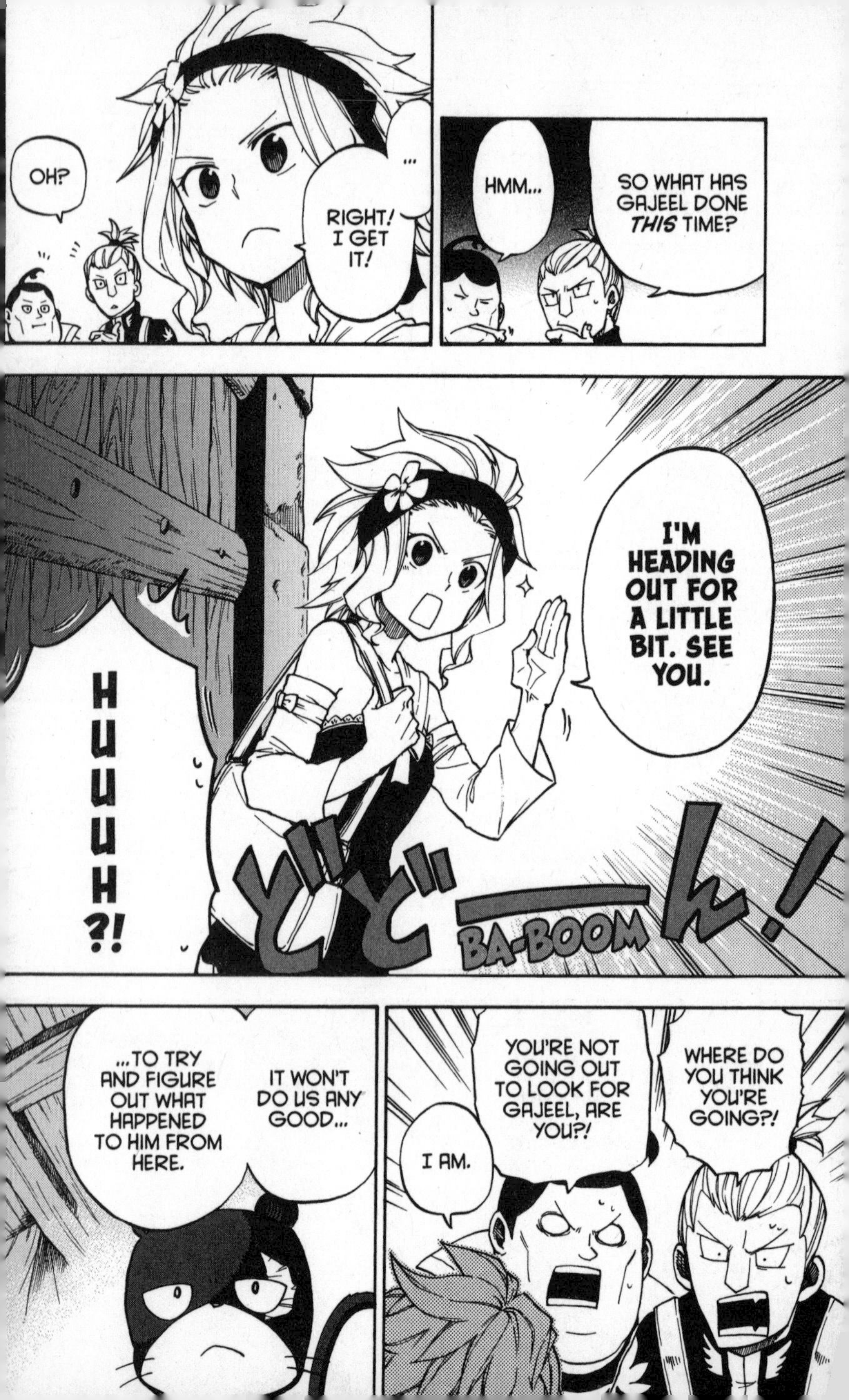
SO WHAT HAS GAJEEL DONE *THIS* TIME?
HMM...
...
RIGHT! I GET IT!
OH?
I'M HEADING OUT FOR A LITTLE BIT. SEE YOU.
HUUUUH?!
BA-BOOM
WHERE DO YOU THINK YOU'RE GOING?!
YOU'RE NOT GOING OUT TO LOOK FOR GAJEEL, ARE YOU?!
I AM.
IT WON'T DO US ANY GOOD...
...TO TRY AND FIGURE OUT WHAT HAPPENED TO HIM FROM HERE.

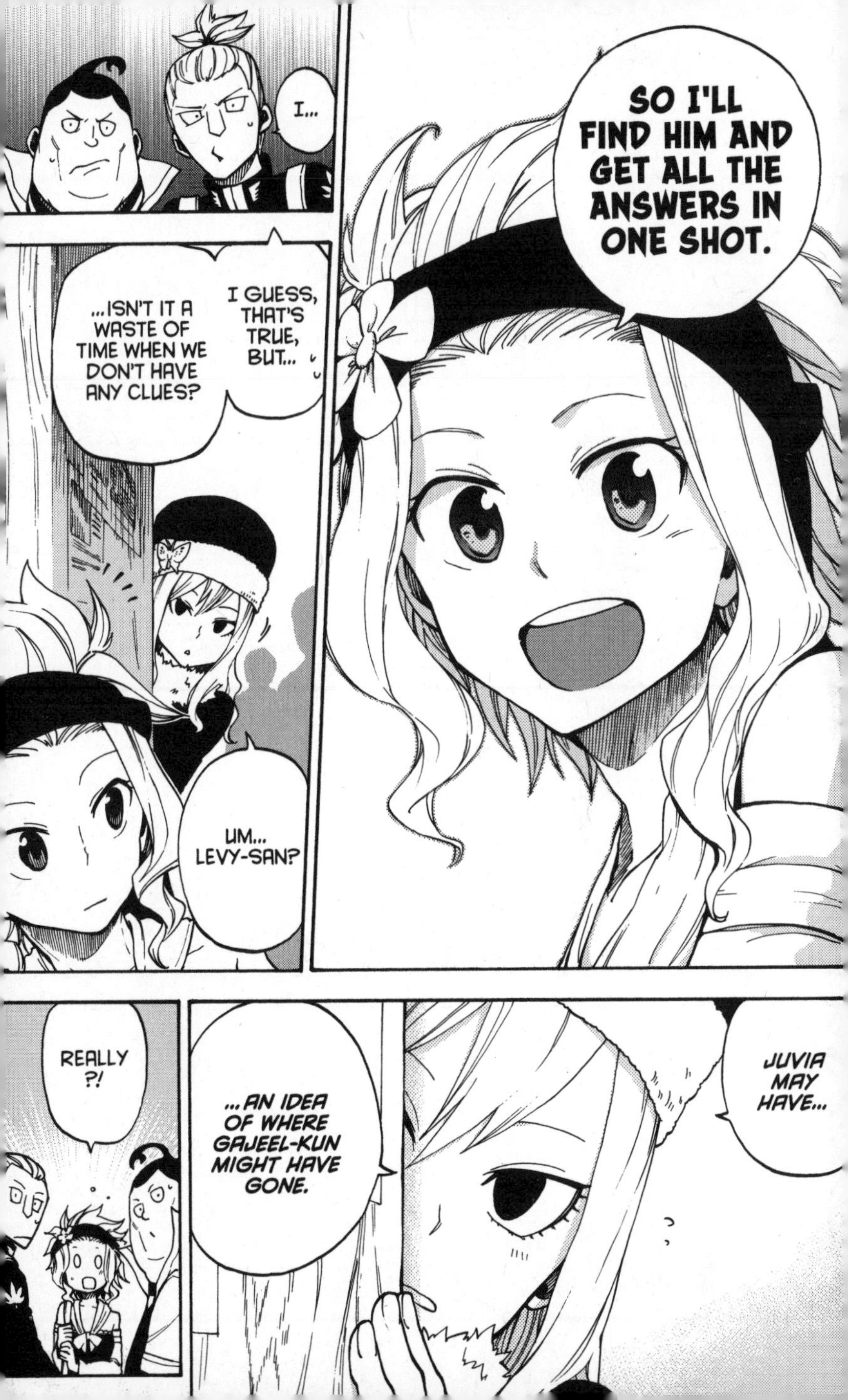
SO I'LL FIND HIM AND GET ALL THE ANSWERS IN ONE SHOT.
I...
I GUESS, THAT'S TRUE, BUT...
...ISN'T IT A WASTE OF TIME WHEN WE DON'T HAVE ANY CLUES?
UM... LEVY-SAN?
JUVIA MAY HAVE...
...AN IDEA OF WHERE GAJEEL-KUN MIGHT HAVE GONE.
REALLY ?!

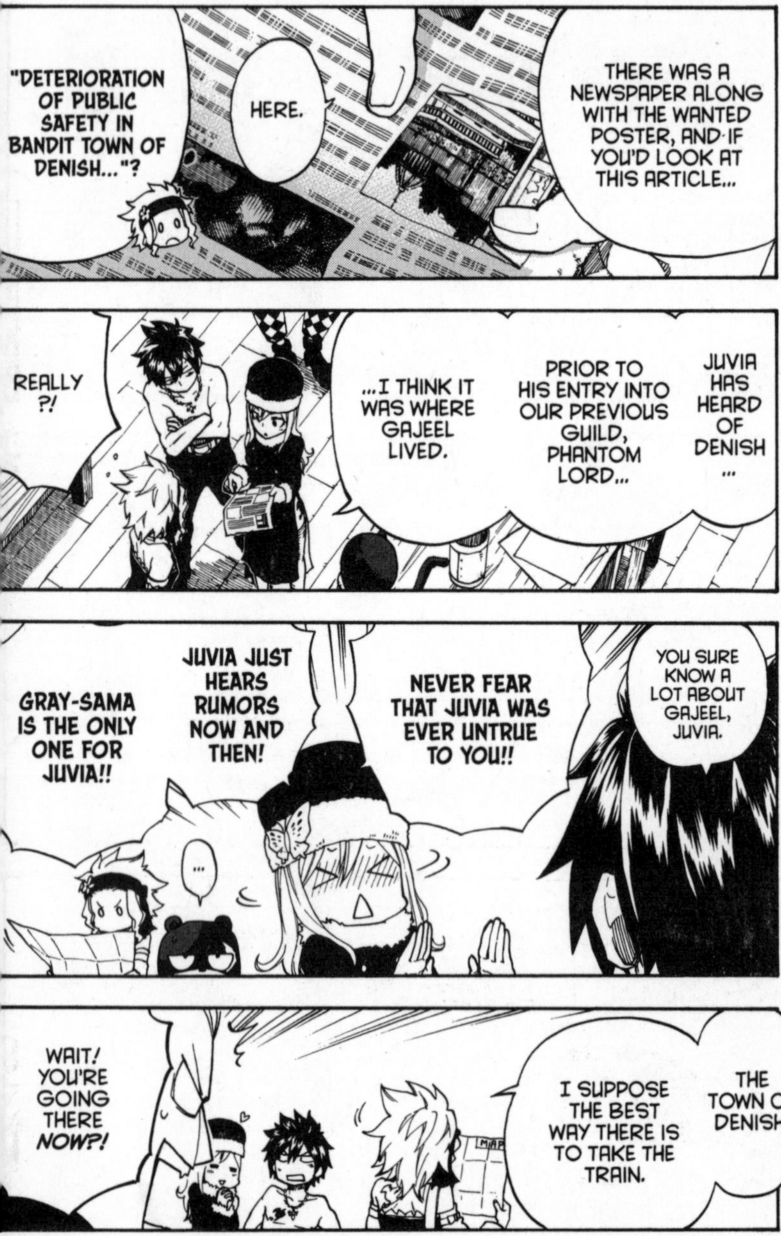
THERE WAS A NEWSPAPER ALONG WITH THE WANTED POSTER, AND IF YOU'D LOOK AT THIS ARTICLE...
HERE.
"DETERIORATION OF PUBLIC SAFETY IN BANDIT TOWN OF DENISH..."?
JUVIA HAS HEARD OF DENISH ...
PRIOR TO HIS ENTRY INTO OUR PREVIOUS GUILD, PHANTOM LORD...
...I THINK IT WAS WHERE GAJEEL LIVED.
REALLY ?!
YOU SURE KNOW A LOT ABOUT GAJEEL, JUVIA.
NEVER FEAR THAT JUVIA WAS EVER UNTRUE TO YOU!!
JUVIA JUST HEARS RUMORS NOW AND THEN!
GRAY-SAMA IS THE ONLY ONE FOR JUVIA!!
...
THE TOWN OF DENISH.
I SUPPOSE THE BEST WAY THERE IS TO TAKE THE TRAIN.
MAP
WAIT! YOU'RE GOING THERE *NOW?!*

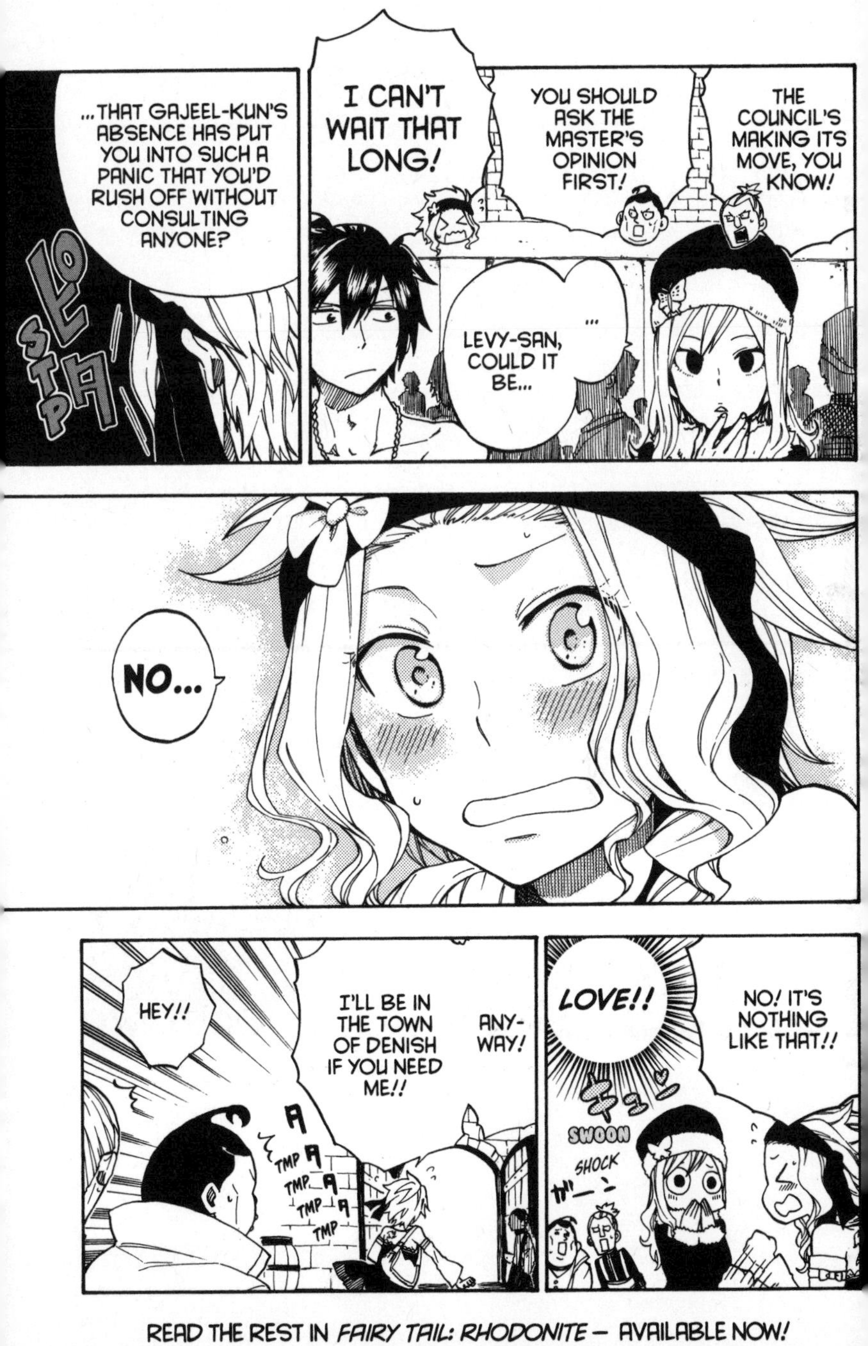
THE COUNCIL'S MAKING ITS MOVE, YOU KNOW!
YOU SHOULD ASK THE MASTER'S OPINION FIRST!
I CAN'T WAIT THAT LONG!
...
LEVY-SAN, COULD IT BE...
...THAT GAJEEL-KUN'S ABSENCE HAS PUT YOU INTO SUCH A PANIC THAT YOU'D RUSH OFF WITHOUT CONSULTING ANYONE?
NO...
NO! IT'S NOTHING LIKE THAT!!
LOVE!!
SWOON
SHOCK
ANYWAY!
I'LL BE IN THE TOWN OF DENISH IF YOU NEED ME!!
HEY!!
TMP TMP TMP TMP

READ THE REST IN *FAIRY TAIL: RHODONITE* – AVAILABLE NOW!

Fairy Tail S volume 1 is a work of fiction. Names, characters, places, and incidents are the products of the author's imagination or are used fictitiously. Any resemblance to actual events, locales, or persons, living or dead, is entirely coincidental.

A Kodansha Comics Trade Paperback Original.

Fairy Tail S volume 1 copyright © 2016 Hiro Mashima
English translation copyright © 2017 Hiro Mashima

Fairy Tail: Rhodonite copyright © 2016 Hiro Mashima / Kyouta Shibano
English translation copyright © 2017 Hiro Mashima / Kyouta Shibano

All rights reserved.

Published in the United States by Kodansha Comics, an imprint of Kodansha USA Publishing, LLC, New York.

Publication rights for this English edition arranged through Kodansha Ltd., Tokyo.

[...] Tokyo

Date: 5/24/18

GRA 741.5 FAI V.1
Mashima, Hiro,
Fairy Tail S. Tales from Fairy
Tail /

9 8 7 6 5 4 3 2 1

PALM BEACH COUNTY
LIBRARY SYSTEM
3650 Summit Boulevard
West Palm Beach, FL 33406-4198

Translation: William Flanagan
Lettering: AndWorld Design
Editing: Lauren Scanlan
Kodansha Comics edition cover design: Phil Balsman